USES OF
EPIDEMIOLOGY

BY

J. N. MORRIS

D.Sc., F.R.C.P., D.P.H.

Director, Social Medicine Research Unit of the
Medical Research Council, London Hospital;
Professor of Social Medicine in the University
of London

SECOND EDITION

REPRINT

E. & S. LIVINGSTONE LTD.
EDINBURGH AND LONDON
1967

FOR GALIA
DAVID AND JULIE

USES OF
EPIDEMIOLOGY

First Edition 1957

Second Edition . . . 1964

Reprinted 1967

PRINTED IN GREAT BRITAIN

PREFACE TO SECOND EDITION

In view of the many criticisms of the brevity of the First, the present Edition is considerably enlarged. As well as expanding the account of epidemiological methods, results and applications, I have included also some background clinical and social information. However, the scope of the book is unchanged and there is no attempt to be comprehensive. I was a long time in rewriting the book and the argument in several places has been overtaken by events; I hope this will be forgiven.

Once again I am deeply grateful for most generous help given me by my friends, abroad and at home, and by my colleagues in the Social Medicine Research Unit. I must name Dr. J. M. Last (Sydney), and Dr. E. Munoz (Cali), sometime Visiting Fellows at the Unit, who produced many of the Tables and Figures. My debt to many others is great, and only part of it can be acknowledged by Reference. The clerical and computing staff of the Unit and in particular my secretary, Miss J. Sullivan, have been endlessly patient. Messrs. E. & S. Livingstone, and Mr. Parker, agreed readily to every request of mine no matter how unreasonable—it has been a real pleasure to work with them.

J. N. Morris.

London, 1964.

FROM PREFACE TO FIRST EDITION

This book is addressed to students of both clinical and preventive medicine, and in it I have tried to indicate how epidemiology can serve as a means of bringing these together. Illustrations are given of the usefulness of epidemiology to clinicians and laboratory workers, and of the possibilities that epidemiology offers for enlarging the traditional field of public health. This is not, therefore, a textbook in the ordinary sense, and there is no attempt to be comprehensive. Thus only passing reference is made to the infections, and a more accurate title would be *Some Uses of Epidemiology in the Study of Non-Communicable Diseases*. Moreover, I have chosen often to illustrate from work with which I have myself been connected in the belief that the reader would prefer generalisations so derived.

I am glad of this opportunity to express by indebtedness to colleagues, past and present, in the Social Medicine Research Unit and to friends who have helped me so generously with ideas and examples. One at least I must mention by name, my teacher, Professor A. Bradford Hill, who has placed a whole generation of medical research workers under obligation. . . .

ACKNOWLEDGEMENTS

I am greatly obliged for permission to quote material to authors, Editors of Journals and Reports, and Publishers, as mentioned in the text: American Heart Association, *American Journal of Public Health, Archives of Diseases of Childhood, British Medical Journal, British Journal of Preventive and Social Medicine, British Journal of Venereal Diseases,* Her Majesty's Stationery Office, *Journal of Obstetrics and Gynaecology of the British Empire, Lancet, Medical Care,* Ministry of Health, Ministry of Pensions and National Insurance, *New Zealand Medical Journal, Proceedings of the Royal Society, Proceedings of the Royal Society of Medicine,* The Registrars General, *The Times,* Tobacco Manufacturers' Standing Committee, *Yale Journal of Biology and Medicine,* and others as specified.

CONTENTS

PAGE

INTRODUCTION 1

I HISTORICAL STUDY 5

Is Health Improving?, 7. Rise of . . . , 12. Modern Epidemics, 16. Change in Character of Disease, 18. Ageing of the Population, 22. Foresight—Young People, 26. Population Explosion, 30.

II COMMUNITY DIAGNOSIS : COMMUNITY HEALTH 34

Statistical Account of Ill-Health in Middle Age, 36. Morbidity Surveys, 40. Populations, 42; Indicators and Measurements, 44; Estimating Mental Disorders, 48. Health and the Mode of Life, 52. Inequality of Opportunity, 56; Affluent Society, 60. Vulnerable Groups, 66. Modern World, 68; New Measurements, 70.

III WORKING OF HEALTH SERVICES . . 75

What is General Practice?, 77. Needs⇌Demand⇌ Supply⇌, 82; Application of New Knowledge, 86; Utilisation, 87. Quality of Medical Care, 89. International Comparison, 96. Community Care, 97; Action Research, 99. New Services for Old, 101.

IV INDIVIDUAL RISKS AND CHANCES . . 102

Tools of Epidemiology, 108.

V COMPLETING THE CLINICAL PICTURE . 110

(1) Completing the Picture in Breadth, 111; Clinical Medicine and Epidemiology, 113. (2) Subclinical Disease—Iceberg Phenomenon, 118; Patients and Populations, 120. (3) Precursors of Disease, 125. (4) Predispositions, 129. Instruments of Research, 130. Natural History of Chronic Diseases—, 133; —And their Prevention, 135.

VI IDENTIFICATION OF SYNDROMES . . 141

Syndromes of Atherosclerosis, 143. Leukaemia in Young People, 147. Two Syndromes of Juvenile Delinquency, 150. High Blood Pressure Without Evident Cause, 152. A Model, 152. Association of Diseases—, 157; —And their Dissociation, 159.

vii

PAGE

VII IN SEARCH OF CAUSES 160

Victorian Thunder, 161; A Modern Hygiene?, 163; Some Epidemiological Contributions, 169. MODERN EPIDEMIC, 172; Hypothesis on Exercise, 174. EXPLORING ESSENTIAL HYPERTENSION, 182; Improvement of Epidemiology, 187. MULTIPLE CAUSES, 188; Theory and Action, 195. EPIDEMIOLOGY OF PERSONAL BEHAVIOUR, 196; Personal and Communal Prevention, 197. BRONCHITIS, 199; Prevention, 210. REDISCOVERY OF BYSSINOSIS, 211; A Dangerous Trade, 217. "ECOLOGY" OF MENTAL DISORDERS, 218; Social Deprivation, 223; Modern World, 224; Social Groups, 226. CANCER IN THE REPORTS OF THE GENERAL REGISTER OFFICE, 229; Morbidity and the NCRS, 241. GEOGRAPHICAL PATHOLOGY, 241; The Appropriate "Universe" in Physiological Studies, 250. HYPOTHESES, 251: (1) Statement, 252. (2) Test of Hypothesis, 254; Experiment of Opportunity, 259; Case-Control and Retrospective Studies, 261. (3) Multiple Causes, 266. (4) EXPERIMENTAL EPIDEMIOLOGY, 268.

RECAPITULATION; GENERAL 274

APPENDIX: COMPLEMENTARY NATURE OF CLINICAL, LABORATORY AND POPULATION STUDIES . . 279

Sir George Baker's Consummate Proof, 283. Occupational Epithelioma of Scrotum, 284; Papilloma of Bladder in Dyestuffs Workers, 285; Leukaemia from Ionising Radiations, 286. Production of Congenital Malformation by Rubella, 288. Chronic Beryllium Disease, 290. Protein Malnutrition in Children, 291; Epidemic Dropsy in Bengal, 292; Cause of Goitre in Tasmania, 293. Sex Ratio in Ischaemic Heart Disease, 294. Psychological Aspects of Duodenal Ulcer, 295. Two Types of Diabetes Mellitus, 296. Discovery of Blood Groups, 298; The Rh Factor, 299; Sickling, 300. Provision of Hearing Aids, 301.

GLOSSARY 302

REFERENCES—

GENERAL 307

SPECIAL 308

INDEX OF SUBJECTS 333

INTRODUCTION

During the nineteenth century death rates in middle age in England and Wales were high (Fig. 1), but about the turn of the century sanitary reform and the rise in the standard of living began to show results in this age group. Death rates began to fall, both in men and women, and they continued

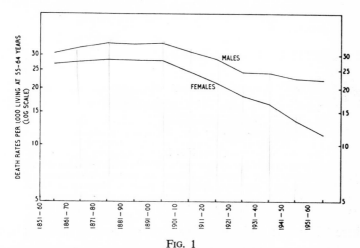

FIG. 1

History of mortality in middle age (55-64) over the past hundred years. All causes of death. England and Wales.
From REGISTRAR GENERAL.[45]

to fall until the early 1920's. Then, rather abruptly, there was a change. Mortality in women kept its downward course; but the decline of male mortality slowed, and for the last twenty years it has hovered around 22 per 1,000. A hundred years ago the death rate among middle-aged men was about 15 per cent higher than in women, after the first world war it was about 33 per cent higher, now the male rate is twice the female.

1
1

What has been happening? The recent course of mortality among middle-aged women is much as expected. This remarkable trend in the male death rate has occurred during years that have seen more advances in medical science than all the rest of history. Middle-aged men have benefited from

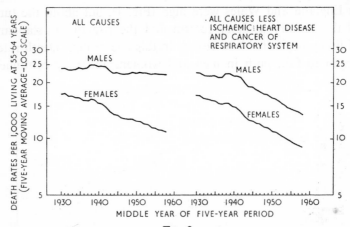

FIG. 2

Mortality in middle age (55-64) from 1928 to 1960. The contribution of ischaemic heart disease and lung-cancer (which constitutes the great majority of cancer of respiratory system). England and Wales. From REGISTRAR GENERAL.[45] [48]

these advances: their mortality from pneumonia is under half what it was before the sulphonamides were discovered, from phthisis only a quarter of that in 1946-7. The rate of cure in men from some cancers has almost certainly improved since the 1920's, mortality from most cancers has fallen, anyhow. Such gains, however, have been wiped out by other changes. The most important is that two diseases, affecting men in middle age far more than women, and highly lethal, have emerged from obscurity to become exceedingly common: " coronary thrombosis " or ischaemic heart disease, and cancer of the bronchus. In 1961 the former killed some 15,000 men aged 55-64 and 4,750 women, the latter over 7,000 such men and about 900 women. (The total numbers of deaths at this age were 55,000 and 31,000.) Fig. 2 illustrates the contribution of these two conditions to the recent trend of mortality; without them the position of the 1920's is almost if not quite regained. " Coronary thrombosis " and lung cancer are " modern epidemics ", and they form a large fraction of the chronic diseases that now dominate the practice of medicine.

Figs. 1 and 2 illustrate one use of epidemiology, in *historical study*, and its basic method. The unit of observation in epidemiology is the group, or " population " as it is called, which may be the actual population of a country, as in the example, or any other defined group of people. Deaths, or illnesses, or any other events are studied only if information can be obtained about the population in which they occurred. The epidemiologist usually starts with a population and seeks the cases, all of them, in it; alternatively, he may start with cases and try to refer them to their population. Always, the epidemiologist tries to reach some estimate of all the cases, as defined, occurring in a defined population, of $\frac{cases}{population}$. The clinician, by contrast, deals only with the cases, with individuals, with his patients and their illnesses. Since these are the concern of both, epidemiologist and clinician sometimes ask the same question, on the natural history of disease for example. Mostly, however, the epidemiologist asks questions that cannot be asked in clinical medicine at all. He is interested in the frequency, or rate of occurrence, of events in a population, in the proportion of it who are affected. Thus, all and particular deaths in England and Wales, in men and women of a specified age, at one time and another, can be counted, and the rate of death in a thousand of these people calculated, to make possible such historical comparisons as in Figs. 1 and 2.

This book is mainly about epidemiology as a means of learning, of asking questions, certain kinds of questions, and getting answers that lead to further questions. As a method, epidemiology may be contrasted with clinical observation of patients, as said, or with the controlled experiment in the laboratory. Traditionally, it has mostly been used in the *study of health and disease of populations*; this is the epidemiology of Farr and Snow, of Hirsch and Goldberger. Today the method is also being applied to a wide range of related problems. Several " uses " of epidemiology will be described in this book, applications of the method, ways of obtaining and analysing data about populations, and illustrations will be given of results.

I

HISTORICAL STUDY

The historical statements commonly made in medicine are by definition " epidemiological ": they refer to the frequency of events among populations at different points in time. Thus diseases wax and wane (tuberculosis, for example), new ones appear (encephalitis lethargica, beryllium poisoning), old ones disappear (chlorosis or, it may be expected, miner's nystagmus). The recent decline from various causes of many of the great infections is often described, and the trends are usually very obvious; they have been enough in themselves to transform the practice of medicine in a single generation. Each specialty has its own examples: ENT surgery with scarcely ever a mastoid; few new cases of GPI; no more ringworm clinics; surgical tuberculosis wiped out; fever hospitals emptied. . . . It is difficult to convey to those with no experience of it, what it meant that as recently as in 1941 2,400 children died of diphtheria in England and Wales, and there were 50,000 cases.[21][45]

Table I, p. 6, is from rheumatic heart disease; it complements the story of " coronary thrombosis " to provide a miniature of modern cardiology and is a contrast in two senses: the steep fall in recent years, and the greater mortality among the poor, illustrated by the high rates in poverty-stricken South Wales when the disease was common. By now there are too few deaths to yield stable rates for such comparisons as are made in Table I. During the four years 1956-9, in fact, there were *no* deaths from heart disease in the children of the big towns of South Wales, nor any certified to rheumatic fever;[32] the national rate in those years was about 1 death in 100,000 children. Juvenile rheumatism is an obsolescent disease, and no longer can clinical students readily be initiated,

5

as they were for so many generations, with mitral stenosis and aortic regurgitation (the other great cardiac infection also has become rare).

TABLE I

*Mortality from (Rheumatic) Heart Disease**

Both Sexes
Ages 5-14 inclusive
Death Rates per 100,000 Children per Year

POPULATION		(1) 1929-33	(2) 1946-49
England and Wales	County Boroughs .	13·4	4·1
	Urban Districts . .	11·2	3·7
	Rural Districts . .	7·9	2·7
South Wales	County Boroughs .	17·9	4·2
	Urban Districts . .	20·1	5·5
	" Rural " Districts .	18·8	3·9

* *I.e.* all certified heart disease except congenital.
Many of the " rural " districts of South Wales are coalmining villages.
Registrar General.

The example from rheumatic heart disease is a good one, because there is little doubt that the recent rise in the standard of living is a cause of the improvement, and no reason to suppose that it alone is responsible. The decline of juvenile rheumatism seems to have begun in the middle 1930's, during the Great Depression.[35] [39] It thus followed late in the wake of the decline in virulence of haemolytic streptococcal infection which began last century and is not just due to mass use of sulphonamides. Penicillin prophylaxis has probably contributed to the latest improvement—I have been unable to get any figures of how assiduously it is being used. In short, a little is understood.

Pages 6-8 illustrate the recent spectacular achievements in child health. Fig. 3 expresses the decline of rheumatism and

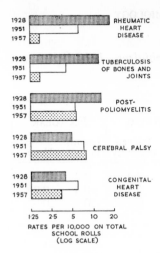

1928 RHEUMATIC
1951 HEART
1957 DISEASE

1928 TUBERCULOSIS
1951 OF BONES AND
1957 JOINTS

1928 POST-
1951 POLIOMYELITIS
1957

1928
1951 CEREBRAL PALSY
1957

1928 CONGENITAL
1951 HEART
1957 DISEASE

1·25 2·5   5   10   20
RATES PER 10,000 ON TOTAL
SCHOOL ROLLS
(LOG SCALE)

Fig. 3

Physically handicapped children in the County of London: prevalence rates in Special Schools over the period, 1928-1957. Total rate for all causes was 64 per 10,000 schoolchildren in 1928; 41 in 1951; 30 in 1957. Palmer, W. T. & Pirrie, D. (1958). *Brit. med. J.* **2,** 1326. (See paper on the comparability of the data.)

tuberculosis in one of its happiest terms. In 1957 the prevalence of handicap from rheumatic heart disease was a tenth that in 1928: there were only 72 children so affected on the school rolls of all of London in 1957, and there were no cases of chorea in either 1951 or 1957. " Cleanliness " in Glasgow, Table II (1) overleaf, deteriorated in fact during 1939-45, and there still are too many verminous heads. But Glasgow is the right context in which to mention another recent revolution in Public Health: the virtual disappearance of gross nutritional deficiencies that was initiated by war-time nutrition policy[21] is as dramatic as the decline in infections. Rickets was epidemic in Victorian Britain and rife till the recent war, particularly among the poor of industrial cities. In the native child rickets is now a rarity. The record with childhood anaemia is almost as good. Table II (2) on the average growth of Glasgow's children gives an overall view of the improvement in nutrition.

Is Health Improving?

By now I hope such a question will appear absurd—there are so many aspects of health. Table III is the main result of an enquiry whether there has been less sickness in the population since the recent advances in therapy, the decline of bacterial infection, and so dramatic a fall in mortality at

7

TABLE II
Health of Glasgow Schoolchildren, 1910-1960

(1)

PERIOD	CLEANLINESS		CLOTHING		FOOTGEAR	
	Verminous		Insuffi-	Ragged	Unsatis-	
	Heads	Bodies	cient	and Dirty	factory	None
1910-19	20·3	2·8	1·3	5·9	2·3	5·2
1930-39	6·7	0·2	0·1	0·5	0·4	0·0
1958-60	7·7	0·0	0·0	0·1	0·1	0·0

Percentages.

(2)
HEIGHTS AND WEIGHTS

Period	Boys				Girls			
	5 years		13 years		5 years		13 years	
	Ht.	Wt.	Ht.	Wt.	Ht.	Wt.	Ht.	Wt.
1910-19	40·4	38·5	55·2	74·5	39·7	37·7	55·5	76·8
1930-39	41·3	39·7	56·8	81·6	41·0	38·3	57·7	85·9
1958-60	42·6	42·4	59·7	95·0	42·3	41·0	60·0	100·0

Inches and lbs.

EWAN, J. (1957). *The School Health Service, Glasgow.* Glasgow; and personal communications.

younger ages. The Government Actuary, advising the Beveridge Committee during the war, forecast an increase in incapacity rates of $12\frac{1}{2}$ per cent as a result of improved social security, rather less for short " sick absence " and more for longer.[54] Of course this was in the days before penicillin and all that followed from it, but he seems to have been uncannily right. Sick absence rates in men show no improvement, over years with available and at all comparable data, in the population at large Table III (1), or in special groups (3), where

TABLE III

Morbidity and Mortality

Men

Per Year

(1) SICK ABSENCE FROM WORK

	Ages					
	16-	20-	25-	35-	45-	55-64
1927	0·8	0·8	0·8	0·9	1·2	1·9
1954-5	0·8	0·9	0·9	1·0	1·4	2·2

Weeks of certified sickness per insured man. First six months only of sick absences are included. Britain. Estimated.

(2) MORTALITY

	Ages					
	15-	20-	25-	35-	45-	55-64
1927	2·6	3·3	3·8	6·6	11·9	25·0
1954-5	0·9	1·2	1·3	2·7	7·9	22·3

Death rates per 1,000 males. Britain.

(3) SICK ABSENCE—LONDON POLICEMEN

	Ages				
	-25	25-	30-	40-	50+
1936-8	2·2	1·9	2·1	2·6	3·3
1955-7	3·1	2·8	2·7	3·1	3·6
1960-2	2·6	2·4	2·5	2·4	2·4

Average absent because of sickness, per cent.

(3) SICK ABSENCE—POST OFFICE

1935-8	9·0	1946-9	11·9
		1950-3	13·9
		1954-7	12·6
		1958-9	11·3

Days of sick absence per man. Established staff, excluding registered "disabled persons". Britain.

(4) ABSENCE FROM SCHOOL

	Infants	7-11 yrs		11-14/15 yrs	
		Boys	Girls	Boys	Girls
1936-8	16	10·7	12·3	10·6	13·7
1956-8	12·8	7·4	8·0	8·1	9·3

Average absent in Jan. of each year, per cent. Birmingham.

Annual Reports of Ministry of Pensions and National Insurance, General Register Offices, Metropolitan Police, The Post Office (Treasury Medical Service), Birmingham LEA; and personal communications, 1959-63.

conditions of employment, social security benefits, and industrial medical provision are relatively unchanged.* Only in

* Indeed, the figures of the Manchester Unity of Oddfellows for 1893-7 corresponding to Table III (1) are remarkably similar:[61]

16—	20—	30—	40—	50—	55—	60—64
0·9	0·8	0·9	1·2	1·5	1·8	2·3

The most recent figures on London policemen, Table III (3), they have just come to hand, show an interesting change after 40 years of age.

children (4) do the morbidity figures show what I hoped to find, and at that age they are especially difficult to interpret.

There are several lines of explanation for what might be happening among the adults. Thus, everyday sickness is mostly due to physical causes which as yet are little amenable to treatment, and to " nerves "—capacity to work is a crude indicator of morale and mental health. Sick absence statistics reflect the medical conditions, obviously; but, it is now realised, they also reflect unemployment pushing the figures down and, as was foretold, social security letting them rise, the social norms of the time and particular work and home situations. All this affects the worker, and also the certifying doctor (who may be well aware of these pressures). This is a char- acteristic modern problem, physical-mental-social, or so it now is characteristic to phrase it. People and the way they live have to be studied, not merely diseases, and no one approach is likely to explain much.

Sick Absence in the 1950's.—Closer analysis is possible for more recent years, [42] [55] and it shows two exceedingly interest- ing features. During the 1950's there has been a rather steady rise, amounting to 25 per cent, in *short absences* among younger men:

Proportion of Insured Men Incapacitated for Periods of Up to One Month

Age	1953/4 %	1960/1 %
15-19	0·82	1·1
20-24	0·98	1·2
25-29	0·91	1·1
30-34	1·1	1·2
35-39	1·0	1·3

Counted in June.

On this increase, about the only thing that needs to be said now is that it is unlikely to be due simply to organic disease; more likely it represents some collective comment on the times, with their rising standard of living, full employment, etc. In middle age, and particularly among men in their early sixties, Table IV, there was a rise of *chronic disability*. Fig. 4 shows the expected reduction at younger ages between 1951

TABLE IV

*Disability in Men
Aged 61-63*

Britain

Year	Proportion of Insured Men Sick Absent from Work for Over Three Months
	Per cent.
1951	8·0
1952	8·2
1953/4	9·0
1955	9·1
1956	9·4
1957	9·5
1958	9·6
1959	10·2
1960	10·6

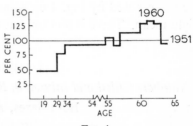

FIG. 4

Disability in men at various ages. Proportion sick absent from work for over three months: comparison of rates in 1960 with those of 1951.

Ministry of Pensions and National Insurance, Annual Digest of Statistics; and personal communications, 1959-63.

and 1960, the triumph of streptomycin alone need be mentioned. There was, however, an appreciable rise of chronic sickness among men in their late fifties, and a very substantial one, amounting to 30 per cent, in men in their early sixties. These rates of disability in middle age, a peculiarly unpleasant form of urban-industrial misery, are equally hard to explain with avaliable data. They may indicate a real growth in the prevalence of chronic disease, and the fall during recent years in the death rate at 45-54 years of age could have contributed a little to this. The spread of pension schemes and other benefits may be encouraging earlier retirement. Disabled men may be retreating in face of more intense industrial production; there is good reason to suppose that many of these men never return to work*.[28] [36]

Rise of . . .

Historical questions about the possible increase of disorders —whether there is a real rise that compares with the decline of infectious diseases and of malnutrition—are often very difficult to answer, and I am not now referring to problems like those posed by Fig. 4 on what an unquestionable increase might mean. There is no doubt about the real rise of casualties

TABLE V

Numbers Killed and Injured in Road Accidents, 1938-1962

Both Sexes, All Ages

Britain

Year	Population '000's	Index of Traffic (Motor and Pedal Cycle)	Killed	Numbers		
				Seriously Injured	Slightly Injured	Total Casualties
1938	46,208	106	6,648	51,000	176,000	233,000
1949	48,992	*100*	4,773	43,000	129,000	177,000
1956	49,812	138	5,367	61,000	201,000	268,000
1961	51,350	187	6,908	85,000	258,000	350,000
1962	51,866	192	6,709	84,000	251,000	342,000‡
1963						

‡ Including, under 15 years of age: 761 deaths, 12,186 seriously injured, and 40,359 slightly injured.

Road Accidents 1961, HMSO; The Royal Society for the Prevention of Accidents (1963), personal communication; Norman, L. G. (1961). *Road Traffic Accidents*. WHO, Geneva.

* These figures on middle-aged men were dug out of the official statistics some years ago, but little analysis by cause, occupation, region and so on, is yet possible. Major new social inequalities could be concealed in such averages. It may be relevant that during this period the number of men in the population aged 65-74 rose about 7 per cent, the number over 65 in employment fell about 7 per cent.[26]

in road-vehicle accidents, for instance, though not latterly in the accident rate per vehicle-mile, Table V, and little doubt about the increase of barbiturate poisoning, though the total rate of suicide is changing little. There *was* no argument over epidemic poliomyelitis or retrolental fibroplasia: history moves fast. But many questions, interesting and important questions, are so bedevilled by uncertainties about nomenclature in the past, and on the standard of diagnosis over the years, that no answer can be given. Consider these figures, of sickness certificates given by doctors about other doctors, and only fifteen years apart: [22]

	No. of cases	
	1937	1952
Muscular rheumatism	18	7
Fibrositis	17	11
Lumbago, sciatica, sacroiliac strain	47	29
Prolapsed intervertebral disc	0	35
Total	82	82

This is a population in which vague diagnoses like " low backache " are unfashionable. It is not necessary to believe that " discs " are a consequence of man's upright posture to wonder . . . (Graunt in 1662 certainly would have wondered.) More serious in trying to judge an historical trend, commonly there are no numerical estimates of frequency for any period: how many cases occurred annually among a thousand specified persons in the 1930's and how many in the 1950's? Or, and this is the crux of it, how frequently were *new* cases arising, which gives the " *incidence* " or baseline of epidemiology.

In several gross organic conditions like brain tumour, dissecting aneurysm, the various collagen and hypersensitivity diseases, it remains quite uncertain whether their recent apparent increase, even if manifestly not a temporary fluctuation, reflects a true rise of incidence. Each question has to be treated on its merits and the evidence, often contradictory as well as scanty, weighed. In mental illness problems are even more complicated. There is no evidence of any overall increase of insanity with " civilisation ", since the French Revolution a controversial issue with a whole literature of its own.[14] On the simplest of theories, the growing number of solitary old women, in a society unprepared for it, provides the kind of situation where a real rise in incidence of psychosis might be expected. In fact, the suicide rate in women over 55 has increased substantially since the War, unlike the rate in younger women and in men. Historical questions on the frequency of the psychoneuroses are particularly hopeless of direct answer, and useful clues are more likely to come from the novelist and the social historian. There is a new interest in emotional disorders today, perceptions are sharper, expectations of happiness as well as of health are rising, so that historical comparison often is hazardous.[18]

Each civilisation, Sigerist has said, makes its own diseases. But it has many ways of doing so : I will illustrate only with the simplest of examples from recent changes.

RELATIVE INCREASE, NOT ABSOLUTE

The first point to settle is—increase of disease in relative terms, or absolute? An apparent increase of some conditions because of real decline of others can come about in several ways, and it is responsible for much of the changing picture of health (the *onion principle*). The death rate falls, and questions of morbidity assume a new importance. With the decline of the crowd diseases, other infections and non-infectious diseases predominate. Lessen physical deprivation, and widespread emotional impoverishment and social incompetence are exposed. Reduce physical disease, and problems of mental health can no longer be ignored. When environmental casualties are controlled, genetic failures receive more attention. As the lives of mothers and children are protected, Public Health activities can also be focused on other vulnerable groups. Problems solved, by definition, are simpler than problems remaining; which is some consolation in our perplexities.

ABSOLUTE INCREASE

Is the number of cases in fact greater? Is the disease commoner per head of population? Are new cases arising more often? The answer to each of these questions matters, if differently.

Increase in Cases, but Not Disease.—In any given population, uncovering more of the cases that are there will swell the numbers evident, although there has been no change in the frequency of disease. Prolapsed intervertebral disc is described, and soon the diagnosis is commonplace. Hashimoto's disease is suddenly in the limelight—everywhere. Cardiomyopathy will inevitably be recognised oftener, and hypertension due to renal artery stenosis become " commoner " in the years ahead. Recorded deaths from pyelonephritis are rising steadily. New possibilities of diagnosis and treatment very likely account for the apparent increase of ruptured cerebral aneurysm. The discovery of venous thrombosis at necropsy seems largely to be a function of the search for it: a fortiori the influence of *believing* on *seeing* must be kept in mind when trying to understand an historical trend. How much is better medical care of old people responsible for the more frequent diagnosis of leukaemia in them? More energetic case-finding could readily double the number of known diabetics. It is anybody's guess what keener law enforcement has done and could do to the number of official delinquents. The supply of health services sharpens perception of need and raises expectations, *i.e.* produces more cases; social security benefits as said raise the rate of declared incapactiy. Disability from byssinosis has increased fifty-fold because of changes in the compensation law.

Fashions of nomenclature and similar artefacts can play havoc with morbidity figures, as already seen, and since 1662 this has been recognised of mortality (*Graunt's law*).[17] " Myocardial degeneration " and " neurasthenia " are unfashionable terms today, and this is probably responsible for part of the recorded increase of " coronary thrombosis ", some of the many diagnoses of " depression ".

Increase in Disease, but Not Rate.—A bigger number at risk, without any other change, will mean a real increase in the number of cases, though there is no rise in frequency per head. Every week in England and Wales nearly two thousand persons over the age of 65 are added to the population, increasing those susceptible to suffer stroke and cataract and fractured neck of femur and other afflictions of old age.

Increase in Rate, but Not Incidence.—More effective treatment can increase the number of survivors and, thus, the number of cases and their rate in the population. There do not seem to be any more mongols born, the incidence does not seem to have risen, but the total of mongols living at 10-14 years of age, their *prevalence,* may be as much as four times what it was thirty years ago, pre-sulphonamides.[5][15] This " survival of the unfit " is becoming characteristic of the serious handicaps of early life.[51] The greater longevity of diabetics is one of the main results of modern therapy, and it means that there are more of them in the population.

Modern Epidemics

Here are two measures, they come from studies we have been making[20][38][44][45][55] and the data were collected in a uniform way over the years, of the recent *increase in incidence,* rise in the the occurrence of new cases, of ischaemic heart disease :

(1) *First clinical episodes of IHD per 1,000 insurance salesmen aged 40-59; all presentations of the disease.* The increase from 1954-7 to 1958-60 = 55 per cent.
(2) *First clinical episodes of IHD per 1,000 London busmen aged 35-64; presentation as " sudden death ".* The increase from 1949-52 to 1957-8 = 42 per cent.

Such figures need to be, and have been, " standardised " or " adjusted " to allow for changes in age composition of the population-at-risk over the years.

Fig. 5 proceeds to mortality: the occurrence of this trend in many hospitals is what impresses, the continued increase in certified mortality long after IHD became widely known

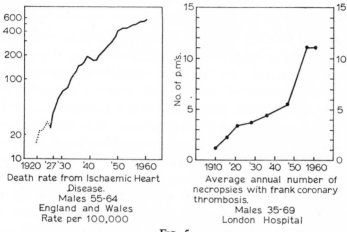

Death rate from Ischaemic Heart
Disease.
Males 55-64
England and Wales
Rate per 100,000

Average annual number of
necropsies with frank coronary
thrombosis.
Males 35-69
London Hospital

FIG. 5
Two (indirect) indicators of the rise in incidence of ischaemic heart disease in middle age.
REGISTRAR GENERAL (log. scale).[45] [58] Archives of the Bernhard Baron Institute of Pathology, London Hospital.[34] [55]

among doctors.[34] In the end, however, it may be the kind of evidence presented in Figs. 1 and 2 which carries most conviction that ischaemic heart disease has in fact increased. Whether it did is obviously a more fundamental question than the previous. The role of environmental causes in the aetiology is involved: possible failures in adaptation to social change, the suggestion of an avoidable rise in ill-health. As a result of much study, it must today be accepted as a working hypothesis and guide for investigation that there has been a true rise during this century of ischaemic heart disease and a fortiori of cancer of the bronchus. A true rise in incidence: apart from the decline of cardiac and pulmonary infections, the ageing of the population, greater appreciation of the abdominal symptoms of cardiac ischaemia and of the true pathology of " mediastinal sarcoma ", the profusion of X-rays and electrocardiography, exceeding medical alertness to both diseases; apart from all of these.

CHANGE IN CHARACTER OF DISEASE

Diseases wax and wane. They also change in character over time, vary in severity, present in different forms. Populations change; organisms also. Influenza, syphilis and poliomyelitis are classical examples. Scarlet fever grew virulent during the industrial revolution, particularly in the second third of the nineteenth century, then began to subside. Tuberculous disease is now being modified, through a combination of less and postponed infection, greater resistance and the loss of allergy, the consequences of new therapy added to old Public Health measures. The mutation of organisms, the emergence of antibiotic-resistant strains to become a grave complication of operations ("hospital staphylococci", for instance), and the new pathogenicity of once harmless *E. coli* and other gram-negative infections represent a forced change of character.[1][7][53][60]

Mental Disorders

A fall of incidence in a psychological disorder may reflect a real improvement in health. But it could also mean no more than a change in the mode of manifestation of the disorder arising from " sociocultural changes which no longer reward (a particular) pattern of ' crying for help ', or which actively suppress the particular symptomatology, or treat it with negative sanctions ". The attitude of doctors and public to deviant behaviour is always changing; and this changes the form that functional disorders take, without necessarily affecting the underlying social problems, of insecurity or repression for example, for which the disorders are " a deviant type of solution ".[8] [18] [29] Perhaps the appearance of " new forms " of juvenile delinquency can partly be explained along such lines: fifty years ago in East London they threw stones at horses, before the 1939-45 War they stole cycles; perhaps taking and driving away motor cars is a compound of these.

It makes better sense to include under this head the war-time changes of neurosis, psychosomatic and functional disorder, rather than simplify discussion in terms of rise and fall, on which a word has already been said. " Shellshock " and conversion hysteria were rife in the first world war, anxiety-depression and " battle fatigue " in the second; epidemic effort syndrome (World War I) in contrast to epidemic dyspepsia (World War II). The useful model of what occurred will include also the notion of exchange of one group of disorders for another. An altogether new psychological sophistication over the years, as well as changes in the current environment of war, the more understanding approach to fear during World War II, and the different attitude to (the possibility of) casualties, these provide a first explanation.

The removal of the overlay of institution-induced deterioration brought about by allowing for the social capacities of patients, by attitudes that no longer regard them as alien, by the movement to provide a " therapeutic community " as environment—and by the tranquillisers—are changing the picture of disease in mental hospitals and, there is a little evidence, in the community also. Psychotic illness is becoming milder and quieter in nature, there is less anti-social behaviour, withdrawal and hostility, less loss of identity (of staff as well as patients), less catatonia, less of violent disturbance in schizophrenia, frank mania is less common and so is classical melancholia.[30] [33]

Remarkable History of Duodenal Ulcer

Last century peptic ulcer commonly took the form of acute gastric ulcer in young women, a condition scarcely seen nowadays. During this century *duodenal ulcer* has become common as a chronic disease of men, and it reached epidemic proportions in the 1930's and 1940's.[23] [24] [40] A survey after the war, made mainly in London, showed that by the time they reach 55, about 6 per cent of men have or have had a duodenal ulcer.[6] Recently, and without warning, it has appeared to decline (Table VI).[44] [57] [62]

TABLE VI

Recent History of Duodenal Ulcer[55]

Men aged 45-64

Rates per 100,000 per Year

(1) MORTALITY

	Gastric Ulcer	Duodenal Ulcer
1936-38	28·8	16·5
1953	13·6	16·3
1961	7·3	9·2

Registrar General, England and Wales.

(2) "ADMISSIONS" TO HOSPITAL

	Total Peptic Ulcer	Perforations GU	Perforations DU	"Cold" Surgery GU	"Cold" Surgery DU
1953-55	584	23	52	97	156
1956	478	16	55	84	126
1959	412	16	40	70	98

Hospital In-patient Enquiry, Ministry of Health and General Register Office, England and Wales; and personal communications.

Because of the secular improvement in the sample, the most instructive comparison is between 1956 and 1959.

(3) INCAPACITY TO WORK

	Spells GU	Spells DU	Spells Gastritis etc.	Days GU	Days DU	Days Gastritis etc.
1951	570	490	1,310			
1954/5	600	450	1,310	38,000	30,000	29,000
1959/60	490	340	1,240	26,000	20,000	23,000

Ministry of Pensions and National Insurance, Britain.

Evidently there has been an improvement. But is it due to a fall in the frequency of the disease, in the proportion of the population contracting it, which is one thing, or merely to a reduction in severity among those affected, even more frequent cure, a change in character which could for example be accounted for by better treatment? Mortality is falling (1) but improving medical care makes this a poor indicator of secular trend in a disease with such low case-fatality. The rate of perforation (an exceptionally hard indicator of historical trends) also is falling (2), but the " epidemic " of partial gastrectomy in the 1950's,* it is conceivable, has freed many from the risk of perforation, reduced population susceptibility to it. Sick absence in industry is less (3) in terms both of spells and their duration, but, judging by the duration of spells, signing victims off work because of ulcer is no longer fashionable treatment except in the most serious circumstances. There is no means of settling this question, in the absence of figures over the years for *new* cases, *i.e.* of the incidence, the basic and crucial figure in all epidemiology as said, and about as difficult a fact to pin down in DU as in any of the chronic diseases. (What is to be accepted as ulcer, and what as its first attack?) No exploitation of available statistics will yield this figure.**

The most interesting possibility of course is that there is a true decline in incidence. In the present context this would suggest to anyone in sympathy with psychosomatic theories (and there are no better ones for duodenal ulcer) that predisposition to the disease is less common, not at present a meaningful proposition, that men are less subject to stress, which is scarcely conceivable—or that under stress they react differently. It is necessary therefore to ask whether any other " disease " that possibly is equivalent, or complementary, is increasing? Another psychosomatic condition? Pill-taking? The overt

---

* During the period 1953-9 it is estimated that 20,000 " cold " operations for ulcer were done annually on men, two-thirds of them for DU.
** National Insurance, it should be clear by now, has a potentially fabulous store of information, and far greater effort should be devoted to realising it.

expression of anxiety, even? Depression? When coronary thrombosis is so common, the gain from the ulcer " sick role "[41] is smaller. Because of the current pace of social change, the highly unstable epidemic constitution[12] of the times, changes in both manifestation and incidence of psychological disorder are to be expected. Meanwhile, it must be noted that these remarkable trends in duodenal ulcer are by no means so clear or consistent at 25-44 years of age, or in women.

Coronary Artery Disease

This seems to have changed in character in the present century.[34] Coronary thrombosis has apparently become commoner (Fig. 5); but there is no evidence of any concurrent or corresponding increase in the underlying coronary atheroma. One atheromatous process, calcification of the intimal lesions, may indeed have become less common; and if calcification represents a healing of atheromatous lesions this, conceivably, is a local cause of the increase in thrombosis. Anyhow, massive thrombosis in atheromatous coronary arteries does seem to be occurring oftener. To identify the social changes which have resulted in this particular biological change is a central problem for modern medicine.

AGEING OF THE POPULATION

A basic fact of our society, dominant in any consideration of social and medical needs, is the ageing of the population; and this is only to be understood from history. Two main movements need to be considered.[2 4 22 47 48]

1. During the second half of the nineteenth century the number of children born in England and Wales rose steeply, from $5\frac{1}{2}$ million in the 1840's to more than 9 million, over 900,000 per year, in the 1890's and in 1901-10. In consequence, during the present century the *number* of old people in the population has been rising steeply.

2. After about 1908 the number of births fell, reaching their lowest, 580,000 in 1933 (and in 1941). Because of this, the

great Victorian and Edwardian cohort as it moves up the age scale has been replaced by smaller numbers, and the *proportion* of old people in the population is increasing; *i.e.,* the population as a whole is ageing.

I have referred to the number of births, which is what matters here, and not to the birth rate per thousand of total population or of women aged 15-44. The birth *rate* in fact stopped rising in the 1870's, and began to fall in the 1880's; but this was not reflected in a fall of the *number* of births till the early 1900's.

The first of these movements will continue till the 1990's; the latter anyhow till the 1970's—what happens then will depend on the current trend of births. Numbers have been rising again since 1955/6, and they topped 800,000 in 1961 and 1962.

Here are the main facts:

Population of England and Wales, 1861-1961

Thousands

	TOTAL	UNDER 15	OVER 65	
			M	F
1861	20,066	7,150	423	509
1901	32,528	10,546	661	857
1961	46,269	10,586	2,120	3,401

The number of old people has almost quadrupled in the present century, the presence of a large army of the retired is something new in history.[16] For the over 75's, the age of disability,[52] the change during this period is even sharper: a fourfold increase in men and fivefold in women. Numbers of these " old-olds " have almost doubled from one to two millions since 1939, and they will continue to grow (page 24), with implications in the number with " intractable physical and mental infirmity ", the number living alone, housebound, bedfast. Their own children coming along to look after them, those presently middle-aged, have increased only by half as much since 1939.

The historic *decline of mortality* at younger ages has also added to the numbers of old people; but not many as yet, because

TABLE VII

Recent, and " Projected ", Growth of Population England and Wales

Thousands

AGE	1939		1961		1981		1991	
	M	F	M	F	M	F	M	F
45-64	4,330	5,085	5,684	6,191	5,628	5,835	5,766	5,790
(% 1961)	(76)	(82)	(100)	(100)	(99)	(94)	(101)	(94)
65-74	1,194	1,477	1,431	2,105	2,058	2,659	2,046	2,601
(% 1961)	(83)	(70)	(100)	(100)	(144)	(126)	(143)	(124)
75+	404	657	689	1,296	965	1,852	1,141	2,089
(% 1961)	(59)	(50)	(100)	(100)	(140)	(143)	(166)	(161)
Total All ages	19,688	21,559	22,448	23,821	25,599	26,503	27,215	27,841

Registrar General and Government Actuary.

substantial gains in the number of survivors from the fall in death rates were not achieved till after the turn of the century when *infant* mortality began to fall. A decline of mortality in children for example, however grand an achievement, can increase the survivors to live (very likely) to old age only by little. These are some examples of the course of mortality:

Average Annual Death Rates Per 1,000 Males [46]

	Under 1 yr.*	5-9	35-44	55-64	75-84
1851-70	168	8·3	13	32	147
1891-1900	168	4·3	12	35	146
1906-10	129	3·3	8·6	31	138
1921-25	86	2·6	6·5	25	136
1961	24	0·5	2·4	22	124

* Infant mortality per 1,000 live births. The rate was just under 160 between 1871 and 1890.
All statistics refer to England and Wales unless otherwise stated.

Death rates are high in infancy, fall to their nadir in school-days, then climb slowly to reach again the same kind of level as in infancy. The epochal, over 50 per cent, drop between the 1850's and the 1900's in the death rate at 5-9 years of age, from 8·3 to 3·3, reduced the number of deaths in a thousand children by five and increased the number of survivors from 991·7 to 996·7 (or fifty in ten thousand children, etc.); *i.e.* the size of the cohort moving onward has scarcely been affected. In other words, the great increase in " expectation of life " among the young (at birth the improvement this century is about 20 years to an expectancy now of 68 in men and 74 in women) has not yet contributed substantially to the growing numbers of old people. Longevity in middle age has also increased during the present century—by about 20 per cent, less in men because of the forces already described and more in women. For example:

Average Expectation of Life at 60 [46] [49]

On Experience of—	Men	Women
1838-54	13·5 years	14·3 years
1891-1900	12·9	14·1
1901-10	13·5	15·0
1920-22	14·4	16·2
1960-62	15·1	19·0

Again, obviously, the contribution to the rising numbers of old people has been comparatively small.

And the same applies to the experience of the aged themselves. In 1920-22 life expectancy at 70 was 8·8 years in men, and 10·0 years in women. Now the corresponding figures are 9·3 and 11·7. . . . Even small increments at this age are a real gain, of course, but they might well represent little more than snatch victories by the antibiotics, etc., and there is little support in such figures for the notion that today's old people are appreciably healthier than their predecessors.

SEX RATIO

Where mortality, including the losses in wars (these were catastrophic for young men in 1914-18) has strongly affected British demographic patterns is in the sex ratio, the *proportion* *of males to females* in the population.[47] The death rate is higher among males at all ages,* the worst periods being 15-19 years (nearly all the excess in males then are accidental deaths, and motor cycles are involved in well over half) and, for very different reasons, the decade 55-64. Far more males are conceived, but by birth the population ratio, M:F, is just over 1:1. It falls, very gradually at first, the number of men and women equalising around 30 years of age. Throughout the 20's, therefore, and particularly the early 20's which are the usual marrying ages, there is now a slight excess of males. From age 55 the fall in the sex ratio of the population is steep, and over 80 years old it now is 0·5:1.

FORESIGHT

For some the main interest of history is the light it can throw on the future. With the help of vital statistics and other " political arithmetic " it is possible to make some reasonable forecasts: prospects vis-a-vis young people will be considered for a change. The " boom " of post-war births** is now the " bulge " in its 'teens, and the school-leavers of 1962 are already having a good deal of trouble finding suitable jobs. Apprenticeships have not expanded; the system is working badly despite the serious shortage of skilled workers. In 1965 there will be nearly 600,000 more 17-19 year olds than in 1960, a rise again of almost a third, with consequences for higher education that are anticipated with considerable anxiety. Thus to maintain the present proportion with university education (but 4-5 per cent of the age group), the number of places will need to be increased by a third or so, *i.e.* by about 35,000, the size of the whole of Oxford + Cambridge +Birmingham + Leeds + Liverpool + Manchester Universities. In fact the position will be even more acute, because the schools are increasing their output of Sixth

---

* Till 104, anyhow. There is no further information.
** Average number of births in 1939-45 was about 650,000 p.a., in 1946-7 about 850,000 p.a.

Formers with the necessary entrance qualifications. Many will be unable to gain admission, present, not to say, rising, expectations will be frustrated.

In Social Medicine, several movements can be foreseen. Without any change in incidence rate, numbers having the serious diseases of young people—" appendicitis " in girls, asthma, osteosarcoma, schizophrenia—obviously will increase. . . . These are not pressing issues; young people are among the " healthiest " in the population, making little demand on ordinary medical care. The incidence of social disorders, however, is rising so rapidly that they have to be monitored from year to year. Motor cycle fatalities in teenagers doubled

TABLE VIII

Mortality of Males Aged 15-19[27][55]

England and Wales

	No. of Deaths in Motor Cycle Accidents	Death Rate from Disease per million	Total Death Rate per million
1951	117	524	887
1952	105	485	900
1953	121	450	822
1954	155	444	814
1955	178	436	880
1956	183	378	788
1957	228	458 ('flu)	914
1958	298	354	835
1959	376	362	936
1960	450	329	905
1961*	463	331	930

* Population-at-risk increased 20 per cent 1951-61, though in face of such figures of motor cycle fatalities it is possible to be sure of the main trend without up-to-date information on the population. Other violent deaths varied little in the period.

between 1957 and 1960, Table VIII: the craze seems to be subsiding, and unless it does the population increase will mean an even bigger increase in these accidents[27] . . . The menarche is earlier (it is about 13½ now in girls and close to a year on average earlier than pre-war[58]), the age of marriage is falling,

TABLE IX

(1) *Maternities Conceived Extramaritally*

Per 1,000 Unmarried Women

England and Wales

AGE	1938	1952-4	1956	1958	1960	1961
15-19	11·8	15·5	19·0	21·2	24·0	27·1
20-24	32·6	42·5	48·6	52·2	58·0	63·1
Total 15-44	18·6	25·3	28·9	31·4	35·5	38·9

The Table includes children born illegitimate and, also, children conceived out of wedlock but born during the early months of marriage. In 1961 this latter group formed 72 per cent. of total " maternities conceived extramaritally " at 15-19 years of age.

Registrar General.[47] [48] [50]

(2) *Number of Patients with Gonorrhoea*

British Co-operative Clinical Study*

AGE	1957	1958	1961
Males			
15-19	828	1,058	1,530
20-24	4,171	4,853	6,612
25+	10,309	11,493	16,229
Females			
15-19	939	1,118	1,677
20-24	1,377	1,654	2,446
25+	1,816	1,955	2,377

* Includes c. 80 per cent of national total.
British Co-operative Clinical Group (1962). *Brit. J. vener. Dis.* **38**, 1.
Willcocks, R. R. (1962). Personal communication.

youngsters have achieved a new independence, in the transition to new standards there is general confusion about sexual behaviour[3]; so it is not surprising that there is more prenuptial conception and illegitimacy, Table IX (1), and more venereal disease (2).[25] [63] Since 1955/6 delinquency, too, seems to be increasing. The greater crowding of the bigger number of teenagers and the greater pressures on them—there is already a portent of unemployment—may well quicken the rising incidence of such casualties among the bigger population at risk, with a sharp increase indeed in the number of cases. . . . Such exacerbation of already serious problems opens up disturbing prospects, is a challenge now to try to be wise before the event.

FUTURE OF THE DEATH RATE IN MIDDLE AGE

Fig. 1 can be projected ahead, though the margins of confidence must be wide. What keeps the trend of mortality in middle-aged men even as moderately satisfactory as it is now, is the balancing of those diseases which are becoming commoner, like ischaemic heart disease, by those which are diminishing, like the infections. If the latter decline is halted before the modern epidemics are brought under control, and if the conditions that have remained stationary, such as bronchitis or cerebrovascular disease, do not show improvements in the meanwhile, the overall middle-aged male death rate will begin to rise.

Two hundred years ago there seems to have been a somewhat analogous situation.

" The yearly sum of the deaths ranged under the heads of apoplexies, suddenly, planet-struck, lethargies and palsies, fluctuates without any constant increase or decrease, till the beginning of the present century: from which time this sum has been perpetually increasing. Is this difference (increase) only an apparent one, arising from the placing of some deaths under these in the latter Bills (of mortality) which formerly came under other articles? There seems no reason for such a suspicion. If the increase be real, is it owing to any alteration in our manners, or diet? And what is that alteration? The practice of drinking spiritous liquors must, probably, answer for some part of this; and it might be of public use, if some attention were paid to the finding out of the other causes.

But there does not appear to be any increase in the distempers just mentioned, or in any other, which is not likely to be abundantly made amends for, by the decrease in the numbers destroyed by the smallpox, which may be hoped for from the practice of inoculation". Heberden, W. 1759. Preface to *A Collection of the Yearly Bills of Mortality,* London.

Prophecy, however, is hazardous. In doctors, a group with exceedingly high incidence—and maximal diagnosis—there is no evidence of a rise of ischaemic heart disease between 1947-50 and 1957-60.[37] [55] Among the general population of men, mortality from cancer of the lung at 55-64 years of age should now steady off: the death rate in men aged 35-44 has not risen since the late 1940's, at 45-54 years of age since about 1953, and at 55-59 since about 1956. The " cohort " born in this century has been fully exposed to cigarette smoke, it may be postulated, unlike all previous generations who had no cigarettes at all, or passed part of their adult life before the habit could be adopted. The decline of duodenal ulcer, the third of the " new diseases " of middle-aged men, has already been described, though of course ulcer has never been a killing disease on a major scale but a cause of misery and inefficiency.*

POPULATION EXPLOSION

With this glance at the recent history of population I must mention, if only as token, what is the world's main problem in social medicine; the world's main problem it might simply be said. The illustration chosen has recently been much in the public eye because natural disaster has piled problems on already insoluble problems.[59] It illustrates several features of the population explosion.

* There is another aspect of the death rate in middle age. Disease that does not become apparent until after the end of the reproductive period is not subject to the forces of natural selection in the same way that diseases effective in younger age groups are. Because selection is less powerful, genetic factors may be particularly strong in the aetiology of disease affecting older age groups.[19] [31] [43] The genes are still likely to have their effects conditioned by the environment, however, and this is in principle controllable. A good example is cancer of the stomach in which (a) there are genetic causes, and (b) which has fallen sharply in the U.S.A. and begun to fall in this country. Environmental causes already are evident in the production of ischaemic heart disease, lung cancer and chronic bronchitis which between them are responsible for half the deaths of middle-aged men. It may be expected that genetic and environmental causes will prove to be linked, the expression of one to be dependent on the other.[9]

30

Malaria is hyperendemic in Mauritius, and in 1949 DDT residual insecticide spraying on a mass scale was begun. The attack was soon successful and the principal vector, *Anopheles funestus*, has been eradicated. The vital statistics tell a story that no longer surprises:

Mortality in Mauritius

	1946-8	1950	1959-60
Death rate per 1,000 .	24·4	13·9	11·1
Infant Mortality . .	147	76	66
Population, '000s .	433	465	630

Death rates have been halved, and are stabilised at that level, with a sharp rise in life expectancy. Changes have been compressed into a few years that in England and Wales took a century—the fall in the general death rate—and half a century—the fall of infant mortality. But the birth rate in Mauritius has not adapted to this revolution in survival; it continues exceedingly high, in the order of 40 and more per 1,000. The " natural increase " of population, the surplus of births over deaths, is now about five times what it was before the anti-malaria campaign. Characteristic of a country with high fertility experience, the *age distribution of the population*, and the burden of dependency, is grossly different from our own:

	Per cent	
	UNDER 15	OVER 65
Mauritius . . .	44	3·1
England and Wales .	23	12

1960.

It is the younger ages who benefit most from a general fall in the death rate: survivors of infancy have risen by 81 per 1,000 liveborn. There has not yet been time, however, for the great wave of children to move far up the age scale. The population " pyramid " in Mauritius thus *is* a pyramid. The 0-4's are the largest group and, typical of a " young " population, successive groups are smaller in size. This is quite unlike the shape of the distribution in Britain for the last 50 years.

The population of Britain is growing by about 0·5 per cent a year, that of Mauritius by over 3 per cent a year, somewhat above the average in the underdeveloped nations. In the world as a whole the annual rate of increase is 1·8 per cent (the rate it so happens in the USA) and world population now some 3,100 millions and increasing by a million a week will, on a conservative projection, be 6,000 millions by the end of the century. Numbers will snowball as the children whose lives have been saved begin, in turn, to bear their own.

Triumph of Public Health

In the underdeveloped countries medicine and Public Health are fulfilling ambitions on a grand scale, death rates are melting away. Besides preventive measures like DDT and cleaner water supplies, sulphonamides for bacterial pneumonia and meningococcal meningitis, penicillin for yaws, and an array of therapies for tropical infections and infestations are now available; the possibilities with tuberculosis have recently been transformed.[11] But measures designed to promote health have not turned out quite as intended. Benefits of medical science and technology are now being applied en masse to populations that are changing little in some other respects and, for example, reducing the size of their families. The great source of the misery of mankind may yet prove to be their numbers and Public Health, in one sense, may be responsible.

More than half the world at present is wretchedly poor and the gap between the haves and have-nots, with all its critical potential, is not narrowing. In the underdeveloped countries, with incomes well below £1 weekly per head (it is over £8 in Britain), economic growth is little more than keeping pace with the growth of population; in some countries like Mauritius the standard of living actually is falling. Mainly cereal diets—and malnutrition, kwashiorkor, anaemia—is the lot of a third to a half of the world's population, 30 or 40 millions may suffer from actual calorie shortage.[10]

The United Nations have now declared a *Development Decade*. The endeavour is to increase economic growth of the underdeveloped countries to 5 or 6 per cent annually, well above the rate of population growth, and thus begin the move towards the " take-off " to economic prosperity. Many countries, our own prominently, have also joined hands with the new nations in Asia and Africa in a *Freedom From Hunger* campaign. World Health Day 1963 is devoted to " Hunger, the Disease of Millions ". Whatever happens in the future to the size of families, a substantial rise of population is now inevitable and these campaigns are urgent.

Population Policy

The most realistic hope for the future of population in the " underdeveloped " countries is that *family planning* will come, but so far this is making little headway. With industrialisation and far more intensive and scientific agriculture, and with mass disease less of a limiting factor, living standards surely will rise; and the growth of education, the enlargement of parochial horizons, the provision of new sources of security, will surely provide the psychological impetus for restriction of size of family—though it cannot be expected to happen quickly.[13] Health, population and social advance form one complex of problems. Meanwhile, WHO, dedicated since 1955 to the eradication of malaria, is prevented from giving a lead in population control. Public Health has been slow in adjusting to the challenge. It has much relevant experience in Maternal and Child Welfare, and epidemiologic observation and experiment too could more often be applied. The social sciences are likely here to find their great opportunity. Chemistry and plastics will help with simpler contraceptives: what is needed are inventions to match those that started the population explosion—and the social and economic incentives to use them. How much misery there will be till a new balance of population is achieved numbs the imagination.

3

COMMUNITY DIAGNOSIS: COMMUNITY HEALTH

Epidemiology provides " intelligence " for the health services. The nature and relative size of problems are described, and indications given of their importance to the community. For example, and illustrating again with the statistics of incapacity for work, in the year 1960-1 the 15 million or so men now insured in Britain (nearly 100 per cent of men at working ages) had over 6¾ million " spells " of absence because of sickness and injuries, totalling some 217 million weekdays lost from work. Twenty-six million days were certified as bronchitis . . . , 20-21 million days were lost for (acute) respiratory infection, including influenza. . . . Ischaemic heart disease, hypertension, etc., accounted for 15 million days . . . , " rheumatism ", arthritis, " sciatica ", etc., for 17 million days . . . , peptic ulcer for 4¼ million, other unspecified gastric and duodenal ailments for 5¼ million. . . . Psychoneurosis, anxiety symptoms and the like labelled as such, were responsible for 10 million days. . . . Industrial accidents caused the loss of 16 million days. . . . The spells of absence included in these figures all lasted four days or more, and to them have to be added the time lost in absences of one, two and three days.[53]

Such facts may be sketchy and very general. How accurate the diagnoses are, and what may lie behind them, often cannot be assessed, not more readily than for death certificates when Farr began his work. Practitioners, for example, are understandably reluctant to certify cancer, with all that it means to the public, when it is the cause of disability. These are figures moreover of capacity to work, which is by no means necessarily the same as clinical sickness. The physician has social as well as medical responsibilities in certifying fitness or unfitness for work, and the interpretation of trends is never simple. I have already touched on this. Another trouble in using such information as a measure of community health is that most of the information is about *spells* of absence. One worker may have several spells in the course of a single year, and routine translation of " spells " of incapacity into *persons* who are incapacitated, providing thus a prevalence rate of morbidity (*i.e.* of all the persons who are affected) is very difficult. Yet the figures are valuable for Government in planning of health services, and as indicators from year to year of one of the main burdens of illness on the community. Thus, nearly a million workers on average are drawing sick insurance—the cost in benefit alone is £150 millions a year—and by virtue of sheer size and numbers, the first and simplest warning of a " flu epidemic " is an increase merely in the total volume of such sick absence. For the clinician these figures provide background and perspective, some idea of the importance in morbidity as a whole of the type of patient he meets and does not meet. The public too is educated about the magnitude of health problems; the figures on rheumatic disorders, for instance, have proved an effective weapon in stimulating public as well as official interest. These statistics have proved useful also in the advancement of knowledge. Thus, inspired observation by Halliday before the war[21] led after it to the epidemiological study of " rheumatism " and occupation that has been so rewarding in the description of miners' disc syndromes and the rest.[31][34]

Table X overleaf shows, with a method borrowed from the Reports of the Ministry of Health, how the picture of ill-health in middle age, and of the work of Medicine, differs at various levels of presentation. And how it does differ! Straightaway it should be said that the selection of " diagnoses " and their grouping must be arbitrary: the main thing is that they should make sense at the level that is being considered. " Middle age " is drawn here in wider terms than in Figs. 1 and 2. Attention is drawn only to a few features.

TABLE X

Statistical Account of Ill-Health in Middle Age

Importance of Different Conditions at Different Levels of Presentation

Ages 45-64

Level of Presentation; and Frequency	Men		Women	
	Condition	Proportion of Total %	Condition	Proportion of Total %
(1) QUESTIONING OF SAMPLE OF POPULATION Persons reporting sickness: *Rate per 1,000 of those interviewed* PER MONTH *in* Men=670 Women=780 Britain, 1950	"Symptoms", often vague, including headache and nervousness	20	"Symptoms", often vague, including headache and nervousness	29
	"Rheumatism", etc.	13	"Rheumatism", etc.	17
	Acute upper respiratory infections	10	Acute upper respiratory infections	7
	Gastric troubles	10	Gastric troubles	7
	Bronchitis	6	Bronchitis	3
			Varicose veins	3
(2) GENERAL PRACTICE Persons consulting the doctor: *Rate per 1,000 on practitioners' lists* PER ANNUM *in* Men=604 for 1,149 illnesses Women=667 for 1,428 illnesses England and Wales, 1955-6	Acute upper respiratory infections	14	Acute upper respiratory infections	12
	Injuries	8	Rheumatism, etc.	8
	Bronchitis	8	Psychoneurosis, and symptoms of nervousness, etc.	8
	Rheumatism, etc.	7	Injuries	6
	Disorders of stomach and duodenum, including ulcer	6	Menopause; and menstrual disorders	5
	Psychoneurosis, and symptoms of	5	Bronchitis	4

Patients discharged from hospital: Rate per 1,000 population of England and Wales PER ANNUM in Men=78 Women=69 1960	Herna Ischaemic heart disease Peptic ulcer Cancer of lung Bronchitis	8 6 5 4 4	disorders: Prolapse Fibroids Injuries Diseases of gall-bladder Varicose veins Cancer of breast	5 3 6 3 3 3
Admissions for mental disease to mental hospital: Rate per 1,000 population of England and Wales PER ANNUM in Men=3 Women=4 1959	% of total admissions to all hospitals	3	% of total admissions to all hospitals	6
(4) CAUSES OF DEATH Persons dying: Rate per 1,000 population of England and Wales PER ANNUM in Men=13 Women=7 1960	Ischaemic heart disease Cancer of lung Vascular lesions of nervous system Bronchitis Injuries Cancer of Stomach	28 13 8 7 5 4	Vascular lesions of nervous system Ischaemic heart disease Cancer of breast Injuries Cancer of large intestine and rectum Chronic rheumatic heart disease	13 13 9 5 5 4

(1) LOGAN, W. P. D. & BROOKE, E. M. (1957). The Survey of Sickness 1943 to 1952. HMSO.
(2) LOGAN, W. P. D. & CUSHION, A. A. (1958). Morbidity Statistics from General Practice. HMSO.
(3) Report on Hospital In-patient Enquiry for the Year 1960. Part I. Preliminary Tables. HMSO.
    Supplement on Mental Health 1959. Registrar General. HMSO.
(4) The Registrar General's Statistical Review of England and Wales for the Year 1960. Part I, Tables. Medical. HMSO.

By way of introduction, the Table starts (1) with the kind of information obtainable by interviewers of the government's *Social Survey*, " knocking on the door " of samples of the population and enquiring about their health. In reply of course they were given a good deal of rather vague description of symptoms causing minor inconvenience, as well as a little —in proportion—of more serious trouble. It should be noticed that about two-thirds of the men and three-quarters of the women per *month* reported some " sickness ", whereas all the other rates in the Table are per *year*. The value of the diagnostic labels attached to these complaints is quite dubious : thus less than 2 per cent of all these middle-aged women's (very many) troubles were recorded as gynaecological disorder, which more likely reflects working-class reticence with a lay person than any other kind of fact.

The " leading causes " of sickness recorded during one year in a study by *general practitioners* in 106 practices of the National Health Service are then quoted (2). The patients in these practices are probably reasonably representative, though the doctors surely (and alas!) are not. Sixty per cent of the middle-aged men in the practice populations consulted the doctor during the year (604 per 1,000), and they reported 1,149 separate " illnesses ", excluding relapses, etc. Diagnostic categories are of course similar to those already given for incapacity to work. Fourteen per cent of the illnesses were acute respiratory infections, and with injuries, 8 per cent, they make up the majority of acute illness. These two groups of disorders were responsible for even less of the total consultations with the doctor, 11 and 7 per cent, respectively. The major chronic diseases accounted for about half of the consultations. (Age-bands in this study unfortunately are too broad to provide any illumination of the trends of Fig. 4.) These particular data are the best now available of the prevalence of morbidity in the general population. Comparing (1) and (2), it can be inferred that most " trouble " with health is not presented to the doctor. Moreover, there is no reflection in the figures of the commonly held view that psychological disorders account for much, a third or even half, of the general practitioner's work, though the Social Survey's data suggest that prevalence of these, including presumably the most trivial, may be as high as about 13 per cent in men and about 23 per cent in women.

Since this book is much concerned with it, details are given of the *prevalence of cardiovascular disease* in middle age in these general practices:

Patients Consulting, per 1,000 on Practitioners' Lists, Ages 45-64

DIAGNOSIS	MEN	WOMEN
Ischaemic heart disease	17	7·4
Hypertension, and hypertensive heart disease	15	37
Vascular disease of nervous system . .	4·3	3·7
Peripheral arterial disease; other " arteriosclerosis ", etc.	5·4	3·8
Rheumatic fever and heart disease . . .	1·6	3·3
Varicose veins, phlebitis, etc.	14	33
Haemorrhoids	12	8·8

Thus, about 7 per cent of the men, and 10 per cent of the women, consulted for cardiovascular disease during the year.

The diseases taking people into *hospitals*, Table X (3), are very different from the diseases bringing them to the general practitioner. By now the acute upper respiratory infections have been shed, but bronchitis continues. It is indeed the only diagnosis that runs through all " levels " of the Table in either sex. Commoner in men than in women from the beginning, at the hospital " level " bronchitis no longer appears as a major cause of serious illness in women. There is a rather even spread of diagnoses in hospitals, nothing to compare with upper respiratory infections in general practice or ischaemic heart disease in mortality. As well as giving about half-a-dozen examples in each section, I aimed at including 50 per cent of the total; this could not be done for the hospitals.

At the hospital stage or " level " there is no doubt about the preponderance of chronic disease, often of course in acute episodes. Again, however, the statistics are unsatisfactory; they represent spells in hospital, not persons, and can only occasionally furnish estimates of incidence or prevalence. The figures on perforations, p. 20, are a good example of how useful such data can be (one perforation/one man is a reasonable assumption).

Finally, the Table (4) gives leading *causes of death*; they are in sharp contrast to those of morbidity, particularly in general practice. The contribution of the two main " modern epidemics " stands out.

With all their limitations, the implications of such facts about the people's health, and of the differences in the Table, extend widely to social policy, medical education and the strategy of research.

MORBIDITY SURVEYS

The diverse figures in the Table illustrate the difficulties of describing health in terms other than mortality! Morbidity means what it is defined to mean: whether a subjective malaise, measurable evidence of disorder, pathology diagnosed by a doctor, or certified incapacity to work. Related, particularly in the chronic non-infectious diseases are the problems of when " morbidity " begins, how long it lasts, how to define its severity and the incapacity it causes. Despite many such difficulties the study of morbidity is expanding rapidly, and it is becoming a main interest of Public Health since mortality is progressively less useful in the diagnosis of community health. There is great scope for field surveys to extend what can be obtained from routine statistics, and to make good their deficiencies. Many are being carried out, and some will be referred to later on, but there is always need for more. How much obesity is there? In middle age, in childhood? What are the dimensions of the allergy—prurigo—asthma problem? Is there any useful idea of how often accidental poisoning occurs in children? Toxic reactions to drugs in adults? Drug habituation, addiction? How many abortions? How common is genital prolapse and other gynaecological misery? Prostatic enlargement? Malnutrition in the aged? Hypothermia? Osteoporosis? Varicose ulcer? Pulmonary thrombo-embolism? Cerebro-vascular disease, major and minor? What in fact is the proportion of children brought up in fatherless families, of young-marrieds without a home of their own, of old people living alone? Is there a lot of untreated but treatable depression, of confusional states in the old, of alcoholism? How common is " school phobia "? How much disruptive sexual maladjustment? How many homosexuals? In no field are modest fact-finding surveys more needed than in mental disorder, of individual and family. But this apart, I doubt if a single community has usable, comprehensive inventories of its recognised chronic physical disease problems, and of the needs for community care and rehabilitation. There has been far too little spill-over from traditional Public Health with its long experience of tuberculosis (and rheumatic heart disease) registration. In general, the Cancer Register and some hospital figures for psychosis apart, there are little data even on a national scale of the incidence and prevalence of the chronic diseases that now dominate the practice of medicine.

Morbidity is but one illustration of the modern community's need to know itself, a need whose wide recognition—anew—represents a striking change in the contemporary climate of opinion. A tragic and shameful growth of homeless families in London was suddenly exposed late in 1961. The country entered the recent war with 9 per cent of the population over 65 years of age, and no problem; at its close there were 10 per cent, and Old Age suddenly was The Social Problem of The Century—but recognised too late to affect the 1948 legislation. From the condition of the recruits in the Boer War to the thalidomide calamity (it surely took far too long for this epidemic to be spotted), and not forgetting the boy whose death led to the Children Act, society is liable to be caught by surprise, and not in all instances inevitably. The growing number of over 75's, and the conditions under which many of them live, must sooner or later present a winter " emergency ". Will there be a crisis in nursing, teaching and social work from the disappearance of the young unmarried woman?*The more complex a society, the more does it need an inquisitive intelligence service to diagnose itself, to seek trouble (and create it), and to probe the consquences of trends and policies. I have already referred to the help of history in looking ahead. That foresight is so rare a virtue is proving a critical factor in everything to do with health and health services. Of course no success can be guaranteed for any line of enquiry, but that does not excuse waiting on events.

*   *   *

NOTES ON PROCEDURES

In this book I can say little about practical matters, on how epidemiologic studies actually are carried out. But illustrations will be given of the kinds of question that arise.

Populations

In making an epidemiological survey of a chosen population the first thing to be determined is who in fact is present during the period of study. The Table shows what was the true state

" Population " of a General Practice [45] [64]

Persons registered	3,611
Persons actually found on search to be present	3,037
Missing persons	574

of affairs when we set out to list the actual membership of an ordinary general practice we were observing, and not merely taking for granted those who were officially " on the books ".

* *Proportion of Women who are Married*: England and Wales[55]

AGE	1911	1938	1961	1963
		per cent		
20-24	24	33	59	
30-34	71	73	90	

The deficit was made up thus:

Found to be represented by duplicate cards	53
Previously died	59
Transferred to another doctor's list . .	178
No trace on other local doctors' lists, or in the district	284
Total .	574

To check all who were registered, account for the 574 " dead souls ", and produce finally the correct figure of 3,037, involved much shoe-leather, hundreds of home visits and many other enquiries. But discharging this most elementary duty of scrutinising the data transformed them, and the value of any sampling that might later be done.*

To proceed. All populations it must be recognised are " biased ". The question, " Who is present? ", must be followed by " How did they get there? "—and " Who got away? " That is to say, it is necessary to consider how *selection* might affect what is being investigated. Thus Ødegard found an excess of schizophrenia in merchant seamen and showed that it was due to selective *entry,* the choice of this occupation by persons with character disorder;[51] Schilling showed that the deficiency of byssinosis in female cotton workers reflected merely their selective *exit* from the mills because of the disease, not any immunity to it.[59] During the decline of coalmining in the inter-war years it was the tougher who got out of the industry; today standards of recruitment in several services have been lowered because of manpower shortages. Studies of whole communities also are liable to significant bias. Thus, what makes people emigrate to New Towns—such causes as their age, family responsibilities, occupation, health and temperament—will affect morbidity rates in these towns; and in the towns that have been left. During the Depression of the 1930's, assessment of the effects of unemployment on health

---

* Though that was not the intention, it also had implications for the administration of the recently established National Health Service.

was bedevilled by the impossibility of dealing satisfactorily with migration, of assessing to what extent the high rates of rheumatic heart disease and phthisis in the young women of the North of England or South Wales, for example, were a result of the departure of the healthier to more prosperous parts of the country, offering better chance of jobs.[47] The continuing drift of population from North to South of England must be one cause of today's continuing North-South, " Two Nations ", gradient of mortality.

Indicators and Measurements

Diagnosis of the " cases " (and, likewise, specification of the biological and social variables which are to be related) present another series of problems. In studying morbidity, the usual problem in epidemiology is to describe every individual in a population, or its sample, so that those having the disease are distinguished from those free of it. Criteria of what is a case must be laid down; they will often be " operational " definitions, adopted for the particular investigation and settled only after pilot, pre-test, studies.

Indicators of morbidity can be discussed under three heads.[19] The first requirement is *simplicity* of the indicator or " instrument " proposed, the utmost simplicity that is consistent with the level of study, and yet will discriminate categorically in terms of the question being put. Thus, it is possible to obtain much information in mass surveys about the mechanics of the lung and the gas exchange from a single breath. The US Army in World War II used a battery of fifteen tests to screen for psychoneurosis among recruits.[3] Later it was found that one of these—a brief questionnaire dealing with psychosomatic complaints—identified 93 per cent of those eliminated by the entire battery. Electrocardiography and the X-ray meet this requirement of being (relatively) easy to apply on a large scale, and they have the further advantage that observations can be assessed for their *reproducibility*, requirement (2). The traditional history and physical examination are often difficult to reproduce; but observer variation matters far more of course in epidemiological surveys[15][74] than in the individual case-study of clinical work with its opportunities for multiple examination and its concern for the total picture.* In a pioneering venture, much effort by Fletcher and others has been devoted to the production of the Medical Research Council's standardised questionnaire on respiratory symptoms[15][24][25][65] which yields a reproducible diagnosis, within known limits, of " chronic bronchitis " as this is defined in terms of cough, spit and chest illness; and which is being tested in various social groups and in different countries.[15][57][59] A lot can be learned from social scientists who depend so heavily on questionnaires and interviews for their data, and have refined the techniques of obtaining reproducibility and assessing it.[14][28][49] In the case of intelligence tests this is established (a) by giving the same test on several occasions and comparing the IQ scores in each; and (b) by split-half methods, where the score on half the items (randomly selected) in the test is compared with the other half. This latter technique has the additional merit of indicating whether the test can be further simplified. The reproducibility of most IQ tests is very high indeed, when the situation remains the same. But reproducibility is not enough.

The *validity* of the indicator, *i.e.* how far it measures what is intended, has also to be assessed (3) if possible by comparing it in action with the best available, the standard method, say in making the diagnosis as defined. It can then be estimated how successful the indicator will be, how closely it measures or distinguishes what it sets out to do: in how many, for example, it is insufficiently specific and the disease is wrongly found to be present (the false positives), and how often it is insufficiently sensitive, how many cases are missed (the false negatives). From the balance of these it can be

---

* Nevertheless, what has been learned in epidemiology can help to raise the accuracy of clinical practice, and of other activities, including the marking of exam. papers.

decided whether the indicator is good enough for the particular investigation. In some enquiries false positives could
be disastrous (*e.g.* when it involves admission to a mental
hospital), in others false negatives could be fatal (*e.g.* in
screening for cancer). Here are two examples, from our own
work, of validation of simple methods against standard. Fig.
6 shows how satisfactory a measure the trouser waistband of
busmen's uniforms, data available by the thousands,[46] can be
in assessing the waist circumference, and *girth,* of these
men. The trouser-size was obtained from the tailors' records
for a sample of men after they had been examined clinically:

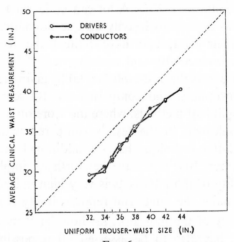

FIG. 6

Survey methods: Validation of uniform
trouser-waist size by clinical measurement
of waist. Comparison of the two measurements in a sample of 365 busmen aged
40-64. London Transport, 1956-8. On average, the clinical measurement was about 2
inches smaller than the tailors'—throughout
the range of nine sizes, and equally in
drivers and conductors.

Brit. J. prev. soc. Med. (1961). **15,** 143.[45] [64]

It has been exceedingly difficult to produce simple and valid
methods of assessing individual *diet* which are suitable for
large-scale field surveys. Our own approach has given promising results for a wide range of foods. . . . Samples of

bank men (97 of them) weighed what they ate for a week or a fortnight and the total *weight* of each food was summed. This method of assessment is probably the best possible under free-living conditions, but it is quite unpractical for big population studies. We then experimented with numerical scores of the number of *times* specific foods were taken in various forms—*e.g.* milk in tea, with cereal, etc.—until a total score was obtained for each food that correlated highly with the recorded weight of that food consumed by the same individual. Next, the method was tested by applying the scoring system that had been developed to other samples of men, *e.g.* a group of busmen, and the correlations were calculated between the scored number of times they had eaten various foods, and the total amount of these foods that was recorded in weighed surveys they had carried out. Here are some examples:

Validation of Simple Method of Dietary Assessment (Derived from Number of Times Food Eaten) By Comparison with Standard Method (Actual Weight of Food as Eaten) [22] [37] [46] [64]

CORRELATION BETWEEN RESULTS OF TWO METHODS

	(1) Original Study of 97 Bank Officers	(2) Independent Test in 53 Busmen
	r	r
Milk . .	0·94	0·88
Butter . .	0·86	0·90
Meat . .	0·77	0·67
Cooking Fats	0·89	0·93

The scoring system is demonstrably as good (or as bad) in the independent group of metropolitan workers as in the original sample of provincial white-collar men, and it encourages the hope that a valid method can be produced for conducting individual diet surveys of big numbers by simple record of food taken without going to the trouble of weighing it.

Note: The word "reliability" means reproducibility and is nicer; but it is sometimes wrongly used for validity, so it is best to stick to the jargon.

The main point, sometimes overlooked in the struggles with methodology and data collection, is that the investigation must ask a meaningful question that elicits a worthwhile answer relevant to the research problem as stated, and commensurate with the effort involved. This, of course, is where the investigator's experience, his judgement—and his ingenuity —as well as his knowledge of the subject matter and its variation are crucial. The investigation can be at different *levels*, and even the crudest can be useful. Thus, description of the epidemiology of myocardial lesions at necropsy may be attempted at these levels: [10] [40] [42]

(1) Representative clinical case-studies, designed to inform about a population, can include much quantitative detail of all macroscopic pathology. (Reproducibility can be tested by " blind repeat " reporting on sample specimens.)

(2) Large-scale ad hoc surveys should permit classification, at least, into infarcts large and small, focal myocardial fibrosis, other lesions, (Validity may be tested by submitting every Xth specimen to detailed clinical scrutiny.)

(3) It may be possible to derive information from local coroners' records on the presence or absence in the population of infarcts leading to ruptured ventricle. (A sample can also be studied microscopically.)

Each study can extract worthwhile information at its own level; but of course both the analysis made and the conclusions drawn must be appropriate to that level.

Estimating Mental Disorders

The greatest difficulties are at present met with in psychiatry: in setting meaningful questions and producing objective and technically satisfactory indicators. Here are estimates from a special sample in a four-doctor *general practice* during one year:

48

Prevalences of Psychiatric Disorder

	PROPORTION OF ALL AGED 15+
(1) Persons referred to consultant psychiatrist	1%
(2) Persons with disorder in defined psychiatric categories of International Statistical Classification of Disease (WHO)	5%
(3) "Conspicuous psychiatric morbidity", as operationally defined	9%
(4) = (3) + other persons with obvious psychological illnesses, or with illness where physical factors were not considered significant in causation	27%
(5) = (4) + other persons with "psychosomatic" or "stress" conditions	34%

In addition, there was an unknown proportion with psychological overlay complicating physical illness.

KESSEL, W. I. N. (1960). *Brit. J. prev. soc. Med.* **14**, 16.

The assessment of " mental health " in this practice obviously depends on the criteria adopted; and it is just as sensible to say that in about 10 per cent there was conspicuous psychiatric morbidity, as that about a third of the population had psychological illness, provided the definitions are stated. In raising the proportions with psychological disorder beyond that in the simple diagnostic categories of Table X, more information about the patients is used, including what was learnt in the attempt to relieve and treat. However that may be, the proportion of the total which is seen in hospitals and, a fortiori, Teaching Hospitals evidently is minute.

Individual doctor-variation for category (3), which was mostly neurosis, ranged from 4·2 per cent to 12 per cent of the population-at-risk. In such a setting the question of what is a psychiatric " case " is beset by particular difficulty in achieving a reproducible answer. There is variability, first, among the doctors in their feel for psychological mechanisms, conscious and unconscious. Second, a subject I have not con-considered,[46] the condition of the patient is liable to vary considerably (there is a whole literature on the variability of the blood cholesterol level[46]). Finally, and even more than in other illness, there is variability also from the interaction of observer and subject. (This is seen at its crudest in the selection of mutually sympathetic doctors and patients, but it also operates acutely by suggestion and in the " uncertainty " effect—the observer influencing the subject by the act of studying him.) Such problems are far from solution. The most hopeful approaches at present are through multiple observations and standardised questionnaires.

A Joint Enterprise

Troubles are by no means over with these questions of criteria and classification. The essence of the epidemiological method, as said, is that the same information must be obtained about all the population or its designated sample. Only thus can numerator appropriate to denominator be produced. So many, x, in the population smoke, the rest, y, don't; $x/(x+y)$ gives the frequency, or rate, of smokers. In health surveys, not everyone invited can be expected to come forward straightaway for examination. It is axiomatic that those who don't " play " are different from those who do, and by now it is also clear that those who participate unwillingly differ from those who are eager or ready. The Fig. opposite is an excellent illustration. We made the same kind of observation, in a social-psychological study of families of patients with duodenal ulcer,[20] when a sample of ordinary families in a local general practice was invited to act as " healthy " controls. This is how they co-operated :

Family Response	Total	No. Eventually Found to Have a Major Problem
" Good " co-operation	20	3
" Fair " co-operation	12	5
" Unco-operative "	17	11

The contrast is striking, even with these small numbers, between the families who agreed at once to participate and those who throughout were unwilling.

The consequences of a high refusal or failure rate may be serious, and every research group will have its own (often horrible) examples of it. The seriousness will depend, of course, on the nature of the question that is asked, and on the

ANALYSIS BY ORDER OF COMING UP

Percent with disease found in volunteers, analysed by order of coming up for examination.

COCHRANE, A. L. (1950). In *The Application of Scientific Methods to Industrial and Service Medicine*. HMSO.

range of difference being observed. Generally speaking it is worth great effort to get 90 per cent co-operation;* reasonable analyses can then be done on the worst interpretation of the missing 10 per cent. In the survey of London busmen some results of which will be presented in later pages,[30] [64] it took as much effort to win the co-operation of the final 15 per cent of the men as of the initial 77 per cent who agreed immediately to be examined. Such a failure rate (8 per cent) however, cannot matter very much in describing anatomical and bio-chemical distributions of drivers and conductors, since the 80 individuals out of the 1,000 concerned are fairly equally spread among the two occupations, and over a span of twenty-five years of age. (Everyone has a height, weight, blood

* Co-operation can be measured in units, or Cochranes: 90 per cent co-operation scores 1 Cochrane, 95 per cent scores 2, etc.

cholesterol level, etc.; the value of these, moreover, is unlikely to affect willingness to co-operate.) But a " lapse " rate even of this size could be fatal in a study of disease, where a difference is being demonstrated between a prevalence of say 2 per cent in one group and 1 per cent in another—especially if there are only a few hundred instead of thousands in each group—since it is entirely conceivable that the sick will selectively decline to participate. Quite a lot may be discoverable, one way and another, about the non-co-operators and it is usually well worth trying to do so.*

*   *   *

Health and the Mode of Life : Social Medicine

Epidemiology may be further defined as the *study of health and disease of populations in relation to their environment and ways of living.* This will involve definitions of: (1) the people being studied; (2) their environment; (3) the aspect of health. Observations will be expressed in such terms as the distribution of casual blood pressure, and the proportion with particular readings, among men of defined age, doing one kind of work and another; the object being to see whether there is an environmental difference, in their occupation, between hypertensives and others.

Social Class

Table XI is a simple social analysis of the first reproductive cycle in the population of this Scottish city with close on 200,000 inhabitants. The ongoing Survey from which the figures are drawn focuses on health, and on the efficiency of this physiological process. The value of an " umbrella " category like social class is well illustrated. This scale, provided

---

* Before condemning anyone as " unco-operative " it may be worth recalling that about 30 per cent of the doctors who were approached in Doll and Hill's classic study did not answer a simple questionnaire on smoking.

by the General Register Office, was devised 50 years ago by Stevenson, a successor to Farr as Chief Medical Statistician. He based it on occupations, on (a) their level of skill and role

TABLE **XI**

Social Class and Reproductive Performance in Aberdeen
1956-60

Married Women Bearing a First Child

Findings in Primiparae	Social Class of Husband		
	I & II	III	IV & V
Age	%	%	%
– 20 years	2·2	14	22
30+ years	19	8·5	8·4
Physique—Height			
Under 5′ 1″ (155 cm)	10	22	30
Education			
Left school above the minimum age	63	20	8·3
Intelligence*			
Higher than average on matrix test	80	42	26
Reproduction			
Prenuptial conception	9·5	21	32
Prematurity	6·6	6·3	11
Perinatal mortality per 1,000 births	23	26	30
Child Care*			
Fully breast-feeding at 3 months	60	37	29
Potting regularly at end of 1st month	72	49	28

5,348 single children.
* From sample studies during 1948-52.
Baird, D., Thomson, A. M., Illsley, R., Billewicz, W. Z. (1962). Personal communication.

in production, and (b) their " general standing " in the community. The population is divided into five classes, as follows:[54]

SOCIAL CLASS	DESCRIPTION	EXAMPLES
I	Leading professions and business	Physician, stockbroker
II	Lesser professions and business	Teacher, shopkeeper
III	Skilled workers : non-manual / manual	Most clerks, engineering craftsmen
IV	Part-skilled workers	Machine minder, most agricultural and fishery workers
V	Unskilled workers	Railway porter, builder's labourer

The proportion of males aged 20-64 in the various classes at the Census of England and Wales in 1951 was: SC 1, 3·4 per cent; II, 15 per cent; III non-manual (NM), 9·4 per cent, III manual (M), 43 per cent; IV, 16 per cent; V, 13 per cent. Wives are " classed " by husbands' occupation, children by fathers'. Broadly, it may be said that social classes I, II and the non-manual " white collar " workers of III constitute the *middle classes*, the manual workers of III, together with IV and V, are the *working classes*.[26] [54]

The two components of this model of society involve (a) broad categories of living standards—of income, housing and education—which are highly correlated with occupation level, and (b) some grading by status and prestige.[66] The scheme is thus a simple picture of poverty/prosperity, privilege/under-privilege, gratification/deprivation; a scale of equality and inequality in "life's chances" in Britain's changing but still class-ridden society. The whole mode of life it has become evident is implicated in "social class": type of family structure, methods of child rearing, language and way of speaking, aspirations, values and attitudes, expectations of health and concern with illness. It is not surprising that, very crude as it is, and blurring now in several respects, this distinction by " social class " is still proving a powerful tool in the exploration of physiological and psychological processes, of physical, mental and social disorder, of the health that people enjoy, the diseases they suffer and, though far less than formerly, the treatment they receive.*

To return to *Aberdeen*: differences throughout the Table are gross. The range of reproductive performance, however, is much smaller than in Scotland as a whole. Contemporary data are not available (in Aberdeen or anywhere in Britain) for relevant incomes or nutrition, but the latter has recently shown satisfactory averages and relatively small differences between the social classes. In 1949-53, in the early years of this study, nutrient intake was like this : [67]

	SOCIAL CLASS		
	I & II & III NM	III M	IV & V
Animal protein, g . .	47	44	40
Calcium, g	1·2	1·1	0·88
Ascorbic acid, mg . .	79	64	61

* Kelsall's figures reflect one of the consequences of the British class structure :

Social Origins of Students Entering Medicine [32]
England and Wales, 1955-6

SOCIAL CLASS			
I & II			78%
III	Non-Manual	8%	20%
	Manual	12%	
IV & V			2%

For males the figure for classes I and II was 76 per cent, for females, 85 per cent; the Scottish rates are little better; physicians' children account for only a small part of the distribution. Of course such figures do not correspond to the talent in the population, or even to the proportions from different classes entering Grammar Schools—still less to the interest in medicine, as many who have served in the RAMC can attest. (In other Faculties, the proportions in England and Wales, M + F, were 63 per cent from S.C. I and II; 33 per cent from III; 4 per cent from IV and V.)

Broadly speaking, then, 80 per cent of the doctors are coming from classes I and II, 80 per cent of their patients—the people—are in other classes. This social distance presents a real problem. [27] [61] The middle-class doctor must not expect the majority of his patients to share *his* values, attitudes and ways of living : to communicate effectively with his patients and get a good history, to be able " to take the social factors of the case " into account, the middle-class doctor must study *theirs*, or learn about them, as the good general practitioner does, through sympathy and experience.

Such figures are too simple, and the ranges in each class are wide. Nevertheless, Thomson could not relate the substantial dietary differences within classes to perinatal mortality or prematurity rates—which is the rigorous test of the hypothesis.

Inequality of Opportunity

The figures of perinatal mortality in Aberdeen understate current social inequalities in infant mortality. Indeed, as seen in Figs. 7 and 8, these remain just about as great as 50 years ago when such analysis was started. This situation, moreover, is not restricted to infant mortality, Fig. 9, p. 58. Despite the achievements already mentioned, the diseases traditionally associated with poverty and the denial of elementary needs are far from abolished. Various explanations have been offered for the situation in infant mortality.

The *first* can probably be dismissed. It is that differences between the social classes in the ages at which mothers bear children, and in the numbers of children they bear, explain the class differences in mortality. Thus, death in the postneonatal period is particularly common in children of young mothers who already have large families, and there are more of these in the lower classes. But taking only this group, Table XII, p. 59, such families in class V had a higher postneonatal mortality than those in class IV, class IV higher than class III, etc. This kind of analysis can be carried through almost the whole range of infant mortality statistics.

Secondly: class lines in Britain are being redrawn, and numbers in the traditional social classes are changing. The modern upgrading of work means that the number in white-collar jobs is growing and there are considerably fewer in unskilled labour, for example. (Social class V in England and Wales included $16\frac{1}{4}$ per cent of men in 1931, $12\frac{3}{4}$ per cent in 1951, and surely less in 1961. Moreover, about 20 per cent of infants were born into Class V in 1931, only half as many in 1951.) This trend reduces the significance of the mortality

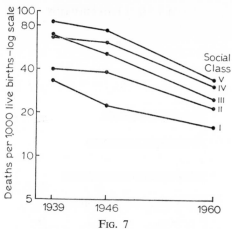

FIG. 7

Community diagnosis: inequality of mortality in first year of life in the different social classes. Scotland.
REGISTRAR-GENERAL,[56] see also Alwyn Smith, E., in the *Report* for 1961, p. 65.

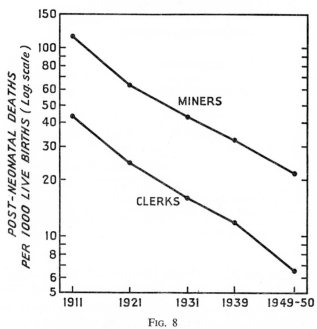

FIG. 8

Mortality at 4 weeks - 1 year of age in the children of miners and clerks. England and Wales.[23] [41] [43] [64]
Lancet (1955). **1,** 554.

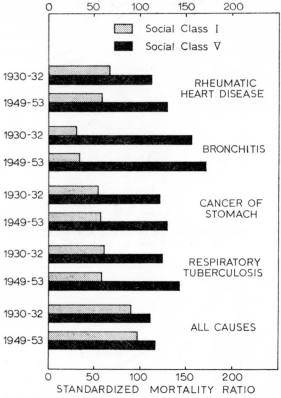

FIG. 9[41] [43] [55]
Differences in mortality between men of social class I
and social class V: most recent data, and 1930-2. Ages
20-64 years. England and Wales. The experience of all
men aged 20-64, in all classes together in each period = 100;
a ratio, standardised for differences in age composition,
is calculated for each social class. (The cause-of-death and
age data in the two periods are comparable.)

gradient that persists, but still leaves much to be explained.
High infant mortality is not confined to a minority " social
problem " group, however much on this and many other
accounts " social class V " has to be studied.

The *third* and most direct explanation is that persisting
unequal death rates reflect persisting social inequality. Money

wages of the poorest have certainly improved with recent affluence, of miners notably—during family building their incomes now are probably as high as clerks'—and it has been common in the past to see quick response of high infant death

TABLE XII

Post-Neonatal Mortality (4 weeks - 1 year)[23 41 43 64]

Social Class; Birth Rank of Child; and Maternal Age
England and Wales
1949-50

Rates per 1,000 Live Births

Social Class	All Children All Causes	Fourth and Later Children			
		Mothers – 30 Years		Mothers 30+ Years	
		All Causes	Infections*	All Causes	Infections*
I	4·8	} 15·0	6·5	} 9·2	3·6
II	5·7				
III	10·3	21·9	12·6	14·3	7·3
IV	13·7	26·4	} 15·6	17·6	} 9·4
V	17·0	29·1		18·1	
ALL	10·8	23·7	13·4	15·0	7·7

Single, legitimate infants.
* Respiratory and alimentary, 1950.
Social Medicine Research Unit and General Register Office, Joint Enquiry.

rates to social betterment. But, as the Aberdeen and other data show, gross differences between the classes remain in what may be regarded as their " capital ".[41 43] Thus there is substantial variation among women in different classes in healthiness and physique, which is related very likely to inequalities in their own childhood experience. Such differences are enhanced by social mobility in marriage, by upward and downward selection in which education plays a crucial role. Their educational inferiority may be reflected in lesser utilisation by the " lower " classes of available health services.[11] [39] [43] [66] At the onset they report pregnancy later, which may be related to the " wantedness " of children and in turn to knowledge of family planning. Present social inequalities in reproductive performance and in the physiological failure often reflected in *perinatal* mortality seem to depend much on earlier environmental experience and the lifetime history of the mother.[6] [29] [67]

Contemporary social differences remain gross in housing as well as education, and Victorian thunder, or a latter-day Boyd Orr, is needed to do justice to the crowding, squalor and lack of elementary amenities in which a large minority of the population are now living.* Yet under half the post-neonatal deaths in class V in Scotland during 1961 occurred in hospital (and there were quite a few in the ambulance).[56] The current environment as illustrated in housing conditions is specially important after the perinatal period, in relation to infectious disease for example, and in the class trends of *post-neonatal mortality.*

Affluent Society

Table XIII gathers together a few of the elementary facts about incomes, prices and living standards in the British version of the affluent society, and Fig. 10 illustrates even if roughly the main facts on nutrition. 1948 is used as marker of the post-war world; the National Health Service began then,

* As it turned out, this task was not left to epidemiology or social medicine. However—
At the *Census of 1961*:

Housing Amenities

POPULATION	PROPORTION OF HOUSEHOLDS			
	Sharing Cold Water Tap	Without Hot Water Tap	Without Fixed Bath	Sharing WC
	%	%	%	%
LONDON (County)	7·3	37	31	30
GLASGOW	2·2	33	39	24
ABERDEEN	5·2	27	37	38

Table XIII
Affluent Society
Britain

	1938	1948	1956	1961	(1962)
Average Weekly Earnings Adult Males in Manufacture°	£3.11s [50]	£7.1s [100]	£12.4s [173]	£15.17s [225]	(£16.5s) [230]
Cost of Living (Retail Prices) Index	50	100	145	163	(169)
Unemployment Rate %	13	1·8	1·3	1·6	(2·2)
Public Expenditure on Social Services (millions)†	£500 app.	£1,551‡	£2,886	£4,223*	
National Assistance, M+F, Adults (excl. Rent)	£1.11s	£2	£3.7s	£4.5s	(£4.15.6)
Dwellings Owner-Occupied %	32	32	32	40	
Households/Families, % Having Washing Machine	?1	3·6	19	39	
TV	0	1	40	78	
Car	?16	15	24	33	
Expenditure on Advertising (millions)	£98	£121	£309		(£475)

° Average weekly wage-earnings for *all adult males in manual work* are up to 6% less.
* 1961-2.
† Central and local government; capital and current; including housing.
‡ 1950.

Abrams, M. (1962). Personal communications. *Annual Abstract of Statistics 1961.* HMSO. Co-operative Permanent Building Society; France, J. C. (1962). Personal communications. London & Cambridge Economic Bulletin, *The Times Review of Industry, Quarterly. Monthly Digest of Statistics.* HMSO. *National Income & Expenditure.* HMSO. *Patterns of British Life,* Hulton Research (1950). London. *Women and the National Market* (1961). London.

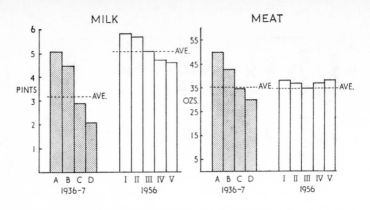

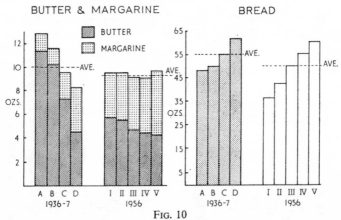

FIG. 10

Contemporary "nutrition" in comparison with pre-war. Estimates of domestic food purchases per person, per week. Britain.[41 43] In 1936-7 all members of each household surveyed were allocated to one social class. In 1956, old age pensioners and others not gainfully employed are included in the averages, but not in any of the class figures.

Proportions in the Social Classes:

1936-7		1956: National Food Survey
(Highest)	A 5%	The distribution of households among the five
	B 20%	social classes in Britain in 1956 was probably
	C 60%	much like that of occupied and retired males
(Lowest)	D 15%	aged 20-64 in England and Wales (Registrar General), as given on p. 54.

The situation in the early 1960's was little different from that in 1956. From CRAWFORD, W. & BROADLEY, H. (1938). *The People's Food.* Wm. Heinemann, Ltd. London. *Domestic Food Consumption and Expenditure* 1950, 1952, **1956,** 1961. HMSO.

Only 50-60 per cent of the sample have co-operated in the National Food Survey. Other, independent, data are also available, and Fig. 10 is probably valid enough for its purpose. For a more complete picture, as well as group *averages* of household purchases (like those in the Figure) the *ranges* within the groups are also required. Because of the method of the NFS these cannot be provided. Individual weighed surveys are now being started.

as did National Insurance income-maintenance of the welfare state. The watershed of 1955-6 (it is not possible at present to do more than draw attention to it) is also specified. Only during the 1939-45 war did Simon's dictum of 1890 begin to lose its force for Britain: ". . . how far the poor can be made less poor. In the whole range of questions concerning the Public Health, there is not any one to be deemed more important than the question which these words raise."[62] There is no doubt again about these averages in the Table, and the comparison for example of the first and second rows of figures. The poorest have been lifted, and in the upper strata of the working classes standards have been merging with those of the lower middle classes. But there still is in this country much primary poverty, and not just temporary, from simple inadequacy of income that is ignored in such a Table. Plimsoll Lines need constantly to be re-set: " people are poverty-stricken when their income, even if adequate for survival, falls markedly behind that of the community. Then they cannot have what the larger community regards as the minimum necessary for decency; and they cannot wholly escape, therefore, the judgement of the larger community that they are . . . degraded for, in the literal sense, they live outside the grades or categories which the community regards as acceptable . . ."[17] That is to say, the poor by definition will always be with us.* Current poverty, as said, may largely be

---

* Contemporary statistics of poverty are unbelievably inadequate for the country that pioneered the Poverty Survey. Estimating broadly, about 10 per cent of households in 1960, comprising 6-8 per cent of the population, between 3,000,000 and 4,000,000 people, were at or little above National Assistance levels[9] (cf. Table XIII). These people were, of course, quite unequally distributed. About 50 per cent of old people so subsisted: and considering the prevalence of disease and disability, it would seem sensible for doctors to suspect that half or two-thirds of their patients over 65 years of age will be very poor. Under 65, the proportion in such distress by comparison is small. In 1959, however, between one-third and one-fifth of men who were " chronic sick " (incapacitated over 3 months) received National Assistance. The other main underprivileged groups are the widows, broken families, and manual workers with large families; in all of these the possibility of serious poverty needs specifically to be kept in mind. The little recent data it must be added refer to periods of full employment.[36] [69]

producing the class gradient of Table XII. In rheumatic heart disease there is little doubt that Fig. 9 represents late effects of the kind of situations described in Col. (1) of Table I. What is responsible for the gradient of bronchitis mortality in adults (Fig. 9); how much this too is a legacy of the past; and what is the contribution to it of downward drift in the social scale because of illness[38]—all this is unclear and badly wants studying. The Victorians were emphatic about the corollary to Simon's dictum: disease begets poverty, disease → poverty → disease, a reflection of one of mankind's most vicious circles, still prevalent in more than half the world.[50] [72] This, too, is a lesson that has to be relearnt by each generation; today the impact on the family of the chronic diseases of middle age is just beginning to be appreciated.

A last word. In diseases associated with poverty it seems that only when they disappear, or reach some apparently basic minimum, do class differences disappear. In British children there is so little rickets now that analysis by social class is no longer meaningful. The history of juvenile rheumatism has already been quoted. Mortality at 1-2 years of age has fallen to very low levels (Table XIV), and little class distinction remains; the same kind of equalisation at very low rates can already be detected in the last three months of the first year of life, though not before.* Meanwhile, it should be remembered that while British infant mortality rates now are 21-26 per 1,000, those of Holland and Sweden are 15 or 16 per 1,000.

This discussion has been extended because it exemplifies the transfer of a pattern from the nineteenth century, where it belongs, to the second half of the twentieth where surely it does not. The modern debate on inequality has moved on from health to education,[16] but it may be wiser still to think in terms of both.

* For various reasons more recent figures are not yet available (1963). The discussion therefore may be quite out of date.

TABLE XIV

Mortality at 1-2 Years of Age[23] [43] [64]
M & F
England & Wales
Annual Rates per 1,000

Period	Social Class					Excess V/I
	I	II	III	IV	V	
1930-2	4·5	7·3	12·6	15·7	23·0	411%
1950-1	1·9	2·2	2·2	2·4	3·1	63%
Proportion 1950-1 of 1930-2	42%	30%	17%	15%	13%	

" New " Diseases and " Old "

Fig. 11, p. 66, shows a characteristic modern change: the " new " diseases show more even spread among the social classes, are less concentrated among the poor than the " old ". The main overall increase of IHD in the population in recent years may well have been among those who *were* the very poor and who, for example, have substantially increased their total fat intake and, possibly, also reduced their physical activity. So far as the evidence goes, in nearly all the important conditions which showed a higher mortality among the upper classes in 1930-2, in breast cancer as well as ischaemic heart disease, the gap between the classes was narrower by 1949-53.

Such analysis of groups, occupations, social classes, and the demonstration of inequalities between them, is a basic task and technique of epidemiology. Within groups there obviously will be individual differences; but resolution of these, and the summary

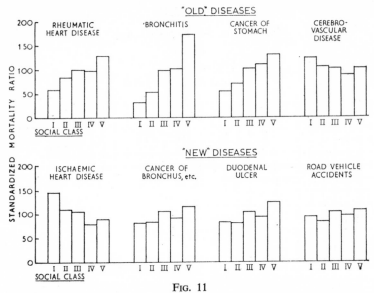

FIG. 11

" New " diseases and " old ". Mortality of men in different social classes
in 1949-53. Standardised mortality ratios at ages 20-64. England and
Wales.[41] [43]

From REGISTRAR GENERAL (1958). *Decennial Supplement on Occupational
Mortality*, Part II, Vols. 1 and 2. HMSO.

of group experience in this way, is useful and tells something that
could not be known before. It often provides the first indication
that there is a problem for consideration. Since Farr such figures
have been a powerful weapon in educating the community in the
need for action. As already seen, description of selective distribution is the beginning of the search for causes of disease—to
analyse *why* infant mortality differs in social classes—and it
can be put to many special uses.

VULNERABLE GROUPS

One of these is to identify those at special risk who merit special
attention by health services. The example chosen is again from
reproduction (Fig. 12) and it uses only " biological " data. Four
vulnerable groups for stillbirth and early natal death are here
defined. In magnitude they accounted for 15 per cent of births, but
for about a third of the perinatal deaths. (And, it may be added,

these women are "vulnerable" also for maternal mortality and much other reproductive casualty.)

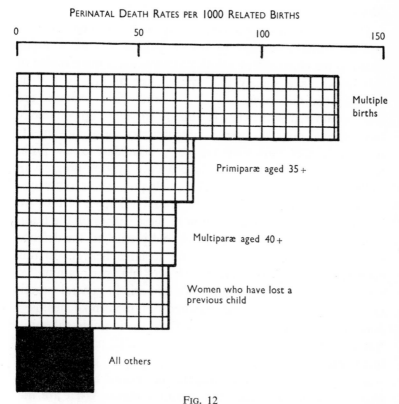

FIG. 12

Four vulnerable groups for perinatal mortality. 1950. England and Wales.[23][43][64] ("Perinatal" includes stillbirths + deaths in the first week.)
Brit. J. prev. soc. Med. (1956). **10,** 97.

Defined groups at high risk have long been a leading concern of Public Health in maternity and in child welfare,[60] and more recently with the handicapped and in old age. Once defined, they have led to action against accidents and other industrial hazards. The protection of "vulnerables" at critical periods of development such as the 'teens (p. 26), or those who are meeting strains of the modern family cycle like widowhood, is beginning to provide a basis for preventive psychiatry. However little is understood of the causes and mechanisms involved, effective practical action may be possible.*

MODERN WORLD

Diagnosis of the state of community health must be dynamic, and the remarkable changes already evident and to be anticipated in the character of health problems are a main theme of this book. In a society that is changing as rapidly and as radically as our own,[1 7 8 12 43 68 73] (and these changes are small compared with what is already in sight), epidemiology has a special duty to observe contemporary social movements for their impact " upon the people ", to be alert to new problems as they arise, to probe where we are making progress in wellbeing and where falling back, to help prepare for tomorrow. Sometimes, dramatic episodes illustrate the impact of how we live on what we are. Observation of these carries on the tradition of the classic studies of famine and pestilence, the defence of the people's health in wars and social upheaval. In this country in recent years there have been " blitz perforations ",[71] a post-war increase of coronary thrombosis in general practitioners,[44] 1952 smog,[48] the hundreds of motorbike deaths,[35] Xmas-drink road slaughter,[58] race riots, thalidomide calamity. But such *epidemic outbreaks* are only a small part of the life that has to be observed.

In the context of demographic, technological and social change specific issues affecting health abound. What are the implications for Public Health of more married women, especially the middle-aged, going out to work? Of failure at the 18 plus? The rising standards of personal behaviour, marriage and family life? New expectations of mental health? The new powers of manipulation of minds? Continuing drift to the South? More living in the suburbs, and the decay of city

* To establish social and cultural group regularities is useful also in trying to understand the individual clinical instance. Thus delinquency is likely to mean something different in one kind of district and another, in a boy from Social Class I and a boy from Social Class V; alcoholism obviously is one thing in an Irishman, another in a Jew; illegitimacy is not the same to a Jamaican and to a Briton.

centres? Over two thousand extra cars on the roads each day? Smokeless zones, still with sulphur? Less physical activity in work, and more bodily sloth generally? Automation, an age of leisure, and unemployment? Our astonishing taste for sweets? Fifty new drugs on the market per year? The multiplying transformations of food? New pollutions of airs, waters, places? More smoking in women? The prodigious increase of antibiotics? The Pill?*

Such questions, about the *history of the present* and the health of tomorrow, could readily be multiplied, and I have already alluded to some. Many are being intensively studied. Thus, the rising number of old people has stimulated a far-ranging programme of medical, social and psychological research. There is growing appreciation of the many forms that social inadequacy may take, the casualties of social progress. Young people are being studied more systematically, not merely as a clutch of problems or in terms of conflict between the generations. We are beginning to spell out the implications for physical and mental health of the increasing numbers of married women in employment, and the effects of this on marital roles and on the upbringing of children. A new literature is helping with the needed transition into family as well as individual medicine. A national—and international—intelligence service on drug toxicity will be set up. With specialised laboratories, investigation of new industrial processes will less often be left to chance. Road safety is being studied by many different methods, though not yet in this country the pollution that cars cause. So far, the nervous cost of motoring has proved too difficult to investigate; the contribution of cars to sedentary living is only too obvious. It is unlikely that Medicine will henceforth ignore its growing

---

* " Health is an expression of fitness to the various factors of the total environment. Any change in the environment demands new adaptive reactions, and disease is the consequence of inadequacies in these adaptive responses. . . . 'It is changes that are chiefly responsible for diseases,' wrote Hippocrates in Chapter XV of *Humours*, 'especially the great changes, the violent alterations both in seasons and in other things'. . ."[13]

power to produce disease: mutations, leukaemia, congenital malformation, blood dyscrasias, the transformation of old and seemingly harmless infections, the anxieties aroused by the discovery of the dangers of the most ordinary behaviour.

COMMUNITY DIAGNOSIS

Information on health is plentiful; but it is never enough, and today this applies particularly in mental health. Medicine could make greater use of other indicators of community health and sickness. There are the statistics of deviant behaviour: the apparent rise in juvenile delinquency, for example, of crimes of " violence " and sex crimes (and, it may be as significant, the still fierce public reaction to these). Such " social problems " illuminate sources of strain in society, they often represent modes of behaviour under stress that are alternative to " disease ". The renaissance of sociology, and their mutual concern with the conditions of mental and social health and with issues of equality, dependency and social inadequacy, is opening up the possibility for Public Health of an altogether more penetrating social analysis. Opinion polling and market research, with plenty of money, are producing information on social trends and on attitudes which is often available long before the results of academic study.* And, of course, in trying to understand the times reliance cannot be placed only on " facts ", or even on theories. Thus artists characteristically capture a contemporary mood and spirit that defeats scientific measurement: Forster's " finely developed bodies, partly developed minds and undeveloped hearts ", Golding's tears " for the end of innocence, the darkness of man's heart ", Trilling's diagnosis of " the modern selfconsciousness and the modern self-pity "....

Many *new measurements* of health on an ongoing basis are needed, locally or nationally: of the proportion of children

* Contemporary writing on society is providing sharp insights, exemplified in *meritocracy, organisation man, subtopia, admass, rat race, fun morality, establishment, anti-hero.*

beginning, continuing, stopping to smoke . . . the number and condition of over 70-year-olds living alone . . . active leisure facilities and their enjoyment . . . the prevalence of obesity from childhood on . . . environmental pollutions . . . noise . . . comparative accident risks . . . radiation hazards . . . the incidence and course of various chronic diseases . . . the conversion of mortality into morbidity, at both ends of life . . . notification of congenital malformation . . . vital statistics adapted to genetic study . . . Tables XV-XX illustrate some of the new measurements already in use to diagnose the condition of the people in a changing society; and others will be mentioned later in the text.

TABLE XV

Boys Smoking

Prevalence in 1961

Social Class	Boys of 15 At School At Work Smokers		Men Cigarette Smokers
	%	%	%
Upper Middle	15	25	60
Middle			58
Lower Middle	15	40	58
Skilled Working	34	64	59
Working	30	60	63

Statistics of Smoking in the United Kingdom. London. Todd, G. F. Personal communications.

TABLE XVI

Air Pollution in London
Winter Averages

Winter	Smoke		SO$_2$	
	(a)	(c)	(b)	(c)
1954-5	49		11·1	
1955-6	52		11·8	
1956-7	45		10·2	
1957-8	41		11·5	
1958-9	43	309	11·9	340
1959-60	32	206	9·6	275
1960-1	24	200	9·7	277
1961-2	—	182	—	302
1962-3	—	173	—	365

(a) Mg of black suspended matter per 100 cubic metres of air.

(b) Parts of acidic gases per 100 million parts of air.

(c) Micrograms per cubic metre.

Average daily readings, 7 stations.
The Clean Air Act became operative in 1956.

Annual Reports of the Medical Officer of Health, London County Council; Scott, J. A. (1963). Personal communications.

TABLE XVII

Strontium-90 in Human Bone
Average Amount at 2 Weeks - 5 Years of Age
Micro-microcuries of Sr-90, per G of Calcium
Britain

1957	1·20			
Jan. - June 1958	1·30		Jan. - June 1960	3·15
July - Dec. „	1·50		July - Dec. „	2·65
Jan. - June 1959	2·80		Jan. - June 1961	2·05
July - Dec. „	3·20		July - Dec. „	1·82
			Jan. - June 1962	1·50

Medical Research Council, Monitoring Report Series.

TABLE XVIII

Mortality in Transportation Accidents, USA
1958-60
Death Rates per 100 Million Passenger Miles
per Year

Mode of Transport	Death Rate
Automobiles and taxis .	2·3*
Scheduled domestic flights	0·73 ⎫
Buses	0·16 ⎬ **
Railroad passenger trains	0·16 ⎭

Drivers of automobiles are considered to be
" passengers ".

* No. of deaths of passengers in 1960 =
24,600; death rate = 2·2;
        (7,750 pedestrians were also killed).

** No. of deaths of passengers in 1960 = 419.
Accident Facts, 1961. Chicago

TABLE XIX

*Some " Diseases of Medical Progress "**
Both Sexes, All Ages
England & Wales
Average Annual Number of Deaths

Hazard	1954-6	1957-9	1960
Adverse reaction to drugs	76	92	100
From radiotherapy .	8	23	42

Registrar General.
The 1961 figures show a further increase of about a quarter.
* Moser, R. H. (1959). Springfield, Ill.

TABLE XX

Years of Working Life Lost

1961

England & Wales

Cause of Death	Years Lost Per 1,000 Population Aged 15-64	
	Male	Female
All causes . . .	75	46
Accidents . . .	9·8	2·7
Ischaemic heart disease	9·2	2·1
Bronchitis, Pneumonia	7·9	4·4
Cancer of bronchus .	4·1	
Cancer of breast . .		2·1

Registrar General (1962). *Quarterly Return* No. 454. HMSO; Benjamin, B. Personal communication.

Deaths at ages 0-64 are included. Infant Mortality accounted for 22, and 16, respectively of years lost.

III

WORKING OF HEALTH SERVICES

From the study of health I come to the study of health services. How is knowledge being applied in the community? To what extent is it being expressed in the development of organised services? The more knowledge there is to apply the more important it is that it should be applied. How then are the health services working, in reality, as distinct from laws, plans and pronouncements about them? What needs are they serving—and how well? How, for example, are the community's maternity beds being utilised in relation to the susceptibilities defined in Fig. 12, p. 67, to stillbirth and natal death? We found in 1950, at the start of the National Health Service, that only two of the four vulnerable groups were accorded priority for hospital confinement. Elderly multiparae and mothers who had already lost a child were delivered in hospital less often than the national average, an average as high as it is because of public wishes and general agreement that " primips " should be confined in Hospital. These are the main facts:

High-Risk Group	Perinatal Mortality Rate per 1,000	Proportion Confined in Hospital, 1950
Multiple births .	131	85%
Primiparae aged 35+	72	88%
Multiparae aged 40+	65	49%
Women who had lost a previous child .	62	51%
All others . .	31	60%

The reports of the Chief Medical Officer show some modest improvement since 1950 in response to an intensive campaign by the Ministry of Health among doctors and midwives.[27] Thus 44 per cent of women aged 35+, and bearing fifth or later children, were confined in hospital in 1954; this figure reached 57 per cent in 1960. The perinatal mortality among such mothers in 1950, corresponding to the figures above, was 48 per 1,000; the overall hospital confinement rate in 1960 was 65 per cent.

The value of such facts for social policy is limited. Investigation of this question in a community would have to be on three levels, and make use of several techniques to provide a basis for action. The first, what may be called the *vital statistics*, states the problem and describes its size and distribution, the short table just quoted is an example. Secondly, general and local *social surveys* are necessary, analysing such issues as the availability and booking of beds, local housing conditions, public attitudes (rational and irrational) including the doctors', effectiveness of the home-help service. Representative *case-studies* ought then to be made to bring the statistics to life and give a picture of what actually is happening in typical situations: how obstetric need and advantage are balanced against other personal and familial preferences, and what in the event governs whether the mother is confined in hospital. Only if informed on all these levels will a campaign to change the situation shown in the Table stand a chance of success. Encouragement of these demands has to be distinguished from the general issue of increasing overall the number of women confined in hospital; though short-stay, " early discharge " schemes are obviously relevant to every aspect.[1][23][25]

Operational Research, which this chapter is concerned with, may be defined as the *systematic study of the working of health services with a view to their improvement.*[52][53] Though it is thus in a strong and direct tradition of English empirical enquiry, operational research is still a slowly developing branch of social medicine, little speeded by the rapid spread of such ideas elsewhere, in industry for example. There may well have been more official and unofficial operational research on social-medical services in mid-Victorian times than there is today.

Of course the epidemiological is not the only method of learning about them. The "chronic" ward, conditions of terminal care, the Juvenile Court, the Old People's Welfare Committee, the Chest Clinic (how effective is its help with bronchitis, its anti-smoking programme?), today these provide particular opportunity for clinical observation of the workings of health services. Econometric analysis,[2] mathematical models,[5] work study,[55] various social science techniques[60 65 68 90] are increasingly being applied to these questions. But population studies of several aspects can be useful: studies of community needs and resources; of the utilisation of services, in general and by those in special need; of the effectiveness of services in improving community health (and of their hazards), studies that can help in setting priorities for service and for research. Methods meanwhile often are primitive, but they will not improve of themselves.

The remainder of this chapter asks simple epidemiological questions on contemporary health services.

MEDICAL POLICE

The simplest sums can be worthwhile. How do boys under sixteen get hold of the 221,000,000 cigarettes they smoke a year?[79] . . . Propaganda has resulted in about 60 per cent of male motor cyclists wearing helmets. The figure has scarcely improved since 1958[66]—what now? . . . In what proportion of the country's factories are safety provisions (including fire precautions) below the legal minimum? In what proportion are maximum allowable concentrations of toxic substances exceeded? . . . How many old people are still living in the workhouse-type institutions?[90] . . .

WHAT IS GENERAL PRACTICE?

General practice is proving the problem child of the National Health Service, as of other systems of medical care. I can glance at only a few of the issues.

In the quite ordinary practice that we studied, as typical as a sample of one can be,[3] [4] 60 per cent of the nuclear families were wholly registered—the frame at least was there for the general practitioner really to be a family doctor:

DEFINITION OF FAMILY	PROPORTION OF FAMILIES WHO WERE COMPLETELY REGISTERED WITH THE PRACTICE per cent
Mother and children . . .	96
Parents and children . . .	60
Parents, children, and relatives living at the same address .	27

Outer London, 1951-2.

Utilisation of the services of the practice was quite unequal. About a quarter of the " population " had no contact with the doctor during the course of a year (Fig. 13). Sixteen per cent, on the other hand, about 500 persons in far fewer " families ", had 10 or more consultations during the year, and they accounted for half the doctor's work. Obviously there was plenty of opportunity for the doctors and these patients to get to know each other.* More than 40 per cent of the work of the practice was with readily definable " serious problems " affecting life or livelihood; and about a third, over all ages, involved " chronic " disease. The National Health Service has great need for this kind of analysis, in simple " shop arithmetic ". These observations were unique when they were made—and the vacuum was filled with declamations about the general practitioner being the " specialist in the trivial ", an " expert in minor illness ", etc.** The relative and absolute

* Scrutiny of the records showed that this concentration was not confined to the year under study. Such figures illustrate the limitations of data about " spells " of sickness as a picture of the health of the population, and they raise questions on causes.
** This situation continues. There is little systematic study of general practice and less planned experiment. Myths continue to flourish, different myths now.

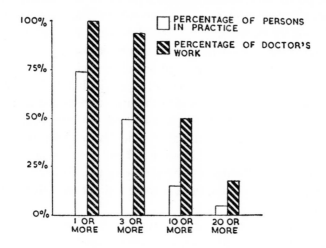

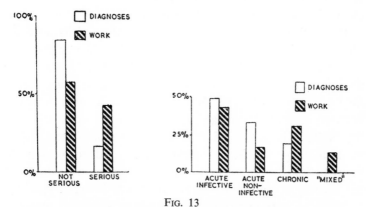

FIG. 13

Work of a general practice. Outer London, 1951-2. Upper figure:
72 per cent had 1 or more consultations; 28 per cent had none;
ave.=5; 16 per cent of the persons in the practice had 10 or more
consultations in the year and accounted for 52 per cent of all the
work. Lower left figure: 16 per cent of the diagnoses were of
"serious" problems, accounting for 43 per cent of the work.
Lower right figure: 18 per cent of the diagnoses were of
"chronic" conditions, accounting for about 33 per cent of the
work (and over twice these proportions after 65 years of age).

Brit. med. J. (1954). **1**, 109.[3] [78]

increase of the chronic diseases, in which hospitals play an episodic role, has transformed general practice—and created a new kind of partnership with the hospital. The general practitioner nowadays ought to have a good knowledge of internal medicine, and be an expert in social medicine, in after-care, rehabilitation and resettlement at work, including housework. (The problem, so often, is with the little understood and long-term social functioning of patients and families, rather than short-term treatment of disease.) The National Hospital Plan " institutionalises " this situation: there is to be no increase in provision of " chronic " beds despite the further ageing of the population. In fact, there is to be a slight reduction in beds for old people.[1]

The impact of the aged on this (one) practice may be stated thus: although the 300 persons over 65 years made up rather fewer than 10 per cent of all on the doctors' lists, a figure below the national average, they were responsible for almost a fifth of the total work, about a quarter of the home visits, a third of all the " serious " work, and half that with chronic disease.

Table XXI, an abstract of available official data, uses a documentary approach in contrast to the " case study " in the field just described. The Table lists the main contacts in 1960 between a really " typical " general practice and the rest of the NHS. There are 2,500 with the hospitals alone, 50 per week, a staggering feat of organisation—and no wonder that many believe communication between doctors to be the key to the success of the whole National Health Service. Attention is drawn to only two other figures in the Table. If maternity work is excluded, the average use of *clinical pathology* in the non-infectious diseases must be well below one " patient request " per week, corresponding to the 100 or so consultations (of a total of 160-180) that this hypothetical general practitioner has with his patients for such conditions. In fact, and wherever investigated, it has been found that many general practitioners do not utilise the service at all[13] [45] although " clin-path " is now freely accessible in very many districts,

TABLE XXI

General Practice in the National Health Service[22 25 26 29 30 38]

Contacts during One Year between an Average General Practice
of 2,250 Persons and Other Branches of the
National Health Service*
1960

	NUMBERS IN YEAR
Admissions to Hospital	208
Admissions to mental hospital 5	
First admissions to mental hospital 2-3	
New *Out-patients*	641
Including "casualty" 277	
Out-patient attendances, total	2,085
Use of Hospital Diagnostic Services	
Pathology	59†
X-ray	99
X-ray by mass miniature radiography, including	
10 referred by GP	177
Domiciliary Visits	
By Consultants	16
Health Visitors	600
Home Nurses	1,134
Patients Attended	
By Home Nurses	45
Home Helps	16
Women attending *Antenatal Clinics*	17
Postnatal Clinics	2
First Attendances at *Infant Welfare Clinics*	31
Children seen by *School Health Service*	107
No. of *Meals* (on wheels) supplied to old people	
in the year	100
No. of *old people living alone* (approx.)	50
No. on *National Assistance*	100

Composition of practice:		-14	15·44	45-64	65+
	M	264	441	276	104
	F	251	446	304	164

No. of Marriages =17
No. of Births =39
No. of Deaths =26

---

* Actually there were 19,928 Principals on the lists of General Practitioner
Executive Councils in England and Wales in 1960, and the Registered
Population was 45,579,598. To estimate the national totals it will do to
multiply the figures in the Table by 20,000. All figures refer to 1960
or a year very close to it.
† Numbers are rising, from 59-74 between 1960 and 1962. No figures are
available on the use of the facilities of the Public Health Laboratory
Service in the diagnosis of infectious disease.

and everywhere, probably, there is some access. (It is a myth
that one of the aids needed for general practice is access to
pathology.) Here surely is a serious issue. Unfortunately, little
is known of what is involved: few studies have been carried
out, though medicine is a learned profession. What is the connection between such facts and the present system of
organisation and incentives? What models have we of good
general practice? Anyhow—what are the ways by which clini-
cal pathology can promote good general practice?[8] [11] [16] [54] [59] [84]
... Turning now to a figure on Maternity, the contrast between
the 17 women attending local authority *ante-natal* clinics and
only two at *post-natal* again raises questions of what is, and
ought to be, done about it? Is the post-natal examination
essential? For whom in particular? And what are the characteristics, the social class for example and the medical state,
of the two?

NEED⇌DEMAND⇌SUPPLY⇌

One value of basing operational research on populations
i.e., an "epidemiology of health services as well as of health",
is that the idea of people, and their changing needs, will not
be forgotten. Here is the other side to the *community diagnosis*
that should provide the basis of planned health services. Needs
have to be felt as such, perceived; then expressed in demand.
Little is understood about this: consider the variability of
angina, or the differences between men and women in complaining of "rheumatism", between Welsh miners and
Lancashire cotton operatives in their endurance of chest
trouble. We visited a sample of 101 "ordinary" families in
the general practice already mentioned, to try to obtain a more
complete view of "needs" than was available through the
general practitioners alone,[72] [73] and found that during a period
of six months almost 40 per cent of 813 manifest health
problems (as we defined them) were unknown to the practitioners and other local health services:

	ALL PROBLEMS		"MENTAL HEALTH" PROBLEMS	
Treated by National Health Service				
G.P. alone . . .	360	} (62%)	18	} (24%)
Otherwise . . .	144		5	
Not treated by National Health Service . .	309	(38%)	73	(76%)
Total	813	(100%)	96	(100%)

These " untreated " problems included a good deal of serious trouble, psychiatric in particular, and this picture alongside that in p. 49 is very different from anything in the general statistics of morbidity, *e.g.* of Table X. The family seemed to be coping effectively with many of these problems, helped often by relatives and friends (the " lay referral system "[17] [18]); in others, especially among children, there clearly was need of further help. So far as we could see, much of this trouble should have presented to the NHS. What we knew about the prevalent " thresholds " in Britain and the public image of the doctors' job—and the services generally provided—made these facts surprising. How much the figures represent a working-class rather than middle-class pattern is uncertain, though there is no doubt that expectations of mental health rise with education. Here is another area awaiting the illumination of the social sciences, with their concern for the subjective point of view, for the irrational in behaviour, for the mores of various groups.[34] [35] [50] [51] [56] [77] [80] People have to learn about needs, all needs except a few biological. The assessment of *need* and not merely *demand* as a basis for planning, then, is a formidable enterprise even if restricted to what is clinically manifest.

Needs often are revealed and demand expressed only when services are supplied. Thus, doctor-consultation rates among women, most of them previously not " insured ", rose far more when the National Health Service was introduced in 1948 than among men who previously were insured, 12 per cent compared with 2·8,[81] and possibly for simple economic reasons.

The provision of out-patient and voluntary treatment by the 1930 Mental Treatment Act revealed great numbers who wanted them. Today, even with a free and comprehensive service, the principle still applies. As facilities for mental defectives are provided, the claims on them grow;[88] start a child guidance clinic in a new area, and very likely it will soon be swamped with work. The absence of services depresses demand; if there is no incentive for people to demand, needs will be less articulate—the kind of negative feed-back that preserves the status quo. The chequered history of Local Authority house-waiting lists is an illustration.* An imperfect equilibrium between supply and demand must be assumed.

Regions have different numbers of hospital beds, 3·4 " medical " beds per 1,000 of the population in Liverpool, and 2·4 in Sheffield;[30] [44] since they are occupied at not a very different rate this is a warning (with contemporary values) against simply increasing the supply. These relativities of hospital service in the Regions are older than the NHS and they continue from year to year: custom and inertia act as a self-regulating device. Parkinson's law may well also be operating. But mostly such facts are just not understood: the necessary medical and social data are just not available. No abundance of information about those who are in hospital beds, moreover, necessarily tells anything about those who are not, but perhaps should be. Some assessment of the load of avoidable misery in Sheffield and in Liverpool could be attempted. (Waiting lists are not enough.)

Provision for Industrial Health.—Since, on analysis, most attendances at these 14 large and representative Industrial Clinics (England 1951) seemed to arise directly out of the job—

No. of attendances in sample week	2,940
Proportion for " occupational " reasons . . .	76%
Proportion for " non-occupational " reasons . .	24%

* How supply can altogether usurp the role of demand is evident in the number of grammar school places: the " demand " equals whatever is supplied.

it must be enquired who does the work of the *industrial medical officer* in the great majority of factories employing the great majority of workers, which still, after 20 booming years, have no such voluntary occupational health service. Do these factories, they are very often small, produce a disproportionate amount of industrial disease?* In the context of the National Health Service—what are the priorities of industrial medicine that ought to be generally supplied? What job analysis of it has been done,[32] must it cost so much? And what is the Appointed Factory Doctor up to (in the small accumulator factories for example) where he provides the only medical service? How to get more doctors into industry? Despite the publicity which followed the reports (in 1958-9) of the Ministry of Labour's special surveys in Halifax and Stoke-on-Trent,[31] the results so far[36] are dismal beyond words:

		1955-7		1962
Halifax	4	part-time IMOs in (of 760) factories	21	4 in 17
Stoke	5	part-time IMOs in (of 298) factories	5	7 in 9

Employers—and Unions—demonstrably are little interested. But where are the doctors to come from anyhow? On what social accountancy?

Shortage of Doctors.—As I write, there is a sharp controversy on the supply of doctors themselves. Unfortunately, many of the essential facts are not available. Each doctor the country trains represents a major investment in time and thought and money (thousands of pounds). But large numbers of young doctors are missing from the statistics. How many of these are married women bringing up a family, how many have emigrated, etc. is not known. A government committee

---

* Less than 10 per cent of the cases of industrial lead poisoning in accumulator manufacture, 24 of a national total of 370 during 1930-61, occurred in the group of large factories with good medical services making 90 per cent of the product.[71]

in 1957 misjudged the situation,[37] foresaw too many doctors.*
Deflation was promptly recommended, but some Universities
were sluggish to respond, which has helped a bit, and recently
there has been a sharp upturn again in the number of students
admitted to medical schools.

Application of New Knowledge

Little systematic is known yet about the time lag in the
application over the community of new tested knowledge.
These *diabetes* figures, *death rates of males aged 20-34*,
suggests that social classes I and II benefited more, or earlier,
from the introduction of insulin than classes IV and V, and
this was true throughout " young " insulin-sensitive diabetes :

Social Class	1921-3	1930-2
I and II	64	26
III	50	25
IV and V	46	35

Rates per million per year. England and Wales.

By 1949-53, mortality in all classes was well down, but the
social class distribution of 1930-32 was accentuated. (There
is continuing evidence that prescription of a diabetic regime
is one thing, following it another.[91]) How are the benefits of
anticoagulants being distributed today? For venous disease,
and for ischaemic heart disease anyhow when bedfast?
(Most " attacks ", that are not rapidly fatal, of " coronary
thrombosis " in middle-aged men, some 40,000 in 1960, seem
to be treated in hospitals.[30]) What about the treatment of
depression in its various manifestations? It may be time
already to begin asking about respiratory resuscitation, and
about ventricular defibrillation, and their implications for
casualty services. How many men might be pulled through?

* In 1956 the Ministry of Education's Advisory Council on the training
of teachers also forecast a surplus and was concerned " that there may
be some difficulty in the early 1960's ", " in maintaining full employment
in the teaching profession ".[14]

How is *cardiac surgery* applied over the country? Differences nowadays, I fancy, are more likely to be regional and local (cf. Table I, especially column (1) of it), than by " class ". The surgery of mitral stenosis may be regarded as a slum clearance job, which should largely be done by now. Is every patient known, assessed, and under observation? There is far less rheumatic fever than formerly, but cases do occur. I have been unable to obtain any figures of how many *re*cur in the absence of prophylactic penicillin.

Utilisation

The free supply of *vitamin supplements* to pregnant women in Aberdeen, it is obvious, is only part of the story:

	SOCIAL CLASS		
CONSUMPTION	I & II	III	IV & V
	%	%	%
Regular . .	60	52	41
None . . .	28	35	49

1948-53.

Less than half the mothers in social classes IV and V regularly took the concentrates.[47] As the authors say, " ignorance and apathy seemed to play a great part. Many women believed that the vitamin A and D tablets were laxatives... The orangejuice concentrate was often disliked, or thought to cause heartburn."* In many of the health services, though much has been learnt through experience, little systematic is known of consumer attitudes, and how the Public perceives the situation, so it is difficult to plan remedial education.[57] To supply facilities often is not enough. How to get the community's medical and welfare services utilised has become a key problem of the chronic diseases and among old people. Even here, in the simpler ante-natal situation, there was least communication with those most in need of the service (p. 55). This is a most

* Quite a number of City Fathers seem to be at this stage of development on the fluoridation question.

elementary kind of enquiry. What actually is happening? Is the service being delivered to the community that which was intended? The increase in 1961 of charges for vitamin supplements sharply lowered consumption, it is not yet clear whether in one section of the population more than another (though there is every reason to fear the worst), nor whether it matters in terms of nutrition. Whatever they are,

TABLE XXII

Utilisation of Hospital Services

Estimate of Admissions in 1957
Both Sexes
All Ages
England and Wales
Rates per 10,000

CAUSES	CONURBATIONS	OTHER URBAN DISTRICTS	RURAL DISTRICTS
ALL	809 (140)	735 (127)	577 (100)
Uterine Fibromyoma (F)	9·3 (143)	7·3 (112)	6·5 (100)
Strabismus	5·8 (164)	5·0 (143)	3·5 (100)
Haemorrhoids	5·9 (168)	5·2 (151)	3·5 (100)
Hypertrophy of Tonsils and Adenoids	42 (153)	40 (145)	27 (100)
Hernia	20 (116)	21 (121)	17 (100)

Hospital In-patient Enquiry, Ministry of Health and General Register Office.
Report for 1956-7; and personal communications.
In fact, these are *discharges,* including *deaths.*
The age structure of the three populations is reasonably similar.
For comparison, rural rates are taken to be 100.

how many of the results were anticipated, intended, planned? Or could have been?

The functioning of Health Services might be described as dynamic " transactions " of need$\rightleftharpoons$demand$\rightleftharpoons$supply$\rightleftharpoons$ utilisation$\rightleftharpoons$need, each of which has to be studied, none of which can be understood apart from the rest, and all of which are changing. Considering hospital treatment in Britain now, in the extreme case, say a perforated ulcer, or grossly deluded schizophrenia, what very likely will happen is that need= demand=supply. Mostly, however, in questions of admission to hospital there are multiple interactions at work, medical and social, involving individuals and institutions. These have already been illustrated with the maternity beds, and they are seen at their extreme in such an area as the disposal of the feeble-minded. Table XXII is again the simplest of arithmetic, but it raises awkward questions. Is there less of these specific disorders in the country than in the towns, less morbidity, less need; or less perception of it, less appeal for help, less service in response, less acceptance of advice, less —? Or excessive utilisation in the towns? By what standards? Speculation is in order, and a lot of study: of this as of pretty well everything to do with health services. (The urban-rural gradient with bronchitis, the kind of condition where such differences are expected, is of course far steeper, more than 3 to 1.)

Quality of Medical Care

The appraisal of what health services are all so busy with, how good they are, is proving exceedingly difficult and investigations—understandably—are few.[11 42 69 74] But they are vital for the future of the National Health Service; and since medical care has become a leading concern of social policy, objective standards of performance are likely increasingly to shape the professional responsibilities of medicine. The profession, it must be admitted, is poorly prepared for this. Questions range all the way from ethics to economics.[7 53 63 67 75 87] I will describe a few sorties in this field, mainly into central areas of efficiency and effectiveness. In a sense the various Tables presented in this chapter interlock, and they are all concerned with quality. No service, whatever the reason, no application of the new knowledge for example—then no quality. Thus the National Health Service by increasing and

TABLE XXIII

Dental Services in England and Wales
1958

REGION	POPULATION PER DENTIST	COURSES OF TREATMENT PER 1,000 POPULATION	RATIO PERMANENT TEETH FILLED: EXTRACTED	PROPORTION OF COURSES THAT INCLUDED FULL DENTURES %
Midlands	5,850	167	1·1	9·2
Wales	5,400	131	0·9	11·7
Northern	5,300	159	0·9	10·8
East & West Riding	5,000	185	1·1	9·2
North Western	4,800	178	1·2	9·3
Eastern	4,600	274	1·8	5·2
South Western	3,900	256	1·9	5·4
Southern	3,400	304	2·2	4·8
London & S. East	3,100	299	3·1	4·7

Ministry of Health, Report, Part I, 1959.

better distributing specialist skills has created quality. A direct linkage of quantity supplied, and quality, is seen in these Regional figures, Table XXIII, on dentistry: the fewer the dentists, the greater the proportion of teeth extracted rather than conserved. The place of the Midlands at the top (or bottom) of the league is unexpected; but for this the Table is another of those bleak " North/South " divides If in the 1950's issues of quantity predominated, the 1960's will very likely see a move forward and those of quality become the public concern. (Trouble can be foreseen. This mood will co-incide with inevitable shortages of staff.)

Historically, diphtheria immunisation provides a text-book case of a simple and valid test of quality, and failure to pass it. The experiments in North America in the 1920's and early 1930's established its value. Yet in this country, as late as in 1941—but the figures have already been given (p. 5). A Report of the Ministry of Health shortly before the War reported that "con-tinuous if slow progress is being made, particularly in some of the larger provincial cities, although none of them has yet succeeded in immunizing the 50 to 60 per cent of the child popula-tion which is necessary before the incidence of the disease is affected. Chester, with an estimated number of 45 per cent, is probably the best immunized town in the country; then follow in close order Birmingham, Walsall, Worcester, Leeds, Manchester and Chatham, all of which are in the neighbourhood of 35 to 40 per cent. . . . London (all the Metropolitan Boroughs combined) appears very low in the list with an estimated number of 5·3 per cent of her child population immunized ".[27] Jameson's leadership in righting this situation is too well known to need description.

What is to be made of the difference in these two estimates of prevalence of *otitis media* :

Defect found at School Health Inspection (1951)
                                7·6 per 1,000 examined.
Cause of rejection for National Service (1954-55)
                                32·0 per 1,000 examined.

The school figures are an average over ages five to fifteen, and the rates at fifteen years were presumably even less than 7·6 per 1,000 since the disease is less common in later than early childhood. Why were so many more cases discovered at eighteen during the National Service examinations? Such an observation is unlikely to be an isolated one and, in fact, Lee identified a whole series of physical disabilities that were found at eighteen and apparently had been missed in the school medical examinations.[39] Are there adequate incentives to quality in the schools' system? Why does another equally " routine " examination detect more? What has now been learnt from the studies of observer error? (With modern data processing, and record linkage, the result of later examinations could routinely be fed back.)

Glover Phenomenon.—The next Table represents a pioneer study, from a quarter of a century ago:

Tonsillectomy Rates per 1,000 School Pupils, 1936-38[21]
Annual Averages

Manchester .	.	. 11	Leeds .	. .	. 38
Bradford	.	. 12	Leicester	. .	. 36
Gloucester .	.	. 12	Exeter .	. .	. 40
Birkenhead .	.	. 3	West Hartlepool .	.	. 39
Isle of Ely .	.	. 4	Soke of Peterborough		55
Cambridge .	.	. 13	Oxford	. .	. 40

But Glover still rules.* The quality of care received by these children surely varies grossly. In how many other examples of surgical—or gynaecological—treatment would such comparative studies of what is happening, such *community* perspective, stimulate fresh *clinical* thinking? Do not such figures raise the question whether there are any valid clinical indications for tonsillectomy, an operation carried out 200,000 times a year?** The same kind of quasi-random local distribution, unrelated to any manifest clinical need, is evident, as might be expected, in many fields: in diagnosis, throughout the work of the School Health Service; in the local provision of many social services that are " permissive ", not compulsory; and not merely in medicine—in Court sentencing, for instance.

* " In children aged 5-6 years", states the Chief Medical Officer in his Report for 1958-9, " the tonsillectomy rate ranges from 0·5 per cent in Merthyr Tydfil to 16·3 per cent in Chester; in those aged 14 years it ranged from 1·3 per cent in Swansea to 36·2 per cent in Kingston-upon-Hull. . . . As was found in the 1956 survey there were wide differences in some comparable areas in the percentage of children who had had the operation. For example, among 14-year-old boys and girls the percentage was 9·2 in Bedfordshire and 34·8 in Buckinghamshire, 1·3 in Swansea and 32 in Newport." [12]

** The peak age for operation is 5-6 years, which is again surprising in view of the natural history of upper respiratory infections in childhood. Including acute otitis media, they seem to peak around 7 years of age.[64]

Table XXIV is a useful way in which to start elucidating the nearing £100 million drug bill. More evidently than in tonsillectomy, there are systematic differences to be elucidated.

TABLE XXIV

Variation of Prescribing in General Practice—
Some Northern English Industrial Towns

NUMBER OF PRESCRIPTIONS PER PERSON PER YEAR

TOWN	1959	1960	1961	1962
Wigan	8·4	8·6	7·9	7·2
Wakefield	7·7	7·6	6·9	6·7
Manchester	6·4	6·5	6·0	5·6
Barrow	6·2	6·3	5·5	5·3
Stoke-on-Trent	6·1	6·1	5·6	5·4
Liverpool	6·1	6·4	5·6	5·3
Salford	6·1	6·2	5·5	5·2
Sunderland	5·6	5·8	5·1	4·9
St. Helens	5·2	5·5	5·1	4·8
Bootle	4·6	4·7	4·0	3·9
Middlesbrough	4·2	4·5	4·0	3·7
ENGLAND	4·8	5·0	4·7	4·4

Joint Pricing Committee for England (P.D.I.).
Charges were increased in 1961.

These figures are based on samples from retail pharmacists. Samples from doctors give very similar results.[33]

Anything to do with drugs is *political arithmetic* indeed—and raises also at once, and very rightly,* the defences of clinical responsibility. But argument could only benefit from knowing what lies behind such figures, from information on local disease patterns, self-medication in the various towns, the public image of Medicine and the NHS, etc. A battery of techniques, including epidemiologic, is now waiting to be applied to such elementary social criticism.

Case-Fatality in Teaching and Non-Teaching Hospitals. Fig. 14 and Table XXV are valuable in themselves; and

* This chapter is full of value judgements.

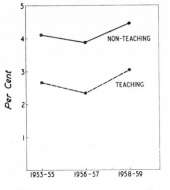

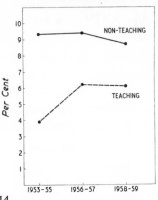

APPENDICITIS WITH PERITONITIS
% CASE-FATALITY

HYPERPLASIA OF PROSTATE
% CASE-FATALITY

FIG. 14

Case-fatality in Teaching and Non-Teaching Hospitals of England and Wales. National Health Service, 1953-1959. The experience of the non-teaching hospitals is standardised to that of the teaching hospitals; in appendicitis for age and sex, and in hyperplasia of the prostate for age and type of admission. Hospital in-patient Enquiry, General Register Office, Ministry of Health; personal communications, 1957-63. The gaps were no narrower in 1960-61. *Med. Care* (1963). **1,** 71.[40] [41] [78]

TABLE XXV

Case-Fatality in Teaching and Non-Teaching Hospitals[40] [41] [43] [78]

1956-59
England and Wales

	TH PER CENT FATALITY	N-TH PER CENT FATALITY STANDARDISED
" IMMEDIATE " ADMISSIONS		
Ischaemic heart disease	23	29***
Perforated ulcer	8·1	10 n.s.
Hernia with obstruction	6·1	9·7**
Hyperplasia of prostate	9·4	13*
Head injury	2·7	3·4*
OTHER ADMISSIONS		
Ischaemic heart disease	9·5	25***
Peptic ulcer c. operation	1·1	1·9*
Hernia	0·26	0·29 n.s.
Hyperplasia of prostate	3·5	6·0**
Head injury	14	4·4***

" Significance " of Differences :

 *   p $<$·05 ** p $<$·01 *** p $<$·001

Standardisation was done on the age (and sex) distribution of the Teaching Hospital admissions.

equally accurate data for morbidity, including cross-infection, and disability are needed. Statistics analysed simply but with a purpose can "discover" problems. Meanwhile, several explanations of the differences in the results obtained by the two types of hospital have been proposed. First, that the figures reflect inferior treatment by the non-teaching hospitals. Staffing ratios are far higher in the teaching hospitals; these however have other roles than patient care and anyhow admit more complicated cases. Alternatively, it has been suggested that teaching hospitals are wiser in the selection of patients for operation, that the non-teaching hospitals operate on the less fit and maybe less sensible patients. There seems to be a higher proportion of patients from social classes I and II in the teaching hospitals: they "shop better" for medical care.

This kind of inter-hospital study could be done regionally as an extension of the medical "audit" to the quality of work done. Comparisons are possible with national experience and, over time, could be made locally. Meanwhile the Table represents the kind of unpleasant social fact that by almost universal agreement is best swept under the carpet.

Two Aspects of Quality

"Quality" even in the present brief discussion can have two meanings.[46] The application of good standard practice is high quality. To make first rate standard surgery everywhere available is the realistic aim of the Ministry of Health and already a great achievement. But is the object of the practice achieved? Is it effective in improving health? Do patients get better? Are they satisfied? Do mothers bring up their children more sensibly? Do fewer adolescents smoke? Are accidents prevented? How quick is the return to work? Can the old people fend for themselves? Availability of the best standard practice obviously is of limited value if health is not improved. Often, however, the main question has not been asked; often the follow-up machinery is not there; often we do not yet know what questions to ask, as in many aspects of community care in the chronic diseases.[76] Many systematic investigations will have to be made if the community's scarce resources are to be used most effectively. Epidemiological investigations of various kinds may be rewarding and should be tried oftener, in particular for common conditions. That assessment in child health of the value of a community's tonsillectomy service has been attempted so little in this country, the home of the Clinical Trial, is depressing: the primary responsibility surely lies here with the surgeons.

Hazards of Health Services

The damage that health services may do is now recognised as an urgent problem in this kind of accounting. Table XIX (p. 73), for example, may be but a token of what in fact is happening, and as already mentioned a notification and registration scheme for toxic reactions to drugs is now being created. Protection from medical radiation is being considerably improved. In the years 1948-61, 357 children in England and Wales having tonsillectomy died of the operation; the number of deaths, though not of operations, has fallen sharply in the last few years.[61] The increase of bilharziasis from irrigation schemes has proved a major tragedy in underdeveloped countries. Notions of "ecology" and of "functional analysis" help in understanding that it is not possible to act on just one chosen part of a working system. The unplanned consequences of malaria control have helped to precipitate a world crisis.

Another word on " quality ". The investigator should remember that, by definition, this is a highly sensitive area and study may be unwelcome. The bureaucrat under the public gaze has his own troubles, the ENT surgeon with what is left of his charisma his. No easy prescription can be offered the investigator; but that he have humility, persistence and a patent concern only with the improvement of services.

INTERNATIONAL COMPARISON

Different countries, with different social systems, have different systems of medical care, but they present serious problems of manpower and money everywhere. These token figures on *general hospitals* for a recent year are remarkably interesting:

	ENGLAND & WALES	USA
Average stay (days)		
Surgical conditions .	11-15	7
Non-surgical conditions	19-20	10
Operation Rate		
per 1,000 population .	40	63
incl. Tonsillectomy .	4·5	6·0

Obviously, the hospital situation in this country could be transformed if "stay" were reduced substantially (without increasing the number of operations), and it would be well worth finding out more on the personal and communal effects of the American system. A complex of financial factors is surely involved, and these too have not yet been analysed. The overall frequency of hospital admission in this country is about two-thirds that in the USA.[10 15 16 19 30 44 58 92]

COMMUNITY CARE

Health services are under great pressure at present, and not merely because of the pace of scientific advance, or the ageing of the population, from growing demands, or the revolution of rising expectations in mental health. Several quite specific problems face us, one being an epochal reallocation of roles between institutions and community. Today the movement is to "admit" the sick, the deviant and the dependent as briefly as possible for active treatment, then to care for them outside—page 98 for example. (The wording is unfortunate, but by now too late to mend. Its "institutions" surely are part of the "community".) "Community care" involves many untested and even unrecognised assumptions about the benefit to patients, the adaptability of families and their role in therapy, and about local government, general practice, social work, not to mention full employment, etc. The chronic ambulant sick may not be a new phenomenon, but their

TABLE XXVI

Statistics of Mental Disorder, 1951 and 1960

England and Wales

Between 1951 and 1960: NATIONAL HEALTH SERVICE

(1) MENTAL HOSPITAL ADMISSIONS

First admissions rose by	51%	from	39,000	to	59,000
Re-admissions „ „	172%	„	21,000	„	56,000
Total „ „	93%	„	60,000	„	115,000

DISCHARGES

Discharges „ „	123%	„	46,000	„	103,000
Discharges of long-stay patients (5 years or more) „ „	157%	„	1,135	„	2,920

MEDIAN STAY

Half the male patients discharged in 1951 had been in hospital 2·2 months or less; by 1960 this " median stay " had fallen to 1·4 months.

RESIDENT POPULATION (AVERAGE)

1951	1954	1960
143,000	148,000	136,000

Resident population, aged 65 +, 1951-60, rose by 25% to 50,000.

(2) PSYCHIATRIC OUTPATIENTS

New out patients rose by	56%	from	107,000	to	167,000
Total attendances „ „	132%	„	545,000	„	1,265,000

Note: *England and Wales*

Home population, 1951-60, rose by $4\frac{1}{2}$% from 43,800,000 to 45,800,000; the population aged 65+ rose by 13% from 4,800,000 to 5,500,000.

Ministry of Health and General Register Office;[6][62][89] and BROOKE, E. (1963), personal communications.

numbers certainly are.[83] Medicine requires a new dimension in terms of the needs of the chronic sick, of their physical potentialities, psychological adjustment, and social functioning.[20][54] Studies have urgently to be made of services, on a population basis, that assesses the hospital sector in relation to community health and welfare services and domiciliary care. This is implicit in what has already been said about general practice. Thus, mental patients, partially recovered, leave hospital quicker than formerly, to what? How is this working out? Is the burden now less or greater or merely redistributed? The Mental Health Act is proving a great catalyst; but surveys of the needs for personnel and for new community instruments, as well as the re-education of all concerned, were insufficient, when begun at all. What the law says is one thing. . . . It would have been greater folly however to postpone the legislation. The epidemiological method with its inevitable questions about communities, about all the patients in them, and about the work of all their interacting and competing services may be able to help.[48][49][92] The frequent absence of services, moreover, gives an unusual opportunity for experiment. Most discussion today is on mental disorder; but other handicaps, ischaemic heart disease and chronic bronchitis prominently, present as many unanswered questions.

ACTION RESEARCH

Graylingwell Hospital serves a community of some 370,000 people, in three districts, Worthing, Chichester and Horsham. The object of " *The Worthing Experiment* ", in the words of its pioneer, is " to discover whether the provision of large scale psychiatric treatment on an out-patient basis could materially affect the great annual increase of admissions to the mental hospital ".[9] There is no doubt of the results, Table overleaf.

Community Care, on a planned and comprehensive basis, to supplement in-patient treatment, was first provided for Worthing and later for Chichester; in both instances the response was immediate. On the other hand, and this may limit the application of the findings, the present overall rate of admission is now much the same as the national, Table XXVI. Formerly it was very high indeed—it could well be,

TABLE XXVII

Mental Hospital; and Community Care

Admissions to Graylingwell Hospital

YEAR	FROM WORTHING	FROM CHICHESTER	FROM HORSHAM	TOTAL*
1956	645	444	219	1,345
1957	284	463	246	1,032
1958	247	228	256	759
1959	269	263	227	786
1960	295	293	239	853
1961	332	329	278	986
1962	325	389	311	1,086

* Including a small number of " out-county " patients.
Domiciliary and day-hospital facilities were specially provided for Worthing and district in 1957, and for Chichester and district in 1958.

CARSE, J., PANTON, N. and WATT, A. (1958). *Lancet* 1, 39; and personal communication, with Sainsbury, P. and Grad, J. (1963).

because of public confidence in the hospital. (Worthing, moreover, has the biggest proportion of old people in any sizeable town in the country, about 25 per cent over 65 years.) Analysis, however, has shown that *all* groups of patients, including the old, were affected by the new programme and showed a fall in admission—not merely those who in other districts might not have been admitted in the first place.

Sainsbury and Grad are also attempting to appraise the experiment by comparing the experience of Chichester with still another and similar population in S. England, served by a similar mental hospital but not provided with such a battery of domiciliary, day-hospital and social facilities.[24][70] The simplest finding is that 27 per cent of the referrals from

Chichester are admitted, against 57 per cent from the control population. Later survey however showed substantial relief in burden to the family of 25 per cent in Chichester, and 37 per cent in the controls. To measure the therapeutic effectiveness of such *community care plus hospital* services, in comparison with *ordinary hospital* service, and to describe any changes in the mental health of the two populations—for example whether there is a decline in prevalence of mental disorder in Chichester, or at least in its severity, through earlier detection and better treatment—will involve prospective study for some years. This is under way.

NEW SERVICES FOR OLD

If there is to be a progressive National Health Service, unencrusted with the past, and sparing of scarce resources, continuing scrutiny and adaptation is essential. Among the many institutions of the NHS several were established to meet needs that have certainly changed, and they may well have served their historic function. For example: specialist child welfare and school health, when the average child is seen about 40 times by the general practitioner (cannot he be educated to take over the lot?); minor ailment clinics (30 years after the depression); the notification of (some of the) infectious diseases; the Appointed Factory Doctor examining healthy youngsters (who are least likely to need his services); the community's Medical Officer of Health in a " closed shop " because of archaic diploma requirements (when the talent of the whole profession should be tapped)—these and others that are obsolescent and may be preventing the future can be cited. Health Services by their nature must reflect history and politics as well as current needs of the people; knowledge will help to create the public opinion and professional mood that can generate change. One of the main uses of epidemiology is that it can help social institutions to apply the scientific method to their own workings, each physician to examine his practice and himself.

IV

INDIVIDUAL RISKS AND CHANCES

The chances of an individual suffering an accident, as schoolboy cyclist, youth on motor cycle or elderly pedestrian; of developing leukaemia after X-ray therapy, X-ray diagnosis; of having a second stillbirth, another neonatal disaster; of producing malformation from rubella, or rheumatic fever after haemolytic streptococcal infection; of contracting poliomyelitis having had one " shot ", two, three, four; of longevity for a man who is very fat or very thin—these chances and probabilities can be estimated *on average* from measurement of the current experience of large numbers of persons with the relevant characteristics. And the experience of appropriate " populations " not so characterised will also be needed for comparison. The actual arithmetic of the individual risk, say of suffering a disease, is for practical purposes the simple addition of annual age-specific incidence rates.

Incidence rates are calculated for each year of age covering the span of years for which knowledge of the risk is required. These rates are added together, and the result, the cumulative individual risk, expressed not as a rate per 1,000 but as a 1 in X chance of developing the disease in that period. For example, if the sum of the incidence rates per 1,000 equals 200, the individual risk is 1 in 5. The incidence measures the rate at which new disease develops in the group, and the risk of it for the individual. If incidence rates are available only in bands of ages (in decades for example), before being added together the age-specific rates must be multiplied by the number of years of age in each band (10 in the example) so as to make a specific allowance for each year of age. When greater accuracy is required, the actuary's Life Table methods are used. These are also necessary for study of such problems as the chances of individuals having repeated accidents —accident proneness—or repeated spells of sickness.

Fig. 15 illustrates what is very likely the best known fact of this kind; these very full data are Australian. The overall frequency at birth of mongolism (trisomy 21) in this European

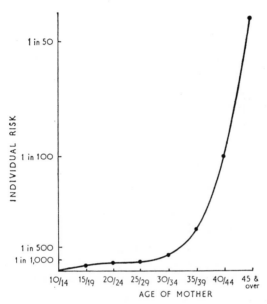

FIG. 15
Individual risk of bearing a mongol child, according to age of mother.
COLLMAN, R. D. & STOLLER, A. (1962). N.Z. med. J. **61**, 24.

population is about one in 700. For mothers under 30 years of age the risk of bearing a mongol child is less than 1 in 1,000; the incidence varies from 0·41 per 1,000 at 15-19 years of age to 0·83 at 25-29 years. There is a smooth and steep rise then through a risk of 1 *per cent* in mothers aged 40-44, till it is about 1 in 45 for mothers over 45 years old.*[5][16]

Fig. 16 gives a rough idea of the cumulative " risks " the average man in Britain now runs during his middle age; it

* It is possible now to go further and calculate the risks of a woman bearing a second mongol child, and the special associations of youth, and chromosomal disorder, with this,[4]

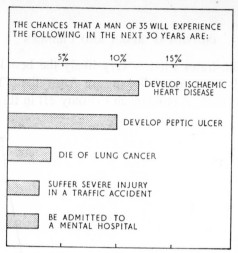

FIG. 16

Some present-day risks and chances of the average man from 35 years through middle age. Approximate figures. Britain.[9] [10] [12] [14] [15] [18]
5 per cent=1 in 20; 10 per cent=1 in 10, etc.

TABLE XXVIII

Risk of Developing Ischaemic Heart Disease[12]

Estimate of the number of male medical practitioners who, not having previously been clinically attacked by it, would get ischaemic heart disease before reaching certain ages

Age x (years)	Of 1000 men aged x, the number indicated below would get clinical ischaemic heart disease before age—					
	40	45	50	55	60	65
35	3	**10**	**27**	**67**	**130**	**200**
40		7	24	65	129	200
45			18	59	124	196
50				43	110	184
55					72	152
60						90

Ischaemic heart disease refers to the clinical manifestations of sudden death, other " coronary thrombosis " and myocardial infarction, angina pectoris, together with a small number of cases of " coronary insufficiency ", etc.

104

TABLE XXIX

Individual Risk of Developing Cancer

The Average Lifetime Risk, on the Experience of
New York State* in 1949-51

MALES		FEMALES	
Site	Probability	Site	Probability
All sites	1 in 4·6	All sites	1 in 4
Skin	1 in 33	Breast	1 in 18
Prostate	1 in 38	Skin	1 in 40
Stomach	1 in 50	Cervix	1 in 43
Large intestine	1 in 52	Stomach	1 in 77
Rectum	1 in 83		

* Exclusive of New York City.

GOLDBERG, I. D., LEVIN, M. L., GERHARDT, P. R., HANDY, V. H., CASHMAN, R. E. (1956). *J. Nat. Canc. Inst.* **17**, 163; (1962). Personal communications.

NOTE. The following are *very approximate* guides to the application of these data to *current* experience in England and Wales:

MALES	FEMALES

All sites: 1 in 4·6 is likely an underestimate, possibly by a third, of risk at present in E & W, because of far greater incidence of lung cancer here, now, than in New York in 1949-51.

Skin: E & W, data not available.

Prostate: Current risk in E & W may be about a third lower.

Stomach: Current risk in E & W may be half as much again.

Large intestine: Current risk in E & W may be about a third lower.

Rectum: Current risk in E & W is similar.

All sites: 1 in 4 is likely an overestimate, possibly by a third of current risk in E & W.

Breast: Current risk in E & W is similar.

Skin: E & W, data not available.

Cervix: Current risk in E & W may be about a third lower.

Stomach: Current risk in E & W may be half as much again.

Registrar General. Report of the Ministry of Health for 1959, Part II. South West Regional Hospital Board Cancer Records Bureau, *Reports* and personal communications.

complements the picture of Figs. 1 and 2. In light of a something like one-in-eight chance of developing clinical ischaemic
heart disease as the Figure suggests (and quite a lot more for
doctors, Table XXVIII), or one-in-ten from peptic ulcer, most
of it duodenal, the popular understanding of the term " epidemic " finds further warrant. Since these calculations were
made in 1955 the probabilities have of course changed, nothing
stays put; but the estimates remain good enough overall. On
present experience, those for IHD in the general population
would be higher, for peptic ulcer lower, for lung cancer very
little different, and so on.[13] [18]

Table XXIX is American. Using it as a baseline, it can
roughly be estimated that rather more than 1 in 4 men and

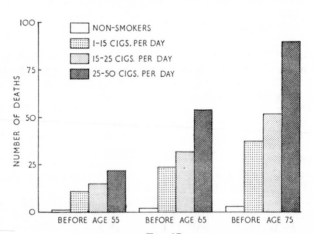

FIG. 17

Individual risks of dying of lung cancer in relation to
smoking habits. Estimates based on the early " case-
control ", " retrospective " studies in English hospitals,
1948-52.[6] Of 1,000 males aged 25 smoking 25-50 cigarettes
per day, 22, on the experience of the patients who were
studied, may be expected to die of lung-cancer by 55 years
of age; 54 (a further 32, *i.e.*) by 65 years of age; and 90, or
1 in 11, by 75 years of age; etc.
Brit. med. J. (1953). **1,** 1105.[18]

rather less than 1 in 5 women may expect to develop cancer, on the current experience of England and Wales. Mortality from lung cancer in men in this country over the whole age span is a good deal higher than in 1949-51, and rates here are twice those of the Americans, so I have not included the New York estimate for that disease. The overall risk or probability of British doctors dying of lung cancer is 1 in 30.*[7][8]

TABLE XXX

(1)

Individual Risk of Dying in Relation to Smoking Habits

Men
All Causes
Experience of British Doctors, 1951-58

SPAN OF YEARS	NON-SMOKERS	EX-SMOKERS	CIGARETTE SMOKERS	OTHER SMOKERS	ALL DOCTORS
35 - 44	1 in 90	1 in 49	1 in 46	1 in 62	1 in 54
45 - 54	1 in 27	1 in 19	1 in 13	1 in 19	1 in 16
55 - 64	1 in 8	1 in 7	1 in 5	1 in 12	1 in 7
65 - 74	1 in 3	1 in 3	1 in 2	1 in 3	1 in 3

(2)

Individual Chance of Male British Doctors Aged 35 Surviving to 65 .

Non-smokers . .	85%
Ex-Smokers . .	81%
Cigarette smokers .	73%
Other smokers .	86%
All doctors . .	79%

DOLL, R. & HILL, A. B. (1962). In *Smoking and Health*. London; and personal communications.

Fig. 17 brings aetiology into the calculation, using early data. From it the conclusion is obvious that on average the

---

* The skin cancer figures show the error of thinking of cancer only in terms of *mortality*. Unfortunately, adequate *incidence* figures for cancer are only now becoming available in this country, and there are none so far for the skin.

heavy smoker is over twenty times more likely to die of lung cancer than the man who doesn't smoke; or, another reading of the data, some 10 per cent of heavy smokers may expect so to die (90 of 1,000 up to the age of 75) compared with less than 0·5 per cent of non-smokers. Considering next the general mortality of smokers from all causes, the average risk of the individual man dying during each of the four decades between the ages of 35 and 75, is illustrated in Table XXX, again from Doll and Hill's data,[7][8] but on this occasion from their study of British doctors. " The significance of these figures may be illustrated in terms of a lottery by supposing that for each ten-year period the man has to draw from a box containing one marked ticket among a number of blanks. If he draws the marked ticket he dies in the next ten years. Thus for a non-smoker aged 35 there is one marked ticket for the next ten years in a box of 90 tickets, but for a heavy smoker of this age (25 or more cigarettes per day) the marked ticket is one among only 23." Among cigarette smokers, the individual risk of dying from 35 to 44 ranges from 1 in 64 for light smokers to 1 in 23 for heavy smokers, with an average of 1 in 46 as shown in the Table on page 107.

The *incidence* (particularly useful in the study of historical trends, and crucial in seeking causes which might be producing cases of disease), *prevalence* (summing the community's burden of chronic disease for example, and indicating the results of treatment), and *mortality* (sometimes the only fact available), are the main tools of epidemiology. This further estimate of *individual risk,* derived from the incidence, has a special value. It has been elaborated in genetics, and is much used practically in counselling as well as in theoretical studies.[2][17] In the chronic diseases, it is indispensable for expressing the impact of conditions with a cumulative and rising incidence over the age span, as in the examples given.[13] Thus at 45-49 years doctors were found to have an incidence of ischaemic heart disease of 3·4 per 1,000 p.a., rising to 17 per 1,000 at ages 60-64; the corresponding prevalence figures were 17 and

90 per 1,000. It tells something different, and more, that the chances of the individual doctor developing clinical ischaemic heart disease during middle age (from 45 to 65) is about 1 in 5 (Table XXVIII). Equally, this may be a particular *in*effective means of expression. There are 350,000 casualties from road accidents a year in Britain, an appalling figure; but the "risk" is about one in a quarter million motor-vehicle miles, a self-defeating kind of "fact". There may be only a 1 in 7,000 or 10,000 chance of dying from tonsillectomy; but it added up to 357 disasters between 1948 and 1961.

This "use" or application of epidemiology is simple, and it is likely to become more popular as forward-looking, "prospective" studies are developed to learn about the conditions of health in middle and old age. What on average are the chances of the athletic, non-smoking Jack Spratt, fully seized of the Sanitary Idea of The Day, having ischaemic heart disease in his fifties, sixties? And are they less than in the mass of the population on quite different regimens? Much that is discovered about the relations of health to the mode of life may be usefully expressed in terms of such individual probabilities; which is one advantage of having a population accustomed to weighing the "odds".

V

COMPLETING THE CLINICAL PICTURE

The clinician is limited in his picture of the chronic diseases. In the less common conditions numbers may be too few, with attendant troubles of chance variation and sampling error. It is to another aspect however that I now wish to draw attention. Numbers can be large and yet the clinician's experience may be incomplete and the patients he deals with unrepresentative of all types and degree, *i.e.* the picture may be biased. The reasons for this are manifold, in personal specialism and reputation, in geographic, economic and administrative situations. Such limitations apply also to the work of a hospital or any other medical facility. Selective processes affecting admission to hospital may be explicit and obvious, in terms of severity for example. They can also be subtle and complicated and, to make things worse, may be working unsuspected and in manner undefined. All this is to refer only to patients who present to medical attention. But even advanced disease may be symptomless, and even those suffering severe disability may not seek help; at the other extreme, much mild illness is ignored. In short, any clinician's experience of a chronic disease is likely to be incomplete; all clinical experience is liable to be incomplete. The epidemiologist, concerned with the total of ascertainable cases in a specified population, and not merely with patients who present in particular hospitals, clinics or practices, can help to provide a fuller picture than is obtainable in any or all of these. This fuller picture may also prove to be a different one. The epidemiological method is thus helping to *complete the clinical picture* and natural history of disease.

1. COMPLETING THE PICTURE IN BREADTH.—*An Illustration from Ischaemic Heart Disease*

Soon after I began to work on the epidemiology of coronary disease in the late 1940's it became clear that the picture of it in hospital is quite unrepresentative. Thus, on searching the pathological archives of the London Hospital I was puzzled at the rarity of *ruptured ventricle,* despite the numerous examples of other manifestations of ischaemic heart disease. The answer eventually occurred to me, and it was confirmed by the pathologist responsible for the medico-legal necropsies of that part of London. " Oh yes," he told me on the telephone, " I get two a week "; the coroner's pathologist (the Medical Examiner) had almost a monopoly of these ruptured hearts.

Some years later we returned to this question, and the detailed results are illuminating.[20] During the two years 1957-8, in all of London's hospitals including the Teaching Hospitals, 80-85 ruptured hearts presumptively from IHD were found at necropsy. But in a 66 per cent sample of coroners' pathology, drawn from the same population during the same period, there were 345 ruptured hearts. On scaling up the coroners' figures to produce an overall estimate for the $3\frac{1}{4}$ million people of London, it is obvious that the condition is by no means rare :

Hospital and Community: Ruptured Ventricle
Estimated Numbers in London[20] [84]
1957-8

AGE (Years)	13 MAIN TEACHING HOSPITALS		OTHER HOSPITALS		CORONERS' MORTUARIES		TOTAL IN LONDON		
	M	F	M	F	M	F	M	F	M + F
- 70	15	4	13	4	86	60	114	68	182
70 +	4	13	11	19	145	240	160	272	432
Total	36		47		531		274	340	614

On these figures, about 300 cases a year are recognised in London, or 100 per million of the population. The rate is much higher in the old; about one in a hundred deaths in old people seems to be due to ruptured heart.

Less than 15 per cent of the total were recognised in hospitals. Some of the answer why these were so few lies in a feature that has emerged clearly only from the coroners' records. Ruptured ventricle is a condition especially of the elderly and, as is only too common experience, there are special difficulties in the admission of old people to hospital. Moreover, the clinical histories are often short and, characteristic of the aged, slight and confused; often, too, the old people were living alone. In consequence, if these people were admitted to hospital it would commonly be as the " B(rought) I(n) D(ead) ". For such, however, other arrangements are made in London through the system of coroners.

The largest number, it will be noticed, was in old ladies. But this does not imply a higher rate in them: as will be expected (p. 24) there are in London more than $1\frac{1}{2}$ times as many females over 70 as males. The number in old ladies, more likely, reflects a trend to a similar frequency in the two sexes among the aged. This recalls a common clinical impression about the natural history of ischaemic heart disease: that female immunity to it diminishes after the menopause and disappears in old age, an impression that so far has been difficult to confirm. Certified national coronary death rates in old age do converge, for what specific cause-of-death data after 65 or 70 are worth (which is probably not very much). But apart from these figures on ruptured heart there are few estimates of the incidence or the prevalence of IHD in old people.

To sum up: the clinical picture in London of ruptured ventricle is incomplete, indeed it is wrong: wrong on size, wrong about sex, wrong on age; and wrong, it may be added, on the share of anticoagulants. These were involved in 16 per cent of the hospital patients, but in only 2 per cent of the total cases.

Clinical Medicine and Epidemiology

The first point to make then is this. Clinicians deal with patients, epidemiologists with populations. In studying the natural history of disease, the epidemiologist, for the numerator of the rates he is always trying to produce, must, as a first step and at the very least, find all the patients in the population—the denominator—wherever they happen to present. Surveys usually are needed for this, and it is to them that the epidemiologist devotes most of his effort. In the instance that has been cited the survey, to find all the ruptured hearts in the population of London, was simple because of the administration whereby nearly every unexplained death in London is routinely investigated by necropsy. Mere addition of hospital numbers and those from the coroners' mortuaries gives a useful picture; though it is certainly provisional, and an underestimate because of cases wrongly diagnosed before death and not brought to necropsy. (Ruptured ventricle from IHD is a foolproof diagnosis—but only if the heart is examined.) The position will be quite different in cities like Glasgow or New York where, I am informed, there is post-mortem examination in only a small fraction of " sudden " deaths that are manifestly due to natural causes. The result of this particular exercise, in what is but a single manifestation of IHD, is bizarre; but further illustrations from ischaemic heart disease can readily be given. Thus of all deaths within five years of the onset of clinical IHD, about half occur within the first hours, or very few days, of the first clinical attack.[74] The *prognosis* in any series will obviously fluctuate drastically according as many or few of such rapidly fatal incidents are included; but, again, they are seen commonly only in the Coroner's Court, and relatively few may be admitted to hospital. For a complete picture of the prognosis of recognised myocardial infarction all patients need to be counted, wherever they present, and whatever the outcome.[75]

Ischaemic heart disease then " presents " in many different places: general practice, consulting practice, the works' clinic,

TABLE XXXI

Clinically Presenting Ischaemic Heart Disease[74 84]

Medical Practitioners

Annual Rates per 1,000

| | AGES | | | |
	45-	50-	55-	60-64
Sudden death[1]	0·6	1·0	3·6	3·1
Other first attack[1]	2·8	6·0	8·3	13·5
(a) Total incidence[1]	3·4	7·0	12	17
(b) Relapse rate[2]	1·7	4·8	6·2	7·1
(c) Attack rate[2]	5·1	12	18	24
(e) Active prevalence[3]	8·3	12	29	42
(f) Quiescent disease[3]	8·3	17	26	48
Total prevalence[3]	17	29	55	90
Total mortality IHD[1]	1·3	2·0	4·7	7·4

[1] 1947-50, annual average.   [2] 1949-50 ann. ave.   (b) is estimate.   [3] 1950.

The following categories can be described:

Men who have an attack starting in the year which is the first clinical manifestation of ischaemic heart disease causing incapacity to work—the *incidence* (a).

Men who have a second or later such attack starting in the year, having had a first attack in an earlier year—their rate of relapse (b).

(a)+(b) constitute the *attack rate* (c), *i.e.* of persons attacked.

Men who had an attack before the beginning of the year, who continue to be incapacitated for part or all of that year, but have no attack starting in the year (d)—figure not given.

(c)+(d) are the *active prevalence* of disease causing incapacity to work and needing treatment (e).

Men who have had an attack of IHD in an earlier year but, having returned to work, do not have an attack starting in the year (the *prevalence* of *quiescent* or inactive disease (f) which is about equal to the active).

a variety of hospitals, general and special out-patients, diverse medical wards, surgical wards, general necropsy rooms, the Coroner's mortuary. IHD also presents in many different ways —most acutely as sudden death in the apparently healthy, as classical cardiac infarction, as an atypical chronic and serious illness, as angina of varying severity, as these ruptured hearts. Since it may present in different ways in different places, more of one type here, of another there, information from any one physician, or any particular facility, is liable to be incomplete and may be misleading. Only a community study can hope to provide a picture, even of clinically presenting IHD, in proportion and as a whole. . . . Table XXXI assembles the clinical data about IHD in a population of physicians. It is probably complete within its limitations that only men who were absent sick on account of the disease for at least six consecutive days during the year are considered to be " patients ". The arithmetic of the various types and stages is highly interesting, for example the picture of the build-up of non-fatal disease. A substantial number of men relapsed during the year. Typical of chronic diseases, of rheumatoid arthritis, multiple sclerosis, many inborn errors of metabolism, affective disorder—and treated cancer—etc., etc., ischaemic heart disease has an intermittent course of *remission and relapse*. This is at present one of the darkest areas (what are the causes of breakdown in patients with ischaemic heart disease?) and the contribution that a complete clinical picture could make is obvious.

Short of trying, there is no means of knowing in how many other conditions the kind of situation that has been described occurs. In cerebrovascular disease, surely. What epidemiological evidence there is gives no support to the reputed concentration, based on hospital experience, of breast cancer in early middle age[5] (or of " coronaries " among men in their late 50's). Whatever it looks like in hospital, there is no evidence that the incidence of congenital malformation as a cause of heart disease in children is rising, or that amyloid disease from rheumatoid arthritis is becoming commoner; it is the other causes, in Britain, that are dwindling (recalling the onion principle, p. 14). Buerger's disease, if it exists at all, is not limited to Russian Jews: " It was Mount Sinai Hospital in New York City which at that time was largely limited to Russian Jews ".[35]

The illustration from ruptured heart has emphasised the inadequacies of hospital data in a grave illness. Even in this instance, however, the picture in the *teaching hospitals,* which are the source of most statements on pathology, was particularly unrepresentative. There is the University Hospital in a northern city which selects its patients from all classes and a wide area, and in which chronic bronchitis and cor pulmonale is uncommon. At a former municipal hospital in the same city, its patients mainly local and often poor, both conditions are common. How can a balanced picture be obtained of chronic chest disease, or of the causes of heart failure? Again—there may be hundreds and thousands of patients on the " books " of a University diabetic clinic, but numbers alone will not ensure that they reflect the occurrence of renal or retinal disorder in diabetes, and not merely in this particular and perhaps quite indefinable group of diabetics. (Patients with such " complications " will often be selected for referral to university clinics, etc.) Having stated a question, say about the frequency of these manifestations, the next step is to ask how to get a correct answer. Multiplying the number of patients will not necessarily help and, indeed, may merely multiply bias. Much better to assure that all patients with diabetes in a sufficiently large population, an appropriate number of general practices for example, are included : this is an epidemiological question and the right way of asking it is epidemiological.*

Clinical Disease That Does Not " Present "

I must continue with the argument. The clinician deals with his patients, and some limitations this imposes on the study of the natural history of disease have just been considered. But some individuals with manifest disease, even advanced disease, and symptoms enough, neglect it; at any

---

* There are of course some conditions among the chronic diseases, where grouped hospital studies, for example, and even a single community-hospital study, may be adequate in contemporary Britain to give a balanced picture of clinically presenting disease. Cancer in the young may be cited, and some cancers, including bronchogenic probably, in middle age. In all, three-quarters of cancer patients are now included in the National Cancer Register which is almost entirely a hospital scheme. Perforated peptic ulcer, schizophrenia with gross disturbance and frank delusions, haemophilia with bleeding, severe accidents are other examples.

rate they do not complain, are not patients. They learn to live with their trouble (migraine, for example), and to put up with it (chronic rheumatism),[32] they are afraid—but mostly it is not yet known why they seek no medical care (p. 83). This is a serious obstacle in cancer control, a recurring tragedy in cataract and glaucoma, an everyday problem with old people. (The question of diagnosis is a separate one that may be ignored here.) It is common for diabetics to give a history of several months' and even years' duration when they first attend (often with a " complication "). Many sufferers from psychological disorders do not appreciate the nature of their symptoms: the depressed, schizophrenics (that they do not call their doctors is an unanticipated difficulty in community care), withdrawn children in particular; and even some with serious anxiety states. In general, there is a good deal of manifest, symptomatic disease that one way and another is not brought to medical attention. For a complete picture of angina pectoris, and of its prognosis, a community survey is needed, not merely a collection of what is known to community services. An operational definition of angina needs to be agreed, and the specified population, or a sample of it, questioned. In 500 working busmen aged 45-64, two per cent, none of them under medical care for the symptom, were found to have angina.

Irregular Epidemiology.—This happy phrase, it has been reported, was coined at a World Health Organisation meeting in a plea for the amateur, for the encouragement of the clinician as " naturalist " to extend his analysis and inference to the population whence his patients are drawn. No one with the sketchiest history of epidemiology (of Pott, Gregg, Burkitt and the rest) can be unenthusiastic about such a plea. The last few pages, however, may be read as a notice of the kind of consideration to be borne in mind when translating hospital numbers, for example, and their (changing) ratios to each other, into statements about the frequency even of clinical disease over time, or in particular race, sex, age or other groups. The general practitioner is better placed to get a correct picture; his troubles are liable to be with numbers and with social selection. In each specific question it is wise to consider of any clinical data how representative they are, what the selective factors are likely to be, and how such bias might limit the lessons that can be drawn.[4 30 31 34 35 39 62 63 70]

The discussion has extended to what will be found on search, not merely what turns up of its own, to " cases " not just to patients. In *completing the clinical picture*, this group with manifest disease that is not brought to clinical attention is the simplest that has to be added to what already does present.

2. SUBCLINICAL DISEASE—ICEBERG PHENOMENON

Shortly before the war, in my first exercise in epidemiology, I made a systematic physical examination of the 1,350 men employed in certain grades by a Midlands municipality and found eight with neurosyphilis.[69] None was disabled, none had any symptoms that bothered him, none had any idea he had syphilis, none was under observation or treatment. Such cases with established, often advanced, disease that is not manifest, maybe is burnt out, with nothing that could be expected to bring them to the physician, must also be included in the " natural history ". The fraction they form of the total should be estimated, though in this instance of neurosyphilis I was unable to take the question any further. Twenty per cent of first incidents of infarction in Framingham are symptomless, diagnosed only on electrocardiography.[22] Mitral stenosis used quite often to be a chance, and inexplicable, finding. Routine physical examination in this country occasionally discloses a symptomless cancer. Much anaemia, severe as well as slight, is unrecognised: the women have only vague symptoms (if they have menorrhagia that also is not perceived) and they adapt at a lower level of efficiency. To detect most anaemia a laboratory test is necessary—clinical diagnosis is reliable only below about 60 per cent Hb.[64] Hypothyroidism will often so be detected, if it is kept in mind. I suppose uncomplicated obesity should also be included here.

The main interest for the natural history of chronic diseases in penetrating beyond the clinical presentation, however, lies in the deeper ranges, in the early, minor stages such search commonly reveals.

Early, Subclinical Disease

Early disease may cause trouble, but often it is symptomless. This is the principal group to be found on search, and I am now referring to it: true *subclinical* disease, asymptomatic, or with minimal symptoms, and not presenting. By " early " I refer to the stage and degree of development of the disease and there are theoretical as well as practical problems in distinguishing early disease from healthy variation, say the upper end of a normal distribution; in their earliest stages, moreover, it must be postulated that the chronic diseases are reversible. This notion derives directly and by analogy from nutrition, from subclinical " malnutrition " or " hidden hunger " which is so much more common, in rickets or kwashiorkor for example, than florid deficiency states—these form the tip of the iceberg. Subclinical infection as in gonorrhoea, and " carrier " states, of upper respiratory or of bowel infection, have long been recognised; appreciation of it in tuberculosis, in meningococcal infection and in diphtheria clarified, indeed transformed, the picture of their natural history. The more recent discoveries of the frequency of merely serological poliomyelitis compared with non-paralytic incidents and the paralytic, and the astonishing story of histoplasmosis in the USA, have stated these issues in striking manner and again enlarged our understanding beyond measure. Mild beginning signs are familiar in toxaemia of pregnancy, or lead poisoning. In many of the chronic non-infectious diseases such early stages are often recognisable, their presence at any rate may be suspected. Only by proper survey, however, will they be detected in proper proportion to the clinical and to the population in which both are occurring. Dental caries, hypertension, rheumatoid arthritis, pneumoconiosis, pyelonephritis, hepatic cirrhosis, alcoholism, depression, schizophrenia, senile psychosis, are examples that come to mind.

PATIENTS AND POPULATIONS

The survey of *diabetes* carried out in Birmingham by the College of General Practitioners and the University,[6] using the glucose-oxidase paper strip together with the oral glucose tolerance test (GTT), provides figures that can readily be referred to the various "levels" that have been considered. There were about 20,000 people in the practices of the general practitioners who participated.

Prevalence of Diabetes per 1,000 Aged 50 +, Both Sexes

CLINICAL	(a) *Patients Presenting*	15
	Discovered on Survey	
	(b) "Florid", with symptoms	4·7 ⎫
SUBCLINICAL	(c) "Florid", without symptoms	3·2 ⎬ 17
	(d) "Early" diabetes	8·6 ⎭
	TOTAL	32 per 1,000

The first line (a) gives the frequency of patients in this population, 15 in each thousand over 50 years of age. Included in line (b) are cases who surely should have complained, but did not. Many of them presumably would have presented to their general practitioners later, with a history—with advanced disease or with "complications". Proceeding, line (c) gives the number found to have serious metabolic disorder, but without symptoms; and the last line (d) represents mild disease, "early" in present terms, with trivial if any symptoms. Since the "disease" diabetes is defined primarily on the presence of glycosuria and the results of the GTT, the division into "florid", "early" (and "healthy") is quantitative and arbitrary. In this study, the GTT was administered to all having glycosuria and, conventionally, the response regarded as diabetic if the blood sugar level at two hours exceeded 120 mg/100 ml. "Florid" implies in addition that the fasting value exceeded 130 mg/100 ml, "early" diabetes a lower fasting level. An issue immediately arises on the relationships of these various figures. In particular: what proportion in lines (c), (b), (a) pass through a recognisable stage of early subclinical but detectable disease, as in line (d)? And over what time interval?

Latent Disease.—This study was continued in depth. A random sample of subjects over 50 years of age who did not have glycosuria were given 50 g of glucose and their blood sugar measured. *Eighteen per cent* now produced a diabetic-type curve, and a sizeable minority also had glycosuria. Meanwhile, this large group may be regarded as having "latent diabetes" though the mere act of calling them so begs a lot of questions. Atrophic gastritis in which pernicious anaemia is latent (because stores of cyanobalamin are adequate) is well recognised. Gout represents another class of disorders which can be mentioned here. An exercise test is suggested for eliciting latent ischaemic heart disease;[18] estimation has scarcely begun of the volume of disease, latent or merely subclinical, that can be detected on special challenge; and which may correspond to the cases that bob into clinical trouble, are activated or (just as mysteriously) reactivated under strain of infection, pregnancy, emotional crisis . . . or for no reason that can yet be discerned.

Page 122 gives (1) the number of patients presenting clinically with various conditions in an average general practice in this country, and (2) estimates of what on average may be found in addition on simple ad hoc search, some being advanced but most of it early subclinical disease. The figures in col. (1) are largely derived from records kept for a single year by the College of General Practitioners and the General Register Office and already quoted in Table X, p. 36. The limitations of such a picture of "clinical" prevalence will be appreciated, though for most conditions these figures are the best readily available on morbidity in the population. Col. (2) gathers data from special surveys, and it illustrates the scope

TABLE XXXII

Clinical and Subclinical Disease[54]

Numbers Adjusted to an Average General Practice of 2,250 Persons
Britain

DISEASE	(1) AVERAGE No. OF PATIENTS SEEN DURING YEAR	(2) APPROX. FURTHER No. OF CASES THAT MAY BE DETECTED ON SURVEY
Pulmonary tuberculosis[41 42 61] incl. new notifications (M & F, all ages) ·	6-7 1	2-3 active cases on mass miniature radiography, and 3-4 suspect cases, probably inactive
Cancer: *New cases*[41 42] Lung (M)	1 (All ages)	1 case in 2 years on MMR (55+)
Cervix (F, 20+)	1 in 4-5 years	
Diabetes[6] (M & F, 50-69)	8	8 69 with " latent diabetes "
Obesity[40 61] (M, 45-64)	2	25
Anaemia[52 61] (F, 15-44)	12	c. 100 with Hb<80%
Psychiatric disorder[51 61] (M & F, 15+)	89	71 with "conspicuous psychiatric morbidity "
Glaucoma[21 59 61] (M & F, 45+)	3	20
Ischaemic heart disease[61 84] (M, 45-64)	5	15
Hypertension[61 66] (45-64)	4 (M) 11 (F)	39 (M), 40 (F), with casual DBP over 100 mm Hg
Bronchitis[18 43 61] (M, 45-64)	24	24
Urinary tract infection[47 61] (F, 15+)	20	33 with symptomless bacteriuria

(Sex, and age, in brackets.)

for detecting disease among those not presently recognised to be ill, or complaining. The contrast between the figures in cols. (1) and (2) gives some idea of " icebergs " that can at present be described in the chronic diseases. I can pause only briefly to comment on the figures. Two of the patients and two of the " cases " of pulmonary tuberculosis are men over 45. The figure in col. (2) gives little indication how often it would be rewarding to use mass miniature radiography in the detection of early lung cancer since this often grows very rapidly. Obesity in col. (2) is estimated from the proportion of London busmen with trouser waistbands of 42 inches and over. Table XXI on p. 81 may be recalled vis-a-vis the low figure for anaemia in col. (1).

This further attempt to complete the clinical picture is only in its beginnings but, as in Section 1, it looks like introducing qualitative changes, yielding a *different* picture. Follow-up of symptomless proteinuria detected at routine examination showed that it may progress to Type II nephritis with oedema, which thus is not necessarily or perhaps even commonly a result of acute nephritis.[95] The sexes are equally affected by early subclinical rheumatoid arthritis, in contrast to what is found among patients.[48 49 50] The relationships of suicidal gestures, occurring mostly in young women, to accomplished suicide, commonest in elderly men, is still unclear.[85 86] Current field surveys could well transform the accepted clinical picture of diabetes.[15]

*   *   *

Natural history is one thing. The other great use of the systematic detection of early disease in population surveys is likely to be in the search for causes of the chronic diseases—the subject of a later chapter. In many of the chronic diseases of middle and old age particularly, clinical states often are advanced and complicated, multiple pathologies often present. To search then for causes of the occurrence of these diseases is to choose the worst time to deal with the most difficult problem.

*   *   *

Problems can readily be stated that might be clarified by assembling the clinical, and seeking at the same time the subclinical—the secret drinkers and undetected offenders, the early cases, the *formes frustes,* the near misses. . . . What makes *juveniles " delinquent "*? The psychiatrist will mostly see severely disturbed children; from my own experience it seems often to be a matter of chance whether these turn up in Out-Patients or the Juvenile Court. The magistrate sees much " apple stealing " among more serious trouble. The youth leader knows how badly youngsters may ordinarily behave; in some districts " delinquent " behaviour is the social norm. No picture of delinquency can be complete that does not attempt to include the current range of normal and extreme, of acceptable and deviant behaviour among young people. (And this is not to raise the question of delinquent " equivalents ", anti-social and hostile behaviour that does not even nominally involve breaking the law.) " It is remarkable how insufficient are the ' known facts ' about the delinquent. The defect of the data, of course, is not that they represent too small a sample, but that we cannot tell what sorts of delinquents and delinquencies may be over-represented or under-represented. We can never lay to rest the ghost of un-representativeness as long as our statistical base of operations is delinquencies known to the courts, the police, or even to the schools and social agencies. Until this defect is remedied, comparisons between delinquents and non-delinquents with respect to their developmental histories, personalities and social position must be received with some scepticism and reserve. In order to remedy this defect, we must start, not with known delinquents, but with representative samples of the juvenile population drawn without regard to their known or probable delinquent histories. Then, we must differentiate these samples into delinquents and non-delinquents of various degrees and kinds ". . . .[17] " The total picture of *schizophrenia* is not conveyed by hospital data. Such figures do not take into account the schizophrenic private patients of psychiatrists, or

the undefinable group on the list of practically every practitioner, patients whose schizophrenic-like reactions continually impair response to treatment for other conditions; or the completely unregistered and undiagnosed schizophrenics not in any institution and under no psychiatric or medical care; or the borderline and mild cases, the ' schizoids ', more or less identifiable in any group of the population at any level ". . . .[65]
If the picture of contemporary *reproductive wastage* is to be at all complete, we need to know much more about abortion than can be gathered from the highly peculiar sample of it seen in hospitals or the fertility clinic. The department of obstetrics is less in need of epidemiological help than others, for it has usually some basis in the ordinary population of an ante-natal clinic (though socially this may be atypical). But this representativeness is unlikely to apply in the first months of pregnancy. Particularly in the abortions,[45] hospital admission policies (as well as medical and legal attitudes) can erect effective barriers to completeness of the clinical picture. . . . The extent of *industrial hazards* it is evident is grossly understated in official statistics,[76] [82] and the clinical picture may be bizarrely inaccurate as well: of skin cancer, or byssinosis, or lead poisoning, or accidents for example. In each of these instances there are special if not extenuating circumstances, but the only safe policy today is to seek out the clinical, however disguised or selected out of the population, and to survey ad hoc for the subclinical. . . .

*   *   *

3. PRECURSORS OF DISEASE

The next dimension to be considered in the natural history of the chronic diseases is, much more tentatively, that of *precursors,* using the term to distinguish abnormalities occurring during the pathogenesis and *before* the actual onset of disease —they may often be discovered many years before.[72] [89] Here the analogy of the present formulation to the study of acute infection and an infectious epidemic begins to break down.

The main finding of the Framingham and similar prospective studies[23] is that apparently healthy men with no evidence of ischaemic heart disease who have a high casual level of cholesterol in the blood are more likely, on average, to develop IHD during middle age than comparable men with not so high levels. And so on, down the scale. Hypercholesterolaemia thus is a disturbance systematically preceding the onset of ischaemic heart disease. The development of bronchogenic carcinoma seems to extend over many years (from initiation, it could be), and abnormal cells, though not yet malignant, are very commonly present in the bronchi of cigarette smokers who die of other causes[3]... The point, and potential value, of such probing of the natural history may be illustrated by the contrast between the known futility of lowering high blood cholesterol levels after ischaemic heart disease has developed —the prognosis is not improved[77]—and today's hope that to reduce them earlier will reduce the chances of the disease developing at all.

Functional and structural *precursors* as diverse as the chronic diseases themselves are progressively being discovered, " qualitative " disorders, and " quantitative "—these will be more difficult to define usefully. The proposition about precursors is that they are important stages in the evolution of the chronic diseases, disorders intermediate in time between the operation of pathogenic causes and the beginnings of disease. Carriage of genetical errors (shown in high uric acid levels, for example); immunologic reactions (*e.g.* the rheumatoid factor, or the presence of antinuclear substance); metabolic disorders (*e.g.* raised intraocular pressure); " precancerous " lesions like carcinoma *in situ*; psychotic " character disorders " such as the schizoid already mentioned; diseases like fatty liver (cirrhosis), or gastric ulcer (for carcinoma) : these exemplify precursors that can at present, if very diffidently, be postulated. There is the smoker's cough that might be a herald of lung cancer, and very likely is of chronic bronchitis.[29][43] Vascular hyper-reactivity in early life may be a precursor in the present sense of essential hypertension. " The high incidence of foetal complications of pregnancy in women destined to become diabetic many years later supports the existence of an active metabolic aberration long before the insulinogenic mechanism becomes

TABLE XXXIII

Precursors of Chronic Diseases
Numbers Adjusted to an Average General Practice of 2,250 Persons
Britain

DISEASE	APPROX. No. OF CASES THAT MAY BE DISCOVERED ON SURVEY
Cancer of cervix[9][41][96]	5 (F, 20+) with carcinoma *in situ*
Glaucoma[87]	17 (M & F, 45+) with ocular hypertension
Ischaemic heart disease[46][66]	18 (M, 35-44), 14 (F, 35-44) with casual DBP over 100 mm Hg
	50 (M, 40-49) with casual plasma cholesterol 250 mg/100 ml and +
Respiratory disease[43]	40 (M, 35-44) with smoker's cough

(Sex, and age, in brackets.)

overwhelmed [and hyperglycaemia appears] . . . This is to speak of a diabetic trait which precedes the beta cell decompensation, the deficient insulin activity; it is prior to diabetes, prediabetes, not mild diabetes ".[19]

There is no formula yet for identifying precursor conditions beyond the need to consider of what is known at the stage of manifest disease whether it could be a precursor, then testing the notion by prospective study. In disease of later life that has important genetic causes, or congenital, that is laid down in childhood or merely takes many years to incubate, it is reasonable to hope that precursor disorders during the long pathogenesis will progressively be discovered. Table XXXIII gives a few numbers, magnitudes, guesses.

Table XXXIV draws on various surveys to estimate the frequency of coronary disease, the term being used to include coronary atherosclerosis and the ischaemic disease of the heart. I am diffident about presenting so tentative a formulation, but the Table does attempt to deal with the different dimensions that have been discussed. It illustrates again the

TABLE XXXIV

Frequency of Coronary Disease [70 71 73 84]
Estimates of Average Rates in Men aged 55-64
Period of One Year
Britain, late 1950's

Between $\frac{1}{2}$% and 1% die of ischaemic heart disease (mortality).

About 1% manifest clinical IHD for the first time (incidence).

About 2% suffer a first or later clinical attack of IHD (attack rate).

About 4% have recognisable IHD.
    About another 4% have a history of IHD.

Some 12-25% have recognisable ischaemic myocardial changes.

About 12% have occlusion of a main coronary artery.

Some 20-25% have narrowing of the lumen of a main coronary artery.

About 25% have extensive, confluent atheroma of the walls of the coronary arteries.

About 60% have moderate or extensive atheroma.

About 95% have naked-eye coronary atheroma.

Prevalence Rates, unless stated.

principle of the " iceberg " phenomenon by its figures of sub-clinical disease. The prevalence of " precursor " atheroma also is indicated, though it would have been more meaningful to describe atheroma at earlier ages. I have already given figures for hypercholesterolaemia and hypertension, a more dynamic approach to the pathogenesis of ischaemic heart disease. The crucial precursor abnormality, the tendency to deposit thrombus in excess, is unrecognisable as yet before too late.

One point needs categorically to be made about these precursor conditions. Prediction is possible in terms of group experience but, of course, only of individual chances.[33] Characteristically, only a minority of men with high cholesterol levels develop ischaemic heart disease, at any rate in middle age, *i.e.* there are very many " false positives ". (How hypercholesterolaemia " works ", moreover, is by no means clear yet. As described it is directly involved in the pathogenesis, an intermediate stage in the development of IHD; in which event lowering of the level would reduce that disease. Conceivably, however, it is merely an indicator or reflection of the significant disorder of metabolism; and this may be the situation also with other precursors that have been postulated. Their discovery in that event would still be worthwhile to indicate vulnerable groups deserving of special effort at early detection of disease).

4. PREDISPOSITIONS

This picture of precursors merges into the earlier stage of *personal predispositions* to disease; by which is meant the operation of adverse causes in individuals and groups who thus are liable to be affected, first by precursor disorder and, later, by the disease.[71][94] Knowledge of causes in inheritance, experience, and the mode of life, and thereby of such predispositions, is meagre as yet in the chronic diseases. Their consideration belongs to a later chapter: anticipating, middle-aged men who have a bad family history, are sedentary, eat a

Western diet, smoke cigarettes, are obese, may provisionally be regarded as predisposed to ischaemic heart disease; cigarette smokers to chronic bronchitis and of course lung cancer; fat men to premature death, hypertension, diabetes, osteoarthritis; men who are blood-group O and non-secretors to duodenal ulcer. The anomaly of androgen excretion in breast cancer illustrates emerging knowledge that cannot yet be classified as causal predisposition, or as precursor.[14]

INSTRUMENTS OF RESEARCH

Several types of investigation are needed to help provide a more complete clinical picture of the chronic diseases, to describe their natural history; and to seek causes. We need to discover precursor states and to relate them to predispositions and subsequent pathology, to identify the beginning undifferentiated stages of disease and unravel the events in progression, in relapse and remission, to diagnose the causes of disability. These tools of research are *chronic disease registers,* the *linkage of health records, cohort studies,* and *family studies.*

The first is the *Chronic Disease Register* (p. 41). The clinical picture " in breadth " of various chronic non-communicable diseases might be transformed, and the transition from subclinical to clinical become easier to study, if all the patients in specified Health Areas, population groups or even general practices were notified and entered on active Registers, as is routine in tuberculosis and some other handicaps, and proved invaluable in rheumatic heart disease before the War. Table XXXI is the beginning of such a Register; the data were used to study individual doctor's chances for survival, for further attack, for return to work and for total disablement. Such Population Registers are more than ever necessary because the " community " rather than the " hospital " now carries the main burden of the chronic sick, as is most evident in mental disorder (p. 98).[68 98]

The second instrument involves the *linkage of records,* medical and social, so that the relevant history of individuals can be pieced together. At present, clinical and administrative records are scattered in files of births and deaths, in general practice and in hospitals, in National Insurance, a variety of social agencies, Criminal Statistics, in special Registers like Cancer and X-ray. During a year in this country something like 500,000,000 relevant entries must be made. (And this is not to include the Census which presents special difficulties.) For research into chronic conditions that may develop over half a lifetime and last the other half, it would help enormously if there were a system of individual identification so that extracts of various documents could be brought together automatically as required.[2] Such machinery is particularly necessary with the shifting population of a mobile society; the growth of medical specialism and of fragmented observation is another factor. Modern computers would be essential in this kind of exercise. And it is not science fiction to think also in terms of family-linked records. Such systems of intelligence would be invaluable also in studying the utilisation of health and other social services—and in evaluating them.

Cohort Studies.—Another instrument consists of the clinical follow-up, over many years if necessary, of whole " populations " of suitable individuals. " Many years " may be the operative words; thus blood lipid patterns of the sexes begin to diverge in the 'teens, though ischaemic heart disease is uncommon till the forties.[37 44] Such cohort studies may be the only way of settling how to distinguish early and maybe fleeting pathology from healthy variation. They could provide perspective among the multiple processes, including ageing, that are involved in ischaemic heart disease or chronic bronchitis. In what circumstances do the ubiquitous predispositions to these conditions go critical—take off—to become dangerous? How and when is benign coronary atheroma changed into malignant coronary occlusion; what are the mechanisms of progression of smoker's cough into chronic bronchitis, and under what conditions is there regression? Longitudinal study could give the answer whether blood pressure rises " physiologically ", or if it is only some individuals who develop hypertension; the notion that essential hypertension is present before 50 years of age or not at all could be tested.[78] There is good prospect with such studies of learning more about the predictive role of early experience for personality disorder in later life. In the clinical instance, the emotional cripple or the chronic offender in particular, it is often only too easy to imagine present disturbance on to past trauma, but few consistent patterns or " prototypes " have been established.[8][25] The evolution of subclinical urinary infections into pyelonephritis and maybe hypertension might be described. Deceptively simple questions of timing like the priority of disability or retirement could be clarified.

Study of cohorts of individuals longitudinally may give the answer to many puzzling questions on the *natural history of old age*. Does blood cholesterol (or diastolic pressure, or body weight) fall in the old, or is the fall of average levels commonly found in population samples the result merely of " selection out ", many of those with high levels having died? Or, again, there is a complex of questions—what is disease and what the physical, mental and social processes of ageing? To appreciate the significance of an observation among the old, moreover (including the question why they have survived), it is of little help to make comparisons with the contemporary middle-aged who may have led quite different lives.[1]

Finally the need for *family studies* must be mentioned. The approach to natural history of the chronic diseases described in this chapter is being applied now to many problems and the interest in heredity is a major stimulus: members of the families of patients (these are the index cases) have been the first to be examined, before studies are extended into the community. It is an interim principle that the chronic diseases run in families, because of common experience as well as inheritance, and there is now a great range of conditions including the psychoses,[83] hypertension,[67][79] various cancers,[26][91] rheumatoid arthritis,[56] [57] auto-immune disease,[36] many of the inborn errors of metabolism,[38] in which family clustering is being studied for overt disease and covert, and for evidence of metabolic predispositions and precursors.

NATURAL HISTORY OF CHRONIC DISEASES—

I try now to abstract the main features of what has been discussed in order to produce a useful if very tentative model, overleaf, of the natural history of the " chronic diseases " —the term that has come to be used, rather loosely, for the malignant, metabolic and mental disorders that present mostly in the second half of life.[34] [58] [70] [72] In the ageing population of an affluent society, which has mastered many of the infections and malnutrition, and has high standards of maternal and child health, these chronic diseases increasingly dominate the practice of medicine. Their juxtaposition emphasises certain features they have in common. By the time they present clinically (Section 1 of this chapter), diseases like cancer, or IHD, or diabetes only too often are irreversible, advanced and severe; the chances of cure often are small, a remitting course is the best that can be expected; social and psychological repercussions may be profound. Of greatest interest in subclinical disease (Section 2) are the slight, early and, even more, reversible lesions that may be detected. The Table presents only the two ends of the spectrum of disease; there are many gradations between and disease may be first detected at any. The beginning, the " incidence ", of the chronic diseases is therefore difficult to define, quite apart from the mystery of the borderlands between health and disease, and operational definitions based on particular manifestations, e.g. first symptom, first notification, or first sick absence from work, are unavoidable. Earlier still come the prodromal, or *precursor,* disorders discovered during pathogenesis and before what is currently recognised as disease develops (Section 3). Here again definitions must be pragmatic. With advancing knowledge the boundaries between

TABLE **XXXV**

Suggestions for a Model of the Natural History and Prevention of Chronic Diseases

"STAGES"	THEORY OF PREVENTION
ADVANCED DISEASE Irreversible (structural) changes are present Often severe disease Mostly clinical, with obvious symptoms, and having medical care Course is chronic, often relapsing—remitting Social repercussions are often serious	**TERTIARY PREVENTION** of *deterioration* of *relapse* of *disability* and *dependency* By (anticipatory) medical and social care
EARLY DISEASE Pathology is reversible in earliest stages Slight disease Mostly subclinical, without symptoms, detected on search; possibly latent, manifest only on challenge	**SECONDARY PREVENTION** of *progress of disease* of *continuation* (thus reducing prevalence and chronicity) of *illness* By early detection and treatment
	PRIMARY PREVENTION of *occurrence of disease* (incidence)
PRECURSOR DISORDERS of function and structure that occur during the pathogenesis Silent, discovered on search (Ageing)	By removal of precursor disorder
PREDISPOSITIONS *i.e.* the presence of causes, genetic, environmental	By specific measures against causes in predisposed subjects
HEALTH	By general and specific measures in the population to promote health, and prevent disease

early and late disease must shift; there is now a prospect of altogether new understanding at the molecular level of precursor disorders and their transition into disease.

—AND THEIR PREVENTION

This model of the chronic diseases is abstracted so that, in turn, a theoretical—and useful—model can be set up of the main possibilities of prevention.[11 53 58 80] At each stage action may be possible; at each stage it is worth trying to identify *vulnerable groups* among whom action is particularly necessary or worthwhile. This presentation also is over-simple, and there are many variants and combinations. The prospects now opening up of a new union between clinical medicine, preventive medicine and Public Health cannot be discussed, nor the practical issues for social services, the organisation of medical care and clinical practice. Logically, it would be preferable to turn the whole Table down on its side so that the traffic of events through the continuum of health to mortality is emphasised, a traffic that till late moves in both directions, at any rate can be halted. But I want to attach the scheme to the clinical picture, to look at these questions from the clinical standpoint.

Tertiary " Prevention "

At the clinical stage, even of advanced disease, good treatment is preventive: of decompensation and deterioration of course. There are more direct targets in trying to prevent relapse, and such " complications " as suicide among the depressed, blindness from cataract, kyphosis in spondylitis, bedsores in the aged, the family disorganisation that so often threatens with the chronic diseases. The most useful thing often that can now be done, as seen most clearly in the elderly, is to seek to prevent disability and sustain independence. Epidemiologic and other studies are identifying physical, mental and social factors affecting the wellbeing and capacity of the patient, and the course and outcome of disease, general factors, and specific. Smoking and its relation to the chronicity of peptic ulcer may be cited;[24] family relations and breakdown from schizophrenia;[13] [98] social circumstances and survival from cancer.[12] A new dimension is beginning to be added to Medicine—built on its own experience, drawing heavily on social work, and learning now from social science—that is concerned with the long-term functioning of the " chronic sick " in the community (p. 80). The need for rehabilitation so as to preserve familial roles and working capacity till normal retirement at least (p. 11) is a challenge that is now accepted.*

The other " preventive " issue at the clinical stage is represented by the florid diabetes with symptoms and often " complications " that commonly remains undiagnosed : three or four cases on the figures already given in the average general practice of 2,250 persons. About these there is no argument on the need for action, only the question of how to take it.

Secondary Prevention

Causes of the chronic diseases are only slowly being found (e.g. most cancer), knowledge is often difficult to apply (e.g on cigarette smoking), and when applied it may be the next generation who mainly will benefit (e.g. much of mental disorder, very likely). Control of the chronic diseases will therefore involve more than the methods developed for the infections and nutritional deficiencies. There is now a hope, a hope rather than a promise, that it may be possible by detection and effective treatment of their early stages to reverse tissue changes, achieve a cure, at the least to halt progression

* Why is it that with similar pathology and clinical disorder some persons can lead independent and useful lives, while others suffer personal *disability* and are socially incompetent? This is a crucial question for a society which increasingly has to learn how to live with chronic diseases that cannot be cured. Obviously these are physical—mental—social problems : the nature of the lesion, the care received, the attitudes to the illness, family relationships, and economic factors (the state of the labour market, for example) probably all are involved. Such issues will surely be easier resolved if, in terms of this chapter, those who are coping are studied as much as those who cannot, *i.e.* if the " careers " of all (or representative) cases in a population who have particular handicaps are studied, whether they are manifestly disabled or no.

to advanced disease. In such ways much personal misery might be avoided, the prevalence of the chronic diseases could be reduced and the burden on the community lightened.

Detection of early and mild cases, the stages previously discussed in Section 2, is already a basis for much Preventive Medicine in the personal health services such as antenatal care, in tuberculosis control, and in industry. Because their development often is slow and their onset insidious, the chronic diseases are specially difficult to deal with—and they may offer special opportunities. The search for valid methods of screening for early disease is eminently worthwhile;[10 90 97] though there will be no point for Public Health practice unless something useful can be done about what is found. Thus the detection of mild subclinical diabetes in middle age is practicable, and high-risk groups are well established; the value of doing so remains to be seen. Infection can be controlled, and such complications as coma. However, it is quite doubtful to what extent the diabetic process itself can be arrested, florid disease avoided by treating mild, and vascular complications escaped. Perhaps in some groups at high risk for diabetes it will prove necessary to intervene at the stage of latent disease, or even in the precursor stage—if and when these can be usefully defined. Randomised therapeutic trials are now under way in subclinical diabetes, and they need urgently to be extended to determine what is reversible and how much renal disease, for example, is already foredoomed from the start, is not in fact a " complication " in the ordinary sense of the term. Meanwhile, the patient with diabetes should be regarded as an index case, first-degree relatives ought to be observed for the disease, and clinical judgement invoked on what to do about the results. The great majority of newly detected diabetics will be found in well recognised vulnerable groups:[93] persons over 45 or 50 years of age, the obese, women who have borne several children, those with a history of diabetes in the family as said. Such subjects in particular will repay the clinician's detection campaign.

In a sample survey of a rural area in Eastern USA, 2,600 medically disabling conditions were found.[92] The investigators considered that with present knowledge only a tiny proportion could have been avoided altogether. But in a third—a miscellaneous group of infective and non-infective, psychiatric and ophthalmic disorders—they suggested that progression might have been stopped. In 40 per cent, made up of cancer, heart disease, rheumatoid arthritis, etc., no secondary prevention was considered possible, a rather pessimistic if sobering view. However, the possibilities of secondary prevention in an ageing population are yet to be charted: whether tissue degeneration in old age will be prevented if earlier disorder is treated in middle age is a question for tomorrow.[7][60]

Primary Prevention

At the stage of discoverable precursors (Section 3) the occurrence of the disease, its incidence, may still be averted. Earlier treatment often is not an answer to the hazards of chronic diseases. Thus a quarter of " coronaries " present for the first time as sudden death, and by the time it is detectable much metabolic disease is florid, cancer incurable. Primary prevention by dealing with precursor disorders is already standard in industry, in seeking punctate basophilia for example, or in monitoring blood cholinesterase levels to anticipate organophosphorus poisoning.[82] If the treatment of hypercholesterolaemia will prevent the development of IHD (and as yet there is no evidence that dietary manipulation will do any good especially if started in middle age) the safe lowering of high cholesterol levels would be a triumph of primary prevention. More confidently, the notion applies to precancerous states, and today especially to *cancer of the cervix*.

By now there is much North American evidence of the value of mass screening by exfoliative cytology for discovery of intra-epithelial, non-invasive, carcinoma *in situ* of the cervix, and in first surveys particularly a bonus of invasive cancer, and of endometrial cancer of the body of the uterus, may also be anticipated. Table XXXVI illustrates one of the most famous experiments.[9] By the close of 1962 over half the adult female population had been screened, and the survey followed-up by definitive biopsy and treatment when necessary. Analysis of the results shows already some overall reduction of incidence in British Columbia though, and this is worrying, mortality has not fallen. (The rise of incidence in 1961 seems to be due to the detection of invasive

TABLE XXXVI

Cancer of Cervix: Precursor Lesions and Invasive Disease
Ages 20+
British Columbia

Year	No. of Women Screened*	No. with Carcinoma *in situ*	Incidence of Clinical Invasive Cancer	Death Rate†
			British Columbia, per 100,000	
1949-54	21,593	108	—	—
1955	11,707	53	28·4	12·8
1956	15,106	77	27·2	11·9
1957	18,719	97	26·0	10·2
1958	29,875	141	23·7	13·5
1959	38,833	142	22·6	13·6
1960	58,109	210	19·7	10·3
1961	81,164	224	23·2	13·3
1962	106,173	296	15·5	16·1

* Total female population aged 20+ averaged 450,000; over half have been screened.
Boyes, D. A., Fidler, H. K., Lock, D. R. (1962). *Brit. med. J.* **1,** 203; and personal communication.
† Renwick, G. (1962). Personal communication.

cancer during the great number of first examinations; the frequency of invasive disease in women previously passed on screening was 3·5 per 100,000.) About a third of the cases of carcinoma *in situ* seem to progress further. Ideas on the development of invasive cancer have emerged from study of these precursor lesions though it is not yet possible to say which women must at this stage have major surgery.

The practical problem in this approach is the human factor in mass cytology; to reduce observer error to a minimum by training the readers and not overloading them. The " positive " yield on average is about 1 per cent, of whom rather less than half will be confirmed as carcinoma *in situ,* and rather more as still earlier dysplastic lesions. Limited resources might therefore be concentrated where they are most likely to be rewarding. Pending the results of ad hoc studies, parous women of the lower social classes from about the age of 35 could be given priority: among them the lifetime probability in this country of developing *invasive cancer* may be 2 per cent, 1 in 50 women, even higher. (There is surely a great future, as in many such schemes of preventive medicine applied en masse to the individual, for automation and the use of computers, in this instance for electronic scanning of the smears.) This is one of the growing points of health services; and the approach to it has to be in terms of defining vulnerable groups with the highest prevalence—and most yield—on the one hand, and of *cost-efficiency* on the other: in particular, how many " false negative " cases will there be when using staff of various levels and combinations of skill? . . . The frequent discovery of atypical cells at necropsy in the bronchi of smokers suggests that it may be possible to identify such changes also by routine cytological study of sputum: which would doubtless concentrate the minds of some at least of our 2,500,000 heavy smokers more effectively than health education on statistics of probability.

*   *   *

As an interim policy, the emergent facts dictate a piecemeal and opportunist strategy for control of chronic diseases: by applying what is known about causes of course—but realistically also by attempts at removal of precursor lesions, however little is understood of the mechanisms involved, and by progressively earlier detection to give treatment the best chance. Of necessity, the policy will vary from one condition to another.

VI

IDENTIFICATION OF SYNDROMES

One of the paths of progress in medicine is to define, and refine, " syndromes " among the undifferentiated mass of clinical data: by the recurrent pattern of symptoms and signs, in regularities of onset, course and prognosis, in common pathology or functional disturbances that arise, by discovering that apparently unrelated phenomena have the same causes. Classically, the Hippocratic contribution distinguishing consumption may be cited or, crossing the centuries, Sydenham's descriptions of acute specific fevers, the separation of gonorrhoea and syphilis, or Kraepelin's classification of the psychoses. In modern times a great many syndromes have been delineated: Sheehan's syndrome and Conn's, for example, Burkitt's lymphoma, echo virus syndromes, malignant hypertension, carotid obstruction, kwashiorkor, phenylpyruvic oligophrenia, the affectionless thief, the authoritarian personality, the varieties of porphyria. One of the great modern achievements is a rediscovery—of the distinction between iatrogenic social breakdown (a) and the illness that occasioned admission to the mental institution (b).[2] The term " hospital-disease " may be recalled from another age for this " social breakdown syndrome " (p. 19).

" Syndrome ", it will be evident, is used here to reflect one of two current trends in medicine: the increasingly specific definition of disease entity, represented by single genemolecular disorders like the haemoglobinopathies at one extreme, and broad description of " reaction types ", like the collagenoses or auto-immune disease, at the other. Each generation will " split " and " lump " to serve its own needs.[7 12 35 38 43]

The epidemiological method has a characteristic " use " here in the study of chronic disease. Analysis of clinical phenomena may show that what is regarded as an entity cannot be so because its parts are differently distributed in the population; conversely, apparently disparate phenomena may be linked by similarities of their distribution. That is to say, the epidemiological behaviour of the clinical phenomena may help in the identifying of " syndromes ".

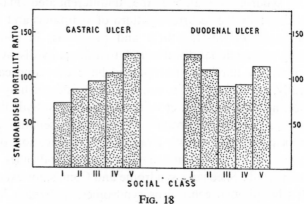

FIG. 18

Peptic ulcer: distinction of duodenal from gastric ulcer in 1921-3 by the social-class distribution of their mortality. Males, aged 20-64. England and Wales.[29] [36]

The mortality from peptic ulcer way back in the early 1920's when there was far less clinical appreciation than there is today that its two main types need to be distinguished, may be cited.[17] [29] Clearly (Fig. 18) there were two ulcerations to be studied, not one; their behaviour in social terms, the fairly strong class gradient in the certifications of gastric ulcer, and the absence of anything like it in the " new " duodenal ulcer, suggested that there are two diseases to be considered. A more recent morbidity study found the same social distributions.[13] The gross international differences in the ratio of gastric to duodenal ulcer point in the same direction.[4] Now there is confirmatory evidence from family studies that indicate specific inheritance of one or other ulcer,[14] and in the differing data on secretor status and blood groups (a smaller increase of group O in the gastric ulcer).[5] [25] The latest evidence (p. 20) shows a decline in DU following 10 or even 20 years after that of GU; the class distribution of DU mortality at the latest analysis was like that of GU (p. 66).

Syndromes of Atherosclerosis

My own interest in this use of epidemiology has been in trying to unravel some of the complex of " atherosclerosis ", by studying the group behaviour of its constituents. Two examples are given.

Simply to lump together *ischaemic heart disease* and *cerebrovascular disease* as " atherosclerosis " is little justified in the light of the anatomy of the affected vessels, by clinical experience, or in the relation of the two conditions to hypertension. Viewed epidemiologically they are again different. Ischaemic heart disease was known last century but apparently uncommon, cerebrovascular disease, as now, was common. IHD is apparently increasing, CVD (congenital aneurysms very doubtfully excepted) shows no such trend. There is a gross excess of IHD among middle-aged males in comparison with females which is not seen in CVD. International figures show striking differences: thus cerebral haemorrhage seems to be common in Japan, but not ischaemic heart disease. The small experience among physicians, Table overleaf, is another bit of evidence making the same point. (The Table incidentally shows how an epidemiological observation can sometimes be made when the population-at-risk, the denominator, is unknown: since these two disorders occurred in the same population, it would not have mattered, to the point being made, if that population could not be counted.)

Two Processes in Coronary Atherosclerosis.—There are many indications that coronary atherosclerosis involves several related, though independent, processes. The main distinction is into (1) *lumen-occlusive* lesions which lead often to ischaemic heart disease, and (2) *mural atheroma* which matters less.

TABLE XXXVII

"Atherosclerosis"—Distinction of Ischaemic Heart Disease from Cerebrovascular Disease among Medical Practitioners[28] [39]

Number of " First Attacks "

Males aged 40-64 years

1947-50

DISEASE	GENERAL PRACTITIONERS	OTHER DOCTORS
Ischaemic Heart Disease .	82	33
Cerebrovascular Disease .	14	13
Man-years of Observation .	10,800	8,620

These again it can be suggested should not be simply lumped together as " atherosclerosis ". Atheroma of the walls of the coronary arteries is far commoner in the population than occlusive disease. The latter arises only on the basis of the former, but many with much atheroma at necropsy show no particular obstruction, while some with little atheroma show a good deal. Historically, Table XXXVIII, there is evidence that acute coronary thrombosis and chronic coronary occlusion, and with them ischaemic heart disease, have increased, none that mural atheroma has done so.* The social distribution of the two processes again is different. Sedentary and light workers seem to have more frequent severe coronary

* These figures for 1908-13 were derived from Turnbull's original Reports which were sought, on his suggestion, after the original paper based on his summary material was published. It was possible to analyse the more detailed reports for lumen-narrowing of the coronary arteries as well as for mural disease: in the interval between the two studies the need to distinguish between these processes had become evident. In the first paper acute coronary thrombosis (and ischaemic heart disease) were distinguished from mural atheroma. Since Duguid's work suggests that organisation of intravascular coronary thrombosis is responsible for most chronic occlusive lesions with severe obstruction of main coronary arteries, it was necessary to distinguish these also from mural disease.[26]

obstruction than physically active and heavy workers—more fatal acute thrombosis judging by the incidence of acute infarction, and more complete or near-complete closures of

TABLE XXXVIII

"Atherosclerosis" : Distinction of Two Processes in Coronary Arteries[26] [39]

Mural Atheroma and Lumen Occlusion

Males aged 45-59 years
1908/13 - 1954/6

CORONARY ARTERIES	DEATHS FROM INJURIES, INFECTIONS, CANCER, ETC.		DEATHS FROM HYPERTENSION, CEREBROVASCULAR DISEASE, ETC.	
	1908/13 (530 cases) %	1954/6 (1394 cases) %	1908/13 (87 cases) %	1954/6 (292 cases) %
Mural atheroma:				
Moderate	53	34	36	32
Much			40	30
Calcification present	19	10	26	22
Coronary stenosis	4·2	13	10	28
occlusion of main artery	0·8	2·1	1·1	5·5
Ischaemic myocardial fibrosis present	1·3	4·4	3·4	17

1908/13, London Hospital; 1954/6, National Necropsy Survey (the modern London Hospital data are similar).
Average annual number of deaths from ischaemic heart disease with recent coronary thrombosis, males, 45-59, London Hospital, 1908/13=1·2 and 1954/8=4·2.

coronary arteries found at necropsy in deaths from other causes. There is no evidence however of major differences among the different types of worker in the amount or severity of mural atheroma. The following figures include both the groups of deaths of Table XXXVIII:

10

Coronary Atherosclerosis and Occupation

Deaths from Causes other than Ischaemic Heart Disease
Males, aged 45-70

CORONARY ARTERIES	OCCUPATION		
	Light (1392) %	Active (1377) %	Heavy (836) %
Much mural atheroma	21	17	18
Calcification present	23	20	21
Occlusion of a main artery	5·9	4	3·1*

National Necropsy Survey.[27] [39]

(Number of cases in brackets.)   * ·01 > p > ·001.

Finally, in trying to set up a " model " from the necropsy data available to us of the contemporary *distribution in the population* as a whole of coronary atheroma and coronary occlusion, there seems again to be a radical difference. Thus close on 100 per cent of men show mural disease at necropsy, Table XXXIV on page 128, most of them having a little or moderate amount. But only a minority have naked-eye narrowing of a main coronary artery and in most of these it is severe, in early middle age amounting to actual occlusion. The occlusive phase having started, it may be postulated that it tends to build up by some positive feedback mechanism (which has its implications for the treatment of ischaemic heart disease once that is established).

Summing up, in peptic ulcer, the group behaviour of the two main ulcers suggested very early that they must be distinguished, and that there was something new in duodenal ulcer. In ischaemic heart disease/cerebrovascular disease, epidemiological support is provided of a distinction for which there was already much clinical evidence. In coronary atherosclerosis, the evidence of two processes, paralleling the morbid-anatomical observations of the British school,[9] [10] [15] raised questions on the correctness of common clinical assumptions that its various constituents are simple functions one of another. In each of these examples, the identification of syndromes may have practical as well as theoretic interest. Issues of causation and pathogenesis—of control and prevention—arise. Thus if the modern epidemic of IHD is due to an increase of coronary thrombosis, to a new frequency of the occlusive phase, two modes of attacking it are open: by reduction of ancient, underlying atheroma; or by prevention of the increasingly common thrombosis which is likely to be associated with far more recent social changes.

Identification of syndromes by their causes is the ideal method but, in the absence of this, useful definition may still be possible. Epidemiology can help by introducing parameters beyond clinical " taxonomy "; and this may lead to the discovery of causes.

I pass now to some further examples.

Leukaemia in Young People

Stimulated by his observation of the remarkable trends of appendicitis in young people, Lee began a systematic search of the vital statistics for this period of life. Soon, p. 148, (1), he noticed a " bump " in the male leukaemia mortality—and why no one had noticed this before. . . . Development is so rapid at this time of life that the conventional five-year statistics (10-14, 15-19, etc.) are too coarse for useful exploration. A request was therefore made to the General Register Office for analysis of death rates by narrower age groups. When these showed the excess of leukaemia among adolescents even more clearly (2), an appeal for similar help was made to the USA, Fig. 19 (3), Canada (4), and Scotland, with the same results. Evidently there is a peak of leukaemia in late adolescence, interrupting the well-known fall in the death rate that occurs from about four years of age.

Next, Lee studied another set of data that also happened to be available, in the National Cancer Register. The cases of leukaemia in young people were extracted and on the suggestion of the late Dr. A. McKenzie the records were first analysed

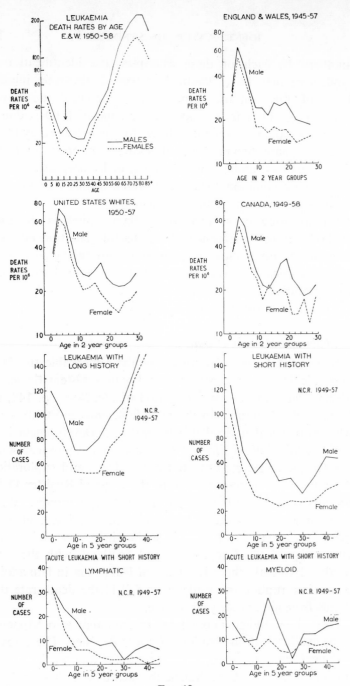

FIG. 19
See Legend Opposite.

for length of clinical history. The result was unequivocal: no peak among patients with a relatively long history (Fig. 19 (5)), and a prominent one in those with a short history (6). The latter were then classified by the reported cell type of their disease, and again the distribution was remarkable. Nothing of interest appeared in those labelled " lymphatic " (7), but the by now familiar peak reappeared in the " myeloid " cases (8).* Analysis by season of onset showed subsequently that the cases of acute myeloid leukaemia are rather irregularly spread through the year, whereas the lymphatic have an excess in the summer months.[21] The syndrome is therefore now defined as *acute myeloid leukaemia of young people*.[8][24]

Several lessons can be drawn from this exercise. First, is the continuing value of the simplest analysis, by age, season, and so on in opening up a problem—epidemiology could scarcely be more classical. . . . The exploitation of routinely collected health information in medical research is well illustrated (though not the practical problems involved). Mobilisation of the whole country's data was necessary to illuminate a specific question in a rare disease. Being truly representative the small numbers which still alone are available are more than otherwise valuable. . . . Mutual aid; this is increasingly on an international scale. . . . Finally; haematologists are reluctant to categorise the acute leukaemias of early life by cell type, and they have little confidence in the

* Data now available for 1958-61 show the same picture.

Fig. 19

Identification of a syndrome: particular incidence of acute myeloid leukaemia in late adolescence. Reading from the top, and from left to right—(1)-(4): average annual death rate per million in three countries, by sex and age. Log. scale, starting at 10 per million. (5)-(8): distribution of cases of leukaemia in the National Cancer Registration Scheme of England and Wales, analysis by sex, age, clinical history and cell-type. (5), history before diagnosis > 2 months; (6)-(8), history before diagnosis < 2 months. Cases in (6) which were not further specified as " acute " are excluded from (7) and (8).

Brit. med. J. (1961). **1**, 988.

results when persuaded to do so. Evidently they are far better at it than they think, and their errors far less, at any rate in identifying granular and lymphatic series. How otherwise explain the consistency in data covering many years of Fig. 19 (7) and (8), the anything but random distribution?

It remains to be seen whether this " syndrome " is telling something about leukaemia or about a critical period in maturation. Are there a small number of persons, programmed to have acute myeloid leukaemia, who develop it prematurely under the stress of growth? Or is there an excess-incidence of the disease at 15-19? Marrow tissue is actively developing at this epoch, unlike lymphoid, whence possibly the cell-selection observed (compare also the excess of osteosarcoma at this age). So far, the picture does not fit the model of radiation-induced leukaemia, which includes all acute cell types. The mortality statistics, moreover, show that this peak in youth was present as far back as the first world war—*i.e.*, before mass irradiation.[8] [24]

Two Syndromes of Juvenile Delinquency

Fig. 20 gives the first results of Power's study of young offenders in East London. Two syndromes seem to be emerging: (1) *dishonesty,* which is maximal at 14 years of age; (2) *disorder,* vandalism and sometimes serious violence, beginning to be common only at about 14, and then rising steadily till the end of the " juvenile " period (and, it is suspected, continuing to do so for some years). In terms of the preceding chapter, a first attempt to " complete " the clinical picture—inclusion *i.e.* of all ascertained delinquent behaviour and not merely the " indictable " cases, mostly of dishonesty, which legal tradition dictates are alone scrutinised in official statistics—together with the simplest analysis by age was enough to expose these two groups of offences.

The analysis is of course very superficial, and does not explain anything either at the social or at the psychological levels. But in approaching the problem of relapse and chronicity, for example, this description of two syndromes is promising. Clinical studies can now be focused on 14-year-old stealers and 16-year-old hooligans. By asking the right question, moreover, a popular myth was dispelled. The well-known

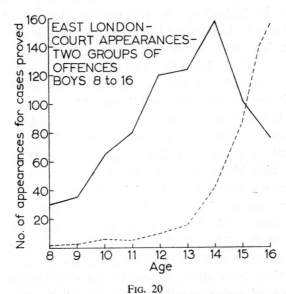

FIG. 20

Juvenile delinquency in the East End of London, 1958-61. Boys. Cases proven. Analysis by age and type of offence. (1) Continuous line=dishonesty, mainly; (2) broken line=disorder, mainly. The distributions are the same for *first offences* alone; and for rates per 1,000 of related population.—*The Times*, Aug. 9, 1962.

peaking of delinquency at 14, the last year at school for nearly all working-class children, is seen to be an artefact produced by ignoring a large number of offences. When all offences that matter are added together, non-indictable as well as indictable, there is a fairly steady rise with age till the end of the juvenile period at the seventeenth birthday and, though there are no data yet to prove it, the rate almost certainly continues to rise year by year for a few years thereafter.

*High Blood Pressure Without Evident Cause—Is There a
Specific Disease?*

Is there a specific syndrome, *essential hypertension,* or do
those having high blood pressure without evident cause merely
represent one extreme of a continuous distribution of blood
pressure in the population? This crucial question has been
debated by Pickering, who proposes the latter explanation,
and Platt who is responsible for the modern statement of the
former. The answer, to date, is equivocal. The evidence,
genetic-statistical, shows that there is a fairly normal distribution of casual blood pressure in the population, individual
levels being determined by multifactorial inheritance to a small
extent but mainly, it seems, by causes as yet unknown in the
environment. Those at the positive end of this distribution
constitute a group with high blood pressure. The majority
having high blood pressure without evident cause, however,
may have a different mode of inheritance and in them the
environment may be of less importance; *i.e.* there may be a
large group qualitatively distinct from the minority who are
merely at the high end of the " normal " distribution. (Comparison can be made with achondroplasics or mongols who
are distinct from others of small stature or low intelligence
but they, of course, constitute only a small fraction of those
at the low end of height and intelligence distributions.) Meanwhile, there is no clinical or biochemical method of further
distinguishing individuals postulated to have this specific entity
of *essential hypertension* from others having high blood
pressure without evident cause, and the epidemiological
evidence is contradictory. Our own contribution to the controversy from an analysis of busmen's pressures—this showed
segregation of a group of hypertensive drivers on the basis of
a presumptive family history of hypertension—has received
no support in much larger studies of miscellaneous industrial
workers.[23] [31] We are now following up the busmen and will
see whether the rise of pressure with age is related to such a
family history. These questions have been more clearly—even

excitingly—argued elsewhere.[32][33][34] Whatever the answer, it is useful to identify persons with high pressure because their expectation of life is reduced; actuarial data, in fact, show that average life expectancy falls rather steadily with the height of blood pressure at acceptance for insurance. . . . Definition of " disease " in syndromes in terms of specified groups at a tail-end of a continuous distribution in the population, and being only *quantitatively* different from the majority (Pickering's definition of essential hypertension), could provide an explanation in much of mental deficiency, neurosis and psychosis,[37] for example, in glaucoma, in hyper- and hypothyroid functional disease, possibly also in diabetes. These situations may be contrasted with the infections, with chromosome abnormalities, and specific gene-enzyme defects which represent *qualitative* changes and syndromes.

Table XXXIX, on pages 154 and 155, is a model of what has been said in this chapter. In the first column several problems are stated, *e.g.* about the nature of the apparent excess of " appendicitis " in young women, or the course of coalworkers' pneumoconiosis. The second column lists the various data that were analysed, *e.g.* large representative series of cases, or vital statistical records. Column 3 shows the criteria on which these data were classified: by clinical condition; by various parameters of host (*e.g.* sex and age) or of environment (*e.g.* occupation, smoking habits); and by making " secular " comparisons, *e.g.* of the site of perforated ulcer last century and this, or of the cell-type of bronchogenic carcinoma during the modern epidemic. In the last column the results are given of the *syndromes* that were identified from the mass-data of column 2. Thus " appendicitis " in young women divides into two, and the surplus of the disease in them beyond what is expected on overall sex and age trends (in any one year it is enough to occupy a 200-bed acute general NHS hospital) is probably not true appendicitis. The common squamous and oat-cell cancer of the lung is related to cigarette smoking—as might be anticipated from the histology—adenocarcinoma has not been so related. This example points directly to aetiology, the main object of such exercises. In the last illustration a vulnerable group for stillbirth is identified; this discovery led at once to successful preventive action, and it has been rewarding, moreover,

TABLE XXXIX

Identification of Syndromes by Epidemiological Methods: Some Examples

PROBLEM	MEDICAL DATA AVAILABLE	EPIDEMIOLOGICAL ANALYSIS	RESULT
HOMOGENEITY OF "PEPTIC" ULCER[17] [18] [22] [29] [36]	National death certificates, 1921-3 Surgical records, late 19th and early 20th century (large series)	By site and— social class secular trend sex	*Duodenal* ulcer distinguished from *gastric*
"APPENDICITIS" IN YOUNG WOMEN[21]	Hospital admissions (national sample) Death certificates	By age By sex By clinical severity By civil state	Large group (7-8,000 per year in England and Wales) which is probably *not* appendicitis distinguished by its peak at 17 years of age, and its occurrence only in females. There is no corresponding excess of peritonitis or fatal cases. Frequency declines with age in both married and unmarried women

Natural History of Pneumoconiosis[6]	Radiological follow-up of populations of coalminers and ex-miners	By exposure to coal dust	*Progressive massive fibrosis* (which can and does develop without further exposure to dust) distinguished from *simple pneumoconiosis* (which doesn't)
Histology of Bronchial Carcinoma[19]	Large (national) series of cases	By smoking habits By historical trends By sex	*Squamous* and undifferentiated, characteristically "exogenous", carcinoma are related to smoking; unlike *adenocarcinoma*
Unexplained Stillbirth[1]	Clinical records of total "population" Stillbirth certificates	By age and parity of mother By period of gestation	A group of "unexplained" stillbirths distinguished by their *post-maturity* and occurrence especially in *elderly primiparae*.
			Action Research—or "experimental epidemiology". In Aberdeen they have begun earlier induction of labour in the vulnerable group thus defined, and caesarean section is done more often. The statistics show a substantial fall of stillbirths and first-week deaths among these women (the lines for Parity 1 at ages over 30 in the first two sections of Fig. 21 indicate the scope for reduction.).

155

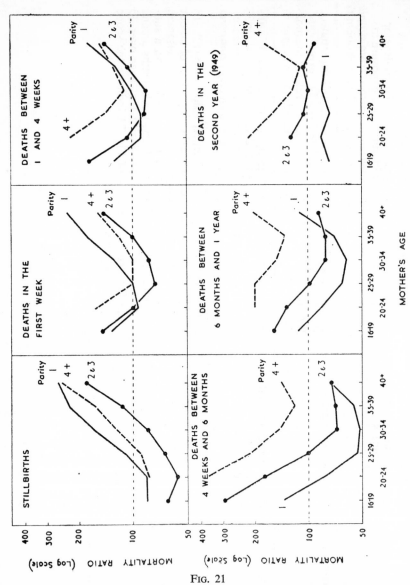

Fig. 21

Stillbirths and deaths in the first week (*perinatal mortality*); deaths in the remainder of the first year; and in the second year. The pattern of mortality, at various stages, on analysis by mother's age and parity (number of children she has borne). Stillbirth rates are calculated per 1,000 total births (live and still), the other death rates per 1,000 live births. In the figure, the various rates have been expressed as mortality ratios (log. scale), the experience of all mothers being regarded as 100.

Single, legitimate births, 1949-50. England and Wales.

to study the group in the laboratory—anoxia was found to accompany the postmaturity and cause the foetal deaths.

ASSOCIATION OF DISEASES—

Clinically and pathologically there are many examples of diseases being connected; with varying degrees of justification. Diabetes and ischaemic heart disease can be cited, peptic ulcer and coronary occlusion, pernicious anaemia with cancer of the stomach and now with hypothyroidism, mental and physical disorder in the aged, ankylostoma and malnutrition; the association of acute leukaemia and mongolism was shown epidemiologically before the common chromosomal abnormality was discovered.[14] As the death certificate is modernised, and as tabulations are done of the multiple associated pathologies, much will be learnt about the association of diseases, particularly in the aged.

The associations of endemic goitre illustrate on a panoramic scale: " Endemic goitre has widespread effects on the well-being of a community: cretinism, feeble-mindedness, and a lowered educational ability are associated with it. Reports have suggested a significant correlation between the incidence of deaf-mutism and that of endemic goitre . . . there is evidence that the incidence of hypothyroidism and carcinoma of the thyroid is higher where endemic goitre is found. . . ."[3]

I wonder if another example of such association of diseases is to be found in the health of the wartime Army.[40] [44] Morbidity among men soldiers from *peptic ulcer* (for example,

---

Figure 21 (*contd.*)

Numbers. Live births: 1,322,150
  stillbirths: 28,956 ⎫ *perinatal deaths*
  deaths in first week: 17,359 ⎭
  deaths between 1 and 4 weeks: 4,095
  deaths between 4 weeks and 6 months: 10,270
  deaths between 6 months and 1 year: 3,952
  deaths in the second year: 1,566.
    Arch. Dis. Childh. (1959). **34**, 101.

  J. Obstet. Gynaec. Brit. Emp. (1959). **66**, 577.

discharge rates in 1945) was far higher, as expected, than among women of similar rank :

(*B.O.R.*) *Males*   (*A.T.S.*) *Females*
216   46

But when figures for " *psychoneurosis* " are added to these, the totals repeatedly are equalised. In the same data, these were the discharges for psychoneurosis :

737   900

Added to the ulcers, there are :

Total   953   946
              ———   ———

(Rates per 100,000)

Does this complementarity point to a common aetiology of the two groups of disorders, to mutual relationships of neurosis and ulcer? The example illustrates also the need to define epidemiological problems not only in " given " terms, but also by examining around them, the notion of " equivalence " or substitution already mentioned. This has to be done at the simple technical level (Graunt's Law, p. 15), and at biological and social levels, p. 21. In the communist countries, mental and nervous disorders are apparently less common than in the West. But hypertension with nervous manifestations is apparently very common. What would be the result of this kind of exercise in simple addition? *

---

* "The question of *associations between diseases*," writes Neel,[30] "has long intrigued medical investigators. So long as the predominant diseases were caused by single agents which, with appropriate techniques, could be isolated, relatively little was done to exploit the potential value to the epidemiologist of disease associations. Now, however, that our attention is more and more occupied by diseases caused by genetic susceptibilities or environmental insults with long lag periods, the question of associations assumes new importance, since a single gene or a constellation of genes may predispose to several apparently distinct diseases, and a single newly introduced environmental insult, such as radiation, may result in abnormal cell proliferations recognisable both as leukaemia and as one or more other types of malignancy."

—And Their Dissociation

This is a fertile field for speculation, *e.g.* cancer and hypertension have been set apart, and recently cancer and multiple sclerosis. Clinically there are well established dissociations, rheumatoid arthritis and jaundice, *e.g.,* or ulcer and pregnancy. The grandest dissociation of course is Jenner's. Discovery of the protection of mottled enamel against dental caries was the beginning of fluoridation.

Fig. 21 provides another illustration, from elementary human biology. The notion of *perinatal mortality* has many origins, in clinical obstetrics, and pathology, in administration and forensic medicine; it has many advantages in making international comparisons. The differences in the figure are a warning on its limitations and against assumptions about aetiology. Mortality in the first week of life—indeed in the very first hours—includes patterns both of *stillbirth* (high rates in elderly primiparae and an association with postmaturity), and of *post-neonatal* mortality (high rates in young multiparae and an association with prematurity). The causes of death moreover may be different in the two parts of the " perinatal " period: for example, anencephaly (stillbirth); and the respiratory distress syndrome (causing death in the first week).

*   *   *

Several " uses " of epidemiology are being proposed, but variations on a theme might have been a better description. Clearly, for example, the more " complete " the clinical picture the more will it be possible to describe epidemiological patterns with enough confidence to identify syndromes; in doing so, moreover, data from historical study and " community diagnosis " has also been exploited. The same epidemiologic data in fact are being organised to ask different questions, serve different purposes.

VII

IN SEARCH OF CAUSES

The main use of epidemiology is to discover causes of disease, and of freedom from disease, so as to increase understanding and help improve the people's health.

Examples can readily be drawn from classical epidemiology, from study of health in relation to the epidemic " constitutions " of the atmosphere—causes in *airs, waters* and *places.* Over the centuries knowledge was built of the influence of climate and season (*e.g.* malaria, rickets); of geography (cholera following the trade routes), and geology (the significance of iodine and of fluoride were so discovered). The "unhealthiness of towns " (bowel infections, bronchitis) and country (pellagra, mental deficiency) were described; and "dangerous trades ". When affected populations are so characterised by their environment and ways of living, the epidemiological method is in fact beginning to discover "causes" of disease, causes which it may be possible to control. Commonly this happens before, it may be long before, the mechanisms of the disease are understood, as in the achievements of Lind and scurvy, Pott and chimney sweeps' cancer, Snow and the cholera.

Ways of living can often be described only very generally, and causes postulated in them have often been in general terms of the satisfaction of elementary needs and their gross deprivation: non-specific causes of disease, or of diseases, have been identified. Such are the relationships of purity (and abundance) of water-supply to bowel infections of many kinds, of living space and population density to respiratory infections as a class, and the manifold connections between income levels and susceptibility to infections, between the standard of living and reproductive performance, child growth and development. Simple observations must not on that account be dismissed. These " general " principles include much of what has been learnt over the centuries about healthy living, and the history of the search for means to prevent disease, and survive at all, shows how the elementary study and courageous generalisation from it (the " filth " theory, for instance) can transform the quality of living. Thus the epidemiological research reported in such publications as the *Sanitary Condition of the Labouring Population* are a landmark in the history of Public Health. The findings of bacteriology were anticipated; published in the middle of the Industrial Revolution, they roused public opinion and showed people how they might better live and work together in the new Britain. Chadwick and the other pioneers campaigned effectively for environmental improvement to check the spread of disease and increase resistance to it—with little real understanding in fact of the mechanisms involved. Table XL is a sample of these Victorian studies.

TABLE XL

Victorian Thunder

(1) " SANITARY RAMBLINGS "[19]

No. of Deaths	BETHNAL GREEN 1839	AVERAGE AGE OF DECEASED
101	Gentlemen, Professional Men and their Families	45
273	Tradesmen and their Families	26
1,258	Mechanics, Servants, Labourers and their Families	16

Gavin, H. (1848).

11

(2) CHANCES OF LIVING IN THE 1840'S, PRESTON, LANCS.[8]

	GENTRY	TRADES	OPERATIVES
Born	1,000	1,000	1,000
Remaining alive at end of:			
1st year	908	796	682
5th year	824	618	446
20th year	763	516	315
40th year	634	375	204
60th year	451	205	112

Clay, The Rev. J. (1844).

(3) AN EXPERIMENT ON THE GRANDEST SCALE[46]

Mortality from Cholera in the Four Weeks ending 5 August, 1854

WATER COMPANY	NO. OF HOUSES SUPPLIED	NO. OF DEATHS	RATE PER 10,000 HOUSES
Southwark and Vauxhall*	40,046	286	71
Lambeth**	26,107	14	5
Rest of London	287,345	277	9

Snow, J. (1855-6).

* Down-river water " containing the sewage of London ".
** Up-river water " quite free from such impurity ".
During the whole 14 weeks of the epidemic the mortality rate from cholera was 153 per 10,000 population supplied by S. & V. Co.; 26 per 10,000 supplied by the Lambeth Co.; and 30 per 10,000 in the rest of London.

(4) In a Three-Hundred Year Tradition[17]

Mortality of Men in Cornwall, Rates per 1,000 per Year

Ages	1849-53 ALL CAUSES		1860-62 PULMONARY DISEASES	
	Metal miners	Males excluding metal miners	Metal miners	Males excluding metal miners
15-24	7·44	7·50	3·77	3·30
25-34	9·57	8·32	4·15	3·83
35-44	15·12	10·08	7·89	4·24
45-54	29·74	12·50	19·75	4·34
55-64	63·21	19·96	43·29	5·19
65-75	110·51	53·31	45·04	10·48

Farr, W. (1864).

A Modern Hygiene?

Epidemiologists are beginning to identify general non-specific causes of the main contemporary problems of ill-health, though formulations often must still be very tentative. Table XLI (on the dangers of being mortal) is a summary of much that has already been spelled out in this book, or will be later. It starts by bringing Graunt up to date on sex and age. *Age* (1) is crucial at the two ends of life; high in utero and infancy, the force of mortality is progressive again from schooldays, p. 164. At the turn of the century about 25 per cent of deaths occurred in infancy and about 25 per cent over 65 years of age. In 1961 corresponding proportions were a little over 3 per cent, and about 70 per cent. . . . The *sex* difference in mortality is illustrated in (2). The higher death rate of males is general. In infancy at any rate " biological " causes can be postulated. Thereafter environment may be very different, *e.g.* occupation, smoking[53]. . . . How much is due to selection, and whether there is also an element of causation, the married state being protective, has not yet been sorted out of these figures on *marital status* (3). The

TABLE XLI

The Death Rate—All Causes
England and Wales

(1) INFLUENCE OF AGE[40]
Death Rates in 1961

	IM	1-	5-	15-	25-	45-	55-	65-	75-	85 + Years
Male	24	1·04	0·44	1·01	1·8	7·3	22·0	54·3	124·0	257·4
Female	19	0·80	0·28	0·45	1·3	4·5	10·7	30·9	87·1	227·1

Infant mortality (IM), deaths in the first year of life per 1,000 live births.
Other death rates, per 1,000 persons living in the specific sex and age groups.

(2) SEX[40]

	IM	1-	5-	15-	25-	45-	55-	65-	75-	85 + Years
Male	126	130	157	224	138	162	206	176	142	113
Female	100	100	100	100	100	100	100	100	100	100

1961; male death rates as percentage of female death rates. Ages as in (1) above

(3) " CIVIL STATE "[42]

	All in Age Group	Married	Single	Widowed/Divorced
Male	100	95	129	139
Female	100	92	112	117

1959. Ages 55-64

In this, and Tables (4)-(7), the specific death rates are shown as percentages of the death rate in the whole group being studied. Thus, married men aged 55-64 in England and Wales during 1959 had a death rate from all causes that was 95% of the death rate in *all* men of that age.

Rate per 1,000	All in Age Group	Rural Districts	Urban Areas: Population −50,000	50-100,000	100,000+	"Conurbations"
Male 14·4 =	100	81	98	101	108	107
Female 8·4 =	100	93	102	98	104	101

1950-3. Ages 45-64.

(5) OCCUPATION[39]

Standardised Mortality Ratios (SMR) *i.e.* Adjusted for Differences in Age Composition

Men aged 20-64   All occupations=100

Teachers (not music)	66	Medical Practitioners	90	Tailors	126	Publicans	150
Farmers	70	Clerks	101	Ticket Collectors	135	Watchmen	163
Drillers	85	Barbers	113	Shoe Repairers	140	Sandblasters	173

1949-53.

(6) WEIGHT[4][25]

Subsequent Mortality Relative to Weight on Taking Out Insurance—For Policies Issued at Ages 40-49

DEVIATION FROM AVERAGE WEIGHT

	−30 lbs.	−20 lbs.	−10 lbs.	AVERAGE	+10 lbs.	+20 lbs.	+30 lbs.	+40 lbs.	+50 lbs.
				Mortality					
(Ht=5′7″-5′10″) Male	100	95	100	100	110	120	125	135	145
(Ht=5′3″-5′6″) Female	85	90	90	100	110	110	120	130	140

USA.   Policies were issued during 1935-53, lives were traced to the end of 1954.

(7) SMOKING[13]

	ALL	Non-Smokers	Ex-Smokers	Cigarettes per day 1-14	15-24	25+
Ages 45-54	100	60	84	90	117	166
Ages 55-64	100	79	94	116	134	168

Male Medical Practitioners, United Kingdom. 1951-8.

165

American (white) figures at 55-64 years of age are even more surprising:

	ALL	Married	Single	Widowed	Divorced
M	100	91	121	127	216
F	100	92	111	112	139

1959.

The contribution of alcoholism, for example, to such figures may be crucial.[1][3][35][48]

There is still with us an overabundance of ignorance, slums and insanitation, failures of the social system, that still contribute only too much in avoidable misery. Thus the trend of mortality with density of population is in large part a measure of the hazards of industrial-urban life. The *unhealthiness of towns* is more evident when the data of Table XLI (4) are recalculated in terms of domestic air pollution:[11][47]

	ALL ENGLAND & WALES	RURAL DISTRICTS		COUNTY BOROUGHS		
		Agric.	Industr.	Clean	Intermed.	Dirty
M	100	73	94	97	112	124
F	100	89	104	94	108	114

and, narrowing down to respiratory disease:

	RATE PER 1,000				
M	3·7 =100	62	93	116	153
F	0·82=100	76	84	118	141

Ages 45-64.

Adjustment for industrial effluent into the air is not readily possible. . . . *Occupation* is also involved in such local figures: byssinosis for example is exceedingly common in the men of some of the Northern towns in the last group, whereas there is an overall SMR of 70 or so in agriculture (5). The figures on occupation are designed to illustrate the various combinations of cause and effect that are responsible for differences in occupational mortality. Thus many watchmen take that job because of ill-health; sandblasting, on the other hand, is a truly " dangerous trade " (silicosis).

To become more particular, *overeating* and *obesity* seem to be involved in a multitude of modern pathologies. The figures in (6) are of course of under- and overweight, not of obesity in terms say of skinfold thickness. Big muscle and bone masses will be " heavy "; but there is little doubt about the obesity at one extreme of the range. Because of selection of applicants for insurance, and exclusion of the grossest, the figures will underestimate the hazards of obesity. The other defect of the figures is that being related to obesity at 40-49 years of age, they do not completely deal with " middle-age spread ". Available British figures[7] (unfortunately they include a small number of women among the large numbers of men) give the record at specific ages. This is the subsequent mortality, at 50-59 years of age, relative to weight when accepted for insurance :

Underweight	80% of Standard Mortality
Average Weight	100% „ „ „
20-30% Overweight	123% „ „ „
30% and more Overweight	165% „ „ „

How many are fat is another question. About twelve per cent of London busmen aged 45-64 ($9\frac{1}{2}$ per cent of the conductors and 14 per cent of the drivers) have a trouser-waist band over 42″, equivalent roughly to a true waist measurement of 40″ + (page 46); correspondingly, in 29 per cent of these drivers and 14 per cent of the conductors who were examined, the sum of the three standard skinfolds was 60mm or over.[22][47]* *Physical inactivity* is manifestly a cause of obesity, probably a cause of disordered metabolism in general during middle age, and possibly of cardiovascular disease[31]. . . *Cigarette smoking* (7) is a major factor of premature death, as already seen, from several diseases and not merely from lung-cancer, though, of course, its relationship to that condition is far stronger than to others. . . .

* Obesity, thus, is so common in the population that the " average weight " may be unhealthily high. In that event the magnitude of this hazard to health will again be underestimated by such ratios as in Table XLI (6).

These last three, overeating, underexercise and cigarette
smoking, are all associated with the rising standard of living
and modern technology. The cigarette is a tragic accident of
human history; but physical inactivity is integral to social
progress and, at the least, overeating is approved behaviour
reflecting success of the social system. Physical inactivity, in
turn, represents an even more general cause, affecting social
and mental as well as physical health, and particularly relevant
to an ageing population. The *exercise of functions* is necessary
for their health, and with disuse comes atrophy—" that which
is used develops and that which is not used wastes away "
(Hippocrates). The need to maintain physical activity and to
exercise the intellect, for sensory stimulus, emotional response
and social interaction, is crucial to healthy functioning,
throughout life. . . . *Environmental strain,* physical, mental,
social, in those who are predisposed, is another example of a
general " cause ". If too great to adapt to, *stress disorders*
result which can delay recovery in the chronic diseases (p. 136),
aggravate and perpetuate existing pathology, produce decompensation and disability in duodenal ulcer and diabetes, in
thyrotoxicosis and phthisis, heart failure even—and not merely
breakdown with neurotic or particular " psychosomatic " disorders. The role of " stress " in the initiation of disease through
physiological disturbance and visceral reaction is often less
clear, though its contribution to deviant behaviour and social
pathology is evident enough.[5] [30] [37] [50] [51]

If these *general, non-specific causes* are at all additive the
mortality problems of the middle-aged Male will not be intractable.

*   *   *

The Tables and Figures in this chapter provide examples of
the " use " of epidemiology in the search for causes, and they
report studies at different levels, from reconnaissance and first
turning of the ground to highly sophisticated observations.
Table XLII is a sample; it recalls some of the great names,

TABLE XLII

In Search of Causes of the Chronic Diseases

Some Epidemiological Contributions

In 1662, Graunt, the London haberdasher, related sex, age, season, place (town and country) to mortality, and he also made preliminary studies of causes of death. Later, in Germany, *Statistics,* the numerical study of matters of state, developed. In the nineteenth century, during the Industrial Revolution, *Chadwick* related mortality to the standard of living: it was his " sanitary idea " that deaths could be reduced by environmental improvement. *Farr* founded modern vital statistics; and he began the use of mortality rates to measure the healthiness of populations—nationally, in districts, and in occupations.[18 20 44 52]

Three Classics—Nutritional Deficiencies[12 28]

Lind and the calamity of sailors, Takaki and beri beri, Goldberger and pellagra: they employed experiment as well as observation.

Discovery of the role of fluoride deficiency in dental caries continues this tradition.

Overnutrition and Obesity[4 12 27]

Actuarial data show premature mortality, in particular from cardiovascular disease, among the obese. In clinical surveys obesity has been related to diabetes, to hypertension, to ischaemic heart disease (less certainly), and to high blood lipid levels; these constituting a characteristic group of metabolic *diseases of affluence.* Epidemiological as well as laboratory studies associate the common obesity with underexercise and overeating.

Blood Cholesterol Levels[24]

have been related to sex and age, and to individual fatness, physical activity, and nervous strain (of occupation). Average levels are lower in underdeveloped than in developed countries, and this has been related to the national plane of nutrition particularly of saturated fats; but in highly developed countries little if any correlation has been found between individual diet and the blood cholesterol level. A grand experiment to prevent IHD by reducing saturated fat intake of volunteers is now being planned in USA.

TABLE XLII (*contd.*)

Environmental Causes of Malignant Disease[14]

Percivall Pott described soot cancer of scrotum: this was the origin of experimental carcinogenesis.

The causes of occupational *bladder cancer* have been demonstrated so that the disease can be eradicated.

Cervical cancer.—Age of onset, and duration, of coital experience is postulated as a principal cause of the common squamous (environmental) cancer;[48] circumcision, penile hygiene, as a primary protection. Epidemiology of precursor carcinoma *in situ* will provide an earlier approach to aetiology.

Leukaemia.—Radiation has been established as a (numerically small) cause. Current work on the seasonal onset of leukaemia and on clustering of cases, " microepidemics "[24] may prove to be complementary to the search for responsible viruses.

Excess of primary *cancer of the liver* in the Bantu is example of gross international differences that are beginning to be investigated for clues to causes.

Disease or Ageing[9] [10] [23]

Changes in physiological variables, increased liability to disease, and the rising force of mortality over the years are basic in distinguishing processes of ageing from " degenerative " diseases. Atherosclerosis, chronic bronchitis and senile psychosis have been established as diseases; discovery of causes could lead to their prevention, not merely postponement.

Congenital Malformations[6] [36] [43]

Rubella has been established as an environmental cause of a small fraction of congenital defect. The thalidomide calamity has led to an intensive search for similar causes. The epidemiologic behaviour of anencephaly points to environmental causation.

Genetics—Population Genetics—Epidemiology[2] [15] [34] [43]

The association of blood groups with predisposition to various diseases is being established.

Sickle-cell trait and immunity to MT malaria have been related. Notion of balanced polymorphism and natural selection is beginning to be considered as possible cause of high frequency of other conditions.

Family relationships of various psychiatric disorders, and of many other diseases, and including their precursor metabolic and immunologic abnormalities, are being described (still mainly in terms of genetic causation).

Mental Deficiency[21] [26] [36]

Inherited, "physical" (e.g. foetal brain damage), and social causes are being identified.

Importance of social definition, and thus of social "causes", of feeblemindedness is evident in the reduction of prevalence as children leave school and change their social roles.

Occupational Hazards[45] [49]

An old industrial disease (byssinosis), and a new one (from beryllium) will be described. The role of occupation in the main chronic diseases (e.g. IHD), and in physical and mental health generally, will be referred to.

Multiple Causes[16] [32]

The notion that there may be several different causes of the same disorder can be illustrated by lung cancer, or by obesity. The notion that a combination of causes operates in any population incidence, or individual instance, is evident again in lung cancer, or dental caries or gout.

General, non-specific causes, like obesity or psycho-social strain, are evidently important in the chronic diseases. Specific agents of the common chronic diseases so far are not much in evidence, and the notion that they have no "necessary" cause is beginning to be postulated for some of the main chronic diseases.

Disease; its Course and Outcome; Illness; Disability

Different causes are being distinguished—of the occurrence of chronic diseases, and of these other phases.

---

illustrates contributions by the epidemiological method to understanding of the aetiology of chronic non-infectious diseases and mentions some of the growing points. A few other relevant facts have also been noted, but there is no attempt to be complete. Sometimes in these examples the epidemiological remains the crucial evidence; there is nothing convincing from clinical observation, nor yet any experimental model.

*   *   *

MODERN EPIDEMIC

None of the causes of ischaemic heart disease so far proposed, saturated fat, physical inactivity, psycho-social stress disorder, cigarette smoking and the rest, alone or in combination, looks like providing a simple answer. Many causes apparently, personal and environmental, biologic and cultural, are involved in IHD. Their unravelling is proving very difficult if only because the ways of living concerned are so common and so widespread, highly interrelated and all pervasive in modern industrial societies. Those with the disease, it is postulated, have more or less of this or that " cause " in their lives. Little is known on the genetic side; but the ubiquity of coronary atheroma, the underlying condition, makes it unlikely that heredity is decisive in this, though conceivably it could be in the production of thrombosis, in the conversion of harmless mural into dangerous lumen-occlusive disease. Recently, a suggestion has been made in terms of balanced polymorphism: that such conditions as obesity, diabetes, hypercholesterolaemia and IHD are so frequent—and so often associated—because they represent the survival of genes that could withstand famine, and other privation, from times when such genes were advantageous to an age of affluence, when manifestly they are not.[23]

If ischaemic heart disease were not so evidently the product of many causes, it would be necessary to invent them: so the natural history requires. The basic local pathology in IHD is coronary—*lumen occlusion*, which develops on coronary—*mural atheroma*. These two processes are related as seen, but they are not the same, nor is the former any simple function of the amount or severity of the latter (p. 145). They must therefore have different causes; and since both pathologies are necessary for IHD, IHD must have multiple causes.

Next, a step back. *Hypercholesterolaemia and hypertension* seem to be precursors, if not actual causes in a meaningful sense, of ischaemic heart disease. Few cases occur in the absence of both; this is the main finding of the Framingham and similar studies in USA.[7][8] Now these two processes are largely independent: those with one are not specially likely to have the other, one alone is often present, the correlation between them in individuals is small, and there are populations in whom one occurs and not the other (in the Japanese and the Bantu *e.g.* hypertension is common, but average cholesterol levels are low). Though, in turn, they may well share causes like obesity, hypercholesterolaemia and hypertension must also have different causes; and since one or the other seems somehow usually to be necessary for IHD, IHD must have many causes.

Thirdly, a look forward. *Cardiac infarction* occurs only with coronary occlusion but is not the inevitable consequence of it; nor is death from infarction a simple matter of the size or speed of the obstruction. The causes of IHD and of coronary occlusion, that is to say, are not just the same, and since it is IHD and not merely coronary occlusion which is of concern, it is evident again that IHD must have multiple causes.

Clinically, the conclusion is the same. Death " out of the blue " in the younger man, post-operatively in the middle-aged, or in the old man shovelling snow or during a smog; infarction in the ovariectomised young woman, in the middle-aged diabetic, or the old lady with ruptured heart; the remarkable differences between such syndromes as angina pectoris and ischaemic " sudden death "; necropsy revealing atheroma smothering the intima or but a solitary plaque, massive fresh thrombosis or none, minimal and maximal infarction: its manifold associations, variety of presentation and unpredictable outcome have accustomed the physician to think of ischaemic heart disease in " multi-factorial " terms, of an extending complex of events in, and interactions between, persons and their environments.

Many pathologies then are involved in ischaemic heart disease; it is the product of many causes, and we have to think of the patterns these form. This is a notion to which study of the infections should by now have accustomed us. The organism is " necessary "; and perhaps one day a specific agent of IHD will be identified, relating fat metabolism to arterial thrombosis it could be. But whatever is found, without many other causes as well, it is unlikely to be any more " sufficient " in causing IHD than the organism is in infectious diseases, and it is even conceivable that there is no specific agent of IHD.[1 4 10 13 16 18 21 22 24 26]

HYPOTHESIS ON EXERCISE

Fig. 22 takes one postulated cause, lack of exercise, and illustrates our attempts, using epidemiological methods,[29] to establish, bit by bit, its reality, importance and mechanisms (pp. 176-7). When government clerks, executive officers and post-office telephonists (males, of course) were all found to have the same kind of excess incidence of IHD, age for age, in comparison with postmen, that the bus drivers had over conductors—*i.e.* more of all presentations of the disease throughout middle age, line 1 (a), and far more of the most severe form in early middle age (b)—we plumped for the possibility that differences in the habitual physical activity involved in these jobs might be responsible for the differences in IHD. The conductors walk along the decks and climb and descend the stairs of these double-decker buses; postmen walk or cycle, carrying and delivering the mail, for about 70 per cent of their working day. This seemed a more sensible proposition than one relating to " stress " arising from the emotional and social demands of the jobs, which was a likely enough cause in bus driving or operating a switchboard (at night often), but did not impress us about clerical work in the bureaucracy. A hypothesis was therefore formulated to guide further investigation that—

> *Physical activity of work is a protection against coronary (ischaemic) heart disease. Men in physically active jobs have less ischaemic heart disease during*

middle age, what disease they have is less severe, and they develop it later than men in physically inactive jobs.

Subsequently several tests of the hypothesis were made, and two are illustrated. The second line of Fig. 22 gives the main results from a *National Necropsy Survey* of ischaemic myocardial lesions, in which the jobs of the deceased were classified by experts as typically " light ", " active ", or " heavy ". Because of selection and bias, necropsy data are usually unsuitable for epidemiological analysis. Here it was warranted because an important—and simple—question was asked, which could not be asked in any other way, because it was possible to designate a national sample, and a variety of built-in checks for internal consistency, etc., were available (cf. page 48). Line 3 is an analysis of the Registrar General's data as well as of these 3,800 necropsies. It explains the well-known social class distribution of ischaemic heart disease in terms of a rather obvious job-association: the higher the social class the less physically active on average the work.*

The original observation, it may be said, has been confirmed, the hypothesis still stands, and it has passed tests unconnected with and well away from the original observation. But it still could be a hypothesis about something else and not about physical activity. Conceivably, nervous strain of occupation is in fact the obverse of physical inactivity—in view of the generality of the occupational findings, lines 2 and 3, a hypothesis would have to be stated in such general terms and not confined to drivers and conductors. Some more likely alternatives can by now be ruled out. Differences in the smoking (and drinking) habits of drivers and conductors are small. Drivers eat more proportionately than conductors,[17] so, not surprisingly, they are fatter; dietary sample studies show no

*A recent report from the Claxton study (Hames, C. G. and McDonough, J. R.) suggests that differences in habitual physical activity may be responsible for the excess of IHD in white men compared with negroes. *Med. Wld News* (1963). **4,** 105.

Light Workers [dotted]   Active [hatched]   Heavy [black dots]

1. Incidence (First Clinical Presentation) of Ischaemic Heart Disease [14 21 27 29]

In London Busmen
(drivers [::] & conductors [hatched])
(a) All forms, ages 35-64
(b) Sudden death, 35-49

In Government Employees
(male clerks [::] & postmen [hatched])
(a) All forms, ages 35-59
(b) Rapidly fatal infarction 35-49

2. Prevalence of Ischaemic Myocardial Fibrosis [20]   National Necropsy Survey

3800 Deaths from other than Ischaemic Heart Disease, men aged 45-70
(a) All forms of ischaemic myocardial fibrosis   (b) Large healed infarcts
(c) Focal myocardial fibrosis in cases with hypertension and
(d) Focal myocardial fibrosis in cases without hypertension

(a)   (b)   (c) and (d)

3. Ischaemic Heart Disease: Physical Activity of Work and Social Class.

Men aged 45-54

Social Class	Light	Active	Heavy
	Rates per 100,000 p.a.		
I	176	–	–
II	167	118	–
III	173	137	111
IV	153	121	116
V	175	145	91
All	173	135	102

(a) Mortality, England & Wales 1949-53 [19 28 29]
Registrar General

(b) Prevalence of ischaemic myocardial fibrosis in deaths from other than Ischaemic Heart Disease [20 29]

Men aged 45-70

Social Class	Light	Active	Heavy
	Per cent		
I	13.7	–	–
II	13.4	9.2	–
III	13.8	8.0	8.2
IV	13.5	10.1	4.9
V	8.9	9.0	7.1
All	13.4	8.7	6.8

National Necropsy Survey

4. Coronary Artery Disease   National Necropsy Survey

Deaths from other than Ischaemic Heart Disease, men aged 45-70
Main coronary arteries only:
(a) Extensive atheroma of walls   (b) Calcification present   (c) Slight narrowing
of a lumen   (d) Complete or near-complete occlusion of a lumen

(a)   (b)   (c)   (d)

5. Essential Hypertension

Evidence at necropsy, men aged 45-70 [20]

(a) E.H. present and related to death
(b) E.H. present and incidental to death
(c) No evidence E.H.

National Necropsy Survey

Casual diastolic B.P. over 100 mm. Hg [14][29]

Age	Drivers	Conductors
	Per cent	
40–49	9.9	14
50–59	23.0	11
60–64	29.0	18

n = 852

6. Blood Lipid in London Busmen [29]

Ages 50-59
n = 272

Lipid	Drivers	Conductors
	mg%	
Plasma Cholesterol	249	·235
β-lipoprotein	202	189
Sf 100–400	61	34

7. Physique and Obesity in London Busmen [14][29]

(a) % Uniform trouser waist
38" and more
n = 958
Ht = 5'8" – 5'9"

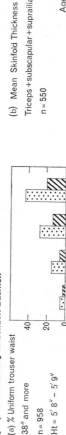

Age 25-34 35-44 45-54 55-64

(b) Mean Skinfold Thickness

Triceps + subscapular + suprailiac
n = 550

Age 45-49   50-59   60-64

(c) "Sudden death" from Ischaemic
Heart Disease   Age 35-49

1949-1958 'Bus Fleet
n = 160,000 man-years

Trouser waist	Drivers	Conductors
	Rates per 1,000 p.a.	
32" and less	0.8	0.2
34"–37"	0.5	0.2
38" and more	1.0	–

When necessary, rates were standardised for age.

Unless otherwise stated the "light" stippled columns = 100%, and the others are in proportion to this.

Fig. 22

Physical activity of work and coronary disease in men. Formulation and testing of an epidemiological hypothesis.
Mod. Conc. cardiovasc. Dis. (1960). **29**, 625.

12

important qualitative differences. Meanwhile, as illustrated in Fig. 23, most studies in other countries are finding the same results.

Pathogenesis.—Possible mechanisms of the occupational difference in ischaemic heart disease were sought in analysis of the prevalence of coronary atherosclerosis, and its two main processes, among men who had been employed in different kinds of work, line 4; and in a clinical-field survey of blood pressure and blood lipid levels. The excess of chronic coronary occlusion found in the national necropsy survey among light workers, line 4 (d), has already been described, page 146. (*Acute* coronary thrombosis—and myocardial infarction—lines 1 (b) and 2 (b), have a similar occupational distribution.) Judging by the Framingham and similar surveys[7] [8] [18] there seems to be enough to the advantage of the conductors in the differences found after 50 years of age in blood pressure, line 5, and from 40 on in blood lipids, line 6, to account for the occupational differences in ischaemic heart disease. (The mean, without a picture of the scatter of observations, is of course a limited indicator. In fact, drivers have high blood lipid levels more than twice as commonly as conductors.[19]) Drivers and conductors provide an excellent population " laboratory " for this kind of research, studying the whole fleet as in line 1, or samples as in lines 5-7. Remarkably similar in their social-economic circumstances, they do very different jobs which have the further distinction of being homogeneous and easily defined. Many further suggestions have of course emerged from the experimental laboratory on possible mechanisms of this postulated cause, *e.g.* the profusion of collateral vessels in the myocardium with exercise,[9] [30] the lengthening of blood clotting time,[11] and the increase of fibrinolysis.[3]

Next, a more fundamental problem was approached. It is axiomatic that men who are different, whether because of inheritance or of experience, will choose different kinds of jobs, jobs that are physically active, for example, or inactive. A

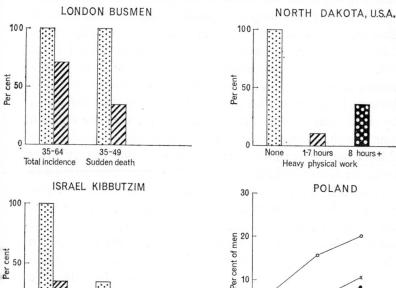

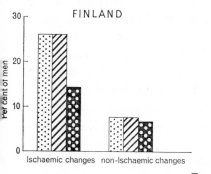

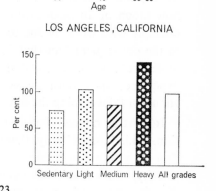

Light workers · · · · Active ▨ Heavy ●

LONDON BUSMEN

Per cent

100

50

0

35-64   35-49
Total incidence Sudden death

NORTH DAKOTA, U.S.A.

Per cent

100

50

0

None   1-7 hours   8 hours+
Heavy physical work

ISRAEL KIBBUTZIM

Per cent

100

50

0

Total incidence . Fatal cases

POLAND

30

Per cent of men

20

10

0

30   40   50-59
Age

FINLAND

30

Per cent of men

20

10

0

Ischaemic changes non-Ischaemic changes

LOS ANGELES, CALIFORNIA

Per cent

150

100

50

0

Sedentary Light Medium Heavy All grades

FIG. 23

Physical activity of work and ischaemic heart disease (IHD) in men.
Recent data from several countries.
London busmen: relative incidence of IHD.[21] [29]
North Dakota: relative incidence of IHD. Ages 35-54.[31]
Israel: relative incidence of IHD. Ages 40-64.[5]
Poland: point prevalence of IHD in bank staff (upper line), electronics
  factory operatives (middle line), and heavy metals workers (lowest line).[2]
East Finland: point prevalence of ECG abnormalities (at rest) in lumber-
  jacks (very heavy workers), and all other (less active) workers in the
  same district. Ages 40-59.[15]
California: relative incidence of IHD in civil servants aged 40-59.[6]

Yale J. Biol. Med. (1961/2). **34**, 359.

tentative approach was made to the question of such " host " factors by way of a study of *physique,* using data readily available for the busmen on uniform size.[14] The validity of the tailor's waist-band measurements has been confirmed (page 46), and clinical measurement of skinfolds, line 7 (b), gives a similar result. The indication is that inclination to obesity is brought by the men with them into their jobs, and more of it by the drivers than by the conductors,* *i.e.* they *are* different men. In the course of the years many more of the sedentary drivers than active conductors become fat, and dietary study indicates that overeating as well as under-exercise contribute to this. Be this as it may, the differences in obesity do not help at all to explain the main differences found in ischaemic heart disease, lines 1 (b) and 7 (c). Measurements are being taken in the clinical sample-survey to give a somatotype of each man—in the prevalent culture photography is impossible—and perhaps this will illuminate the occupational differences in IHD. (We can already say that height and breadth are no more rewarding to study than obesity.) The general problem is a crucial one for the understanding of the chronic diseases: to disentangle how much of an association found with the environment, for example with work, is due to initial selection—and how much to the consequent fact that 20, 30, or 40 years are then spent in different ways. The initial selection and the environmental experience may both be systematically associated with the chances of developing the disease that is being investigated.

It must be noticed that all these observations are on occupation. This kind of study, therefore, is unlikely to give information on habitual or sudden over-exertion. The type of physical activity, whether static or dynamic, may also be relevant: such exercise as the drivers do on the job is more " static " and less

---

* An independent study is now being made[25] of recruits to driving and conducting, aged 23, though in recent years the situation has been much complicated by recruitment of Irish and West Indian immigrants. The former already are a large proportion of young conductors in particular, but still (1962) less than 10 per cent of the total men in either job over 40 years old.

dynamic than that of the conductors. Finally: it is evident that physically active workers still have a great deal of ischaemic heart disease, far too much. If this is a cause, evidently there are greater.

*   *   *

The main significance of lack of exercise may be its contribution to the recent increase of coronary thrombosis and ischaemic heart disease. Because of recent technology, there has been a drastic reduction in physical effort of work, transportation and leisure, and automation promises to finish the job. This is one of the epochal changes in the " epidemic constitution " of modern times, and conceivably it has mass physiological consequences. Men have been affected more than women; perhaps this is one of the social changes underlying the biological changes of Fig. 1. Ischaemic heart disease may be in some senses a deficiency disease, representing the pathology of inactivity. To maintain any sort of ecological balance today, the reduction of exercise in vocation will have to be made good in avocation: relationships of ischaemic heart disease to physical activity *in work* is increasingly an academic issue for preventive medicine.[12][21] Few data are available so far on the value of exercise in leisure, whether for metabolism in middle age or the prophylaxis of ischaemic heart disease, although the Russians with their different approach have instituted mass physical culture in the factory. Properly this question would be studied first by observation. Do sedentary workers who walk to work and garden a lot have a lower incidence of ischaemic heart disease than their fellows who don't? Secondly, experiments will need to be done. Some thousand sedentary workers, persuaded to exercise regularly, might be compared with colleagues of the same age left to their own devices and most of them probably exercising little. Both kinds of study have defeated us to start; the methodologic problems of assessing the activity of " gardening ", for example, have so far proved insoluble. These questions are central to the Public Health of the coming age of leisure, to *re*creation in it.

EXPLORING ESSENTIAL HYPERTENSION

Next, pp. 184-5, an area in an even earlier stage of investigation. Fig. 24 represents some current attempts to clarify the great mystery of high blood pressure without evident cause, a disorder predominantly of middle age. Such is the ignorance of the natural history of essential hypertension that even this apparently innocuous statement should certainly be disputed. The search for causes is proving exceedingly hard; most studies have to deal also with problems previously mentioned in Chapter V; on the other hand, the detection of cases early represents one of the main hopes of finding causes.

Some results from a survey in Scotland are given in Fig. 24 (1). The Fig. shows the increase with age of average systolic and diastolic blood pressures found in population samples. It is a typical report with its crossover (because of the menopause, it may be) to produce the higher figures among women during middle age that were already noticed on page 39. The greater rise of systolic than diastolic pressure is also expected; it may be a simple statistical expression of rigidity in large vessels, unrelated *i.e.* to the central problem of essential hypertension.

Figs. 24 (2) and (3) present contrasts from " geographical physiology ". Fig. (2) is from random sample studies by Miall, who made the same observations in Southern Welshmen and Jamaica Negroes. It has long been known that Negroes have higher blood pressure than whites, higher average pressure, and more with high pressures.[20] But the inherited and acquired causes that are involved are still largely unknown; the epidemiological lead has been little taken up by clinicians and laboratory workers. Bacteriuria (and pyelonephritis) among the

Jamaicans does not seem to be a major factor.[8] Also to be noted here is the gross difference between the frequency of high casual pressure on survey in South Wales and of morbidity from hypertension in the sample of British general practitioners' records (p. 39), a difference between about 16 per *cent* and 19 per *mille*. The " plane " of diagnosis is surely only one of the factors involved, and the lability of the casual pressure another; but the complex of hypertension/anxiety/ atherosclerosis/cardiovascular hypertrophy/morbidity (no chain of events implied) urgently requires sorting out in long-term follow-up studies. Fig. 24 (3) shows that the rise of blood pressure in populations during middle age is not universal or inevitable. The top line is from the sample of Pickering and his group in London, the Indians and Fijians are described in a study of Lovell and colleagues. Genetic as well as environmental hypotheses need to be tested in these geographic studies, including the difficult question of who survives to middle age.

Fig. 24 (4) proceeds to family studies and compares the experience during middle age of relatives of normotensive and of hypertensive subjects.[25] The average increase among the former is less—scarcely any in diastolic pressure—the rise among the latter is " excessive ", in Allbutt's phrase. Here again is an example of the wrong way of asking the right question: such cross-sectional *averages* of blood pressure in varying categories of relative are a poor substitute for the direct follow-up of individuals to determine what happens to the level in *individuals*.[14] The study of the disease in families, with the clustering of cases that will be found, is an illustration of " clinical epidemiology ",[19] another meeting ground for clinician and epidemiologist. But in interpreting what is found it must be kept in mind that a great deal is shared in the family: genes; character development, the learning of patterns of behaviour and human relations; the physical environment. Present-day family studies can scarcely be called population genetics, but here again is a growing point.

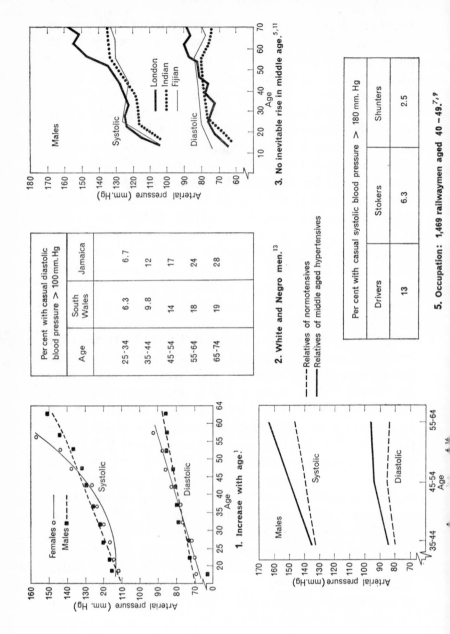

1. Increase with age.[1]

Females o ———
Males ■ – – –

Systolic

Diastolic

---

2. White and Negro men.[13]

Per cent with casual diastolic blood pressure > 100 mm. Hg		
Age	South Wales	Jamaica
25-34	6.3	6.7
35-44	9.8	12
45-54	14	17
55-64	18	24
65-74	19	28

- – – – Relatives of normotensives
- ——— Relatives of middle aged hypertensives

Males

Systolic

Diastolic

Arterial pressure (mm.Hg)

---

3. No inevitable rise in middle age.[5,11]

Males

Systolic

Diastolic

——— London
· · · · · Indian
——— Fijian

Arterial pressure (mm.Hg)

Age

---

5. Occupation: 1,469 railwaymen aged 40 – 49.[7,9]

Per cent with casual systolic blood pressure > 180 mm. Hg		
Drivers	Stokers	Shunters
13	6.3	2.5

184

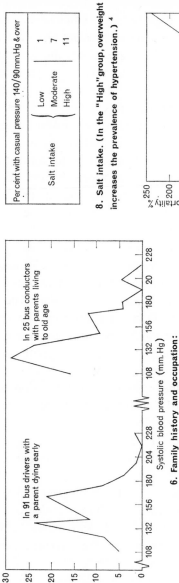

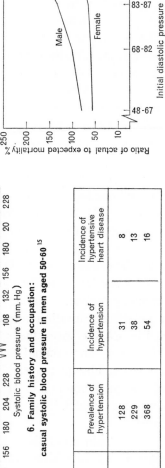

	Per cent with casual pressure 140/90mm.Hg & over
Salt intake { Low	1
Moderate	7
High	11

8. Salt intake. (In the "High" group, overweight increases the prevalence of hypertension.) [4]

9. Sex: actuarial experience. [2]

6. Family history and occupation: casual systolic blood pressure in men aged 50-60 [15]

Obesity	Prevalence of hypertension	Incidence of hypertension	Incidence of hypertensive heart disease
None / slight	128	31	8
Moderate	229	38	13
Marked	368	54	16

7. Obesity : rates per 1,000 men, aged 50–59. [26]

Fig. 24

In search of causes of essential hypertension.
Mod. Conc. cardiovasc. Dis. (1961). **30**, 633.

Fig. 24 (5) is from an occupational study in Czechoslovakia. East European research in hypertension emphasises the nervous strain involved in the job (stationmasters also had a high rate), although without knowing more about the particular situation it is difficult to dissociate this from physical activity. The frequency of hypertensive disease in categories of light workers has already been illustrated, Fig. 22, lines 2 and 5. The epidemiological method could be useful in testing the neurogenic hypothesis of essential hypertension, as presently stated by Russian investigators,[17] if only better measurements or classifications of nervous and emotional factors were available for application in large-scale prospective studies.

Fig. 24 (6) is a primitive attempt to relate inheritance and environment. Comparing drivers with a parent who died prematurely, and conductors whose parents lived to 75, reveals indeed a contrast (P<·05). The drivers in this Fig., it may be postulated, manifest two unfavourable features, their family history and their job—the conductors seem to have two favourable features. The main lead from current controversies on the nature of essential hypertension is the need to attempt studies combining " genetic " and " neurogenic " hypotheses, to seek for patterns of causation in terms of both.

Stamler, Fig. 24 (7), gives the rates with hypertension at start of his study, and annual incidence (detection) rates for the four years subsequent. Dahl's figures (8) are a token of the work on the hypothesis that salt ingestion is a cause of hypertension; the epidemiological evidence at present is contradictory.[3] [10]

Fig. 24 (9) is again about host factors; it illustrates from actuarial data (using Life Table methods) how females have more hypertension, yet cope better with it than males. The Fig. estimates the individual chances, on the average, and at any rate in this kind of (selected) population.

Fig. 24 (10), alas, is missing. I have been unable to discover for the population at large even limited data on something I wished to include, namely, the frequency of various types of

" secondary " hypertension compared with cases having no evident cause, even for young people and for severe disease. It is an urgent responsibility of epidemiologists to attempt to provide representative data on this question, beginning perhaps with necropsy surveys. With each improvement in diagnosis and each recognition of new syndromes (p. 15) the need for this grows.

As clinician and laboratory worker, Wilson looks for contributions from epidemiology to these problems[27] : is essential hypertension a specific disease (qualitative); or merely the extreme of the normal distribution of blood pressure in the population (quantitative)? Is inheritance multifactorial,[21] [22] or by a single gene or small number of genes?[23] [24] Is a rise of pressure in middle age physiological; or does it occur in only a minority of individuals suffering from a specific disease— and what is the role of environment in them? What are the relationships between the differing mean levels of pressure that are found in population groups and their modes of life?

IMPROVEMENT OF EPIDEMIOLOGY

In field studies of blood pressure the first casual reading on a standard instrument is the principal measurement used. That this may often be the only practicable thing to do is scarcely virtue enough. Here is a problem urgently requiring joint work between clinicians, laboratory workers, and epidemiologists : to decide how blood pressure should be measured and recorded for population studies in this electronic age, what readings are worth taking, and what other investigations can and must be made in large-scale surveys of " essential hypertension ". Meanwhile an English instrument that eliminates a good deal of observer error and of subconscious rejection of " significant " digits is giving promising results.

This questioning of the basis of most population studies of blood pressure is but one illustration of the imperative need to improve the methods of epidemiology. Many others can be cited : standardised questionnaires on angina and intermittent claudication; streamlined electrocardiograms, and their reading by computers; simple renal function tests; biochemistry of the drop of blood; methods of classifying individual diet on a mass scale; brief psychological tests, diagnostic and predictive; " Jones criteria " for hypertension and coronary disease like those available for rheumatic heart disease; agreed semi-quantitative assessment of arterial lesions; economical designs for genetic-environmental studies; measurement of personal physical activity. Work is badly needed in all of these problems, and these are not all.[28] [29] [30] [31]

*   *   *

MULTIPLE CAUSES

The notion of " pattern of causes " is a relatively modern restatement. For half a century and more the triumphs of bacteriology, and the liberation they brought from filth and multiple vagueness, led to emphasis on " the germ theory " and other such specific formulations. Now there is progress to a new synthesis.[4] [5] [7] [9] [23] Today interest centres not merely in the production of syphilis by the *treponema pallidum;* the object rather is to understand the occurrence of venereal disease among causes in host and environment as well: causes in sex and age; and causes in the psychology of promiscuity, the economics of prostitution, the horrors of war, the life of the merchant seaman, the disruption of the family with migration, the sex mores of the times, etc.—causes which in one combination or another can result in a case of syphilis or a rising incidence in the community—and without which there will be neither. Much more than the spirochaete is involved in primary syphilis and, a fortiori, GPI; more than the haemolytic streptococcus in scarlet fever or juvenile rheumatism, more than Koch's bacillus in the manifold tuberculous diseases.[19]

In some situations of course one cause will be of overwhelming importance: hereditary haemophilia (though even
here more than deficiency of AHG seems to be necessary to
tip the balance into bleeding), or acquired measles (and when
measles is caught can be very important); in malignant disease,
retinoblastoma (genetic) or cancer of the lip (environmental)
could be cited. There are other situations where inherited
aptitudes matter most (asthma, for instance), or external
agents (an earthquake—or prussic acid poisoning). But even
this type of emphasis is deceptively simple. Childhood
poisoning is apparently becoming commoner: because of the
increasing number of drugs (cause), titivated oftener as
coloured pills (cause), for which the popular appetite is
voracious and readily indulged (in the grocer's shop as well
as by the National Health Service). It is the carelessness of
adults, however, chance, and the sex and stage of development
of the child—exploring, putting things into his mouth—that
often are essential links (or causes).[12] [22] Though predispositions
of inheritance or previous experience are crucial as said in one
kind of asthma, there often are multiple environmental causes,
psychological and infective, which makes for illness or no, as
well as the conjunction of allergic person and allergen. Genetic
and environmental causes together are responsible for disease.
Duodenal ulcer increased this century, under environmental
pressures it may be postulated. Two distinct genetic predispositions to it have also been identified: blood group O
non-secretors have a $2\frac{1}{2}$ times greater chance of developing the
disease than group A, B and AB secretors.*[3]

A case of disease, then, or a population incidence, like any
historical event or social fact, commonly has many causes.
Various overlapping schemes, classifications of pattern, have
been suggested; chance and accident need to be mentioned in
all of them. Thus there are interacting *chains of events*: the

---

* This discussion is of the multiple cause of *disease*. The causes of
illness and of *disability* raise further issues (cf. pages 82 and 136).

child's poisoning, perhaps. Or, in juvenile epilepsy, predisposing inheritance may be identified, provoking brain damage at birth, precipitating fever in infancy, aggravating and perpetuating causes, perhaps, in a miserable home life and a generally unsympathetic environment. . . .[21] And there are *chain reactions.* For example: heredity → cystinuria → urinary calculi → pyelonephritis→ hypertension and/or renal failure → death. . . .* Another formulation groups causes into (a) *stress*ful experiences, and (b) *deprivation,* affecting homeostasis; to which are added (c) harmful *external causes* such as poisons and germs.[14] Kwashiorkor is thus explained by (a) the physiological and psychological strains of the weaning period, (b) the deprivation of protein and possibly excess of calories from CH in the diet, and (c) the frequent coincident infections; all of these combining to disrupt the metabolism of the child. " Deprivation ", the denial of elementary human needs, was dominant in disease aetiology till recently in the West, and it still is very much so in most of the world, the most general, and the most powerful, of the non-specific causes previously mentioned. The notion can be elaborated in personal-clinical terms of an individual mother and her child, or in the sociological dimensions of kwashiorkor: poverty and ignorance, the lack of protein-rich foods and the failure to make use of such as are available (including UNICEF milk) because of " tradition, taboo and magic "; and rapid industrialisation with its disruption of family life including the employment of women away from home.[1][13] My own interest in epidemiology began with Dr. F. J. Poynton's descriptions of the life of the under-privileged child as a cause of its juvenile rheumatism.

For convenience, if not in logic, the pattern of multiple causes of an instance, or an incidence, of a chronic disease may tentatively be summed up like this; at any rate, I have found it helpful. First, a necessary cause, the specific *agent*

* Natura in reticulum sua genera connexit, non in catenam: homines non possunt nisi catenam sequi, cum non plura simul sermone exponere.[10]

that has to be present before the disease can develop may be distinguished, and *other* causes:

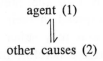

agent (1)

other causes (2)

The significance of the *necessary* cause lies in the direct and immediate opportunity it opens up for a " magic bullet " to achieve specific prevention and cure. BCG immunisation can be cited, or antituberculous chemotherapy now proven effective in Madras under environmental conditions scarcely to be graced with the name of slum, and defying clinical tradition and Public Health practice alike.[6] Such situations are little evident yet in the chronic non-infectious diseases, though cigarette smoking seems to be the agent of the modern epidemic of lung cancer, there are the inborn errors of metabolism like gout, and such environmental situations as the deficiency of light in miner's nystagmus or the X factor in the leaves of the cotton plant which is the cause of byssinosis. In keeping with the rest of this discussion necessary *sets of causes* is a more useful notion. The great majority of those exposed at Hiroshima and Nagasaki did not have the indispensable set of causes to produce leukaemia. The particular asthma occurs only on exposure to the specific pollution of Yokohama and Tokyo—but cigarette smokers alone are affected.[20] In conditions like cancer, anyhow in the exogenous tumours, there is still reason to hope that specific agents will eventually be identified.

More commonly, therefore, another model is required. The chronic diseases obviously are products of interaction between host and environment, of causes in these :

(2) environmental causes $\rightleftharpoons$ causes in host (1)

Causes in the host (endogenous, autogenous, personal causes) are *inherited,* and *acquired* in early experience that is internalised and in later experience. Environmental causes occur in the *physical*, and in the human or *social* environments. The environmental causes of chronic diseases currently being investigated (as described in the previous sections of this chapter) often are widespread in their operation, ubiquitous. But relatively few persons may suffer from them. There is today an upsurge of interest therefore in individual differences in response to these insults, in protective and pathogenic causes in the host: in genetic endowment and the childhood environment, in physiological ranges and personality, in adaptive and maladaptive responses under stress that have been learned, in autoimmune reactions, in the ways that present environment are interpreted in light of the individual past. The study of environmental causes and causes in the host thus is now very complex.

This also is too simple. " Causes in host " and " environmental " causes cannot be so simply distinguished because of the role of *personal habits and behaviour,* deriving from both, as in diet or exercise. Thus it is useful to describe:

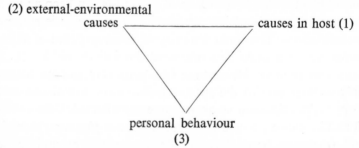

(2) external-environmental
         causes   causes in host (1)

personal behaviour
(3)

Simple examples are inherited predispositions (1), atmospheric pollution (2), cigarette smoking (3). The external environment (2), and personal habits and behaviour (3), are often described as *ways of living;* (2) and (3) together as the *mode of life.* . . . The pattern of causes is made up so, and true *primary prevention* of the chronic diseases may be achieved by disrupting the pattern: by change in presently responsible external environment or personal behaviour, and by alterations earlier in life so that resistance is enhanced and predispositions are not acquired. An endless range of activity is involved, from genetic counselling to elimination of toxic hazards, from bringing up children the right way (!) to eating moderately, from catching rubella in good time to removal of opportunities for crime.

Cardiovascular Disease in Middle Age.—In terms of this discussion causes can be postulated (1) in male sex, or diabetes (personal predispositions); (2) in the hardness of the local water supply (external environment); (3) in physical activity in leisure (personal behaviour). Or there are evident endogenous variations in metabolising fat which, it may be presumed, interact with the food consumption, the mode of life, which is a matter of the prevalent plane of nutrition and local culture patterns and of personal habits and preferences.

Variations on the Theme

Multiple causes combine in the single instance or incidence; but different combinations of causes operate in different populations or individuals; particular causes may be effective in some and weak or absent altogether in others. Hypertension is present in a third or perhaps half the cases of ischaemic heart disease, and absent in the remainder. Obesity also seems to be important for IHD—sometimes, and perhaps only at its grossest. Physical inactivity is clearly of no significance in these Californians (p. 179); perhaps there is too little difference of activity between these occupation groups to show up in this way. Social class, with its known and unknown components, manifestly affects reproductive performance and influences stillbirth rates. But the last two columns, overleaf, show the class factor being overwhelmed in particularly favourable biological situations (young mothers who are not " primips "), and particularly unfavourable ones (the " grand multip "). Contrariwise, in a neutral age group in biologic terms, neither particularly favourable nor particularly unfavourable for age and parity—for example, mothers in their late 30's bearing a third child—the social class range is considerably greater, extending in this instance from 14 in Class I to 33 in Class V. Two further corollaries. The same cause can be involved in the production of different diseases—and of none. The notion of non-specific causes has already been mentioned, but we need not be so general. Smog can kill by cor pulmonale

TABLE XLIII

Biological and Social Factors in Stillbirth[11][18]

1949-50

England and Wales

Rates per 1,000 Total (Live and Still) Births

SOCIAL CLASS	MOTHERS		
	Of All Ages and All Parities	Aged 20-24 Bearing Second Child	Aged 40+ Bearing Sixth or Later Child
I	16	—	—
II	19	11	52
III	21	12	56
IV	23	12	56
V	26	13	56

Single, legitimate births.

or ischaemic heart disease. Coxsackie B virus produces various diseases, so does Koch's bacillus. The same drug can produce manifold toxic reactions. The stereotypes of the unconscious are manifested in a multitude of disorders. Eighteen-year-olds joining the same military depot will range in their response from those who become twice the men they were, to those who have a psychotic breakdown; in between a great variety of positive and negative physical, mental and social adaptations will be detectable. Reference has already been made on p. 158 to the possibility that the association of diseases may point to a common cause.

Finally, multiple different causes can produce the same disease, depending again presumably on the other personal predispositions and on the rest of the environment. Hormonal and immunologic mechanisms are common to many situations, the pathological processes of the body are few, and final common paths limited—whether of inflammation, or liver damage, or the organic mental reaction type. There are many causes of septic or aseptic meningitis. A variety of known causes produce leukaemia. Different external causes acting on the growing embryo at a particular time can cause the same deformity, and different genes may also do so. The same histological lung cancer is found with quite different external causes—cigarette smoking, uranium, nickel; atmospheric pollution possibly. There are many known causes of " industrial " dermatitis. The same symptom or piece of (disordered) behaviour can originate in many motivations.

THEORY AND ACTION

To sum up: it is obligatory now in any situation to think of its multiple causes, variously combining together and of varying import, theoretical and practical. *Theoretical*—in terms of the explanation provided, and of the predicted fall in disease should causes be removed. *Practical*—in terms of the possibility of doing so. These two may be quite different. It is a classic situation in Public Health that there is no need to await full understanding before sensible action is taken, for example in trying to change the mode of life. Multiple causes offer multiple possibilities of action. The great hope of preventive medicine in the chronic diseases is to learn enough of the causes for a regimen to be stated that will disrupt the pattern, and reduce the frequency of disease at a known and worthwhile cost in other trouble. The attack may be on a single cause or on several, major and minor, among the many that have been identified.[2][8][15][16][17][18]

EPIDEMIOLOGY OF PERSONAL BEHAVIOUR

A fundamental question for modern preventive medicine has been raised by the preceding discussion. The chronic non-infectious diseases are increasingly seen to be associated with the mode of life, but with personal habits and behaviour that are distinguished in this rather than with impersonal external environment.

Cancer of the lung, squamous, epidermoid or undifferentiated, *i.e.,* exogenous and " environmental ", provides an extreme illustration. In terms previously stated, two specific agents in the physical environment may be selected, radiation and tobacco. The Schneeberg-Joachimsthal tumour was due to the *industrial process,* the modern epidemic is the consequence of the *personal habit* of cigarette smoking. The former is of course far easier to control than the latter, whence today's great hope of preventing the disease is to remove the carcinogen from smoking. The contrast is not usually so decisive: in most situations there are significant personal and impersonal components, but the point I hope is made.

Knowledge is small on many aspects of personal behaviour. Getting the facts to relate to health and disease is difficult and expensive; often it hasn't yet been attempted. And there are far more private and difficult areas to investigate than smoking. In the absence of systematic study a baleful mythology about the isolated nuclear modern family was allowed to spread. At a time when sexual behaviour may be changing drastically, there is little accurate information for the community as a whole, still less for social classes and for any age (p. 28), on how people in fact behave, or want to; as distinct from what it is believed they do, or what is considered the right thing to do, or what the law says. (Sensibility about this is also changing, of course, and we should soon know a lot more.)

It follows that in the production of disease individual differences in behaviour matter more and more rather than membership of the customary social categories. This is manifestly true of smoking, exercise and diet—say its fat content in a country with full employment, high earnings, and cheap fats. Our recent studies in London and the Home Counties of men in early middle age have shown a range in individual fat consumption of 73 to 216 gms per day: the average among bank managers was 125, and for bank clerks 133 gms; in bus drivers 127 gms, and conductors 124; the range was similar in each occupation-group. To study possible connections between fat consumption and heart disease, direct comparisons of the experience of individuals eating less than 100 gms should obviously be made with that of men eating 100-125 gms, etc. It would be a waste of time to study the role of diet in heart disease in terms of the experience of drivers and conductors *as such*. Work is becoming increasingly sedentary: what is, or will be, significant for health is personal exercise in leisure and in getting to work. The important differences in smoking habits in England and Wales are between *individuals,* and they cut across customary *classes, occupations, regions, towns: e.g.* Table XLIV, when compared with one's everyday experience of men who smoke from 0 to over 20 cigarettes per day. (Among boys the situation is interestingly different, Table XV, page 71, and we ought to be finding out why—is it just a question of the available money? Or is this the beginning of the long haul?) New meaningful groupings are needed for social-medical research; this is another area where the help of the social sciences is badly wanted.

Personal and Communal Prevention

This shifting emphasis to the individual, and personal behaviour, has its correlates: it is one of the changing characters of health problems, the new sanitary idea (though as old as the Greeks, and the eighteenth century pioneers laid plenty of emphasis on it) that prevention of disease is likely increasingly to be a matter of individual decision and personal action. There still are abundant problems of environmental hygiene for Public Health to solve, but the point again I hope is taken. Compare the Victorian programme for laying drains, and today's campaigns on washing the hands;

the prevention of undernutrition, and of obesity; the fencing of machinery, and the control of accidents in the home; Legge's principle of industrial safety,* and the Highway Code; fluoridation (old type and, goodness knows, difficult enough) and not eating

TABLE XLIV

Smoking Habits in England and Wales

1961

POPULATION	MALE		FEMALE	
	Proportion of adults smoking any form of tobacco	Average no. of cigarettes smoked per adult in population per day	Proportion of adults smoking any form of tobacco	Average no. of cigarettes smoked per adult in population per day
	%		%	
England & Wales	72	10·7	44	4·6
London County	73	10·3	54	6·7
Conurbations	72	11·4	48	5·2
County Boroughs	73	11·9	44	4·7
Other Urban Areas	74	10·7	41	4·2
All Rural Districts	67	8·9	40	3·6
" Truly Rural " Districts	(68)	(8·2)	(39)	(3·9)

Statistics of Smoking in the United Kingdom (1962). London: Todd, G. F. Personal communication.

Adult=ages 16 and over.

sweets (new); the satisfaction of children's physical needs, *e.g.* Table II, page 8, and of their need for emotional security. Today's world problem in social medicine is that of over-population, due to the progress of environmental death control compared

* " If you can bring an influence to bear external to the workman (*i.e.*, one over which he can exercise no control) you will be successful; and if you do not or cannot you will not be successful."

with personal birth control. Between the two agents of lung cancer that have been mentioned, and a theoretical link, is urban air pollution which has obvious individual components in what is classically a community problem. I am referring to the millions of domestic coal fires, the main source of smoke pollution of the air we breathe; the community components include education to overcome one of the most " English " of traditions and the organisation to replace these fires, the supply of smokeless fuels, economics, legislation, enforcement.

All this is going to be very difficult to deal with. Successful health policy will depend more on the individual, and the changing of individual habits presents problems that at present are often insurmountable: it is already evident that finding the causes of the chronic diseases will be far easier than putting what is found into practice in preventive medicine. But the individual is of course a social being. A new kind of partnership needs building between community and individual, in place of the old where so often in Public Health the community did things for the individual, external to him. On smoking, the family doctor (himself being rapidly persuaded of the dangers of cigarette smoking) will increasingly be discussing with families their responsibilites, and with the teenager his. But the community " image " will be the counterpart—is it manly to smoke or not to smoke? Do the adolescent's heroes set an example? Does the National *Health* Service shirk its share of action? and Parliament look the other way as the tobacco industry spends more on advertising? How much effort are we devoting to changing individual behaviour? and how much science, including the new knowledge of mind? In a democratic society, how much ought to be?

*   *   *

BRONCHITIS

The smog of December 1952 (p. 200) was followed by an epochal revival of interest in chronic bronchitis and in the relationships of atmospheric pollution to health. Many of the four thousand deaths caused by that disaster were in elderly sufferers from chronic bronchitis. (Subjects with ischaemic

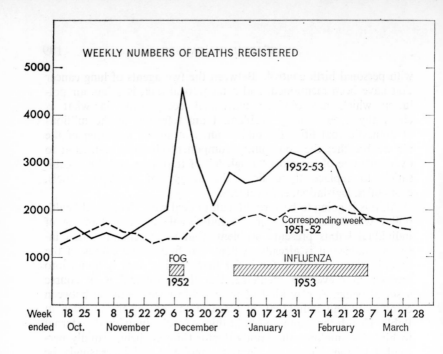

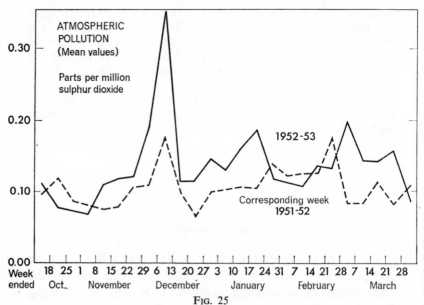

FIG. 25

The great fog of December 1952. Weekly numbers of deaths registered in Greater London (upper fig.) in relation to levels of air pollution, indicated by SO$_2$ (lower fig.). Comparison of 1952 with ordinary year, 1951. All causes of death; all ages. both sexes. Effects of the 1953 influenza epidemic are also shown.

Rep. Publ. Hlth med. Subj. No. 95 (1954). HMSO.

heart disease also could not take the extra strain.) On the *onion principle,* the increasing control over pulmonary tuberculosis and pneumonia might anyhow have drawn attention by now to bronchitis. Be that as it may, its importance to the community can be only too readily illustrated (*e.g.* page 34). Bronchitis moreover is by far the main certified cause of chronic sickness in the working population,* and there is good reason to suspect that it is much involved in the remarkable trend of Table IV, page 11.

The main components, or stages, of the disease can tentatively be described like this:[7]

(1) *Chronic, productive cough*—subjects have excess bronchial secretion with irritant cough and expectoration of mucoid sputum, but usually are little troubled otherwise. This may also be called " simple bronchitis ".

(2) *Bronchitis with infection*—there are recurrent chest illnesses; infection may become established with irreversible damage to lungs and bronchi. Coughing is increased, and the sputum becomes purulent. Morbidity and incapacity to work are common and death from pneumonia may occur.

(3) *Bronchitis with airways obstruction*—at first this may be demonstrable only by physiological tests; but later there is wheezing, shortness of breath, and persisting disability. Respiratory crippling may ensue, and death from cor pulmonale. Emphysema is often found at necropsy.

These disorders, separately and together, and kindred pictures, are generally recognised as " chronic bronchitis " in Britain, and as " chronic non-specific pulmonary disease " in the rest of Europe and the U.S.A. The essential feature of the disease is the hypersecretion of mucus (Lynne Reid). Stage (1)

---

* In Britain during 1959-60 insured men (of all ages) had 298,000 spells of incapacity from work lasting over three months. Twelve per cent of these were certified to bronchitis, 9·8 per cent to accidents, 8·5 per cent to psychiatric disorder, 7·9 per cent to ischaemic and other " degenerative " heart disease. . . .

may be considered " simple bronchitis ", as said, and the precursor of the disabling chronic disease. In some men, the disease is progressive from chronic productive cough, through a period of infection into a stage marked also by respiratory obstruction. The productive cough with sputum often continues for many years, and winter infections recur before chronic infection becomes established, usually in early middle age. But the disease often stops at simple bronchitis (1) and it may progress variously, for example from (2) directly into cor pulmonale. Using the standardised questionnaire on symptoms, and thus reducing the observer variation inherent in clinical assessment (page 45), sample population surveys show that up to a quarter or even a third of the men in this country, from their 40's on, have a persistent productive cough. By 55-64 years of age, it may be estimated, chronic bronchitis is present in 10-15 per cent of men; who are often a misery to themselves and their families, and a grievous burden on the community's health and welfare services.[8][9][10][11][16]

MULTIPLE CAUSES

Much has been learnt in recent years about the aetiology of bronchitis, though it is not yet possible to describe a pattern of causation.

Cigarette smoking, the surveys show, is nowadays much involved in the stage of productive cough. (Surveys are essential, if only because these cases often do not present to medical attention, cf. Chapter V.) This condition, indeed, is indistinguishable from " smoker's cough ": it is quite uncommon in non-smokers, less common in pipe than cigarette smokers, and commoner in heavy cigarette smokers than in light. Productive cough occurs more often in men than in women, but this seems to be a function largely of sex differences in smoking habits.[19] Pathologically, smoking is associated with hypertrophy of the mucus glands and goblet cells in the bronchial walls, and cilial stasis; later, atypical cells with squamous metaplasia of the epithelium occur.

Chest infection also is commoner in smokers, but there is little relationship between its frequency and the amount smoked—moderate smokers seem to suffer as much as heavy smokers. Moreover, as said, in only a proportion of those with productive cough does the condition progress. Much evidently remains to be explained about the pathogenesis of the chronic infective and obstructive disease and its connections with smoking,[22] and a long-term prospective study has been started in an attempt to answer some of these questions.[7]

Unhealthiness of Towns

Living in towns (Table XLV) is manifestly important in the aetiology of chronic bronchitis. Cigarette smokers in London and the county boroughs of England and Wales (the large towns mostly) have about twice as much of the disease as

TABLE XLV

Bronchitis in Town and Country

Prevalence Rates

Ages 40-64

	TYPE OF DISTRICT								
	Rural Districts			Urban Districts and Municipal Boroughs			London and County Boroughs		
	No.	% B	% SD	No.	% B	% SD	No.	% B	% SD
Males	158	12	3	355	15	7	274	23	13
Females	170	8	2	332	7	2	280	9	6

College of General Practitioners (1961). *Brit. med. J.* **2,** 973.
B=Bronchitis on clinical diagnosis.
SD=Bronchitis on standard questionnaire.

smokers living in rural districts. Within each smoking category pulmonary function is lower in town than in country, and the volume of sputum greater (objective methods of assessment are being developed rapidly). Chronic *air pollution* is the urban-environmental factor under most suspicion of causing the chronic disease. In a fine piece of " clinical epidemiology ", one in which subjects were their own controls, exacerbation of their symptoms in London samples of patients with chronic bronchitis accompanied acute increase in intensity of air pollution (smoke and SO_2).[13] [14] [25] Absence from work, and invaliding, on account of bronchitis in postmen doing similar outdoor work over the country have been associated with an index of local air pollution.[6] Mortality in the county boroughs correlates highly with a crude index of

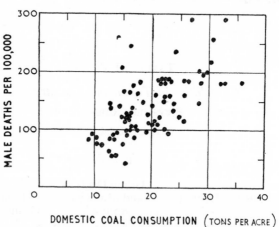

DOMESTIC COAL CONSUMPTION (TONS PER ACRE)

FIG. 26

Mortality from bronchitis, in relation to an estimate of chronic air pollution, in large towns (83 county boroughs) of England and Wales. Death rates of men aged 45-64 in 1948-54.[2] [3] [24] The correlation in women was similar.

Brit. J. prev. soc. Med. (1959). **13**, 14.

REGISTRAR GENERAL (1956). Appendix D, *Quarterly Return* No. 432.

pollution—the amount of coal burnt in domestic fires (Fig. 26). Analysis of the average rate of disease in different towns and the direct observation of individuals thus give the same kind of result.

Chronic bronchitis, in particular, and respiratory disease more generally, are responsible for most of the historic *urban/rural* and *North/South* differentials in mortality. If mortality is recalculated for bronchitis for example, and by degree of " domestic " air pollution, the ratios of Table XLI(3) on page 164 become:[24]

Rate per 1,000		ENGLAND & WALES	RURAL DISTRICTS	COUNTY BOROUGHS		
				CLEAN	INTERMEDIATE	DIRTY
M	1·2	= 100	52	80	126	176
F	0·27	= 100	59	71	132	186
	Ages 45-64.					

In the " truly rural " districts (the data are not available) the ratios are surely below 52-59, so that the true gradient is probably even bigger. The results of experiments of opportunity under the 1956 Clean Air Act are awaited.* In some areas, however, as permitted by the type of legislation, progress is very slow. Thus, of the 13 " dirty " county boroughs, only Manchester plans to be rid of its smoke pollution by 1970, and Barnsley's " target " is 1981 (a date that could be as late as it is, alas, because of the situation of the town on the Yorkshire coalfield). In general only one-sixth of the dwellings in the country's " black " areas were smoke-controlled after six years' operation of the Act.[12] It has proved politically impossible to carry out planned epidemiologic experiments in cleaning the air of particular towns, while designating others as controls, so as to obtain a clearer picture of the relations of air pollution and its various ingredients to health.

* In the great London fog of 1962, excess mortality was much smaller than in 1952. SO_2 concentration was similar in the two episodes, but there was less smoke in 1962 (cf. page 72). Detailed comparisons of the two episodes have not yet been published.

Standard of Living

The background of bronchitis as an epidemic disease is the standard of living, the satisfaction and denial of elementary physiological needs. For a change, I will illustrate from

TABLE XLVI

Percentage of Children Having Bronchitis, in Relation to Food Expenditure

1937-9

Britain

AGES	WEEKLY FOOD EXPENDITURE PER PERSON			
	-5s.	5s.-7s.	7s.-9s.	9s.+
	Boys			
	%	%	%	%
2- 4	21	15	10	4·3
5- 9	11	11	15	6·4
10-14	5	4	3·2	2·1
	Girls			
2- 4	17	11	7·1	0
5- 9	8·4	6·7	3·4	4·3
10-14	4·1	2·8	1·4	1·5

3,502 British children were surveyed, in their families, on a countrywide basis.

Family Diet and Health in Pre-War Britain (1955). Carnegie United Kingdom Trust, Dunfermline.

childhood, Table XLVI, for example, with its wide range in frequency particularly among young children—from 0 to 21 per cent. Classically, in middle age, mortality from bronchitis in both the men and married women of the " working classes " is far higher than that in the middle classes; and the College of General Practitioners' morbidity survey gave similar results:

		SOCIAL CLASS				
MORTALITY		I	II	III	IV	V
AGES 45-64						
per 1,000	Men	0·40	0·62	1·1	1·2	2·1
population	Married women	0·07	0·11	0·22	0·28	0·37
MORBIDITY						
AGES 40-64						
per cent examined						
Clinical	Men	(6)	11	18	19	26
Diagnosis	Married women	—	7	10	10	15
Diagnosis on Standard						
Question-	Men	3		10		10
naire	Married women	4		3		9

Average annual death rates, 1949-53, England and Wales; prevalence of morbidity during 1958, Britain.*

* The *sex difference* in mortality has been apparent from the beginning of death certification more than a hundred years ago, and it is increasing because of a decline in mortality among women. Bronchitis is the third of the great trio of diseases that particularly affect men, and it might well have been considered with Figs. 1 and 2. Average differences in smoking habits may be responsible, occupation, and the fact that middle-aged men dying of chronic bronchitis have also a very full share of coronary occlusion

TABLE XLVII[17] [24]

Coronary Atherosclerosis in Deaths from Chronic Bronchitis

Men aged 45-70   Britain

| | MAIN CAUSE OF DEATH | |
PATHOLOGY	Chronic Bronchitis	Cancer, Accidents,etc.
	%	%
Much coronary atheroma	19	15
Coronary stenosis including coronary occlusion	25 4·3	18 3·0
Ischaemic myocardial fibrosis	12	6·5
Nos.	255	2,530

Age distributions are similar.
National Necropsy Survey, 1954-6.
Deaths from other than IHD, cerebrovascular
disease and associated conditions.

and ischaemic heart disease—for example table XLVII. The strong class trend in *females* points to important general, social-economic, causes rather than to specifically occupational causes.

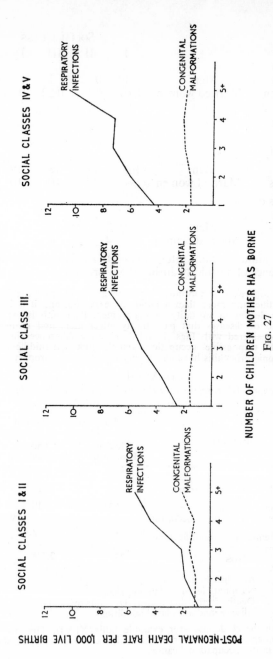

FIG. 27

Mortality from bronchitis and pneumonia, four weeks to one year of age. Relationship with social class, and size of family. 1949-50. England and Wales. (cf. Table XII, p. 59.)[24]

208

The difficulty with such a discussion is that social-economic circumstances and air pollution are so highly interrelated. Thus the more prosperous will live in the cleaner parts of towns from which, as Farr in his time already showed, the prevailing winds carry away the smoke. The " social conditions " long known to foster bronchitis, however, are not just a question of dirty air, nor does atmospheric pollution simply reflect social deprivation. Here is one way of expressing this:

Correlation
r bronchitis mortality and domestic air pollution (a) $+ \cdot 68$
r bronchitis mortality and social index*   (b) $+ \cdot 72$
r bronchitis mortality and (a), keeping (b) constant $+ \cdot 33 \cdot 01 > P > \cdot 001$
r bronchitis mortality and (b), keeping (a) constant $+ \cdot 44$

Combining the index of domestic *air pollution* in the county boroughs (a) with the index of *social conditions* (b) their joint correlation with the bronchitis mortality of these towns is 0·82. That is to say, two-thirds of the " variance " between the county boroughs in mortality from bronchitis among middle-aged men is so explained (0·82 × 0·82 = 0·67). This is a remarkably high value in view of the inaccuracy of some or much of the diagnosis, and the crudeness of the environmental measures.

Poverty may operate by lowering general resistance, and through such special causes as inadequate convalescence from acute respiratory illness. Jobs in social classes I and II differ manifestly from those in classes III-V; it is not yet clear to what extent dusty work, in foundries for example, is a cause of chronic bronchitis.[11] As said, outdoor workers in heavily polluted towns have more of the disease than indoor workers.[6] There is little of interest in comparison of adult smoking habits in different social classes, page 197. The infective component is probably crucial in Fig. 27 but, in general, little is known about the connection of children's illnesses—they are usually acute— with the chronic disease of middle age; they could be

---

* A composite one, using six measures of adverse social conditions. Males aged 45-64, 83 County Boroughs of England and Wales, 1948-54.

precursors.[23] (An observation which may be relevant is that early life in Britain is associated with a higher risk of lung cancer among emigrants to S. Africa and New Zealand,[4][5] conceivably as the result of early imprinting of pathology in the lungs.) The concentration of bronchitis in the lower social classes is probably due to a combination of actual " breeding ' of the disease by unfavourable environment, and of downward " drift "—many bronchitics have to give up customary outdoor and strenuous jobs and take less skilled work on account of their disability.[15] To disentangle the effects of these various possible causes cannot be done at the stage chronic bronchitis commonly presents in hospital. It requires prospective study of the disease from its beginnings, including the precursor cough, in defined populations (cf. page 131). Many individuals will need to be followed; and in relation to better environmental data.[7]

ENGLISH DISEASE

Rickets, the other English Disease, was also associated with atmospheric pollution. . . Certified mortality from bronchitis (chronic) in North America and in Scandinavia is only a small fraction of that in Britain, and differences in diagnosis, in the conventions of death certification, and in classification by the National Offices of Vital Statistics, probably account for little of this contemporary disgrace. (Mortality is now rising in the U.S.A.; it is not yet clear to what extent this is due to the greater interest in these conditions, and their better recognition, that has been stimulated by international comparative study, cf. page 15.) The childhood history—including the conditions of urban squalor in which so many contemporary middle-aged Britons were brought up—continuing air pollution, our climate perhaps, ubiquitous winter infections, and heavy cigarette smoking could all be responsible in some part. Research in a number of countries is now under way, using the MRC questionnaire,[1][18] and it appears that the main difference is the excess in the U.K. of chronic infection, rather than merely of the earlier productive cough.

PREVENTION OF CHRONIC BRONCHITIS

The suggestion, thus, from current work is that many causes are contributing to the incidence, prevalence, severity and mortality of chronic bronchitis.[1][20][23] Only a minority of persons exposed to these insults suffer from the disease, but characteristic of the whole field of chronic disease little is known of what is involved in this predisposition and selection. There is no sure indication yet of any specific cause, though there is a strong hint of it in cigarette smoking. In view of the manifold processes that are involved, the variety of clinical pictures, and the apparent multiplicity of interacting causes it would not be surprising if it turns out that there is no necessary agent, and that several distinct clinical-social syndromes eventually are identified within " chronic bronchitis ".

However much remains to be discovered, there is plenty of indication for action that offers hope of relief. For example: *primary* prevention by a reduction in cigarette smoking, by helping smokers to give up the habit when they start the " precursor " cough, and by lessening pollution at the least to levels where the symptoms of those with the disease are unaffected by it; *secondary* prevention, by early treatment of infection and, possibly, by change of residence and job for those with increasing infection; *tertiary* prevention, by anticipating trouble—in cold weather, in fog and in 'flu epidemics, for the vulnerable people with established disease; and possibly by using antibiotics through the winter to prevent increase of tissue destruction and of disability.

REDISCOVERY OF BYSSINOSIS[1][2][3][4][5]

In the six years following the establishment of the compensation scheme in 1941, 39 men of some 15,000 cotton workers at risk were certified as " totally disabled " by byssinosis. Lancashire regarded the disease as a small and diminishing problem. Modern methods of dust control were generally believed to be successful, and the few men developing byssinosis were thought to be victims of environmental conditions that had been overcome. Chronic bronchitis moreover is the plague of air-polluted Lancashire, and local people considered the little byssinosis that was recognised to be part of this prevalent chest disease aggravated by exposure to an irritant dust. Unexpectedly, in 1947, the health of cotton workers was brought to the fore. On the basis of occupational mortality rates, the *British Medical Journal* suggested that they suffered excessively from hypertension and heart disease, and Schilling carried out a field survey to test this notion. He found little of interest in the blood pressures: instead a quite unexpected amount of respiratory disease was exposed. Of 131 typical middle-aged card and blowroom workers he examined, two-thirds suffered from " Monday feeling ", the characteristic symptom of byssinosis—a tightness of the chest, which may be exceedingly unpleasant, after the weekend break—and 12 per cent were severely disabled. The common impression that byssinosis had been conquered seemed to be grossly overoptimistic, based obviously on the tip of an iceberg.

Schilling then made a further survey, focusing now on respiratory disease and, since there are no characteristic X-ray findings in byssinosis, he took particular care to standardise the " history " and produce a questionnaire that would be reproducible and valid. The table shows good agreement between the observers engaged in this survey:

Prevalence of Byssinosis: Comparison of Gradings by Two Observers

183 Male Cotton Workers aged 40-59

			OBSERVER A		
			Normal 79	Grade I 67	Grade II 37	Total 183
B Normal	78	72	6	0
OBSERVER Grade I	70	6	47	17
Grade II	35	1	14	20
Total	183			

Complete reproducibility in $72+47+20=139$ (76%); agreement on the presence or absence of byssinosis in $139+14+17=170$ (93%).

Normal = no evidence of byssinosis.
Grade I = chest tightness on Mondays only.
Grade II = chest tightness on Mondays and other working days.

Observer A found 79 men normal; Observer B 78; they agreed about 72 of them.

Half the men, the observers thus agreed, were suffering from the disease (and none of the " controls " examined in a local engineering works gave the pathognomonic history). In addition, a test of ventilatory capacity was used and it was found that among men of the same age, maximum breathing capacity was lowest in those with grade II byssinosis, intermediate in the presence of grade I disease, and highest in cotton workers who were " normal ". The more objective test, *i.e.*, confirmed the validity of the classic symptom.

By now it was clear from the field studies that the clinical syndrome of byssinosis is quite different from chronic bronchitis. In early byssinosis there is little cough, spit, or chest infection but, instead, tightness of the chest and a fall in ventilatory capacity. In the later stages the clinical picture does become confused, operatives frequently suffer from both these common diseases, chronic bronchitis as well as byssinosis; and cor pulmonale leads only too often at the end to the misleading occupational mortality statistics of " heart disease " among cotton workers. Extension of the survey to Holland confirmed the distinction between the two diseases. Byssinosis is almost as common in Dutch as Lancashire mills spinning similar types of cotton, but chronic bronchitis is of course the " English disease " and there is less of it in Holland.

By leaving the hospital, with its concentration of advanced and complicated cases, and moving into the community and the cotton mills, Schilling was able to detect the disease at its beginnings and to observe its unfolding. He was also able to complete the clinical picture in other ways. Thus the reputed absence of byssinosis in women is a fallacy: most of the women disabled by it presented themselves at the chest clinic or general practitioner's surgery as Lancashire housewives suffering from " bronchitis ", and the occupational history to disclose they had left the mills because of chronic respiratory trouble was not taken. The same is true of the reported immunity of old men. That is to say, the clinical picture of byssinosis based on hospital experience was as wrong in its way as the mortality statistics: wrong about sex and age, wrong also on the natural history and, above all, tragically wrong on the size of the problem and its impact on the population. How it comes about that so much was missed is another of those mysteries. . . . For the individual operative in his forties and older, the prospects of a job in his home town, apart from cotton, is often bleak, and there is an understandable if inexcusable reluctance to probe—and draw the lessons —by management and Unions, by a contracting industry already under grave strain, and a community chronically beset by economic crises. The contrast with Welsh miners and their pneumoconiosis however remains remarkable. In Lancashire it is at least true that native understatement, belittling the symptoms, was in some measure responsible; and this may be connected with the peculiarity of an industry in which men and women work alongside each other doing the same jobs.

In Search of the Agent

To incriminate the specific cause in cotton manufacture may be crucial for prevention; and it is being progressively achieved. Surveys of different mills showed that the disease is far commoner when medium and coarse grades are spun:

Prevalence of Byssinosis and Type of Mill
Men aged 40-59 Years

COTTON MANUFACTURE	NUMBER AT RISK	NUMBER WITH BYSSINOSIS
Fine	51	18
Medium	75	46
Coarse	75	52

$X^2 = 15 \cdot 06$, $P < 0 \cdot 001$.

The attack rate is remarkably high. Next, a strong and direct relationship was shown between the prevalence of symptoms and proximity to the carding engines, the dustiest process. These figures for female operatives with similar years of exposure are typical:

Prevalence of Byssinosis and Type of Work
Women aged 40-59 Years

OCCUPATION	NUMBER AT RISK	NUMBER WITH BYSSINOSIS
Near card engines	109	51
Distant from card engines	109	25
Ring spinners	61	2

Such findngs removed the last doubt that there is a specific cause in the local working environment. Incidentally, because there are more women than men working in the card rooms, more women than men in fact suffer from byssinosis. It was now possible to begin to define the *risk* in terms of dose-response relationships, of prevalence of disease and dust exposure. These are the details of a combined clinical-environmental survey:

YEARS OF EXPOSURE TO COTTON	PREVALENCE OF BYSSINOSIS	CONCENTRATION OF DUST MG PER M^3				
		0 –	1·0	1·75	2·5	3·75+
-9	No. at risk	31	79	37	28	34
	No. affected	0	0	2	5	15
10-19	No. at risk	23	30	29	22	26
	No. affected	0	1	4	9	14
20+	No. at risk	27	51	24	9	8
	No. affected	0	5	5	4	5

(The investigators looked at sex and age separately but did not find them to be important factors.)

While exposure for less than 20 years to dustiness less than 1·75 mg/m³ seems reasonably safe, the target clearly should be 1 or less mg/m.³ Above 3·75 mg/m³ the prevalence levels off at 50-60 per cent of the operatives exposed-to-risk. Here already is an instrument for primary environmental control; and it is time now to campaign for this knowledge to be applied in the mills, and to study the technical, educational and financial issues that are involved. An additional approach to prevention—secondary—also awaits implementation: to detect workers with the beginnings of " Monday feeling ", or subclinical disease as evidence by impaired ventilatory function, and advise them to leave the industry. Possible implications of that, in present-day Lancashire, have already been indicated.

Cigarette smoking, it has been suggested, is a general factor of respiratory disease. It reduces ventilatory capacity, damages the bronchial mucosa, may initiate chronic bronchitis and be the specific agent of epidemic lung cancer. As expected. smokers are vulnerable to byssinosis, these operatives for example:

Prevalence of Byssinosis : Smokers and Non-smokers
Female Card-room Workers

	NUMBER AT RISK	AFFECTED WITH BYSSINOSIS	MEDIAN AGE	MEAN YEARS OF EXPOSURE TO COTTON
Non-smokers	144	62	39	14
Smokers	82	52	28	9

$X^2 = 7.87$, $P < 0.01$

Field Survey and Laboratory Experiment

In the advance of medical knowledge, the three main methods of learning—clinical observation, laboratory experiment, population survey—have their characteristic parts; each makes its own contribution and raises questions for study by the others as well as testing notions derived from them. The recent exploration of byssinosis illustrates a particularly fruitful collaboration between laboratory workers and epidemiologist, clinicians having described the disease for them over

100 years ago. Much is being learned on mechanisms of byssinosis (pathogenesis), and on the nature of the agent and other causes (aetiology).

Field studies, continuing those described, showed that exposure to very small particles of cotton dust had an acute and specific lowering effect on ventilatory capacity in the cotton operatives, thus indicating that a substance in the dust produced bronchial constriction or mucosal swelling. The *pharmacologists* confirmed that extracts of cotton dust did indeed contract smooth muscle preparations in animals and in isolated human bronchial muscle. *Field* study then showed that this extract is unlikely to arise, as often suggested, from bacterial or mould action on the bales of cotton which commonly lie for months in damp warehouses in Liverpool: the disease was discovered also in the earliest processes of handling cotton, before it is baled for export, among the ginnery workers engaged in the first cleaning of the cotton when it is picked in Egypt—they have chest tightness on Saturdays! These various experiments of opportunity in Africa and Holland and elsewhere rule out the notion that the climate of Lancashire—admittedly unspeakable—or the local air pollution, are important causes of the disease. (The role of bronchial infection has yet to be clarified.) What may prove to be a crucial contribution was next made in the *laboratory*: that the toxic extract causing muscle constriction is present in the leaves only of the cotton, and not in the cotton fluff or in the seeds. This finding may transform the problem of primary prevention—it should be easier to remove the leaves at source than it is to extract the very fine dust in the mills.

A Dangerous Trade

Present estimates, after many years of improved ventilation, are that 3-4,000 of 10-15,000 workers exposed to cotton dust may be suffering from byssinosis. These are the *figures* for *disability* including *partial disablement* from the disease, in both sexes, since 1956:

	1957-9	1960-2
New Disability Pensions	910	1,172
Recorded Deaths	122	110

These pensions figures underestimate somewhat the total misery because some workers compensated under another scheme are excluded.

" ECOLOGY " OF MENTAL DISORDERS[2 9 18 20 36 40 45]

The title pays tribute to Faris and Dunham's study in Chicago (1939) which opened the modern era of research into the epidemiology of psychosis. Examining mental hospital admissions for schizophrenia these investigators found a striking excess from the slum centre of the city, from the " skid rows " near the railway termini with their seedy rooming houses and population of down-and-outs; the lowest rates, conversely, were among the stable population of the outer residential areas. Manic-depressive and senile psychoses showed quite different distributions.[12] In recent years there have been many such observations—evidently, mental disorder is strongly connected with the mode of life. It is equally evident that multiple causes, genetic and environmental, biologic as well as social, are somehow involved, and since epidemiology offers the main hope of investigating such situations psychiatric population studies have multiplied in recent years. Up to now, unhappily, this activity has yielded few new facts, a deficiency somewhat obscured by the communicativeness of psychiatrists and social scientists.

It is scarcely surprising that little has been learned of aetiology, so intractable is the nature of much of the material.[18 25 39 50] Earlier (p. 48) I have remarked how troublesome it is to agree on what is a " case " and achieve a reproducible diagnosis. Recognition is easy only when there is gross disorder of mental function and social relations. When disorder does not involve the whole personality, and is of minor severity, it can be very troublesome to state criteria on which a person is to be regarded as ill or not. Definition of what is healthy or unhealthy in human behaviour is usually quantitative, differing from the average merely in degree, but over a great range. The definition will vary according to the culture, which means shifting in time as well as relative to place.[9] [22] Practical problems of investigation are handled often by description of symptoms. This of course may be rewarding: symptoms have meaning, but various and perhaps opposite meanings. That a person is anxious tells us little, if anything, about aetiology. A family may be peaceable because harmonious, or it may merely be conforming and liable to crack under the first stress. It is essential if often very difficult to know what lies beyond the surface of the behaviour being observed. On the other hand the same psychological forces can result in diverse mental, physical and social effects—consider the many faces of violence, of depression, or self-destruction. The same kind of " overprotective " family situation seems to be found as often as it is looked for in a multitude of " psychosomatic " and other disorders.[15] Be all this as it may, there is a tragic dearth at present of hard fact on the causes of many mental disorders, though in some, suicide and senile psychosis for example, we already know enough to begin to think of programmes that will disrupt the pattern of causation.[3]

Faris and Dunham's observations touched off a controversy that is still very much alive. Is it that these unsatisfactory social circumstances with their multiple deprivations *breed* an excess incidence of schizophrenia? Or, interesting enough but less explanatory, is it merely that victims of such illnesses—perhaps in their early subclinical stage or even in precursor disorder of personality—*drift* down the social scale because of their illness, gather in these areas of the city because of their inability to cope and their need to withdraw from emotional ties and demands? Classically in the old, deteriorated city centres, often crowded and squalid, there is, or was as in Chicago, a clustering of social pathology, of poverty and crime, prostitution and venereal disease, broken families and deprived children, premature death, mental disorder. A transient population is attracted, standards of behaviour are often ill-defined, there is poor communication and little social cohesion, individuals are isolated. Does the personal chaos of schizophrenia derive from the social disorganisation that so moulds the thought patterns of the child genetically predisposed to the disease? Or is there a high prevalence of schizophrenia in these areas for the same reasons that bring others there who are incompetent or incapacitated? In brief, is there social generation of the disease, or social segregation and selection by it?

The answer from two complementary studies of occupation and social class in schizophrenic patients and their families seems clear enough for this country, at any rate, and for the present time.[16][46] (Straightaway it must be said that further studies of the schizophrenia rate in various places, areas of cities for example—the kind of community diagnosis that used to be called " ecology "—is unlikely to take this particular question much further. What are needed are direct studies of the careers of appropriate individuals and families.) Goldberg made a *clinical field-survey* of a consecutive series of young men admitted for schizophrenic disorders to an ordinary district mental hospital, not a very tidy sample even of this particular universe, but common sense suggests unlikely to be misleading. The clinical material breathes life into the statistics; it assures some uniformity of diagnosis, the considered assessment of practising psychiatrists over a period of years and reflecting probably the current mode in Britain; and it also provides much sociological data. She found that the paternal social-economic career and the outward situation of the families were quite unremarkable (this applied also to grandfathers, uncles and sibs): there was nothing unusual in the occupational models that were presented to the children Table XLVIII (A). The failure of the young men on the other

TABLE **XLVIII**

Social " Drift " and Schizophrenia[16][46]

(A)

SOCIAL CLASS OF CONSECUTIVE SAMPLE OF MALE PATIENTS
UNDER 30 YEARS OF AGE ADMITTED TO A MENTAL HOSPITAL
IN GREATER LONDON; AND OF THEIR FAMILIES
1958-62

SOCIAL CLASS	PATIENTS		FATHERS	OTHER MALE FIRST-DEGREE RELATIVES Main Job
	At First Admission	Last Known*	Main Job	
I and II**	8	1	15	54
III	21	15	25	129
IV	7	11	5	21
V	14	7	7	24
No occu-pation	—	18	—	11
?	2	—	—	26

* After 2-4 years' follow-up.
** Including students.

(B)

SOCIAL CLASS OF NATIONAL SAMPLE OF MALE PATIENTS
AGED 25-34 YEARS ADMITTED FOR THE FIRST TIME TO A
MENTAL HOSPITAL; AND OF THEIR FATHERS WHEN THESE
PATIENTS WERE BORN

1956

England and Wales

SOCIAL CLASS	PATIENTS		FATHERS	
	Observed	Expected*	Observed	Expected*
I	12	12	14	8
II	21	44	42	42
III	178	203	192	191
IV	52	55	66	68
V	90	39	55	59
?	18	—	2	—

* " Expected," on the national distribution at the relevant Census.

hand was striking. At school sometimes, but commonly in late adolescence, as the case studies showed, they proved unable to make the grade. Some did not start at all on the jobs that were hoped for them, some dropped after a while into routine or unskilled work carrying little responsibility, others in whom the illness developed acutely collapsed shortly before admission into unskilled work or out of the labour market altogether. Thus by the time they arrived in a mental hospital the social-economic status of the patients was often much below that of their family. (The " incidence " is the crucial figure of course in studying aetiology; it is often very difficult to date the beginning of a condition like schizophrenia, but definition of incidence by the " first admission to mental hospital " is manifestly too late.[6][33]) Morrison, Table XLVIII (B), corroborated this observation by a *documentary study* of specially drawn national samples of first admissions to mental hospitals. He found the customary excess of young men diagnosed schizophrenic in Class V, the miscellaneous labourers, kitchen hands, etc. Then he confirmed from the birth certificates of the young men that when they were born their fathers at that time were normally distributed by social class.* The sons *i.e.* were not born disproportionately into social class V and, again, there is wide discrepancy between performance of father and son. The correct answer was obtained by asking not merely what social class the patients were in, but how they got there (p. 43). Both studies depended on hospital data with their many limitations. But there was nothing in the composition of the clinical series, the picture of disease severity for example, to suggest that selection of patients for admission was responsible for the deficit from social classes I-III or the excess from class V.

The fact that " drift " downwards is responsible for the social concentration of schizophrenia has thus been established

---

* This is another example of the use of official, administrative records for medical research; on this occasion two routine documents (the mental hospital admission card and the birth certificate) were linked in a new way to provide valuable data on familial aspects of disease (p. 131). The information used is simple and probably unbiased, therefore valid enough— and there is a lot of it.

in two independent studies, a decline between the generations as well as in the subjects themselves. The relationship of schizophrenia and social class evidently is close, but, the evidence suggests, the social distribution is consequence not cause of the disease.[6][21][31][34] The production of schizophrenia is widespread through the population; the disease indeed seems to be common throughout the world, which points to major genetic rather than environmental causes.

Social Deprivation

The consequences of social pathology for psychopathology may be evident in other mental disorders than schizophrenia. Multiple genes evidently are involved in *low (measured) intelligence,* the feeble-minded " subnormal " end of the distribution curve. It could be that an element of foetal brain damage also is often present. But the poor performance of deprived groups, racial as well as social-economic, in meeting the demands of the " culture " is compounded, it becomes increasingly apparent, by the denial of elementary physical, emotional and economic needs. Children in these circumstances suffer from lack of stimulation (" input "), of opportunity to develop and exercise intellect and communication—in bad schools for example—from the wasting away of that which is not used. Their low IQ may also be a result of the differing outlook and motivation, and the lower standards of these underprivileged groups.[4][26][28][35][37][42][48] (Of course some will have drifted down into them because of their low intelligence —that is another side of it.)

Early experiences and interpersonal relationships are crucial in personality development. The " complete disruption of *mother-child* relationship by death or serious illness is much less common now than it was fifty or even thirty years ago ", writes Carstairs; " but what of the quality of that relationship when it is not interrupted? Bowlby claims that a child experiencing maternal deprivation in infancy may become peculiarly susceptible to psychiatric disorders in later life (and that) maternal deprivation occurs when mother and child fail to establish a ' warm, intimate and continuous relationship in which both find satisfaction and enjoyment '. . . It is difficult to believe that maternal care of this quality was very common in the slums of our large cities either in the early years of the century or during the depression of the 1930's— or even today. Close family ties can exist in spite of overcrowding and poverty, but on the whole the younger children of a large slum family are unlikely to enjoy relationships with their harassed mothers ' in which both find satisfaction and enjoyment ' . . ."[10] relative, at least to the more privileged sections of the community. Supporting epidemiologic—and other—data are conflicting as well as scanty, but the hypothesis makes very good sense. Relevant information is now being drawn from studies ranging widely from " problem " families to the ethology of animal development.[1 5 6 27 38 47]

(2) MODERN WORLD

Where epidemiological enquiry, illuminated by the social or " behavioural " sciences, should be making a solid contribution is in helping to define typical contemporary social strains and pressures, and investigating whether they result in changes in the nature, presentation or frequency of mental disorders. I have already referred (p. 14) to this classic and most difficult of questions that has been asked very often since the upheavals of the American and French Revolutions,[43] but as yet there are few answers. History may well repeat itself and study of disease lead to the identification of significant social pressures—and not vice versa. Perhaps it is too much to expect anything else, but the epidemiologic notion of vulnerable groups is surely applicable here. Physical, mental and social health are now being studied in the " acculturation " of the developing nations, often exposed overnight to independence, urban life and advanced technology, uprooted and deprived of the traditional supports of tribal custom and kinship. Peculiar neurotic and psychosomatic disorders are being seen, the exacerbation of violence, and such " Western " phenomena as rising juvenile delinquency.[23][24] The biologic and social results of the disruption of a stable culture that accompanied the rapid growth of towns and factories during the Industrial Revolution in England may be recalled. Responses to the social upheavals of modern Britain, to its confusions and absurdity, have been little identified as yet in greater, or lesser, or different mental illness. Delinquency may be increasing and other social pathology in young people probably is (p. 27). There seems to be a great deal of minor depression in the population nowadays, but no statistics and little social analysis of it. Likewise, the causes of epidemic cigarette smoking and alcohol addiction, of modern-epidemic dependence on barbiturates, tranquillisers and amphetamine are being little studied. (Each society has its tensions and stress disorders, and its legitimised modes of relief.)* The rise of the suicide rate in middle-aged and elderly women has already been mentioned; many causes are surely involved, but loneliness and isolation may be increasing[45]—and " resignation "[11] and " retreat ".[29] In middle-aged men, the new vulnerable group, nothing specific has yet been described on the psychological aspects, and the functional component of Table IV (page 11) for example, remains to be investigated. Investigators in the USA[44] are relating a behaviour pattern of competitive striving dominated by time schedules on an incessant treadmill of work, the victims never having " a

---

* I cannot forbear to pass on this comment about the fashionable notion of a sick society: " To say that a society is neurotic may mean that institutions and practices characteristic of the society contribute significantly to the development of neurosis in individuals, and that their behaviour, in turn, reinforces those very practices. A society which ceaselessly stimulates sexuality while condemning its gratification, that rewards competitiveness while extolling benevolence, that values ends for which it denies the means —such a society might be expected to generate conflicts, guilt, and anxiety in its members. And we can also expect that they, in turn, will seek out and support those institutional patterns which answer to their neurotic needs. . . There are those who see the individual and society as caught up in a vicious circle: a sick society cannot nurture the growth of a healthy personality, nor can sick minds create and sustain healthy institutions. But we need only read the circle in reverse, and it is no longer vicious. Mature individuals, rational and realistic, can make some contribution to social sanity; and as social patterns improve, we can look to the growth of freer and more creative personalities. . ."[8]

day to call their own ", to the prevalence of ischaemic heart disease both in men and women. So far, this psychological explanation is the only one to be offered of the peculiarly high rate of IHD in America. A prospective study now under way will test this hypothesis, and at the same time estimate its contribution to the total picture of ischaemic heart disease. Meanwhile, it must be noticed that Russian descriptions of psychological factors in the disease are similar to the American.[32]

(3) SOCIAL GROUPS

The third theme I want to take up in this section is that of the social group and its influence on mental health. Many of the " populations " and " groups " that have been described in this text are, in fact, " aggregates " of individuals with particular properties, often collected and defined ad hoc for the purposes of study. Thus the shape of *8,400 busmen* was investigated, or a *sample* of *young men* admitted to the country's mental hospitals for *schizophrenia* was drawn from the records. By " aggregate " the point is intended that either there is no interaction, mutual influence, feedback, between them—any contact between the schizophrenics obviously was coincidental —or, if there is such interaction—as there must be among the busmen—this, so far as present thinking goes, is not relevant to the question at issue.

Groups in which interaction does occur between its members are true *social groups,* and the term is used to denote that this property is involved. (Unfortunately, there is no better name that avoids altogether the ambiguity in the word " group ", and its specific meaning has often to be taken from the context.) The social groups to which people belong, family, work the larger community; special groups like the hospital; groups of fellow-casualties; normal or deviant groups, seem to be of great moment in mental function. What individuals feel and think and see (and complain of), the kinds of relationships they have with others, all these it may be postulated are potential in inheritance, developed in the family, and continuously relearned through life-experience in the changing groups to which they belong. Modes of perception, norms of behaviour, the predominant system of values are properties of social groups (and the institutions they build) and they profoundly affect the members with their manifold inheritance and early experience. The incidence, form and concentration of mental disorders, it must therefore be expected, will be closely related to the nature of group relationships in the social environment. Bowlby's " separation " hypothesis is about the long-term consequence of elementary social deprivation in the family at the most critical period of development. The " breeder " hypothesis on schizophrenia is very crudely about the way children with particular predispositions fare in particular families and communities. The hypothesis that social isolation is a cause of senile psychosis and of suicide is about communication (and the lack of it) in groups.[17][45] The " social breakdown syndrome " that may arise from the dehumanising effects of life in institutions—any institution—(page 141), is the most tragic of the disorders produced by faulty social relationships;[3][14] (in contrast the potential therapeutic role of a hospital community is beginning to be appreciated, and again mainly in the mental hospital).[39] The changing manifestations of neurosis and psychosomatic disorder (p. 19) are to be regarded in terms of changing people in a changing social environment. As I write, another race riot, in the North-east of England this time, is a reminder of " socially shared psychopathology ".[19] Psychic " epidemics " have long been recognised; analogies with the propagation of infectious disease are evident in the spread of neurosis or delinquent behaviour, they were obvious to the Greeks and the point need not be laboured. What we have come to appreciate better perhaps is how much mental health, too, is communicable.

Social Relations in Industry.—I have already referred to the role of work in physical metabolism. However boring and

unsatisfying it may be, work also plays a key part in the psychological equilibrium of the individual, attaching him firmly to
reality.[13] The work group is the principal social group after the
family, and mental health at work must again become a central
area for social-medical enquiry.[30] Epidemiological study has

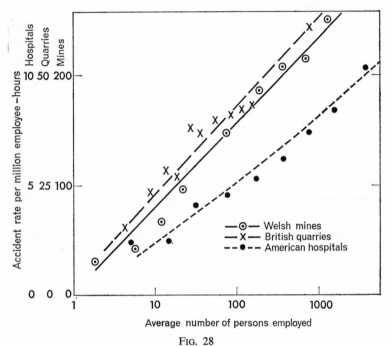

Fig. 28

Accidents in employees of Welsh mines, British quarries and American
hospitals: the average rate in a recent period in relation to the size of the
social unit.

REVANS, R. W. (1960). In *Modern Trends in Occupational Health.* Ed.,
Schilling, R. S. F. Butterworth & Co. (Publishers) Ltd. London.

made several kinds of contribution. Fig. 28 illustrates a correlation between occupational-social structure and individual
functioning. Both quality and quantity of social interaction,
informal as well as formal, will vary with the size of the unit,
and the technology thus represented. Such observation can be
the basis of a hypothesis, though in interpreting the findings
it should be remembered that the larger units may also have

the more efficient reporting systems, etc. (life is like that, especially for social scientists).

*   *   *

Social groups then are a large part of the social environment that is crucial in mental health. There has been far too little systematic study of individual capacity and social well-being, and of neurosis and incapacity, in relation to group membership; and epidemiological methods have been too little applied to these questions. Experiments of opportunity are ubiquitous and promising: it is often a reasonable beginning that people bring similar personal predispositions with them into different social environments. Different schools drawing the children from families living in the same neighbourhood—yield very varied delinquency rates;[46] recruits may in effect be randomly selected into different military units—with what consequences in health?; different factories engage workers with presumably similar personality difficulties—and produce diverse rates of accidents, sickness-absence, labour turnover, etc.; similar patients are admitted to district mental hospitals—with what variation in secondary disability?. . .[7][49] The prospects are bright for the joint enterprise of epidemiologists, students of social structure and of group dynamics.

CANCER IN THE REPORTS OF THE GENERAL REGISTER OFFICE

A hundred thousand deaths per year are certified to cancer in England and Wales. Since William Farr's days the staff of the GRO have used death certificates as an instrument for learning, and in cancer as in many other fields much interesting and important information has accumulated. The Tables that follow are all taken direct from publications of the GRO, or calculated from raw data they provide. I try to illustrate the range of available information on natural history as well as aetiology, and some of the highlights, but make little comment; and needless to say there is no attempt to be comprehensive about what indeed is now a whole literature.

TABLE XLIX

Mortality from Cancer at Different Ages[7][8]

1958-60

England and Wales

Rates per 100,000 per Year

	AGE			
	35-	45-	55-	65-74
MEN				
ALL SITES	53	203	596	1,160
Stomach	6·6	29	87	190
Lung, etc.	17	91	280	414
Prostate	0·1	1·6	16	91
Bladder	0·9	4·8	20	52
WOMEN				
ALL SITES	70	186	348	619
Stomach	3·8	13	36	97
Lung, etc.	4·9	14	29	42
Breast	20	56	76	106
Cervix Uteri	10	17	22	29
Corpus Uteri	0·8	4·2	13	19
Ovary	5·7	19	32	35

Sex and Age

Analysis of cancer mortality by sex and age makes an admirable introduction to the RG's data, so many questions immediately arise, there are so many possible clues to causes. The *Commentary* volume for 1952 which should be in every medical library contains much historical material, and the information is brought up to date annually.[8] Considering first the force of mortality with age in *women* (Table XLIX), the differences are very interesting. In fact, mortality in cancer of the cervix rises sharply till the late forties, in breast cancer till the early fifties, in ovarian cancer till the late fifties and in cancer of the corpus uteri till the early sixties; after these ages the death rates climb only a little.

In *men* total cancer mortality quadruples, broadly speaking, from 35-44 to 45-54 years of age, trebles from 45-54 to 55-64 years of age, then doubles again from 55-64 to 65-74 years of age. In cancer of the stomach (?strongly environmental) the trend with age is steeper; in prostatic cancer (?hormone-dependent) there is no appreciable mortality till the late fifties, then it soars. Such facts may be crucial when formulating theoretical models of the mechanisms of carcinogenesis.[1] Lung-cancer has a peculiar trend that rises sharply till the late fifties or early sixties, then flattens, then actually falls.*

Cohort Study.—Table LI has already been anticipated, p. 30, and the remark on age just made is pertinent. " The danger when studying age-specific death rates " writes Case[3] [4] " is that it is easy to be misled into thinking that the rates for consecutive age groups in any given year, say the age groups 45-49, 50-54, 55-59 and so on, form a series of rates that reflects (only) the effect of age on susceptibility to cancer, an error that may sometimes cause serious misunderstanding. The people in the age group 55-59 in 1960 are, of course, the sur-vivors of those who were in age group 50-54 in 1955, who are in turn the survivors of those in age group 45-49 in 1950, and so on: that is to say, they are the survivors of those born in the years 1901-1905. If we wish to study the effect of age on the death rate we must, therefore, go back into the past and study

---

*

TABLE L

Lung-Cancer Mortality in Men

1960-1

Rates per 100,000 p.a.

AGE	40-	45-	50-	55-	60-	65-	70-	75-	80-84
	24	57	123	232	361	436	447	401	288

England and Wales.

The correct term is cancer of the bronchus, or bronchogenic cancer.

the age-specific death rates of a group of people born within a fairly small defined number of years, and the survivors of that group through the ensuing years "—thus including the effects of experience as well as of ageing itself.

A group of people born in a defined period is called a cohort; and a study of the future history of such a group, of what happens to them, is called " cohort analysis ". This method makes it possible to associate the changing age-specific death rates with relevant environmental changes during the lifetimes of survivors from successive cohorts. It may be that a particular environmental influence asserts itself at different ages, in only one sex, or in varying sections of the whole community, and that the mortality in consecutive age groups in any given year reflects such influences as well as the effect of ageing. " Cohort analysis thus offers better chances of distinguishing between nature and nurture, and of correlating changes in the death rate with the social history of the period."[3] [4] [17]

For example : following the male cohorts born in successive periods from around 1875/6 onwards (the centre of each cohort being spaced five years apart), and studying their death rates from lung-cancer, we can see that the changes in mortality accord with the innovation of the cigarette, now postulated to be the agent of the modern epidemic of the disease. Since smoking of these in any quantity began during the first world war, the generation born around the turn of the century or born subsequently will have been maximally exposed : they were able to start smoking cigarettes in their 'teens. Previous generations will have developed the habit later in life, and exposure in consequence increased progressively in cohorts born during the latter part of the nineteenth century. Examining Table LI, it will be seen that this history of exposure is reflected in the increasing mortality from lung-cancer at each age of death in the cohorts born up till the turn of the century, and a levelling of these death rates in later cohorts. Moreover, the oldest now living will have spent a smaller part of their total adult life in the Age of the Cigarette, and in them it may be

TABLE LI

Cohort Analysis of Lung-Cancer Mortality in Men[7][16]

England and Wales

Age-Specific Death Rates of " Cohorts " Born Around 1875/6, etc.
per 100,000

COHORT BORN AROUND	AGE AT DEATH				
	40-44	45-49	50-54	55-59	60-64
1875/6	1·5	4·4	11	35	65
1880/1	2·7	7·6	26	59	102
1885/6	5·2	19	43	88	172
1890/1	8·7	27	60	135	255
1895/6	15	38	95	200	332
1900/1	19	54	122	232	—
1905/6	24	58	125	—	—
1910/1	25	59	—	—	—
1915/6	25	—	—	—	—

Death Rates in the Year:

1960*	24	58	123	234	(358)
1961**	24	55	123	229	(363)
1962**	22	56	124	234	(371)
1963**					

* Included in the last figure in each column of the Table.
** Not included in Table.
(The rates at age 60-64 seem to be settling now.)

postulated that the increasing predisposition to cancer with age has been counteracted by smaller exposure to the carcinogen—whence the peculiar trends of Table L.

Recent History of Cancer Mortality

Table LII, to return to a more conventional analysis, brings out the fact that, the lung apart, overall mortality from cancer in men has been falling. (The age illustrated has been selected to correspond to the discussion that opens this book.) Cancer of the bronchus is less common in women, and their total death rate from cancer has fallen appreciably. The historical trend now to be watched carefully is that of cancer of the stomach, the mortality of which recently began to fall in this country—about a quarter-century later than in the USA. The most remarkable feature in female mortality is the stability of the rate in cancer of the breast during a period that has seen heroic adjustments in therapy. The figures raise acutely the issues broached at the close of Chapter V. Little is known about the causes of these tumours, and less that can be applied. An attempt is now being made to study prospectively whether abnormalities of steroid (androgen) excretion that have been found in advanced disease are in fact *precursor* disorders which, at the least, indicate women particularly likely to be affected.[2] Present methods of detecting *early disease* are of doubtful efficacy, and the possible usefulness of soft tissue X-ray mammography is being investigated. About 5 per cent of women in this country may be expected to suffer cancer of the breast (p. 105), and about half of these to die of it. There is good evidence that in many of them the tumour is not so inherently malignant as to be hopeless from the start. In brief, here is a situation where a multiple and opportunist attack is needed to answer questions of control and prevention.

Town and Country

In Table LIII, page 237, the mortality of lung cancer in relation to the density of population or " urbanisation ", is

TABLE LII

Recent History of Mortality from Cancer[7] [8]

Ages 55-64

England and Wales

Death Rates per 100,000 per Year

SITE	1921-30	1960-1
MEN		
ALL SITES	467	602
Lung, Bronchus	13	288
All, less Lung, etc.	454	314
Mouth, tongue, etc.	46	5·7
Oesophagus	38	12
Stomach	106	86
Colon	51	31
Rectum	48	26
Liver, etc.	30	9·8
Pancreas	13	23
Prostate	16	15
Bladder	13	20
Brain	10*	14
Leukaemia	5·1*	11
WOMEN		
ALL SITES	417	350
Lung, Bronchus	5	31
All, less Lung, etc.	412	319
Stomach	67	34
Colon	51	33
Rectum	25	15
Liver, etc.	33	7·6
Pancreas	7·5	12
Breast	78	79
Cervix	22**	20
Corpus Uteri	3·9**	13
Ovary	16	33
Leukaemia	3·7*	7·9

* 1936-8.
** 1940-4.

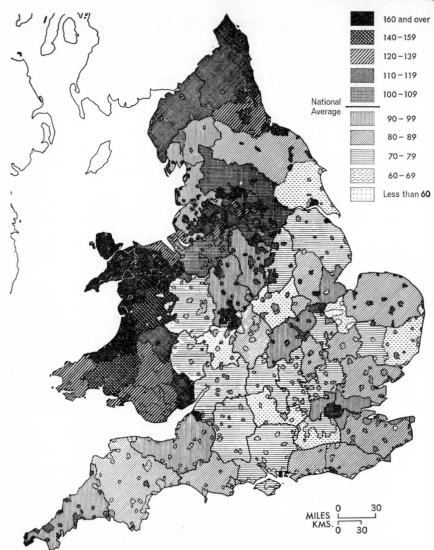

160 and over

140 – 159

120 – 139

110 – 119

100 – 109

National
Average

90 – 99

80 – 89

70 – 79

60 – 69

Less than 60

MILES
KMS.

0   30

0   30

CANCER OF THE STOMACH (MALES)

FIG. 29

Local differences in mortality from cancer of the stomach in England and
Wales. 1954-8. Men, all ages (the local rates are standardised by the
national average for differences in age composition).

HOWE, G. M. (1963). *National Atlas of Disease Mortality in the United
Kingdom.* Nelson & Sons. London.

The high mortality (≡incidence) in the districts of North and West Wales
was reported also in 1950-3.[9]

illustrated. The rate for men in London is three to four times that in the " truly rural " districts of England. The search for carcinogens in the atmospheric pollution that follows from urban-industrial living is now a very active field of inquiry.

TABLE LIII

Area Differences in Lung-Cancer[7] [9]
1950-53
England and Wales
Standardised Mortality Ratio*

POPULATION	MEN	WOMEN
England and Wales	100	100
London County	156†	149†
Conurbations	126	121
Urban Areas Population 100,000 + „ 50-100,000 „ -50,000	111 95 84	101 89 86
All Rural Districts " Truly Rural " Districts England „ „ „ Wales	64 48 33	76 67 56

* All ages; adjusted for age composition to the national experience.
† 1950-2[11]

Table XLIV, page 198, will be recalled; but of course smoking of cigarettes also started later in the rural districts, so these lung-cancer figures may underestimate the contribution of cigarettes to the areal differences in mortality. Another clue that has emerged from this kind of elementary " community diagnosis " and *analysis by place,* is the excess of cancer of the stomach in North and West Wales,[18] Fig. 29. This lead is now being followed-up by a large-scale ad hoc field survey: are there special diagnostic problems in this district?, have the inhabitants a special genetic composition?, do they have special dietary habits, etc.? Numbers are small in these counties, which presents its own problems of interpretation.

TABLE LIV

Mortality from Cancer in the Five Social Classes[10]

1949-53

England and Wales

Standardised Mortality Ratios at 20-64 Years

All Classes=100

SITE	SOCIAL CLASS				
	I	II	III	IV	V
MEN					
Stomach	57	70	101	112	130
Lung	81	82	107	91	118
Prostate	128	99	102	93	102
Testis	164	121	92	98	90
MARRIED WOMEN					
Lung	119	95	102	98	96
Breast	137	110	104	84	85
Cervix Uteri	64	75	98	105	134
Corpus Uteri	110	93	110	85	95

Social Class

Two trends are very clear among the women, Table LIV, above. The strong " poverty " trend in cervical cancer cannot be accounted for statistically by the excess of childbearing in social classes IV and V. The lower mortality ratios in these classes from cancer of the breast should also be noted (the gradient was far steeper in 1930-2). No ready explanation can be suggested for the experience in cancer of the lung which is so different from that in men.

Cancer and Fertility

If the death rate at 45-64 years of age among married women who have borne at least one child is regarded as unity, the differing ratios in Table LV for these four cancers are

TABLE LV

Fertility and Cancer in Women[8][13]

Mortality of Other Women Proportionate to that of
Fertile Married Women
1950-53
England and Wales
Ratios at Ages 45-64 Years

SITE	MARRIED AND FERTILE*	MARRIED AND INFERTILE	SINGLE
Breast	1	1·2†	1·4†
Cervix Uteri	1	0·7	0·4
Corpus Uteri	1	1·6	1·3
Ovary (and Fallopian Tubes)	1	1·7	1·4

* *i.e.* who have borne a child.
† 1948-9; estimated.

striking. The association of *cervical cancer* with the married state, and with the bearing of children, is particularly significant. Like the social class distribution (and the relationships with race and religious practices) it could be contingent on the factor of coital experience and personal (penile) hygiene.[19]

To sum up for two other cancers: there are several " clues " to causes in (fatal) *cancer of the breast*. The steep rise in mortality is co-terminous with the child-bearing period, the disease is less common among married women, in particular among women who have borne a child, and in the poorer sections of the population. These facts support the hypothesis that lactation is protective against the disease.[6][14][15]

In *cancer of the stomach,* the social class distribution is reminiscent of that for gastric ulcer (Fig. 18, page 142). The main points that have emerged from the Registrar General's Tables about this cancer are the trend of mortality with age, the secular decline, and the excessive rates in the lower income groups and in Wales: two of these facts at least point to strong environmental causes of this malignancy.

Operational Research into the workings of death certification as a step towards its improvement, appraisal of the quality of the certificates—how accurate they are, how complete, and what inferences may safely be drawn from them—is gradually being developed. The General Register Office have published interesting figures, for example these from a sample study of the standards of death certification for bronchogenic and stomach-cancer:

Accuracy of Diagnosis of Cancer on Death Certificates
Special Sample Study
Men and Women Under 65 years of age
1955
England and Wales

		FINDINGS		
SITE	No. OF CASES	Diagnosis *established* by post-mortem, operation, etc.	Diagnosis *supported* in consultation, etc.	Diagnosis unconfirmed, etc.
		%	%	%
Lung	361	68	28	4
Stomach	164	73	21	6

McKenzie, A. (1956). *Brit. med. J.* **2,** 204.
(There was c. 80% response to the study.)

In middle age, at any rate, neither the social class distribution of cancer of the stomach, nor the excess of lung-cancer in the great towns, are likely to be artefacts of errors in diagnosis. After 65 the diagnosis is so much less valid that it is highly questionable what the specific cause-of-death statistics are worth.*

* " In Sweden the reliability " (surely validity is intended?, p. 45) " of information on causes of death is checked by means of a stratified random sample of certificates from local registration areas representing the whole country. This might include 3-5 per cent of the total number of deceased persons, and every available measure is taken to ascertain the exact cause of death (*e.g.,* consultation of hospital case histories and information on post-mortem examinations). This sampling technique permits the establishment of confidence limits for estimates covering the whole country ".[5]

Morbidity—and the National Cancer Registration Scheme (NCRS)

Epidemiological data are beginning to be available from the NCRS which, as said, includes about three-quarters of the cancer that is now recognised in England and Wales. Lee's study of season and leukaemia (p. 149) depended entirely on such morbidity data.[12][16] The summer peak in the onset of acute lymphatic leukaemia of young people was evident only for the date of the first symptom, and not for the date of death (or of diagnosis). Unfortunately the NCRS is designed mainly for the routine gathering of information on questions of therapy and prognosis. It was by very good fortune that the date of the first symptom was available for the leukaemias. If the Registration Scheme is to fulfil its promise for epidemiological study, in particular of aetiology, it will need considerable modification. Readers working in British hospitals might enquire how the records are completed in their hospital and consider also how the Forms might be altered to serve more purposes than at present.

* * *

GEOGRAPHICAL PATHOLOGY [4][6][20][21][22][26]

The local variations in mortality from cancer of the stomach and cancer of the lung that are found within so small a country as our own are a further illustration of the potential value of comparative studies. (In conditions with such high case-fatality the death rate also measures, near enough, prevalence and incidence.) The term " geographical pathology " is usually reserved for comparisons between countries; it is one aspect of World Medicine. In seeking clues to causes, the geographical method has been particularly fruitful in ischaemic heart disease and in cancer.

As is well known, one of the few facts about ischaemic heart disease is that the half or even two-thirds of the world which is very poor suffers little from it. This observation has led to much enquiry and speculation and it is a main plank of the current dietary hypothesis. The low incidence of IHD among peoples at an early stage of social and economic development is associated with low mean blood cholesterol levels; these, it is suggested in turn, reflect poor nutrition and in particular a low intake of animal and dairy (saturated) fats. Genetic factors also may well be important in the immunity of such populations to IHD. It is interesting therefore that mortality in men from IHD among the (selected) middle-aged Japanese emigré population in Hawaii is substantially higher than among coevals in Japan and, a move further West, mortality among Japanese men in USA resembles that in white Americans.[7] [9] The other " geographical " observation that has strongly affected recent thinking was made in Norway: during the war the death rate from cardiovascular disease fell, and, of course, there was a concurrent reduction in fat intake. It is an equally interesting " international " fact that in early middle-age IHD mortality is two or three times higher in the USA than in Sweden, the English rate lying between. *Cardiovascular* mortality in American men under 65, indeed, is about the same as *total* mortality in Sweden.* The same kind of contrast is found also among comparable cities in these countries.[25] The existence of so wide a range among advanced

* *Mortality from All Causes, and from Cardiovascular Disease*
1960
Rates per 1,000

	MEN				WOMEN			
	45-54		55-64		45-54		55-64	
	All	CVD	All	CVD	All	CVD	All	CVD
USA Whites	9·3	4·7	22	13	4·6	1·5	11	5·1
England and Wales	7·2	3·1	21	9·8	4·3	1·3	11	4·7
Sweden	5·1	1·8	15	7·4	3·8	1·0	9·2	3·5

Vital Statistics of the United States, Washington, D.C.; Registrar General; World Health Organization.

Western countries raises the hope that ischaemic heart disease
may eventually be controlled without having to scrap Western
civilisation.

Cancer is apparently common in all countries, though
localisation of the new growths shows striking differences, the

TABLE LVI

*Mortality from Cancer in England and Wales
and in Japan*

Ages 55-64

1957-59

Rates per 100,000 per Year

SEX AND SITE	ENGLAND AND WALES	JAPAN
MEN		
ALL SITES	594	475
Stomach	88	266
Lung, Bronchus	276	33
Prostate	15	2·6
WOMEN		
ALL SITES	352	316
Stomach	37	120
Breast	76	11
Cervix	23	12

World Health Organization (1962). *Epidem.
vital stat. Rep.* **15**, 308.

explanation of which is increasingly being sought in differences
of the environment and of personal habits. The Japanese experience may again be quoted (Table LVI). They have a
remarkable excess of cancer of the stomach among both men
and women, the highest rate recorded in WHO statistics; in
Japanese women a remarkable immunity to cancer of the
breast has been found. So far, there is nothing to explain the
former difference: the latter provides further support for the

hypothesis that incidence of breast cancer is reduced by lactation which tends to be prolonged in Japan.

A Disease of Civilisation?

Is cancer in general actually less common in " primitive " than in highly developed communities? The difficulty in answering this very important question lies in the frequent absence

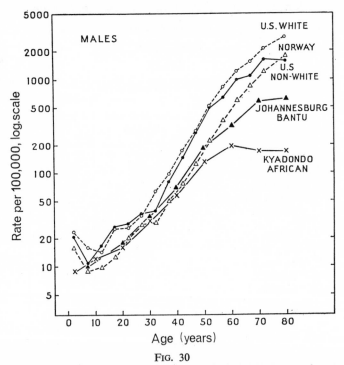

FIG. 30

The incidence of cancer at different ages in two Western and two African countries. Men. All sites.

DAVIES, J. N. P., WILSON, B. A. & KNOWELDEN, J. (1962). *Lancet*, **2**, 328.

of reasonably valid statistics from underdeveloped countries: these usually are without adequate death registration, not to say cause-of-death certification. (There are more than enough clinical impressions, including travellers' tales, and hospital statistics are liable to give biased pictures, cf. page 117.) In

Uganda a special area with 150-200,000 inhabitants is now being systematically surveyed and every case of cancer studied. Age-specific rates among people who are far removed in their own mode of life from Western civilisation are being obtained. From middle age on the results show overall a much lower rate among these people than in the West, Fig. 30 for example.

TABLE LVII

Incidence of Cancer in Three Countries

Standardised for Age*

Rates per 100,000 per Year

SEX AND SITE	KYADONDO, UGANDA	NORWAY	U.S. WHITES	U.S. NON-WHITES
MEN				
ALL SITES	45	93	172	135
Stomach	1·9	20	15	19
Liver, etc.	6·2	0·8	2·2	3·1
Lung, etc.	0·4	4·9	15	13
Prostate	2·4	11	14	21
WOMEN				
ALL SITES	62	104	193	178
Stomach	0·8	12	8·3	11
Breast	6·8	24	44	34
Cervix	17	13	22	49

Knowelden, J. (1963). *Proc. roy. Soc. Med.* **56,** 529.
* On the basis of a " young " African standard population.

It is impossible, meanwhile, to assess the bearing of differential survival on this question: in such underdeveloped peoples only a minority reach the ages when the force of malignant disease becomes strong (perhaps a fraction between the " Gentry " and " Trades " on page 162). These data, however, do suggest, first, that most cancers are induced by external agents rather than by ageing itself and, second, that while some carcinogenic hazards may be common to Western and primitive communities, and some different, the total carcinogenic impact is increased by modern civilisation. This view is supported by current laboratory-experimental work which is revealing an ever-growing list of substances used in Western technology that are potentially carcinogenic. In theory, then, much cancer of older age-groups is preventable. Moreover, since in many of the cancers that occur in such areas as the Kyadondo there are clues pointing to carcinogenic causes in that environment, the total amount of malignant disease resulting from external and preventable factors may be even greater than can at present be postulated. Be the grand picture as it may, there are remarkable differences in cancer by site between this African population and Western experience (Table LVII).

Special Situations

These are now being recognised on a world scale. There is little atmospheric pollution in Venice[35] and in Iceland,[5] but the population smoke tobacco so the opportunity has been seized to make a particular study of lung-cancer in these places. In Kerala, South India, there is high background radiation: what is the incidence of congenital malformation, leukaemia, etc.?[32] Is the hypertension of American negroes the same as that found so commonly in the West Indies, and commonly enough in US and UK whites—and is it not time to carry out a study among the various immigrants to the UK? The Somalis in Somalia and the Masai in Kenya eat a high animal fat diet, but have low blood cholesterol and apparently little IHD.[15][16][24] The Yemenites in Israel present a unique opportunity for observation of the effects of rapid social change and abrupt exposure to the Western mode of life. Since all of them have immigrated to Israel, family-genetic studies can be done concurrently with environmental, and because the Yemenites have settled in the midst of an advanced country, surveys should be relatively easy.[3][10][20][29] Table LVIII illustrates the kind of analysis made possible in Israel by the "ingathering of the exiles". The identification by Burkitt, O'Connor and Davies of a

TABLE LVIII

Frequency of Glucose 6 Phosphate Dehydrogenase Deficiency

Males of Some Jewish Communities in Israel

CONTINENT: AND ETHNIC GROUP	PER CENT AFFECTED*
Europe: Ashkenazim	0·4
Asia: Non-Ashkenazim	
From Yemen	5·0
From Cochin	10·0
From Iraq	25·0
From Kurdistan	58·0

* The gene is carried on the X chromosome so that the *percentage of males affected* is the same as the gene frequency and is a direct measure of the prevalence in the community. Random sample studies.

Sheba, C., Szeinberg, A., Ramot, B., Adam, A., Ashkenazi, I. (1962). *Amer. J. publ. Hlth.* **52**, 1101. Personal communication.

Genetic Polymorphisms and Geographic Variations in Disease (1962). Ed. Blumberg, B. S., New York.

remarkable syndrome of multiple malignant lymphoma among children in Uganda, and later in a circumscribed if large area of Africa (p. 248) has led to the most intensive work on the hypothesis that some arthropod vector is involved in the transmission of the tumour and that an actual specific agent—a virus—is carried by the vector.*

* *Special Situations* are legion. These make the beginning of a list, sampling only situations with particularly high frequency: alcoholism in Scotland,[19] amyloid disease in Israel,[8] amyotrophic lateral sclerosis in Guam,[13] bronchitis in *Britain* (more accurately), Buerger's disease in the Orient,[17] byssinosis in Egypt,[1] cerebrovascular disease in Japan, chorionepithelioma in the Phillipines, cirrhosis in France, disseminated sclerosis in Canada,[12] depression in England,[11] drug addiction in USA . . . or, cancer of mouth in India, of oesophagus recently increasing among the Bantu, of stomach in Finland.[8] [23]

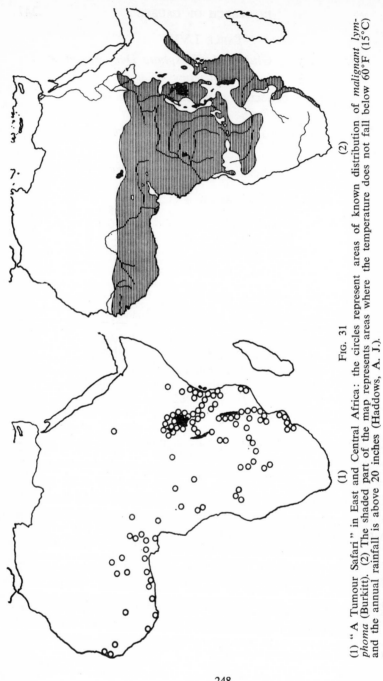

(1)

(2)

Fig. 31

(1) "A Tumour Safari" in East and Central Africa: the circles represent areas of known distribution of *malignant lymphoma* (Burkitt). (2) The shaded part of the map represents areas where the temperature does not fall below 60°F (15°C) and the annual rainfall is above 20 inches (Haddows, A. J.).
Burkitt, D. (1962). *Brit. J. Cancer*, **16**, 379; (1961). *East Afr. med. J.*, **38**, 511. (1963). *Cancer: Progress*, Ed., Raven, R. W., p. 102. Butterworth & Co. (Publishers) Ltd., London.

TABLE LIX

Two Populations in Yugoslavia; Studies of IHD and its Aetiology[18]

Men aged 40-59

POPULATION	ECG ABNORMALITY		Diastolic blood pressure mm. Hg	Serum cholesterol mg. %	Skinfolds triceps and subscapular mm.	DIET - % CALS*	
	S-T Depression %	T-ve %				From fats	From saturated fatty acids
Slavonia	8·9	7·0	81	197	14	32	13
Dalmatia	3·8	1·8	82	185	14	31	6·7

* By ad hoc local chemical analysis. 93 per cent of the 1,371 men who were eligible were examined. Figures are averages. Keys, A., Anderson, J. T., Brozek, J., Buzina, R., Ferber, E., Fidanza, F., Mohacek, I., Punsar, S., Rautaharju, P., Simonson, E., and Tiefenback, B. (1960). Personal communication.

The essential prerequisite for any form of co-operative international study, in the words of the World Health Organisation, would be " standardisation of nomenclature, of definitions, of techniques. . . That postulate accepted, the following are among the categories of inquiry which are regarded as appropriate for international collaboration.

(1) Certain large and comprehensive problems for which world experience is the unit of knowledge. Such are demography, the genetic description of populations, the incidence and prevalence of disease.

(2) Communicable diseases which are of world-wide distribution—such as tuberculosis, and certain virus diseases, or of regional distribution, like malaria.

(3) Diseases in the study of which contrast between the experience of countries or regions might be stimulating. Here, cancer, coronary thrombosis, rheumatoid arthritis are typical examples.

(4) Rare conditions, intensive study of which can illumine thought in other fields. Many genetically determined conditions are of this nature. . ."[34]

The preamble contains the crucial point; useful comparison of experience depends on the *comparability* of data, which cannot be assumed to be high between populations of similar social development, and when the stage of development is different must be assumed to be slight. Joint *expeditions at a distance* are one answer, for example Keys' study in Yugoslavia (Table LIX); the conduct of *parallel studies* with the same criteria in several countries under central control is another, for example the Inter-American[27][28] and the European[33] investigations of coronary atherosclerosis.

*   *   *

The Appropriate " Universe " in Physiological Studies

Among the prospects now opening up for international study is the opportunity to redefine the *healthy,* or *" normal"* (not just the common, or average). Western populations, as said, have higher blood cholesterol levels than those of underdeveloped countries, and a steeper rise with age. The question at once arises what are the normal ranges of blood cholesterol? What is universal in the blood cholesterol level? And what is specific to each community—what are the inherited and acquired, racial and social, factors that produce a community's characteristic blood cholesterol picture? May it be that most people in the West have pathologically high levels? That is to say, it must always be asked what is the appropriate population or " universe " for the study of physiological variables: gross variability between populations as well as within them needs to be considered, and notions of the ranges in health reviewed in light of this.

This anthropological, " cross-cultural " approach to biology offers exciting possibilities. My own first introduction to it was the other way round, when I was told of the laboratory technician in China who believed that what *we* call megaloblastic degeneration of the bone marrow was " normal ".[4] Psychology, in its widest sense, has so far derived most benefit from such an approach: from observation of what is regarded as " normal " and " abnormal " behaviour (healthy and unhealthy) in different cultures, from appreciation of the tremendous range of permissible characteristics, what others fancy as the right way to run a family, bring up children. . .[2][14][30] Every medical student reads Margaret Mead (at least my generation did). " A number of related forces ", she writes, " have combined to make the adolescent in America (and I would add England) stand at the point of highest pressures and difficulty, just as another set of forces place her at the lowest point of pressure in Samoa ". It is obviously misleading to base notions of human behaviour and mental functioning on one culture only. With the post-war immigration into this country from India and Pakistan, the West Indies and Africa, Cyprus and Malta (a half million *net*, and goodness knows how much coming and going), the appreciation of such cultural differences in family structure, child care, short and long-term values and goals—as well as in the diseases of these people and their special problems of adaptation—has suddenly acquired a new significance for local medicine in Britain.

* * *

HYPOTHESES

The *search for causes* of the chronic diseases may be abstracted in a model something like this:

(1) Statement of a hypothesis,

(2) Test of the hypothesis, and of deductions from it,

(3) " Crossing " of the postulated cause with others,

(4) Proof in practical application.
Straightaway it must be said that in real life such tidy progression is rare.

(1) STATEMENT OF HYPOTHESIS

How useful hypotheses are generated is little understood. They are products of their Age—of what is known and thought, what is " in the air "—and of the individual imagination: in epidemiology, ranging over social life and medical discovery, absorbed in data and imposing order upon them, seizing on the unexpected and anomalous incidence, discerning the critical connection among the welter of statistics or a handful of cases. The source also of epidemiological hypotheses is interesting. They emerge—from everywhere: from clinical experience, suggesting a link between occupation and cancer; from laboratory work, which prompted the search for a thyroid-blocking agent in an unusual outbreak of goitre; from watch on changes in the environment—are diesel fumes carcinogenic?; by serendipity—a survey for hypertension in cotton workers disclosed instead epidemic respiratory trouble; and from nowhere in particular—do business executives suffer an excess of " stress " disorders?   Put like this, the last question just makes the grade as a hypothesis : it makes sense (just), is just testable, the answer is not known already and it is worth having.

Any of the *uses of epidemiology* previously considered may turn up clues, be the start of aetiological hypotheses for testing. *Historically,* is the increase of thrombosis in atheromatous coronary arteries related to the consumption of hardened—and mostly saturated—fat which increased contemporaneously after the first world war?[30]   Rising Customs and Excise statistics helped to focus the study of increasing lung-cancer on cigarette smoking; and in an epochal " before and after " change men have shown a disproportionate increase in mortality since the introduction of the cigarette.* Cohort study suggested that rising delinquency after the war was related to the particularly traumatic experience of that generation during it,[48] a hypothesis with a convenient built-in test: the passage of time and a further rise of delinquency in the late 1950's gave no support... *Community Diagnosis* is always turning up aetiological questions. Why do radio and telegraph operators have the highest mortality from ischaemic heart disease? (They certainly are New Men.) How come that Rochdale and Glasgow have so much cardiovascular disease? Hindsight, alas! now suggests that the softness of the local drinking water and not their unnoticed affluence may provide an explanation.[33] The higher prevalence of pernicious anaemia in the less prosperous north and west of Britain[41] prompts a generalisation about the environment—could this be related to the incidence of atrophic gastritis? The excess of cancer of the stomach in North Wales started a search for trace elements in the local soil, and revived the study of blood groups and disease...

A " hunch " may be produced straightaway—by generalising from facts already observed—or only after long and patient special exploring of trends and distributions. In stating a hypothesis an attempt must be made to reduce it to its essentials and make it specific, to isolate it as far as possible from related factors. This will often be a most difficult step to take. Thus, nutrients are complementary; studying saturated fat intake implies the study of unsaturated fat; a high animal fat diet is usually high in animal protein also. In psychiatry, statement of a simple single causal hypothesis may do violence

* *Annual Death Rate from Cancer of Lung*
England and Wales
per 100,000

	MEN		WOMEN	
AGE	1911-15	1960-1	1911-15	1960-1
45-49	3·0	57	2·0	12
60-64	7·0	361	3·9	37

to existing notions (and be traumatic for the psychiatrist); in the end, however, to extract one element from a dynamic system like a family situation, and then to try and put it all back into context again, may be the only way of making progress.

(2) TEST OF HYPOTHESIS

The proposition now stated should be tested in as many, as different and as independent ways as possible. Individual investigations are usually limited and always biased; but it may be possible to draw a cumulative lesson from the consistent behaviour of multiple pieces of evidence that are none of them in themselves as " hard " as could be wished. This is the procedure we adopted in stating a hypothesis relating physical activity of occupation to ischaemic heart disease (p. 174).

Direct Test, and Indirect.[6][36][50] The testing of a causal hypothesis should include a *direct study of* persons

TABLE LX

Smoking and Cancer of Lung

(A)

MORTALITY FROM LUNG CANCER IN THE
COUNTY BOROUGHS OF ENGLAND AND WALES[43]
Males
Ages 45-64

AVERAGE NO. OF CIGARETTES SMOKED IN TOWNS*	ANNUAL MORTALITY FROM LUNG CANCER PER 100,000**
-10 per day	127
10-14	141
15-19	145
20 +	155

* Information from trade sources. 1952-5. Estimated.
** 1948-54.

categorised for example in terms of their smoking habits
—their mortality from cancer of the lung is then analysed.
This is a far superior method to the *indirect study* of
places, of the lung-cancer death rate in countries, say,
or cities, which have been graded by the average amount of
cigarettes smoked in them. How wrong—how diminishing—a way the " indirect " can be of asking the right question
is illustrated in Table LX(A) (in the towns where the men
smoked, on average, less than ten cigarettes per day the
mortality from lung-cancer was 127 per 100,000, and so on
through a shallow gradation). Or I could quote Infant Mortality, in which maternal age and parity do not show up at all
as " causes " when the death rates of the county boroughs are
analysed—there is little variation in the average age of the
mothers of the different towns or in the number of children
they have borne—whereas in our direct study of large numbers
of mothers and infants both variables—as might be expected
—are seen to be very important determinants of IM rates (cf.
Fig. 27).[19] [34] These are examples of factors in the host or in
personal habits and behaviour where individual differences
obviously are crucial, and they have to be studied as such. On
the other hand, in dealing with characteristics of the external
environment it is reasonable to postulate that the differences
between places will be greater than the differences among
individuals *within* them. Thus the study of air pollution levels
of the county boroughs has proven very useful (as in Fig. 26).
In the case of the X factor that matters for health in the water
that is drunk, differences between English towns are also likely
to be greater than differences within them: the range of individual drinking of water does vary of course, it may be 3, 4,
or 5-fold; but the range of water hardness among the county
boroughs is ten or twenty-fold. In such situations, therefore, it is worth investing in " indirect " " ecologic " study
(*e.g.* Table LXI). The trouble is that towns differing in their
water supply are likely to differ in so many other respects, and
the problem is to know what in fact is being studied. The

softness of the local water, for example, was one of the reasons the cotton industry—and the industrial revolution—started in Lancashire. Is the correlation with water hardness merely a roundabout way of describing an association between heart

TABLE LXI[32]

Mortality from Cardiovascular Disease and the Hardness of the Local Drinking Water

83 County Boroughs of England and Wales

CAUSE OF DEATH	CORRELATION (r) Between Death Rate* and Total Water Hardness (ppm)**			
	45-64 Years		65-74 Years	
	M	F	M	F
Cardiovascular disease***	− 0·54	− 0·48	− 0·54	− 0·43
Other disease	− 0·19	− 0·28	− 0·24	− 0·25

* Ave-annual rate 1948-54.
** 1951.
*** WHO, ISC nos. 330-334, 410-468.

Significance Levels of r for 83 Pairs of Observations:

$r > 0·22$	$P < 0·05$
0·28	0·01
0·36	0·001
0·42	0·0001

disease and social conditions? In this instance, painstaking search revealed only trivial correlations between water hardness and such urban-social variables as could be studied—size of town, occupational composition, housing conditions, wages, history of unemployment, etc. Making allowance for these factors scarcely affected the values in the first line of Table

LXI, but they were enough to drop those of the second under a " significance " level of 5 per cent.*

To return to another example: fat consumption in Norway fell during the Occupation, and so did the incidence and mortality of IHD; after the war a more usual Western diet was resumed and IHD increased. But calories, too, were reduced during the war; there was more physical activity; average weight fell; cigarettes became rare; mental health improved—anyhow the suicide rate dropped—and the mortality statistics themselves are a bit dubious.[30][44] How can the dietary hypothesis be sorted out from these alternative explanations except by studying directly the experience of large numbers of individuals, each of them classified by the relevant variables? In theory, yes; but it is only now becoming possible to classify large numbers of individuals by their diet and the exercise they take. At that time in Europe, repetition of the same kind of analysis in different but comparable places was the only practical thing to do. In these places, perhaps there was no dietary change or, with any luck, the change of diet was accompanied by *other* environmental changes. The best has to be made of what is possible, while seeking to improve it. There are plenty of examples in classical epidemiology in malaria, *e.g.*, and in tuberculosis, in goitre or dental caries, where elementary ecologic observations have opened up new territory, led to viable hypotheses, and provided highly relevant evidence in support—or refutation. . . Unfortunately for this particular dietary hypothesis, direct study of individuals in countries with

---

* There is more to it than that, of course.[32][33] The correlation between " water hardness " and cardiovascular disease has been found by three different groups of workers in three very different countries, Japan, USA and Britain; which encourages perseverance in the search for an explanation. In Britain the association, as seen, is specifically with cardiovascular and with no other disease, which is further encouragement. The association, furthermore, is a graded phenomenon, mortality varying rather steadily with degree of water hardness. In brief, if this is *not* a story about *water*, it is an important story about something else. In the absence of any hypothesis on possible mechanisms whereby the effects of hard or soft water might be produced, a tedious chemical screening of the drinking water of various English towns has been started. More recent data for cardiovascular mortality in 1958-62 show rather higher correlations than in Table LXI. Confirmatory *morbidity* data are also becoming available.[43]

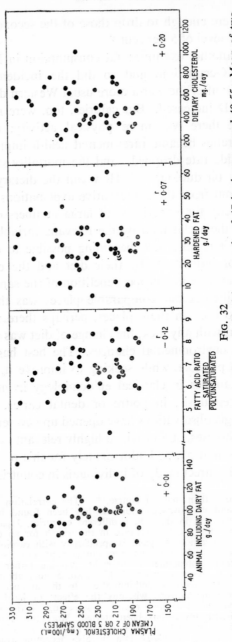

FIG. 32

Individual dietary intake and "casual" plasma cholesterol level in a sample of 47 bank men, aged 40-55. Mean of two separate weeks' weighed surveys carried out by each man, and of two or three blood estimations. London and Home Counties. The association between several categories in diet and the cholesterol level. Results were similar for single foods, *e.g.* milk or eggs; and for sample of 99 men making 1-2 weeks' weighed surveys and having 1-3 cholesterol estimations.

Brit. med. J. (1963) **1,** 571.[35] [43]

high fat consumption is producing results in flat contradiction of these indirect studies. Thus, in Fig. 32 little if any correlations could be found, in samples of bank men we have observed, between their individual diets and their blood cholesterol levels.[31] [35] [43]

Experiment of Opportunity

The epidemiological imagination will be alert to seize the opportunity of an " experiment " like the Norwegian. Snow ascertained the mortality from cholera in persons happening at the time to have clean up-river water, in comparison with a similar population having a down-river contaminated supply, page 162. The effects of social change on individual physiology and pathology are being studied (too little and sometimes already too late) in the new countries, notably in Israel. The hypothesis about radiation was confirmed, if the idea is not blasphemous, by subsequent leukaemia in Hiroshima and Nagasaki. Here at home, the occurrence of bronchitis is being watched in some of the new smokeless zones, " before and after " and in comparison with the experience of still polluted neighbours. The air in these smokeless zones still contains a lot of sulphur, so the opportunity to study high sulphur concentrations in industry is being exploited.[23] The health of immigrants into new towns and housing estates is a traditional field of enquiry.[29] [45] Occupational mortality statistics of British physicians will henceforth be examined with particular interest. Many of them have been health-educated by recent discoveries —and the recurrent horror in their clinical practice—to give up cigarettes; unlike their patients, the general public. Workers in automated processes are being compared with their fellows engaged in more traditional production. . . Snow's was the perfect *experiment of nature* (the alternative name) though, as often, man-made: it was as near a controlled experiment in the laboratory as could be desired, those studied had in effect been " randomised " between the two water supplies. In Snow's words, they were " divided into two groups without their choice, and, in most cases, without their knowledge ", there was no self or other selection of the drinking water by " rank or station, condition or occupation ", characteristics that might themselves be associated with the incidence of cholera and thus confound the comparison between the two groups. The other British examples listed above are progressively less satisfactory on this essential criterion by which the experiment of opportunity, and all epidemiologic observation, has to be judged—and the proof they can provide is thus by no means " incontrovertible ".

Many hypotheses on cause do not survive this stage of testing. Some associations are seen to be chance phenomena; but even when statistically significant many correlations are only too obviously not causal, preferable alternative explanations are only too freely available. One of the troubles of epidemiology is the ease, the inevitability almost, of finding interesting differences, commonly over time and between places. Some hypotheses however do survive, even if changed out of recognition in the process of testing. They explain something, deductions from them " work ", and they make sense: common sense, and/or sense in terms of what else is known and thought in epidemiology, in clinical medicine, in laboratory science.*

---

* There are special difficulties in testing *single* postulated causes, when many causes are operating. Customary logic helps only with necessary causes: if these fail to pass a test the hypothesis is falsified.[38] However, the reality of other causes cannot be tested by such methods of " affirmation, and demolition ". Cigarette smoking seems now to be a leading cause of chronic bronchitis, but last century there was a lot of the disease—and no cigarettes. The driven, striving, competitive person surely was familiar in Victorian England, but it is quite conceivable that he rarely suffered from ischaemic heart disease. Such refutation would not dispose of these hypotheses. Other *patterns* of causes presumably were operating last century, the epidemic constitution was different, other things never are equal. The cigarette, and the personality type, are not " necessary " causes of bronchitis or IHD—that is the only inference to be drawn. Conceivably we have to think in " open-ended " terms, and there is no indispensable cause of either disease; this could be the outcome also of the current controversy on hypertension without evident cause. In time cybernetic models[27] should help with these dilemmas, and field theory already does.[25]

*   *   *

CASE-CONTROL AND PROSPECTIVE STUDIES[5 8 10 13 18 24 26 51]

Page 263 (B) is taken from a study of large numbers of patients with cancer of the lung,[11] Table LX (C) summarises the results of the quite different—and independent—study of British doctors.[12] There are two main ways of testing directly a hypothesis on a cause of disease. The first is " retrospective ", backward looking, historical. It starts with *cases* of the disease, patients who already have it, and matches them for history of the suspected cause, smoking say, with *controls*—usually patients with other diseases. A large series of cases is desirable, and they should be as typical of the disease as can be defined and found. The assumption is that the controls represent the general population, so they too need to be chosen carefully. Sources of bias are endless, as many as the selective influences in hospital admission for a start, and the safest course may be to take for controls as random a sample of as general a collection of patients as possible, matching only for sex and age. Even so, it is now known that patients with ischaemic heart disease and bronchitis, for example, should not be used for controls on questions of cigarette smoking—as they were in the early lung-cancer studies. Fortunately, this error was in the right direction, reducing as it did the contrast that was discovered between the smoking habits of the cases with cancer of the lung and of the controls.

The second method is *" prospective "*, forward-looking, a method already advocated for study of the natural history of disease (p. 131). It starts by defining a population, every individual in which has been characterised by the variables being investigated, smoking for example. The whole cohort, as it may be called, is then followed to see who develops the disease, as this is defined, and how this is associated with smoking habits; the incidence—or mortality—is observed, and compared in smokers and non-smokers, heavy and light smokers, of the same sex, age, domicile, etc. If smoking habits change, this too will be measured so that any change in incidence can be interpreted. There is much to be said for and against each of these methods.

Case-control, retrospective studies are relatively easy to start —there may be only too many patients with cancer of the lung in local hospitals—and they can often be done quickly if necessary. Something like 100 per cent co-operation is common, and much information can be obtained from each patient. This is the method of choice, therefore, in the early stages of enquiry; and the pioneer studies of smoking and disease were of this kind.[3] As with lung-cancer, and the hypotheses on oxygen excess and retrolental fibroplasia, or irradiation and leukaemia,[47] first hunches on possible causes of disease have often come from clinical observation, and formal case-control studies followed. . . . The trouble with retrospective studies lies in the validity of the information that is obtained. Patients with chest illness often feel guilty now about smoking, a history of alcohol consumption is notoriously unreliable, mothers racking their brains for what might have gone wrong will recollect—something, old men just forget—selectively. Moreover, pressure by the investigator (of which he may be unaware) to elicit an answer, a particular answer, may be greater with the cases under suspicion than with the controls, and these may also vary in their suggestibility. *Prospective studies* (" follow-up ", " longitudinal ") overcome many of these difficulties. Since all questions are asked before the diagnosis of the disease, these studies reduce error, conscious and subconscious, in observer and observed—in the investigator who is asking the questions and the subject who is giving the answers.

In some situations the prospective is the only way of getting satisfactory information. Study of many of the personal characteristics of men dying suddenly in their first attack of ischaemic heart disease must be prospective; questioning widows is not the same. Even when both have agreed to participate in a study, the ability of patients with emotional disorder and of controls not so suffering to give private infor-

TABLE LX

Smoking and Cancer of Lung

(B)

RETROSPECTIVE STUDY OF PATIENTS OF VARIOUS AGES
WITH LUNG-CANCER AND OF MATCHED CONTROLS

| AVERAGE NO. OF CIGAR-ETTES (OR EQUIVALENT IN PIPE TOBACCO) SMOKED DAILY OVER 10 YEARS BEFORE ILLNESS | PROPORTIONS IN EACH GROUP | | | |
| | MALES | | FEMALES | |
	1357 Cases %	1357 Controls %	108 Cases %	108 Controls %
Non-smokers	0·5	4·5	37	55
- 5	4·0	9·5	15	23
5-14	36	42	22	17
15-24	35	32	13	5·6
25-49	22	11	13	—
50+	2·8	0·9	—	—
TOTAL	100	100	100	100

Doll, R., & Hill, A. B. (1952). *Brit. med. J.* **2**, 1271.

(C)

PROSPECTIVE STUDY OF BRITISH DOCTORS
Death Rates from Lung-Cancer per 1,000 Men per Year
1951-8

| AGE | NON-SMOKERS* | EX-SMOKERS** | CIGARETTE SMOKERS | | |
			-14/day	15-24/day	25+/day
35-44	0·0	0·10	0·0	0·0	0·12
45-54	0·0	0·10	0·41	0·55	0·58
55-64	0·0	0·49	0·63	1·96	4·29
65-74	0·0	1·44	1·9	4·72	6·04

* This population is very small. Lung-cancer does undoubtedly occur on occasion in non-smokers (cf. (B)).
** Including ex-pipe smokers, etc.
Doll, R., & Hill, A. B. (1962). In *Smoking and Health* (1963).
Personal communication.

mation may be quite unequal; questioning before the event could help. Histories of " chest illness " and of the onset of respiratory symptoms have proven so feebly reproducible that only a prospective study stands a chance of elucidating the personal and environmental causes that lead to the establishment of chronic bronchitis.[15] The diagnosis of rubella may be so uncertain that neither positive nor negative history of it is sufficiently valid. . . The other great advantage of prospective studies is that they provide good estimates of the strength of the association being postulated, first, by estimating the *relative risk,* for example of non-smokers, and of light, moderate, and heavy smokers. Second : since all the cases of the disease, as previously defined and occurring in a defined population are known, it is possible to produce the actual incidence rates of disease in these various categories and thus to give the *individual chances.** [42]

Prospective studies are not ipso facto perfect. They test hypotheses more strictly, and, because the element of prediction is strong, more convincingly. But they cannot " prove " cause and effect as in symbolic logic or as in planned experiments, whether of natural science or clinical trials—even epidemiology. Thus, 30 per cent of doctors in the UK did not participate in the smoking study. More important, within the population of respondents both smokers and non-smokers have further selected themselves, subjects have not been " randomised " (the magic word again). It cannot yet be said for sure whether such self-selection indicates some inheritance or experience that is connected with " proneness " to cancer and to other diseases; prodigious research has so far revealed rather

---

* The *relative risk* can also be estimated from case-control study.[8] The validity of the estimate will depend (a) on how typical the " cases " included are of all who have the disease (on which something has just been said, and see Chapter V; the situation with depression, say, or duodenal ulcer, will be far less satisfactory than in lung-cancer); and (b) on how representative the " controls " are of the general population which does not have the disease. Estimates of *individual chances* can only be made from case-control data by using a lot of assumptions, and they are usually less satisfactory than figures based on prospective study. Fig. 17, page 106, quotes an early attempt to estimate individual risks from case-control data.

little. The interested reader should acquaint himself with the literature of this controversy,[1] [2] [14] [40] [51] and reconsider the variety of evidence outlined in the present book. I hope Fig. 33 nevertheless will give him furiously to think, as it did me,

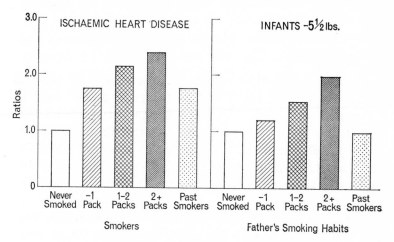

FIG. 33

Mortality from ischaemic heart disease in men aged 50-69 in relation to cigarette-smoking habits.

HAMMOND, E. C. (1960). *Amer. J. publ. Hlth* **50**, March, Pt. II, 20.

Frequency of " prematurity " (birth weight up to 5½ lbs.) in relation to father's cigarette-smoking habits. Data from the Co-operative Study of Child Development.

YERUSHALMY, J. (1962). In *Tobacco and Health.* Ed., James, G., Rosenthal, T. C. C. Thomas, Publisher, Springfield, Ill.

Rates have been expressed as ratios of the experience among those who have never smoked.

about the relationships of smoking to cardiovascular and other conditions. Because of their size the probability of direct causation with lung-cancer and with bronchitis, in Hammond's data as in the British, is in a class apart.

In the study of chronic disease, prospective studies may mortgage energy and resources for years, possibly many years, ahead. Even with so common a condition as ischaemic heart disease very large numbers exposed-to-risk are needed, and all must then be kept in sight. Before undertaking prospective study, therefore, there should already be a strong indication that gold is there to be found, and where it is to be looked for.

*   *   *

(3) MULTIPLE CAUSES

Notions of " multiple causality ", to continue the previous discussion (p. 188), imply that postulated " causes " must be "crossed " with each other to determine their interrelationships: the search for causes of the chronic diseases is a dialogue between the isolation of single causes and describing their patterns. At this stage what is liable to happen is that apparently different causes turn out in fact not to be so. The excess of chronic bronchitis in males may be mainly a sex difference in smoking habits expressed in a roundabout way. Do foundry workers in fact suffer more than others from bronchitis, or is it simply that common chronic diseases tend to be blamed on occupation, and not for example on the filthy air breathed in so many industrial towns? The concentration of juvenile delinquency among Roman Catholics or Negroes may merely be reflecting that both commonly are underprivileged groups. . . . If causes are independent, make their own contribution to the aetiology, it must be asked whether they add together, how much explanation they add up to, and whether they compound and interact. It is urgently necessary to know this of the causes now postulated for ischaemic heart disease; the design of a preventive programme may well depend upon the answer. The study of lung-cancer in relation jointly to smoking and atmospheric pollution attempts to settle just this kind of question. Fig. 34 opposite tries to keep one cause constant while varying the other. The result is another argument if such were needed to clean the air; but at high rates of smoking atmospheric pollution seems to lose its power to affect the death rate, is overwhelmed by the cigarette.[4]

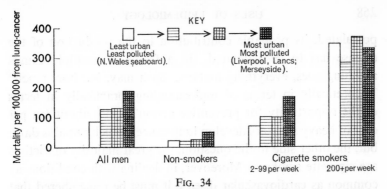

FIG. 34

Two postulated causes of lung-cancer: cigarette-smoking and "urban" environment (air pollution). Estimated annual death rates, men aged 35-74, 1952-5. (Rates are standardised for age.) Areas in N.W. England and in N. Wales. Mortality in moderate smokers (100-199 cigs. per week) was highest in the most urban—most polluted area, but there was no trend with degree of "urbanisation".

From STOCKS, P. (1957). *Suppl. to Part II of the 35th Ann. Rep.* of the British Empire Cancer Campaign, London.

... In our infant mortality studies a collection of largely "independent" causes were identified: maternal age (physiological and social efficiency); "parity", the birth rank of the infant (related to these and also to infection); rapidity of childbearing (personality and social environment are obviously involved as well as physiology); loss by the mother of a previous child (specific responsible pathology is usually not evident); paternal social class (with its correlates of past and present environment); the region of the country (introducing biological as well as social variables). Various combinations of these causes yield ranges in stillbirth from 8 or so per 1,000 births to rates of 70 and 80, and in post-neonatal mortality from 3 or 4 per 1,000 to ten times as many.[19][34][43] (Goodness knows what high and low rates would be found if numbers permitted all these causes to be included simultaneously in the calculations. The clinical situation is familiar, for example in ischaemic heart disease or in juvenile delinquency as well as in infant mortality, where there is so much "overdetermination", saturation with so many causes, that the unfortunates "just don't stand a chance".) The weight or strength of each cause being

267

postulated, its probable contribution to the production of the disease has to be estimated. In a frame of multiple causes anything goes, everything matters. So it may, but how much? Theoretically in terms of understanding, practically in terms of the opportunity for preventive action? Only about ten per cent of heavy smokers develop lung-cancer, much remains dark; but, the other side to the question, the great majority of victims are cigarette smokers. Moreover, in dealing with conditions as common as cardiovascular disease it must be remembered that removal of even a small effect could yield a considerable gain: smoking could be of great importance for Public Health if it is in fact only a minor cause of IHD, the hardness of the local drinking water may yet prove to be a major factor in mortality during middle age.

A last word. If " causes " are related in a dynamic way, and one or more performs a homeostatic function, simple intervention may not have simple results. Any evidence on this aspect will be particularly valuable. It is basic to nutrition policy, corollary of the theoretical point already made, that correcting one of the deficiencies of an inadequate diet, in respect of the B vitamins for example, can make things worse. Men who give up smoking may become more nervous and they often put on weight (the " claw of the seapuss " that gets you in the end?). It is reassuring that the death rate of ex-smokers is lower than that of continuing smokers, though it has not yet been possible to compare the hazards of obesity and of smoking better than done in Table XLI (6) and (7), page 165. A main lesson of ecology and of social science is about interrelatedness—one effect cannot be produced without a lot of others, intended and unintended.

(4) EXPERIMENTAL EPIDEMIOLOGY[16 17 20 21 46]

Quite early in hypothesis-testing it may be possible to take the critical step from observation to experiment. The *planned experiment* carries most conviction—not just the marshalling of circumstantial evidence, which is all that has so far been considered even in the boldest deduction and all but the most perfect natural experiment. Planned experiment may be the only way of ending argument about causes when the evidence is indirect, multiple causes obviously are involved, the " naturally " occurring groups demonstrably are selected—when the results of observation lack conviction. If reasonable doubt persists the epidemiological experiment may be unavoidable before mass attempts at health education to change the mode of life will stand much chance of success. Even then it may not be plain sailing for Public Health services, as is evident again today in the frequently tepid or worse reception of the splendid results, in terms of benefits gained and safety assured, of the British fluoridation experiment (overleaf—and, I may recall, Fig. 35).[28] [37] [39] The possibilities of experiment in therapeutic services have already been mentioned (page 99), but the traditional field is in prevention; a cause isolated, then tested by changing a population or its environment under controlled conditions. This is to achieve the equivalent of the experiment in the laboratory (including experiments in the production and prevention of infectious epidemics).

There are many examples from history: trying the effect of adding iodine to salt as goitre prophylactic, preventing pellagra by improving the diet, Corry Mann's demonstration that giving milk improved the growth of underprivileged children—this is already history. It is now taken for granted that mass trials of vaccines will be conducted before they are introduced into general use, and some of the recent trials have been most remarkable enterprises.[7] Cochrane sought to prevent progressive massive fibrosis of coalminers in South Wales by eliminating tuberculosis from the area (this imaginative scheme has not proved successful). Many experiments have been made in the prevention of road accidents by correction of particular black spots. Results of such experiments may be assessed in simultaneous comparison of randomised " treated " and " untreated " groups, as in immunisation; or, where this is realistic, " before and after " in the same population, as in many experiments in industrial safety.

TABLE LXII

Experimental Fluoridation in Britain

Children aged 4

DENTAL CONDITION	EXPERIMENTAL AREAS		CONTROL AREAS	
	Base 1955-6	1961	Base 1955-6	1961
Average number of carious teeth per child (dmf)	5·4	2·3	5·2	4·8
Proportion of children free from caries (%)	22	42	21	27
Proportion of children with 10 or more carious teeth (%)	21	3·6	19	19

Matched pairs of areas were studied in Scotland, England and Wales. Fluoridation began in 1955-6, and on average reached 0·92 ppm.
d=decayed   m=missing   f=filled.
Reports on Public Health and Medical Subjects. No. 105 (1962). H.M.S.O.

Experiment in the Prevention of Chronic Diseases

There are three points of attack: (1) at the stage of precursor abnormalities; (2) personal habits of living; (3) environmental control. Preventive medicine faces its main challenge today in the second. A good experiment to prove that cigarette smoking is a major cause of cancer of the lung would involve large numbers of smokers and their allocation at random into two groups one of which is persuaded to stop smoking. If such an experiment could be made, and motivation and discipline

BEFORE FLUORIDATION
1944 - 46

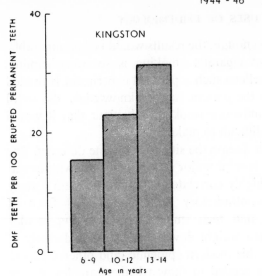

KINGSTON

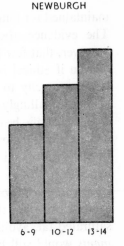

NEWBURGH

AFTER 10 YEARS OF FLUORIDATION IN NEWBURGH
1954 - 55

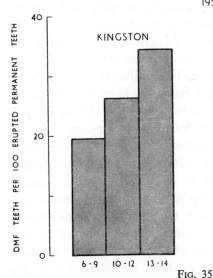

KINGSTON

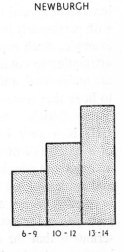

NEWBURGH

FIG. 35

Experimental fluoridation in New York State: Newburgh, experimental area; Kingston, control area. Base 1944-6; further observation after 10 years in 1954-5. Prevalence of dental caries in children aged 6-14. D=decayed teeth, M=missing, F=filled.

HILLEBOE, H. E., SCHLESINGER, E. R., CHASE, H. C., CANTWELL, K. T., AST, D. B., SMITH, D. J., WACHS, B., OVERTON, D. E., HODGE, H. C. (1956). J. Amer. dent. Ass. **52,** 290; and personal communication.

maintained for long enough, the results would be incomparable. The evidence about cigarette smoking is so overwhelming, however, that few believe such a planned experiment is needed —even if ethical in the present state of knowledge. (So small is our capacity to influence smoking behaviour that it would also be appallingly difficult to make.)

In ischaemic heart disease the situation is quite different. The evidence implicates several major causes which are widespread in our society and highly correlated—and on the main dietary hypothesis it is contradictory (cf. page 258). Even if *observation* shows that men smoking little, taking regular exercise, keeping their weight down and eating moderately of saturated fat, avoid this modern epidemic (and others), *experiments* would still be needed to show whether samples of men not naturally so virtuous, but persuaded to change their mode of life for long enough, derive the same benefits. The time has therefore come for experiments on the grandest scale. These could be on free-living population samples; on " captive " populations, such as servicemen or monks or, doubtfully, the inmates of mental hospitals; or in vulnerable groups, all the men with particularly high blood cholesterol levels in a large city for example. Such experiment would be in the classic tradition of attempting to control a disease before its intimate mechanisms are understood, and in the process there is reason from the past to hope that something will be learnt about these mechanisms. These "trials" will be difficult to make. By definition, IHD is a very long-term condition; though the suggestion of a quick fall of the disease in Norway and, more recently, among those who have given up smoking, and the pathological and epidemiologic distinction of the role of acute *thrombosis* in producing ischaemia as distinct from chronic *atheroma*, give reason for optimism. One obstacle which may yet prove serious is that the mere effort of doing something active may have considerable beneficial effect on an experimental population (the "Hawthorne", general, non-specific effect), and realistic control populations may be hard to define.

It is premature to be categorical about the necessity of planned experiment in preventing the chronic diseases (" only nature can do the experiments that you want "[22]). Quite likely, experiment will prove to be impossible in many of the chronic diseases; though a braver new world may be readier for this kind of social engineering. The other major field now ripe for experiment, to my mind, is the attempt to improve health in old age by care of the middle-aged. Since the interaction of physical and mental health is nowhere more evident than among the old, even the simplest approaches may have worthwhile results. This would be experimental of both phases that have been previously discussed: in delivering a health service, and in testing notions of aetiology.

18

RECAPITULATION; GENERAL

The epidemiological method is the only way of asking some questions in medicine, one way of asking others, and no way at all to ask many. Several *uses of epidemiology*, actual and potential, have been described:

I. To study the *history* of the health of populations, and of the rise and fall of diseases and changes in their character. Useful projections into the future may be possible

II. To *diagnose the health of the community,* and the condition of the people, to measure the present dimensions and distribution of ill-health in terms of incidence, prevalence, and mortality; to define health problems for community action, and their relative importance and priority; to identify vulnerable groups needing special protection. Ways of life change, and with them community health and health problems; new indices of health and disease must therefore always be sought.

III. To study the *working of health services* with a view to their improvement. Operational research translates knowledge of community health in terms of needs and demand. The supply of services is described and how they are utilised; their success in reaching standards and in improving health ought to be appraised. All this has to be related to other social policies and to resources. Knowledge thus won may be applied in experiment, and in drawing up plans for the future. . . . The regular supply of information on health and health services is itself a key service needing as much scrutiny as any.

IV. To estimate from the group experience what are the *individual risks* and chances, on average, of disease, accident and defect.

V. To *complete the clinical picture* of chronic disease, and describe its *natural history*: by including in proportion all kinds of patients wherever they present, and by following the course of remission and relapse, adjustment and disability; by detecting early sub-clinical disease and relating this to the clinical; by discovering precursor abnormalities during the pathogenesis. Longitudinal studies are necessary to learn about the mechanisms of progression through these various stages, each of which may offer opportunities for research into causes and for preventive action.

VI. To *identify syndromes* by describing the distribution, association and dissociation of clinical phenomena in the population.

VII. To *search for causes* of health and disease by studying the incidence in different groups, defined in terms of their composition, their inheritance and experience, their behaviour and environment. To distinguish causes, describe their patterns, and estimate the relative importance of different causes in multiple aetiology; to investigate the mode of operation of the various causes. With knowledge of causes comes the possibility of preventing the incidence of disease. Postulated causes will often be tested in naturally occurring *experiments of opportunity,* and sometimes by *planned experiments* in removing them.

These various uses—classical approaches in I, II, and VII, and more recent applications in III, IV, V, VI—all derive from the principle that in epidemiology whole " populations " (or their samples) are studied and compared, and not particular individuals or patients. Information thus gathered, by including all degrees of disease and manner of involvement, may change the picture of the natural history. Description of the community's burden of disease and disability is useful in itself; enquiry into its distribution may reveal groups that are vulnerable; analysis of these is often the beginning of the study of causes—and so of prevention.

In recent years there has been a great increase of epidemiological research, and it is now being applied to the study of health at all levels of organisation, from the molecule to the social group, from the prevalence of sickle cell trait to the conditions of industrial morale. Advances have been recorded in the study of various cancers, of atherosclerosis, ischaemic heart disease, hypertension, of bronchitis, industrial pulmonary disease—and a number of other fields, some of them previously mentioned in this text. . . . New ground is being broken in investigation of health, and in the determination of physiological norms and their range and variability among different populations; in chromosome studies, population genetics, family studies; in surveys of morbidity; in the study of individual and social psychology; in " ops " research. . . . Techniques of investigation are being developed: in population sampling and the assessment of bias, the standardisation of criteria and methods of diagnosis, screening devices, laboratory estimation needing little material; in multiple factor analysis by computers and in the storage and retrieval of information; in health-record linkage; in Chronic Disease Registers. . . . Prospective study of cohorts is increasingly being used, and so are combined survey and case studies, international comparisons by uniform methods, and field experiments on populations. . . . Nevertheless, epidemiology continues the Cinderella of the medical sciences, quite inadequately supported in most countries. The proposition might be advanced that Public Health needs more of the scientific endeavour of epidemiology, so does the whole of medicine and, it may be said, society at large: more of the method, and more of its results.

Epidemiology provides intelligence for *Public Health* services. It is the necessary basis for action by the community

in promoting health, in preventing disease, and in providing
medical care. Health problems are revealed and measured,
and indication given where in the population preventive and
therapeutic action is most urgent, and likely to be useful.
Forecasts helpful to social policy can often be made. Much
epidemiological research is based on the—improving—routine
records of Public Health.

Medicine as a whole needs more epidemiology. With its
help biological variation and distribution can be studied more
systematically. Medicine is social science as well as human
biology, and the epidemiological is the main method of studying
the social aspects of health and disease. Epidemiology is fertile
with suggestions for clinical and laboratory research, and
groups specially worthy of study may be identified. Hypotheses
emerging from clinic and laboratory may be tested epidemiologically (such test indeed is obligatory before new discoveries
can be put into practice). The concern of epidemiology with
causes of health and disease provides a corrective to the
tendency, in both medicine and social science, to concentrate
on " how " and neglect " why ".

The main relations of epidemiology with *clinical medicine*
may be restated thus: Epidemiology studies disease in various
kinds of population, and it is concerned with all the cases that
occur in them. In the chronic diseases these will include, and
in their due proportion, the manifold clinical manifestations
(so yielding a truly representative picture), subclinical and often
reversible disorders, and even earlier precursor abnormalities.
Epidemiology thus helps to *complete the clinical picture* and
to clarify the natural history of disease. Furthermore, epidemiology *supplements the clinical picture* by asking questions that
cannot be asked in clinical medicine; it provides a different
view of the world of medicine. Clinical problems are set in
community perspective, the physician's experience can be compared with the health of the population. Group regularities
that are established will help to explain the individual instance,
or draw attention to its peculiarity. Measurements can be made

of the needs for clinical services and of how they are being met; an indicator is thus provided of the quality of medical care.

Finally, epidemiology may help to *abolish the clinical picture*. One of the urgent needs of highly developed societies is to identify *ways of healthy living*, the wisdom of body and mind and the principles of social organisation that will reduce the burden of the chronic diseases and improve the quality of life. The quest for this knowledge is the main use of epidemiology.

APPENDIX

Complementary Nature of Clinical, Laboratory and Population Studies

We are most of us interested not only in our own part of the job but in how it relates to the rest. Thus, throughout the foregoing account of epidemiologic methods and findings, their relevance to the clinician has been emphasised. As conclusion, this theme will be taken up in another way. An attempt will be made to spell out by example how the main methods of learning in medicine complement and supplement each other, and how this has led to greater understanding of problems that are the concern of the whole of medicine. These methods are the clinical observation of patients, controlled experiment in the laboratory, and the study of populations.

The kind of thing I mean is illustrated by the question of the streptococcus and its relationship to juvenile rheumatism. The original *clinical* observations connected the disease, though there was obviously something special involved, with tonsillitis and scarlatina. From the *laboratory* came facts about the role of Group-A β haemolytic streptococci; and peculiar antibody responses that are found help to explain the long incubation period. Outbreaks of rheumatic fever have been described in various kinds of *population,* adult and child, civil and military, following upon outbreaks of upper respiratory streptococcal infection; the social distribution of the disease further illumines the role of infection. Significant parallels and contrasts, moreover, have been drawn between the recent decline in frequency of rheumatic fever in Britain and the decline in severity of other streptococcal diseases. Nothing predisposes to an attack of rheumatic fever so much as a previous one: in what is something of a " combined operation " of all three methods of study field trials of sulfa- and, later, penicillin prophylaxis have shown that it is practicable to prevent recurrences, and perhaps also first attacks, of the disease.

This is an example of how, by using the three methods—clinical observation of the natural history, isolating a process for laboratory study, describing the disease as mass phenomenon—a particular phase of rheumatic fever, namely its infective nature, was elucidated. Other examples readily come to mind. " The historical sequence through which an understanding of the aetiology of pellagra was gained, and particularly the evolution of Goldberger's work in South Carolina, exemplify these interactions. *Clinical* observations, from the eighteenth century on, defined the disease entity and its many manifestations in man. *Studies on the population* revealed the relationship of poverty and peculiar diet, poor in animal food, to the incidence of the disease; and explained its increase in the rural South of the USA, and its social distribution, by the recent adoption there of single-crop agriculture. Additional *clinical-epidemiologic* studies brought out that in institutions the disease did not affect the staff, was not spread from patients to attendants, was not infectious—a necessary proof in the contemporary climate of opinion. Moreover and taking nothing for granted Goldberger found that patients and attendants had different diets, not the same as was supposed. *Epidemiologic* experiment demonstrated the effects of diet in alleviating manifestations of the disease (in an orphanage), and in producing them (in a prison). *Population* surveys further particularised the relationship of incidence to availability and consumption of certain foods; investigations in the *biochemical laboratory* identified the possible significant nutritional elements deficient in the diet; *animal experiment* (on black tongue of dogs, for example) combined with biochemical analyses approached the isolation of the substance, nicotinic acid, needed to prevent the disorder. . . . With each advance, economic and social policy, Public Health practice, and therapeutics were influenced toward more effective action for the prevention and control of pellagra."[45] Now, with rise in the standard of living, diversification of agriculture and of the economy of the South, and greater understanding of the causes of the disease, pellagra as a public health problem has been eliminated from the USA.

Having stated a question, the common reaction today is to seek to simplify it in controlled laboratory experiment. It may also be rewarding to translate it into epidemiological terms—if only to identify where laboratory studies might most usefully be made. The growth of research departments using all three methods of investigation is one of the most promising developments in modern medicine; and which method or approach to use in any particular situation may sometimes be a strategic question, not merely tactical. The crash programme in search of *viruses* that may be related to the lymphoma of central Africa is based on the most acute *clinical* observation connecting a motley of tumours in children, followed by virtuoso *map-making*. The current attempt to deal with toxic hazards from the fifty or so new drugs being introduced annually, will be using clinical experience *e.g.* for "early warning" signals; laboratory experiments to explain what is happening; and population surveys for assessing the risk from the suspected drug in comparison with that of the untreated disease and of other therapy, and the magnitude of the problems arising.

*   *   *

The tables that follow provide illustrations in outline but not, I hope, too condensed a fashion. Where the sequences of events are clear, this has been indicated by (1) (2) (3); though I have made little attempt to go beyond this and tabulate more complicated cross-fertilisation and feedback. It is characteristic for the *clinical* observation to be the point of departure.

TABLE LXIII

Sir George Baker's Consummate Proof that the Devonshire Colic Was Due to Lead Poisoning[2] [62]

CLINICAL MEDICINE	LABORATORY STUDY	EPIDEMIOLOGY
Baker (1767) noticed that the Devonshire Colic, commonly ascribed to the acidity of the cyder that was drunk in large quantities locally, may terminate in colic, palsy and epilepsy, *i.e.* was clinically identical with lead poisoning. (1)	By *chemical analysis* he confirmed the presence of lead in Devonshire cyder, but not in samples of cyder from Herefordshire. (3) " Under the influence of his discovery a grievous endemic affliction rapidly became extinct."	Baker observed that the colic was rare in cyder-producing areas other than Devonshire, *e.g.* in Hereford. He found that lead was used in the construction of the cyder presses in Devonshire, and that the apple juice was in direct contact with the metal. Lead was rarely so used in other counties. (2) " Cognitio causae morbum tollet."

CAUSES OF CANCERS

TABLE LXIV

Occupational Epithelioma of Scrotum[14 28 32 38 73]

CLINICAL MEDICINE	CHEMISTRY, PHYSICS, EXPERIMENTAL PATHOLOGY	EPIDEMIOLOGY
Pott in 1775 described scrotal tumours in chimney sweeps who when young had been forced to the job. The long incubation period was emphasised. He made an eloquent plea for action against this exploitation of the boys. (1) Later it was observed that the disease may develop many years after exposure to the hazard had ceased.	Kennaway and his co-workers in 1932 identified the policyclic hydrocarbon 3:4-benzpyrene as the responsible carcinogen in soot. The tumour was reproduced in animals.	In 1946, 150 years after Pott, using mortality data, "shoe-leather" epidemiology, and taking detailed occupational histories, Henry confirmed that there was a gross persisting excess of the disease (nearly 200-fold) in men who had been chimney sweeps. Recently the tumour has become rare: no-one climbs chimneys for a living; soot is removed mechanically; people are cleaner.

284

TABLE LXV

Papilloma of Bladder in Dyestuffs Workers[9] [10] [31] [32]

Described by Rehn in 1895, among workers engaged in the manufacture of magenta from aniline. He considered the latter the most likely agent—whence "aniline tumours". (1)	In 1937 Hueper et al. were able to produce bladder tumours in dogs by exposing them to β-naphthylamine. (2)	Ad hoc *cohort studies* by Case, Pearson et al., 1954, revealed a gross excess incidence of bladder cancer in workers making and handling β-naphthylamine, α-naphthylamine, benzidine (and probably also magenta and auramine). Routine occupational mortality statistics had failed to reveal the problem because the groups of workers are too small. These tumours characteristically occurred at younger ages than the non-occupational papillomata of the bladder. The incubation period of occupational cases was found to be very variable, most frequently between 15 and 20, but ranging from 4 to 48 years. *Individual risk* of workers developing the disease on conditions then prevalent was found to be exceedingly high, between 1 in *10* and 1 in *5*. *Epidemiological control:* Use of β-naphthylamine, the most lethal substance, has been prohibited by international agreement. The Code of Practice also includes standards of plant operation, and details of medical supervision.

TABLE LXVI

Leukaemia From Ionising Radiations[15] [17] [26]

CLINICAL OBSERVATION

In 1911 the association between leukaemia and previous exposure to X-rays was first observed in a radiologist.

A high incidence of leukaemia was noticed in patients with spondylitis ankylopoietica who had received radiotherapy.

LABORATORY EXPERIMENT

Production of leukaemia by X-irradiation of mice.

POPULATION STUDIES

In USA an excess incidence of leukaemia has been found in radiologists compared with other physicians, and with the general public; there is some confirmatory evidence also from Britain.

Survivors of Hiroshima (and Nagasaki) have shown a high incidence of the disease:

Incidence of Leukaemia in Residents of Hiroshima
1947-58

DISTANCE FROM EXPLOSION HYPOCENTRE IN METRES	PERSON-YEARS AT RISK	NO. OF CASES OF LEUKAEMIA	INCIDENCE PER MILLION PERSON-YEARS AT RISK
0 - 999	14,638	20	1,366
1,000 - 1,499	126,446	39	308
1,500 - 1,999	214,629	9	42
2,000 - 9,999	747,827	21	28
Total	1,103,540	89	81

BRILL, A. B., TOMONAGA, M., HEYSSEL, R. B. (1962). *Ann. intern. Med.* **56**, 590.

The estimated incidence in Japan as a whole is 20-30 cases per million persons, per year.

Radiotherapy

National follow-up survey in Britain has provided large-scale confirmation of clinical observations on treated spondylitis: a ten-fold increase of incidence of leukaemia was found. Relation of risk of leukaemia to dosage of X-rays could be postulated on a quite small number of *cases* of leukaemia (28) because the " population ", in this instance *all* the patients who were irradiated for spondylitis, could be defined. There was no evidence of excess of leukaemia in those suffering from ankylosing spondylitis who had not had radiotherapy.

Diagnostic X-ray

Excess of leukaemia has also been found among children subjected to X-rays ante-natally—diagnostic dosage to mother:

Frequency of Prenatal X-ray Examination in Children 0-9 Years with Malignant Disease

DISEASE	PRENATAL X-RAY	
	OBSERVED	EXPECTED*
LEUKAEMIA		
Lymphatic	57	29
Myeloid	10	5
Stem Cell	9	9
Monocytic	1	2
Unspecified	19	9
ALL	96	54
OTHER MALIGNANT DISEASE	115	63

* Expectation based on all controls in 1 year age-groups.

STEWART, A. M. (1961). *Brit. med. J.* **1**, 452. Personal communication.

Individual risk of a child under 10 dying of malignant disease is about 1 in 1,200.[57] If the child is X-rayed prenatally the risk may be estimated at about 1 in 800 or 900.[43] About half this risk is for leukaemia.

A much smaller excess of myeloid leukaemia has been observed in *adults* having diagnostic X-ray to the trunk.

*   *   *

There is no indication from present epidemiological evidence that ionising radiations, therapeutic or diagnostic, are responsible for more than a small fraction even of that part of leukaemia (acute leukaemia and chronic myeloid) with which they are associated.

TABLE LXVII

Production of Congenital Malformation by Rubella[7 23 27 33 34 41 67 81]

OPHTHALMOLOGY, ETC.	LABORATORY STUDY	EPIDEMIOLOGY
An inspired observation was made by Gregg, and others, in Australia during the routine recording of clinical case histories. They associated an unusual frequency of congenital malformation—cataract, deaf-mutism, heart disease—with rubella in early pregnancy. This was in 1940-1 when rubella had been unusually common. The clinicians recognised the importance of this observation and thereby opened up a whole new area of research into possible environmental causes of malformation. (1)	*Embryology.*—By special observation of humans and animal experiment it has been demonstrated that during a critical period of early embryonic life, when differentiation and growth are taking place, organs are specially vulnerable to damage. This suggests a possible mechanism of the disease: the specific malformations found after rubella are thought to be due to exposure of the mother to the infection during this vulnerable period, the 6th - 8th weeks of embryonic life possibly	*Testing of the hypothesis.* Looking back, and making use of routine official census statistics, a high rate of congenital deaf-mutism was identified in the cohort of births exposed to the epidemics of rubella that occurred in Australia during 1898-9 and other years, as well as in 1938-41. *Estimate of individual's risk* of producing malformation in pregnancy can be made. Because of the nature of the disease and the frequent difficulty in diagnosis, this requires "prospective" study including *all* pregnant women recognised at the time to have rubella or to be exposed to it, and appropriate controls. The *size* of the average individual risk is very relevant to questions of prophylactic abortion.

Results of prospective surveys have varied. These are the main findings of a co-operative study by British Medical Officers of Health:

Individual Risk of Major Malformation in Infant

567 Pregnant Women with Rubella

All mothers with rubella:
  Risk to infant = 1 in 14
Maternal rubella in first 12 weeks:
  Risk to infant = 1 in 6
Maternal rubella at 13-40 weeks:
  Risk to infant = 1 in 34
5,611 mothers who did not have rubella:
  Risk to infant = 1 in 36

There was also an excess of abortion, still-birth, infant death and low birth weight in the rubella cases.

A later audiometric survey in exposed children detected considerable subclinical hearing loss in addition to the clinical deafness.

Estimate of proportion of malformation that is due to rubella is difficult to make but it is almost certainly very small.

Search for evidence of special incidence of congenital anomalies in relation to *other viral infections* has so far yielded little result, excepting possibly with influenza where there seems to be a somewhat higher risk; pregnant women can therefore be reassured with a fair degree of confidence.

Teratology.—Congenital malformation has been produced in animals by many different causes, singly or in combination. For example: chemical or hormonal imbalance, vitamin or oxygen deficiency; but always by degree of malnutrition or other damage insufficient to kill the embryo. It can be postulated that it is the mildness of the infection in the case of rubella which is responsible for the frequent malformation rather than death of the embryo that occurs.

Virology.—The rubella virus invades the embryo. It also appears that the interferon antiviral mechanism is absent in early embryonic life.

TABLE LXVIII

Chronic Beryllium Disease[6] [25] [32] [69]

CLINICAL MEDICINE	LABORATORY STUDY	EPIDEMIOLOGY
Chronic beryllium disease was distinguished from the acute form by its duration (1 yr.+), and by the characteristic non-caseating granulomatous reaction in the lungs—where beryllium deposits can be demonstrated.	Animal experiment has shown that beryllium combined with a protein provokes a typical granulomatous reaction in the lung.	The industrial distribution of initial cases was described, and their localisation to particular factories confirmed. Exposure to beryllium in manufacture of fluorescent lamps, a new industry, was shown to be the common factor. Cases have been identified not merely in process workers but in clerks, in people living near beryllium extraction plants ("neighbourhood" cases) and in wives, "conjugal" cases.
It was first described in 1946 in Salem, Mass., having previously been confused with silicosis; miliary T.B.; and pulmonary sarcoidosis, whence "Salem sarcoid".	Beryllium can usually be demonstrated in the urine and affected tissues, but the amounts detected are not related to the occurrence or severity of the disease.	Estimates of case-fatality were made from the overall experience: it is probably about 30-40 per cent in untreated cases.
The idea of beryllium arose when it was noticed that all the early cases came from the same fluorescent lamp factory.		A Case Register has been established in Massachusetts.
The disease may appear long (e.g. 10 yrs.) after exposure. Prognosis is poor. Steroids may produce some improvement of symptoms.	A skin-patch test of hypersensitivity to beryllium has been devised which can be used in diagnosis (it may produce flare-up of the pulmonary condition). A positive test may revert with steroid therapy.	The individual risk on exposure has been estimated, and found often to be small and unrelated to size of dose. Personal susceptibility or hypersensitivity seems to be a crucial factor.

TABLE LXIX

Protein Malnutrition in Children (Kwashiorkor)[3 35 60 61 71 76 77]

CLINICAL MEDICINE	LABORATORY STUDY	EPIDEMIOLOGY
In 1933 (as late as this) Cicely Williams described *Kwashiorkor*, a syndrome occurring shortly after weaning and characterised by failure of growth and muscle wasting often masked by oedema; apathy; and skin and hair changes. She suggested that "some amino acid or protein deficiency" could be the cause. A broader concept of protein-calorie malnutrition in early childhood has since developed, including Kwashiorkor, Marasmus and other less definite syndromes. All occur during the transition from adequate breast-feeding to a diet largely composed of starchy foods.	A deficiency of protein and calories in the diet has been demonstrated. This leads to a failure of protein synthesis in the tissues which prevents normal development. Total body water may account for 80 per cent of body weight. Serum albumin level is always low and electrolyte disturbances are evident.	Malnutrition of children is common in under-developed countries: Kwashiorkor is a major public health problem in 19 of 21 countries in the Americas; all countries of Africa south of the Sahara; India, and most countries of the Middle and Far East. Lack of suitable foodstuffs due to low productivity, poor processing and distribution; and a general failure to use the available resources are the main causes in the country. Early weaning, because mothers go out to work, and (inadequate) bottle feeding with its added risk of infection, are results of changes in the traditional way of life, with immigration to towns, etc. *Point prevalence* by a house-to-house survey gives a good estimate of frequency. The crude mortality rate at 1-4 years, regardless of certified cause, is suggested as a useful index of nutritional status of a community: *Mauritius* 10·7; *England and Wales* 0·87 per 1,000 in 1960 (cf. pp. 24, 31). Work by UN Agencies and INCAP is aimed at the development and production of inexpensive, balanced and acceptable protein-food mixtures, and in making these available to vulnerable groups within the population.

SOLVING A NUTRITIONAL PROBLEM

TABLE LXX

Epidemic Dropsy in Bengal[40][43][59]

CLINICAL MEDICINE	LABORATORY STUDY	EPIDEMIOLOGY
Description of the syndrome : it is characterised by oedema, tachycardia, diarrhoea, pyrexia and a raised ESR. The infrequency of peripheral neuritis distinguishes it from beri beri, and the normal level of plasma proteins from hunger oedema. The clinical "hunch" associated the disease with a diet in which mustard oil was used in the preparation of curries. (1)	Laboratory experiment showed that the disease is due to poisoning by Mexican poppy seeds which contaminate the mustard oil. The symptoms were so reproduced experimentally in human volunteers and in animals. (3)	The disease was found to occur in *clusters*. For example, it was observed in Calcutta and district; in particular villages; among Bengalis, especially middle-class; in particular households; in Indian nationals living abroad. (2)

TABLE LXXI

Cause of Goitre in Tasmania (Clements)[12 13 20]

CLINICAL MEDICINE	LABORATORY STUDY	EPIDEMIOLOGY
Observation in 1949 of high frequency of goitre in Tasmania. (1)	Twenty-five years before, Chesney had demonstrated the goitrogenic action of an agent in *brassica* seeds (*e.g.* Kale). "Goitrin" has now been isolated from these vegetables and roots, and shown to block the uptake of iodine by the thyroid. *Radioactive Isotopes* Clements and co-workers showed that there was interference with uptake of I^{131} in adults who drank milk from cows fed on choumollier, one of these vegetables. (3)	A special survey in 1949 during routine school medical inspection confirmed the clinical impressions of increased incidence of goitre among children in Tasmania. Mass distribution of K1 was organised, but re-survey five years later showed a further rise of incidence in the children, *i.e.* the customary response to iodine was not obtained. Moreover, boys were affected as much as girls, unlike the picture in iodine-deficiency goitre. In the period between the two surveys there was considerable increase in milk consumption by children. To meet the demand for milk, production of forage crop choumollier—a Kale—was greatly increased. (2) Selective distribution of the goitre showed that personal susceptibility was probably also involved.

293

TABLE LXXII

Sex Ratio in Ischaemic Heart Disease[16 37 39 48 52 53 57 63 64 65 68 70]

CLINICAL MEDICINE	LABORATORY STUDY	EPIDEMIOLOGY
Women rarely have ischaemic heart disease before the menopause and usually there are special circumstances when they do: in particular, early impairment of ovarian function (premature menopause), or diastolic hypertension.	Evidence on relevant mechanisms: The serum cholesterol level in women is lower than in men until the menopause, after which it increases steeply to a higher average level. β lipoproteins are higher in men than women. Similarly, mean BP levels until middle age are somewhat lower in women (see pp. 184 and 39). On present information these differences are too small to account for the sex difference in IHD.	*Coronary atheroma* is less severe in women, age for age, than in men and *coronary occlusion* less common. On prospective study, *incidence of IHD* through middle age is higher in men than in women. *IHD mortality* under 45 years of age is eight times higher in men than in women. From 45 it rises far more steeply in women, and in old age the male rate is only about twice the female (cf. p. 112). A simple expression in vital statistics of an accurate clinical observation. There is some evidence that this sex ratio is a feature of populations with a high incidence of IHD.
There is some evidence of regression of coronary atheroma in males on oestrogen therapy for carcinoma of prostate. Clinical trials of oestrogens in men surviving a clinical episode of IHD have yielded conflicting results.	Lipoprotein pattern in males changes to a "female" pattern with oestrogens. Coronary but not aortic atheroma in cockerels has been cleared by oestrogen therapy.	The prevalence of coronary atheroma and IHD mortality is nearly as high in US negro women as in negro men; this may be related to the great frequency of hypertension in these women.

TABLE LXXIII

Psychological Aspects of Production and Course of Duodenal (Peptic) Ulcer[4] [5] [21] [24] [36] [44] [46] [49] [63] [78] [79] [80]

CLINICAL MEDICINE	EXPERIMENTAL PHYSIOLOGY	EPIDEMIOLOGY
Characteristic features have been described in the *childhood experience* and adult *personality* and behaviour pattern of patients with duodenal ulcer. This remains a controversial field; among other reasons because often little attempt has been made to study a complete clinical picture of DU, *i.e.* a representative series of cases, and because other diseases have not been studied as well. The notion is that particular individuals become prone to (duodenal) ulcer. Several studies have related the production of symptoms and relapse with DU, to the *life situation*: to interpersonal, work and other strains, including what is symbolic of them, that represent a threat to the subject. In this sense, *i.e.* an attack of duodenal ulcer is one form of behaviour under stress. The greater the external strains. it may be postulated, the less important the personal predisposition. "Cures" of the disease in concentration camps during the war have been reported, related conceivably to psychological and social causes (*e.g.* the handling of aggression) as well as to physical causes (*e.g.* the starvation).	It is postulated that high blood pepsinogen levels represent the physiological predisposition, "organ inferiority", of the disease. In these subjects, strain during development or in adult life may precipitate hypersecretion and ulceration. The influence of conscious and unconscious feelings and ideas have been demonstrated experimentally on gastric functions—motor, secretory, and vascular. Ulceration has been produced in monkeys under periodic psychological stress.	There is evidence that DU is commoner in towns than in country. Agricultural workers seem to be relatively immune to the disease. Prevalence of DU in a field survey was found to be higher in men in social classes I and II, and in those engaged in jobs involving responsibility. Outbreaks of perforation were recorded during the "blitz". Recently DU has appeared to decline; so far without explanation (p. 19).

IDENTIFICATION OF SYNDROMES

TABLE LXXIV

Two Types of Diabetes Mellitus[8] [11] [18] [29] [30] [55] [63] [66] [72]

CLINICAL OBSERVATION

It is possible to group most diabetic patients into two syndromes: (1) the young and thin, ketosis-liable, insulin-requiring type, or (2) the adult and obese type in which often there is recovery from the diabetic state on a low CHO diet, and which responds to oral hypoglycaemic drugs. The mode of onset also differs. The diabetes which begins during childhood and adolescence usually is acute, with loss of weight, dehydration or coma. In middle-aged and elderly patients (more than 75 per cent of all attending diabetic clinics) the onset is usually insidious, the patient presenting with classical symptoms of thirst, etc., with " complications " (retinopathy, neuropathy, skin sepsis, etc.); or asymptomatic glycosuria is found at routine examination. Because of the frequent undramatic nature of the presentation, ad hoc detection of diabetes is a feasible exercise after 45 or 50 years of age in clinical practice.

LABORATORY STUDY

Bioassay of insulin has become sufficiently sensitive to measure the circulating levels of insulin-like activity, *i.e.* the balance between insulin and synergists, and their antagonists. Such measurements have revealed low levels of insulin-like activity in juvenile-type diabetics, but relatively normal levels in adult-onset, obese diabetics.

ANTHROPOMETRY

Somatotype and simpler studies confirm the differences in body build between the two types of diabetics.

FEATURES FOR COMPARISON	YOUNG DIABETICS	MIDDLE-AGED DIABETICS
MORTALITY RATES (ENGLAND AND WALES)		
(a) With food restriction during and after 1st World War	Little change in rates	Rates fell
(b) With the introduction of Insulin	Rapid and sustained fall in rates	Little immediate change in rates
(c) With food restriction during and after 2nd World War	Rates continued to fall	Rates fell
(d) In men (1930-2) in relation to *occupation*	No relationship	Higher rate in sedentary and " light " workers than in " heavy ", the rate in "active" workers being intermediate
CLINICAL - PREVALENCE STUDIES Sex ratio	M : F, is 1 : 1	M : F, is $1 < 1$ (partly due to excess of women in general population in this age group)
Prevalence and parity	No relationship	Frequency rises with increasing parity. (A woman with 5 children has 3 times as much chance of developing diabetes as a woman with none.) Parity is main factor in overall excess of disease in women.

POPULATION GENETICS

TABLE LXXV

Discovery of Blood Groups[47 50 56 58]

CLINICAL MEDICINE	LABORATORY STUDY	EPIDEMIOLOGY
In 1829 the first beneficial blood transfusion was given, to a post-partum patient. Subsequently, however, many accidents resulted from incompatible transfusion.	Following earlier work in animals, Landsteiner in 1901 discovered the ABO blood groups and recognised their role in blood transfusion. Later, with other workers, he described MNP and Rh blood group systems. With this knowledge the development of cross-matching techniques led to safe transfusion.	Blood groups are ideal as markers for fundamental genetic investigation because of their precise, qualitative and clearly classifiable inheritance. They are extensively used in anthropological studies; racial and geographical frequencies have been described.

The systematic relationships of blood groups with various diseases, *e.g.* cancer of stomach and duodenal ulcer, are being determined. |

TABLE LXXVI

The Rh Factor[42][74]

CLINICAL MEDICINE	LABORATORY STUDY	EPIDEMIOLOGY
Investigations of intrauterine and neonatal deaths resulted in the description of syndromes of erythroblastosis foetalis: (1) with hydrops foetalis in stillbirth and (2) with haemolytic jaundice, kernicterus and haemolytic anaemia in the newborn.	In 1939 abnormal antibodies were detected in the serum of an Rh negative woman recently delivered of a stillborn infant. Levine postulated that immunisation by cells from the foetus had taken place. Four years later isoimmunisation in pregnancy was found to be the basis of haemolytic disease of the newborn. In the majority of cases it is due to Rh incompatibility, but other blood group systems can be responsible. Abnormal antibodies in the serum may also result from previous transfusion. Screening tests for abnormal antibodies in pregnant women have been developed, together with methods designed to protect the foetus from the effect of antibody; (the greatest progress so far has been in the treatment of the affected infant).	Population differences in incidence of erythroblastosis foetalis were first described and then explained. For example, Rh negative individuals are uncommon among negroes. Frequency in this country of the disease in the newborn is about 1 in 180.

In England and Wales, the mortality from erythroblastosis rose between 1940 and 1950, possibly because of greater recognition of the condition, and fell between 1950 and 1960 probably because of greater anticipation with early diagnosis and effective treatment. |

TABLE LXXVII

Sickling[1 19 51 54]

CLINICAL MEDICINE	LABORATORY STUDY	EPIDEMIOLOGY
A haemolytic anaemia described in negro children and young adults was called sickle-cell anaemia because of the histological appearance of the erythrocytes.	An abnormal haemoglobin molecule S has been demonstrated electrophoretically, and it is now accepted that the anomaly is caused by a single mutant gene. Homozygotes for the sickle-cell gene develop a profound anaemia which is usually fatal before puberty. Heterozygotes for the gene are carriers of the sickle-cell trait, have a mixture of normal and abnormal haemoglobin, and do not develop haemolytic anaemia.	Sickle-cell genes are constantly lost through deaths from anaemia, but a high frequency remains. There is a 20 per cent gene frequency in a broad belt across Central Africa, and in some villages it is as high as 50 per cent. It is found almost exclusively in negroes. The high frequency of the sickle-cell trait is explained by the selective advantage of the genotype; the abnormal erythrocyte is less easily parasitised by *P. falciparum* and thus a considerable degree of protection against MT malaria results. The relative selective advantages of the genotypes, homozygous normal: heterozygous sickling: and homozygous sickling, are in the ratio 1:32:0. Sickling is infrequent in the American negroes, presumably because the heterozygous state confers no selective advantage in a non-malarial region. This breakthrough has stimulated vast interest in genetic polymorphisms and their possible relationships with (common) diseases.

INTRODUCTION OF A NEW HEALTH SERVICE

TABLE LXXVIII

Provision of Hearing Aids[22][75]

CLINICAL MEDICINE	LABORATORY STUDY	EPIDEMIOLOGY
Diagnosis of different types of deafness. Importance of otitis media in childhood.	*Acoustics, Electronics, Plastics* Provision of efficient and cheap apparatus. Fine diagnosis by audiometry.	*Social surveys* were carried out by the Government's agency, at the start of the National Health Service, to estimate how many of the hearing aids would be needed; and later, to ascertain how much they were being utilised and the satisfaction they gave. These surveys overcame the difficulty inherent in generalising from clinical experience (*i.e.* from what presents) to the community which includes people not ordinarily seen and who may well be different.

GLOSSARY

The main tools of epidemiology, as used in this book, and with particular reference to the study of *chronic, non-infectious diseases,* are the Incidence Rate and Prevalence Rate, which are needed in the study of morbidity, and the Death Rate. The *incidence* is a measure of new cases of a disease, the *prevalence* a measure of all cases. Crude rates refer to whole populations; specific rates to specified sex(es), age groups, etc., in them. What is recognised as " disease " has to be defined on stated criteria.

In practical terms, and in the way they are usually calculated, as proportions of 1,000 population, these rates may be expressed as follows:

The *Incidence Rate* of a disease during a year, the *Annual Incidence* =

$$\frac{\text{No. of specified persons newly manifest-ing a disease in a stated year}}{\text{Ave. no. of such persons at risk during that year}} \times 1,000.$$

Persons may be " specified " as said by their sex, age, occupation, etc. " Newly manifesting " a disease will be defined in terms of what is regarded as the first attack, and its date of onset. These will be arbitrarily defined, depending on the particular circumstances, to give a valid and reproducible indicator of *new development, first occurrence,* of the condition being studied. Three situations are common in the chronic diseases. (1) In *clinical* disease, the incidence will be defined by the appearance of the first symptom (*e.g.* cardiac pain) or, when it is convenient, by first absence from work (*e.g.* in cardiac infarction), even by first admission to (mental) hospital. (2) In cases of *subclinical* disease the incidence can be defined as the first detection of a sign (*e.g.* ECG ischaemic change) in persons previously known to be free of it; (3) such previous knowledge is not necessary where the natural history of the disease indicates that what is detected is obviously the first attack (*e.g.* lung-cancer detected on routine X-ray). Definition (2) can readily be extended to the discovery of silent *precursor abnormalities* (*e.g.* cervical carcinoma *in situ* in women with previous normal cytology).

In acute conditions, subjects previously attacked who have recovered may again be regarded as at risk and liable to further fresh attack. This is an uncommon situation in the chronic diseases.

Characteristically, chronic diseases remit and relapse. *Relapse Rates* can be calculated of second, or later, attacks, as required; and an *Attack Rate*. This is the proportion of a population having attacks that begin during a stated period, and includes in the numerator of the rate all individuals attacked for the first time (the incidence) or in recurrences.

The *Prevalence* of a disease is determined by its incidence, its course and duration. It is usually measured in one of two ways.

The *Point Prevalence Rate* =

$$\frac{\text{No. of specified persons manifesting a disease at a stated point in time}}{\text{No. of such persons at risk at that time}} \times 1{,}000.$$

Another measure of prevalence, the Period Prevalence, is the proportion of persons having a disease during a stated period. For example, the *Annual Prevalence Rate* =

$$\frac{\text{No. of specified persons manifesting a disease in a stated year}}{\text{Ave. no. of such persons at risk during that year}} \times 1{,}000.$$

In a stable population the period prevalence thus equals the point prevalence at the beginning of the period, plus the attack rate during the period; except that each person is counted only once.

In studying morbidity multiple measures are needed, and they will often have to be specially defined for the particular study. The incidence, and some measure of prevalence, usually are required and I hope that by now it is beyond doubt how different these are. The " incidence " of new events is a necessary measure for historical study, in seeking causes that might be producing a disease, in estimating individual risks and, of course, in assessing attempts at primary prevention. The " prevalence " measures the burden of (chronic) disease, on the community at large or on particular population groups, and it is needed to assess the benefits of treatment, including attempts at secondary prevention. The more " chronic " a condition the more important is it to have good measures of prevalence; in the most acute, *e.g.* the common cold, there is no meaningful distinction between incidence and prevalence.

The *Individual Risk* of developing a disease during a stated period closely approximates the cumulative incidence during that period. For practical purposes it may be taken as such, and expressed as a *1 in x* chance of developing the disease between the beginning and end of the period. Life Table methods will be used when greater accuracy is required (for example when the incidence is high particularly at younger ages, or where mortality from diseases other than the one being studied is high).

All the above rates refer to *persons*, and a person can appear only once in the numerator (and of course the denominator). It is often necessary, in administration for example, to know also the frequency of *episodes*, of attacks of myocardial infarction in middle-aged men for example, spells of sick absence from bronchitis in insured workers, or admissions to hospital. In these circumstances, the numerator of the rate equals the number of relevant episodes (attacks, spells, admissions) occurring during a stated period, and the denominator is again the average number of persons at risk during that period.

Duration of disease is often a straightforward measurement. But there are many problems with *severity* and *disability*; these are insufficiently standardised as yet to be included in any Glossary, and they will be defined operationally for the particular context.

Mortality

The *Death Rate*, or *mortality* for short, is the proportion of a population dying of a disease or set of diseases, *i.e.* a " cause " or " multiple causes "; or dying from " all causes ". As reckoned in official statistics, the death rate from a disease means the frequency of death during a year in which the disease, as named in the WHO I(nternational) S(tatistical) C(lassification), was the main or underlying cause. The *death rate* thus =

$$\frac{\text{No. of specified persons dying of a disease in a stated year}}{\text{Ave. no. of such persons at risk during that year}} \times 1,000.$$

When convenient, *e.g.*, when numbers in the numerator are small, death rates are reckoned per 10,000, 100,000 or million population.

Infant Mortality refers to deaths in the first year of life. IM = the deaths under the age of one occurring in a stated year per 1,000 live births during that year. In this country the *Stillbirth Rate* (of late foetal deaths) is calculated per 1,000 *total* births, live and stillborn; internationally, the trend is to exclude stillbirths from the denominator so that both IM and stillbirth have the same denominator. This makes it tidier to calculate *perinatal mortality*, which = stillbirths + deaths in the first week of life.

The death rate, as in the above examples, applies to the population at risk of having a disease. When the death rate among those known to have a disease is required, the term *Case-Fatality* is used. In that event the denominator includes a defined group having the disease, and the numerator is the number of them who die of it in a stated period. This notion can be extended to other aspects than fatality, *e.g.* to the numbers having relapses and remissions and, with Life Table methods, to prognosis.

REFERENCES

GENERAL

ACKERNECHT, E. H. (1945). *Bull. Hist. Med.* Suppl. No. **4**, 1.
American Journal of Public Health. Bookshelf series, annually.
BENJAMIN, B. (1959). *Elements of Vital Statistics.* London.
CASSEL, J., PATRICK, R. & JENKINS, D. (1960). *Ann. N.Y. Acad. Sci.* **84**, 938.
CAUDILL, W. (1953). In *Anthropology Today.* Ed. Kroeber, A. L. Chicago.
COHN, A. E. & LINGG, C. (1950). *The Burden of Diseases in the United States.* New York.
COPEMAN, S. A. M. & GREENWOOD, M. (1926). *Rep. publ. Hlth med. Subj. Lond.* No. **36.**
CRUICKSHANK, R. (1961). *Measurements in Medicine.* Edinburgh.
FRANCIS, T. (1954). *J. med. Educ.* **29**, 15.
FRANCIS, T. (1961). *Publ. Hlth Rep. Wash.* **76**, 963.
FARR, W. (1885). *Vital Statistics.* Ed. Humphreys, N. A. London.
FINAN, J. L. (1964). *Open vs. Closed System Models of Causation in Epidemiological Research.* In press.
FROST, W. H. (1941). *Papers of W. H. Frost.* Ed. Maxcy, K. F. New York.
GALE, A. H. (1959). *Epidemic Diseases.* London.
GOLDBERGER, E. *Collected Papers of E. Goldberger.* Ed. Terris, M. In press.
GOODALL, E. W. (1933). *A Short History of the Epidemic Infectious Diseases.* London.
GORDON, J. E. (1953). In *The Epidemiology of Health.* Ed. Galdston, I. New York.
GORDON, J. E. (1963). *Amer. J. med. Sci.* **246**, 354.
GREENWOOD, M. (1935). *Epidemics and Crowd Diseases.* London.
GREENWOOD, M. (1948). *Medical Statistics from Graunt to Farr.* Cambridge.
HILL, A. B. (1961). *Principles of Medical Statistics.* London.
HILL, A. B. (1963). *Statistical Methods in Clinical and Preventive Medicine.* Edinburgh.
KARK, S. L. & STEUART, G. W. (1963). Ed. *A Practice of Social Medicine.* Edinburgh.
LEAVELL, H. R. & CLARK, E. G. (1958). *Preventive Medicine.* London.
LOGAN, W. P. D. (1950). *Popul. Stud.* **4**, 132.
MACMAHON, B., PUGH, T. F. & IPSEN, J. (1960). *Epidemiologic Methods.* London.
McKEOWN, T. (1961). *Milbank. mem. Fd. Quart.* **39**, 594.
MAY, J. (1958). *The Ecology of Human Disease.* New York.
MISHLER, E. G. & SCOTCH, N. A. (1963). *Psychiatry* **26**, 315.
MORRIS, J. N. (1947). *Lancet* **2**, 341.
MORRIS, J. N. (1955). *Brit. med. J.* **2**, 395.
ORR, J. B. (1937). *Food, Health and Income.* London.
OSBORNE, R. H. (1961). Ed. Conference on Genetic Perspective in Disease Resistance and Susceptibility. *Ann. N.Y. Acad. Sci.* **91**, Art. 3, 595.
PAUL, J. R. (1958). *Clinical Epidemiology.* Chicago.
PEARL, R. (1928). *The Rate of Living.* London.
PEMBERTON, J. (1963). Ed. *Epidemiology. Reports on Research and Teaching 1962.* London.
PEMBERTON, J. & WILLARD, H. (1958). Eds. *Recent Studies in Epidemiology.* Oxford.
PICKLES, W. N. (1939). *Epidemiology in a Country Practice.* Bristol.
ROSEN, G. (1947). *Bull. Hist. Med.* **21**, 674.

ROSEN, G. (1948). *Milbank mem. Fd. Quart.* **26**, 7.
ROSENAU (1956). *Preventive Medicine and Public Health.* Ed. Maxcy, K. F. New York.
RYLE, J. A. (1948). *Changing Disciplines.* London.
SCHILLING, R. S. F. (1960). Ed. *Modern Trends in Occupational Health.* London.
SCHUMAN, L. M. (1963). Ed. Conference on Research Methodology and Potential in Community Health and Preventive Medicine. *Ann. N.Y. Acad. Sci.* **107**, Art. 2, 471.
SCOTCH, N. A. & GEIGER, H. J. (1962). *J. chron. Dis.* **15**, 1037.
SHEPS, C. G. & TAYLOR, E. E. (1954). *Needed Research in Health and Medical Care.* Chapel Hill.
SIGERIST, H. E. *On the Sociology of Medicine.* Ed. Roemer, M. I. (1960). New York.
SMITH, G. (1941). *Plague on Us.* New York.
STOCKS, P. (1934). *Proc. R. Soc. Med.* **27**, 1127.
STOCKS, P. (1938). *J. R. statist. Soc.* **101**, 688.
SWAROOP, S. (1960). *Introduction to Health Statistics.* Edinburgh.
SYDENSTRICKER, E. (1933). *Health and Environment.* New York.
TAYLOR, I. & KNOWELDEN, J. (1957). *Principles of Epidemiology.* London.
TOP, F. H. (1952). *History of American Epidemiology.* St. Louis.
VERNON, H. M. (1939). *Health in Relation to Occupation.* London.
VON PETTENKOFER, M. (1873). *The Value of Health to a City.* Transl. Sigerist, H. E. (1941). *Bull. Hist. Med.* **10**, 597.
WORLD HEALTH ORGANIZATION (1959). Immunological and Haematological Surveys. *Wld Hlth Org. techn. Rep. Ser.* No. **181**.
WINSLOW, C-E. A. (1944). *The Conquest of Epidemic Disease.* Princeton.
WITTS, L. J. (1959). Ed. *Medical Surveys and Clinical Trials.* London.
ZINSSER, H. (1960). *Rats, Lice and History.* London. (Re-issue.)

CHAPTER 1

[1] ANDERSON, T. A. (1962). *Scot. med. J.* **7**, 44.
[2] BENJAMIN, B. (1957). In *The Biology of Ageing. Symposia of the Institute of Biology.* London.
BENJAMIN, B. (1962). Personal communication.
[3] CARSTAIRS, G. M. (1963). *This Island Now.* London.
[4] CARRIER, N. H. (1962). In *Society.* Ed. Welford, A. T., Argyle, M., Glass, D. V. & Morris, J. N. London.
[5] CARTER, C. O. (1956). *Gt. Ormond St. J. No. 11,* 65.
CARTER, C. O. (1958). *J. ment. Defic. Res.* **2**, 64.
[6] DOLL, R., JONES, F. AVERY & BUCKATZSCH, M. M. (1951). *Spec. Rep. ser. med. Res. Coun., Lond.* No. **276**.
[7] DUBOS, R. (1959). *Mirage of Health.* London.
[8] ENGEL, G. (1962). *Psychological Development in Health and Disease.* London.
[9] EPSTEIN, F. H. In press.
[10] FOOD AND AGRICULTURE ORGANIZATION (1963). *Third World Food Survey.* Rome: FAO.
SUKHATME, P. V. (1961). *J.R. statist. Soc. Ser. A,* **124**, 463.
[11] FOX, W. (1962). *Lancet* **2**, 413, 473.
[12] GALDSTON, I. (1942). *Bull. N.Y. Acad. Med.* **18**, 606.
GALDSTON, I. (1951). *Bull. Hist. Med.* **25**, 8.
GALDSTON, I. Personal communications.
[13] GLASS, D. V. (1963). *Fam. Plan.* **12**, 5.
GLASS, D. V. (1963). *Malay ec. Rev.* **8**, 29.
GLASS, D. V. (1963). Personal communication.

[14] GOLDHAMER, H. & MARSHALL, A. W. (1953). *Psychosis and Civilisation.* Glencoe, Ill.

[15] GOODMAN, N. & TIZARD, J. (1962). *Brit. med. J.* **1,** 216.

[16] GORER, G. *Proc. R. Soc. Med.* In press.

[17] GRAUNT, J. (1662). *Natural and Political Observations made upon The Bills of Mortality.* London.
   BENJAMIN, B. (1963). *Proc. R. Soc. B.* **159.** In press.
   GLASS, D. V. (1963). *Proc. R. Soc. B.* **159.** In press
   SUTHERLAND, I. (1963). *J. R. statist. Soc.* Ser. A, **126,** 537.
   MANN, G. V. (1957). *Amer. J. Med.* **23,** 463.

[18] GROUP FOR THE ADVANCEMENT OF PSYCHIATRY (1961). *Problems of Estimating Changes in Frequency of Mental Disorders.* Rep. ho. 50. New York.

[19] HALDANE, J. B. S. (1954). *The Biochemistry of Genetics.* London.

[20] HEADY, J. A., MORRIS, J. N., KAGAN, A. & RAFFLE, P. A. B. (1961). *Brit. J. prev. soc. Med.* **15,** 143.

[21] MINISTRY OF HEALTH. *On the State of the Public Health.* Annual Reports, and corresponding volumes. London: Her Majesty's Stationery Office (HMSO).

[22] HEATH, E. A. J. (1954). *J. Inst. Actu.* **8,** 32.

[22a] HOBSON, W. (1961). Public Health Problems of an Ageing Population. In *The Theory and Practice of Public Health.* Ed. Hobson, W. London.

[23] JENNINGS, D. (1940). *Lancet* **1,** 395, 444.

[24] JONES, F. AVERY (1957). *Brit. med. J.* **1,** 719, 786.

[25] KING, A. J. (1958). *Lancet* **1,** 651.

[26] MINISTRY OF LABOUR (1963). Personal communications.

[27] LEE, J. A. H. (1963). *Proc. R. Soc. Med.* **56,** 365.

[28] LE GROS CLARK, F. (1960). *Growing Old in a Mechanized World.* London.

[29] LEWIS, A. J. (1953). *Brit. J. Sociol.* **4,** 109.
   LEWIS, A. J. (1962). *Yale J. Biol. Med.* **35,** 62.

[30] MACMILLAN, D. (1963). *Lancet* **1,** 567.

[31] MEDAWAR, P. B. (1952). *An Unsolved Problem of Biology.* London.

[32] MEDICAL OFFICERS OF HEALTH, Cardiff, Merthyr Tydfil, Newport, Swansea (1962). Personal communications.

[33] *Mental Disorders: A Guide to Control Methods* (1962). New York: American Public Health Association.

[34] MORRIS, J. N. (1951). *Lancet* **1,** 1, 69.

[35] MORRIS, J. N. (1951). *Brit. med. J.* **2,** 548.

[36] MORRIS, J. N. (1961). In *The Theory and Practice of Public Health.* Ed. Hobson, W. London.

[37] MORRIS, J. N. (1963). *Proc. R. Soc. B.* **159.** In press.

[38] MORRIS, J. N., HEADY, J. A., RAFFLE, P. A. B., PARKS, J. W. & ROBERTS, C. G. (1953). *Lancet* **2,** 1053, 1111.

[39] MORRIS, J. N. & TITMUSS, R. M. (1942). *Lancet* **2,** 59.
   MORRIS, J. N. & TITMUSS, R. M. (1944). *Med. Offr* **72,** 69, 77, 85.

[40] MORRIS, J. N. & TITMUSS, R. M. (1944). *Lancet* **2,** 841.

[41] PARSONS, T. (1951). *The Social System,* chaps. 7 and 10. Glencoe, Ill.
   PARSONS, T. (1958). In *Patients, Physicians and Illness.* Ed. Jaco, E. G. Glencoe, Ill.

[42] MINISTRY OF PENSIONS AND NATIONAL INSURANCE. *Annual Reports; Annual Digests of Statistics Analysing Certificates of Incapacity.*
   MINISTRY OF PENSIONS AND NATIONAL INSURANCE (1954). *Reasons Given for Retiring or Continuing at Work.*
   MINISTRY OF PENSIONS AND NATIONAL INSURANCE. Personal communications.

[43] PLATT, R. (1956). *Lancet* **1,** 61.

[44] PULVERTAFT, C. N. (1959). *Brit. J. prev. soc. Med.* **13,** 131.

44a RAFFLE, P. A. B. London Transport Board, Medical Dept. Personal communications.
45 46 REGISTRAR GENERAL. England & Wales. *Tables, Part I Medical;* and corresponding annual volumes. London: HMSO.
47 REGISTRAR GENERAL. *Population;* and corresponding Part II, annual volumes. London: HMSO.
48 REGISTRAR GENERAL. *Commentary;* and corresponding annual volumes. London: HMSO.
49 REGISTRAR GENERAL. *Life Tables;* and *Quarterly Returns.* London: HMSO.
50 REGISTRAR GENERAL. Personal communications.
51 ROBERTS, J. A. F. (1961). *Proc. R. Soc. Med.* **54,** 841.
52 SHELDON, J. H. (1948). *The Social Medicine of Old Age.* London.
SHELDON, J. H. (1960). *Brit. med. J.* **1,** 1223.
53 SIMON, H. J. (1960). *Attenuated Infection:* the Germ Theory in Contemporary Perspective. Philadelphia.
54 *Social Insurance and Allied Services.* Report by Sir William Beveridge (1942). London: HMSO.
55 SOCIAL MEDICINE RESEARCH UNIT AND COLLABORATORS. Work in progress.
56 STEWART, A., PENNYBACKER, W. & BARBER, R. (1962). *Brit. med. J.* **2,** 882.
57 SUSSER. M. & STEIN, Z. (1962). *Lancet* **1,** 115.
58 TANNER, J. M. (1962). *Growth at Adolescence.* Oxford.
59 TITMUSS, R. M. & ABEL-SMITH, B., assisted by LYNES, T. A. (1961). *Social Policies and Population Growth in Mauritius.* London.
ANNUAL REPORTS, Government of Mauritius. Colonial Office, London. Personal communications.
60 THOMSON, D. (1955). *Mon. Bull. Minist. Hlth Lab. Serv.* **14,** 106.
THOMSON, D. (1957). *Mon. Bull. Minist. Hlth Lab. Serv.* **16,** 124.
61 WATSON, A. (1927). *J.R. statist. Soc.* **90,** Part III, 433.
WATSON, A. (1931). *J. Inst. Actu.* **62,** 12.
62 WEIR, R. D. (1960). *Scot. med. J.* **5,** 257.
63 WILLCOX, R. R. (1963). *Brit. J. vener. Dis.* **39,** 149.

CHAPTER II

1 ABRAMS, M. (1961). *The Teenage Consumer.* London.
2 *Amer. J. publ. Hlth* (1962). **52,** 759. Wegman, M., Mattison, B. F., et al.
3 *American Soldier* (1950). *Studies in Social Psychology in World War II.* Vol. IV. Chaps. 12-14. Stouffer, S. A. & Starr, S. F. Princeton.
4 BACKETT, E. M., SHAW, L. A. & EVANS, J. C. G. (1953). *Proc. R. Soc. Med.* **46,** 707.
5 BACKETT, E. M., HEADY, J. A. & EVANS, J. C. G. (1954). *Brit. med. J.* **1,** 109.
6 BAIRD, D. (1962). *Bull. Wld Hlth Org.* **26,** 291.
7 BUTLER, D. E. & ROSE, R. (1960). *The British General Election of 1959.* London.
8 CARSTAIRS, G. M. (1963). *This Island Now.* London.
9 COLE, D. & UTTING, J. E. G. (1962). *The Economic Circumstances of Old People.* Welwyn.
COLE WEDDERBURN, D. (1962). *Soc. Rev.* **10,** 257.
LAFITTE, F. (1963). Personal communication.
NATIONAL ASSISTANCE BOARD. *Annual Report for 1962.* London: HMSO.
10 CRAWFORD, M. D. & MORRIS, J. N. (1960). *Brit. med. J.* **2,** 1624.
11 DOUGLAS, J. W. B. (1951). *Lancet* **2,** 440.
DOUGLAS, J. W. B. & BLOMFIELD, J. M. (1958). *Children Under Five.* London.

[12] DUBOS, R. (1959). *Mirage of Health*. London.
[13] DUBOS, R. (1960). In *Disease and the Advancement of Basic Science*. Ed. Beecher, H. K. Cambridge, Mass.
[14] FESTINGER, L. & KATZ, D. (1954). *Research Methods in the Behavioural Sciences*. London.
[15] FLETCHER, C. M. (1964). *Proc. R. Soc. Med.* In press.
[15a] FLETCHER, C. M. & OLDHAM, P. D. (1959). In *Medical Surveys and Clinical Trials*. Ed. Witts, L. J. London. (Methodology.)
[16] FLOUD, J. E., HALSEY, A. H. & MARTIN, F. M. (1956). *Social Class and Educational Opportunity*. London.
[17] GALBRAITH, J. K. (1958). *The Affluent Society*. London.
[18] GALDSTON, I. (1954). *The Meaning of Social Medicine*. Cambridge, Mass.
[19] GILSON, J. C. (1959). *Proceedings of the Pneumoconiosis Conference, Johannesburg*, p. 348. London.
[20] GOLDBERG, E. M. (1958). *Family Influences and Psychological Illness*. London.
[21] HALLIDAY, J. L. (1948). *Psychosocial Medicine*. London.
[22] HEADY, J. A. (1961). *J.R. statist. Soc.* **124**, 336.
[23] HEADY, J. A. & HEASMAN, M. A. (1959). *Social and Biological Factors in Infant Mortality*. London: HMSO.
[24] HIGGINS, I. T. T. (1957). *Brit. med. J.* **2**, 1198.
HIGGINS, I. T. T. (1959). *Brit. med. J.* **1**, 325.
[25] HIGGINS, I. T. T., COCHRANE, A. L., OLDHAM, P. D. & GILSON, J. C. (1956). *Brit. med. J.* **2**, 904.
[26] HOGGART, R. (1957). *The Uses of Literacy*. London.
[27] HOLLINGSHEAD, A. B. & REDLICH, F. C. (1958). *Social Class and Mental Illness*. New York.
[28] HYMAN, H. H. (1955). *Survey Design and Analysis*. Glencoe, Ill.
[29] ILLSLEY, R. (1955). *Brit. med. J.* **2**, 1520.
[30] KAGAN, A. R. & PATTISON, D. C. In preparation.
[31] KELLGREN, J. H. & LAWRENCE, J. S. (1952). *Brit. J. industr. Med.* **9**, 197.
[32] KELSALL, R. K. (1957). *Applications for Admissions to Universities*. London.
[33] KESSEL, W. I. N. (1960). *Brit. J. prev. soc. Med.* **14**, 16.
[34] LAWRENCE, J. S. & AITKEN-SWAN, J. (1952). *Brit. J. industr. Med.* **9**, 1.
LAWRENCE, J. S. & AITKEN-SWAN, J. (1955). *Brit. J. industr. Med.* **12**, 249.
[35] LEE, J. A. H. (1963). *Proc. R. Soc. Med.* **56**, 365.
[36] LYNES, T. (1962). *National Assistance and National Prosperity*. Welwyn.
[37] MARR, J. W., HEADY, J. A. & MORRIS, J. N. (1959). *Proc. Nutr. Soc.* **18**, xii.
[38] MEADOWS, S. H. (1961). *Brit. J. prev. soc. Med.* **15**, 171.
[39] MILLER, F. J. W., COURT, S. D. M., WALTON, W. S. & KNOX, E. G. (1960). *Growing up in Newcastle upon Tyne*. London.
[40] MORRIS, J. N. (1951). *Lancet* **1**, 1, 69.
[41] MORRIS, J. N. (1959). *Lancet* **1**, 303.
[42] MORRIS, J. N. & CRAWFORD, M. D. (1958). *Brit. med. J.* **2**, 1485.
[43] MORRIS, J. N. & HEADY, J. A. (1955). *Lancet* **1**, 343, 554.
[44] MORRIS, J. N., HEADY, J. A. & BARLEY, R. G. (1952). *Brit. med. J.* **1**, 503.
[45] MORRIS, J. N., HEADY, J. A., RAFFLE, P. A. B., PARKS, J. W. & ROBERTS, C. G. (1953). *Lancet* **2**, 1053, 1111.
[46] MORRIS, J. N., MARR, J. W., HEADY, J. A., MILLS, G. L. & PILKINGTON, T. R. E. (1963). *Brit. med. J.* **1**, 571.
[47] MORRIS, J. N. & TITMUSS, R. M. (1942). *Lancet* **2**, 59.
MORRIS, J. N. & TITMUSS, R. M. (1944). *Med. Offr* **72**, 69, 77, 85.
[48] Mortality and Morbidity During the London Fog of December 1952. *Rep. publ. Hlth med. Subj. Lond.* No. **95**. HMSO.
[49] MOSER, C. A. (1958). *Survey Methods in Social Investigation*. London.
[50] MYRDAL, G. (1952). *Economic Aspects of Health. Chron. Wld Hlth Org.* **6**, 203.

[51] ØDEGÅRD, Ø. (1932). *Acta psychiat. neurol. scand.* Suppl. 4.
ØDEGÅRD, Ø. (1956). *Int. J. soc. Psychiat.* **2**, 85.
[52] MINISTRY OF PENSIONS AND NATIONAL INSURANCE. *Annual Reports Annual Digests of Statistics Analysing Certificates of Incapacity.*
MINISTRY OF PENSIONS AND NATIONAL INSURANCE. Personal communications.
[53] *Sickness Absence Statistics. Health in Industry* (1956). London: London Transport Executive.
[54] REGISTRAR GENERAL, ENGLAND AND WALES. *Classification of Occupations 1960* (1960). London: HMSO.
[55] REGISTRAR GENERAL. *Decennial Supplement on Occupational Mortality* (1958). *Commentary* volumes (Marriage). London: HMSO.
[56] REGISTRAR-GENERAL FOR SCOTLAND. *Annual Reports.*
REGISTRAR-GENERAL FOR SCOTLAND. Personal communication.
[57] REID, D. D. AND COLLEAGUES. Work in Progress.
MORK, T. (1962). *Acta med. scand.* **172**, Suppl. 384.
[58] ROAD RESEARCH LABORATORY (1960). *Road Accidents—Christmas 1959* London: HMSO.
[59] SCHILLING, R. S. F. (1956). *Lancet* **2**, 261.
SCHILLING, R. S. F., *et al.* Work in progress.
[60] SHERIDAN, M. D. (1962). *Mon. Bull. Minist. Hlth Lab. Serv.* **21**, 238.
[61] SIMMONS, O. G. (1958). *Social Status and Public Health.* New York Social Science Research Council.
[62] SIMON, J. (1890). *English Sanitary Institutions.* London.
[63] *Social Changes in Britain.* From Central Office of Information (1962) *New Society* **1**, No. 13, 26.
[64] SOCIAL MEDICINE RESEARCH UNIT AND COLLABORATORS. Work in progress
[65] STUART-HARRIS, C. H. (1954). *Brit. J. Tuberc.* **48**, 169.
[66] SUSSER, M. & WATSON, W. (1962). *Sociology in Medicine.* London.
[67] THOMSON, A. M. (1958). *Brit. J. Nutr.* **12**, 446.
THOMSON, A. M. (1963). *Mod. Probl. Pediat.* **8**, 197.
THOMSON, A. M. (1963). Personal communications.
[68] TITMUSS, R. M. (1958). *Essays on the Welfare State.* London. Reissued 1963, with paper on *The Irresponsible Society.*
[69] TOWNSEND, P. (1962). *Brit. J. Sociol.* **13**, 210.
TOWNSEND, P. (1962). Personal communications.
[70] WHITE, K. L., WILLIAMS, T. F. & GREENBERG, B. G. (1961). *New Engl J. Med.* **265**, 885.
[71] WINSER, D. M. DE R. & STEWART, D. N. (1942). *Lancet* **1**, 259.
[72] WINSLOW, C. E. A. (1951). *The Cost of Sickness and the Price of Health* Geneva: WHO.
[73] YOUNG, M. (1958). *The Rise of the Meritocracy.* London.
[74] YERUSHALMY, J. (1947). *Publ. Hlth Rep.* **62**, 1432.
YERUSHALMY, J. (1956). *Bull. int. Un. Tuberc.* **26**, 110.
YERUSHALMY, J. (1956). Personal communications.

LAMBERT, R. *Nutrition in Britain 1950-1960* (1964). In press.

CHAPTER III

[1] *A Hospital Plan for England and Wales* (1962). London: HMSO.
[2] ABEL-SMITH, B. & TITMUSS, R. M. (1956). *The Cost of the National Health Service in England and Wales.* London.
[3] BACKETT, E. M., SHAW, L. A. & EVANS, J. C. G. (1953). *Proc. R. Soc Med.* **46**, 707.
[4] BACKETT, E M., HEADY, J. A. & EVANS, J. C. G. (1954). *Brit. med. J* **1**, 109.

[5] BAILEY, N. T. J. (1954). *Appl. Stats.* **3**, 137.
BAILEY, N. T. J. (1956). *Appl. Stats.* **5**, 146.
BAILEY, N. T. J. (1962). In *Towards a Measure of Medical Care.* London
[6] BROOKE, E. M. (1962). *Lancet* **2**, 1211.
BROOKE, E. M. Personal communications.
[7] BROTHERSTON, J. H. F. (1962). In *Towards a Measure of Medical Care.* London.
[8] BROTHERSTON, J. H. F. (1963). *Lancet* **1**, 1119.
[9] CARSE, J., PANTON, N. & WATT, A. (1958). *Lancet* **1**, 39.
[10] CHESTER, T. E. (1960). *Hospital (Lond.)* **56**, 731, 848.
[11] DAVIES, J. O. F. (1962). In *Towards a Measure of Medical Care.* London.
[12] MINISTRY OF EDUCATION. *Health of the School Child.* Biennial Reports. London: HMSO.
[13] EIMERL, T. S. (1962). *Lancet* **1**, 851.
[14] *Fifth Report of the National Advisory Council on the Training and Supply of Teachers* (1956). London: HMSO.
[15] FORSYTH, G. & LOGAN, R. F. L. (1960). *The Demand for Medical Care.* London.
[16] FORSYTH, G. & LOGAN, R. F. L. (1962). In *Towards a Measure of Medical Care.* London.
[17] FRIEDSON, E. (1960). *Amer. J. Sociol.* **65**, 374.
[18] FRIEDSON, E. (1961). *Patients' Views of Medical Practice.* New York.
[19] FRY, J. (1961). *Brit. med. J.* **2**, 1705.
[20] GALDSTON, I. (1954). *The Meaning of Social Medicine.* Cambridge, Mass.
[21] GLOVER, J. A. (1950). *Mon. Bull. Minist. Hlth* **9**, 62.
[21a] WILSON, N. (1938). *Public Health Services.* London.
[22] GODBER, G. (1958). *Lancet* **2**, 1.
[23] GODBER, G. (1963). *Lancet* **1**, 1061.
[24] GRAD, J. & SAINSBURY, P. (1963). *Lancet* **1**, 544.
[25] HEADY, J. A. & MORRIS, J. N. (1956). *Brit. J. prev. soc. Med.* **10**, 97.
[26] MINISTRY OF HEALTH, *Annual Reports, Part I.* London: HMSO.
[27] MINISTRY OF HEALTH. *On the State of the Public Health.* Annually. London: HMSO.
[28] *Health and Welfare. The Development of Community Care* (1963). London: HMSO.
[29] HEASMAN, M. A., (1961). *Mass Miniature Radiography, 1955-1957.* London: HMSO.
[30] HOSPITAL IN-PATIENT ENQUIRY. *Annual Reports.* London: HMSO.
[31] *Industrial Health* (1958). A Survey in Halifax. London: HMSO.
Industrial Health (1959). A Survey of the Pottery Industries in Stoke-on-Trent. London: HMSO.
[32] INTERNATIONAL LABOUR CONFERENCE (1959). *Recommendation 112.* Geneva: ILO.
[33] JOINT PRICING COMMITTEE FOR ENGLAND. *National Health Service Reports.* London: HMSO.
[34] KOOS, E. (1954). *The Health of Regionsville.* New York.
[35] KNUTSON, A. L. (1954). *Publ. Hlth Rep. Wash.* **70**, 1129.
KNUTSON, A. L. (1963). In press.
[36] MINISTRY OF LABOUR (1963). Personal communication.
[37] LAFITTE, F. & SQUIRE, J. R. (1960). *Lancet* **2**, 538.
[38] LAST, J. M. (1963). *Lancet* **2**, 28.
[39] LEE, J. A. H. (1958). *Brit. med. J.* **1**, 573.
[40] LEE, J. A. H., MORRISON, S. L. & MORRIS, J. N. (1957). *Lancet* **2**, 785.
[41] LEE, J. A. H., MORRISON. S. L. & MORRIS. J. N. (1960). *Lancet* **1**, 170.
[42] LEMBCKE. P. A. (1952). *Amer. J. publ. Hlth* **42**, 276.
[43] LIPWORTH, L., LEE, J. A. H. & MORRIS, J. N. (1963). *Med. Care* **1**, 71.
[44] LOGAN, R. F. L. Personal communications.
[45] MACAULAY, H. M. C. (1962). *Lancet* **1**, 791.

[46] MacMahon, B., Pugh, T. F. & Hutchison, G. B. (1961). *Amer. J. publ. Hlth* **51,** 963.

[47] Marr, J. W., Hope, E. B., Stevenson, J. D. & Thomson, A. M. (1955). *Proc. Nutr. Soc.* **14,** vii.

[48] McKeown, T. (1961). *New Engl. J. Med.* **264,** 594.
McKeown, T. (1961). *Lancet* **2,** 1.

[49] McKeown, T. (1962). *Lancet* **1,** 923.

[50] Mechanic, D. & Volkart, E. H. (1960). *J. Hlth hum. Behav.* **1,** 86.

[51] Mechanic, D. & Volkart, E. H. (1961). *Amer. social. Rev.* **26,** 51.

[52] Morris, J. N. (1957). *Lancet* **1,** 41.

[53] Morris, J. N. (1958). *Proc. R. Soc. Med.* **51,** 139.

[54] Morrison, S. L. & Riley, M. M. (1963). *Med. Care* **1,** 137.

[55] Nuffield Provincial Hospitals Trust (1953). *The Work of Nurses in Hospital Wards.* London.

[56] Paul, B. D. Ed. (1955). *Health, Culture and Community.* New York.

[57] Paul, B. D., Gamson, W. A. & Kegeles, S. S. Ed. (1961). *J. soc. Iss.* **17,** No. 4.

[58] Peterson, O. L. (1962). Personal communication.

[59] Peterson, O. L., Andrews, L. P., Spain, R. S. & Greenberg, B. G. (1956). *J. med. Educ.* **31,** Pt. 2, 1.

[60] Polgar, S. (1962). *Curr. Anthrop.* **3,** 159.

[61] Registrar General (1963). Personal communication.

[62] Rehin, M. A. & Martin, F. M. (1963). *Psychiatric Services in 1975.* London: Political and Economic Planning.

[63] Report on Confidential Enquiries into Maternal Deaths in England and Wales, 1958-1960 (1963). *Rep. publ. Hlth med. Subj. Lond. No.* **109.**

[64] Report of a Survey by the Medical Research Council. Acute Otitis Media in General Practice (1957). *Lancet* **2,** 510.

[64a] Lowe, J. F., Bamforth, J. S. & Pracy, R. (1963). *Lancet* **2,** 1129.

[65] Revans, R. W. (1962). *J. Chron. Dis.* **15,** 857.
Revans, R. W. (1962). *Sociol. Rev. Monog.* No. **5.**

[66] Road Research Laboratory (1962). Personal communication.
Moore, R. L. (1962). *New Sci.* **15,** 288.

[67] Roemer, M. J. (1954). *Canad. J. publ. Hlth* **45,** 133.
Roemer, M. J. (1959). *Hum. Org.* **18,** 75.
Roemer, M. J. (1962). In *Research in Social Welfare Administration.* New York.
Roemer, M. J. (1962). *Amer. J. publ. Hlth* **52,** 8.

[68] Roemer, M. I. & Elling, R. H. (1963). *J. Hlth hum. Behav.* **4,** 49.

[69] Rosenfeld, L. S. (1957). *Amer. J. publ. Hlth* **47,** 856.

[70] Sainsbury, P. & Grad, J. (1962). In *The Burden on the Community.* London.

[71] Schilling, R. S. F. (1963). *J. R. Soc. Arts* **111.** In press.
Schilling, R. S. F. Personal communications.

[72] Shaw, L. A. (1954). *Case Conf.* **1,** 9.

[73] Shaw, L. A. (1954). *Sociol. Rev.* **2,** 179.

[74] Sheldon, J. H. (1961). *Report on Geriatric Services.* Birmingham.

[75] Sheps, M. C. (1955). *Publ. Hlth Rep. Wash.* **70,** 877.
Sheps, M. C. (1956). In *Transactions of the Fourth Conference on Administrative Medicine.* New York: Josiah Macy Jr. Foundation.

[76] Silver, G. A. (1963). *Family Medical Care.* Cambridge, Mass.

[77] Simmons, L. W. & Wolff, H. G. (1954). *Social Science in Medicine.* New York.

[78] Social Medicine Research Unit and Collaborators. Work in progress.

[79] *Statistics of Smoking in the United Kingdom* (1962). London.
Todd, G. F. Personal communications.

[80] Steiger, W. (1963). *Publ. Hlth Rep. Wash.* **78,** 431.

[81] Stewart, W. H. & Enterline, P. E. (1961). *New Engl. J. Med.* **265,** 1187.

[82] Susser, M. W. (1963). *Lancet* **1,** 315.

[83] Susser, M. W. & Watson, W. (1962). *Sociology in Medicine*. London.
[84] Taylor, S. (1954). *Good General Practice*. London.
[85] Terris, M. (1962). *Amer. J. publ. Hlth* **52**, 1371.
[86] Titmuss, R. M. (1950). *Problems of Social Policy*. London: HMSO.
Titmuss, R. M. (1958). *Essays on the Welfare State*. London.
[87] Titmuss, R. M. (1962). *Lancet* **2**, 209.
[88] Tizard, J. (1964). In press.
[89] Tooth, G. C. & Brooke, E. (1961). *Lancet* **1**, 710.
[90] Townsend, P. (1963). *The Last Refuge*. London.
[91] Tunbridge, R. E. (1953). *Lancet* **2**, 893.
[92] USA National Health Survey (1959). *Publ. Hlth Serv. Publ. Wash.* No. **584-B7**.
[93] White, K. L., Williams, T. F. & Greenberg, B. G. (1961). *New Engl. J. Med.* **265**, 885.

Chapter IV

[1] Bolt, W. & Lew, E. A. (1956). *J. Amer. med. Ass.* **160**, 736.
[2] Böök, J. A. (1958). *Eugen. Quart.* **2**, 174.
[3] *Build and Blood Pressure* (1959). Society of Actuaries. Chicago, Ill.
[4] Carter, C. O. & Evans, K. A. (1961). *Lancet* **2**, 785.
[5] Cohen, B. H., Lilienfeld, A. M. & Sigler, A. T. (1963). *Amer. J. publ. Hlth* **53**, 223.
[6] Doll, R. & Hill, A. B. (1952). *Brit. med. J.* **2**, 1271.
[7] Doll, R. & Hill, A. B. (1962). In *Smoking and Health*. Report of the Royal College of Physicians. London.
[8] Doll, R. & Hill, A. B. (1963). Personal communications.
[9] Doll, R., Jones, F. Avery & Buckatzsch, M. M. (1951). *Spec. Rep. Ser. med. Res. Coun., Lond.* No. 276.
[10] Heady, J. A. & Barley, R. G. (1953). *Brit. med. J.* **1**, 1105.
[11] Kallman, F. J. (1946). *Amer. J. Psychiat.* **103**, 309.
Kallman, F. J. (1953). *Heredity in Health and Mental Disorder.* London.
[12] Morris, J. N., Heady, J. A. & Barley, R. G. (1952). *Brit. med. J.* **1**, 503.
[13] Morris, J. N. (1963). *Proc. R. Soc. B.* **159**. (See pages 16, 20 and 233 in this text.)
[14] Registrar General, England and Wales (1953). *Supplements on General Morbidity, Cancer and Mental Health, 1949-59*. London: HMSO.
[15] Ministry of Transport. *Return of Road Accidents for 1949 et seq.* London: HMSO.
[16] Penrose, L. S. (1961). *Brit. med. Bull.* **17**, 184.
[17] Roberts, J. A. F. (1963). *Brit. med. J.* **1**, 587.
[18] Social Medicine Research Unit and Collaborators. Work in progress.

Chapter V

[1] Abrams, M. (1962). *Memoranda* to National Old People's Welfare Council, London.
[2] Acheson, E. D., Truelove, S. C. & Witts, L. J. (1961). *Brit. med. J.* **1**, 668; and subsequent correspondence.
[3] Auerbach, O., Stout, A. P., Hammond, E. C. & Garfinkel, L. (1962). *New Engl. J. Med.* **267**, 111, 119.
Auerbach, O., Stout, A. P., Hammond, E. C. & Garfinkel, L. (1962). Personal communication.
[4] Berkson, J. (1946). *Biometrics Bull.* **2**, 47.

[5] BERKSON, J. (1955). *Proc. Mayo Clin.* **30**, 319.
[6] BIRMINGHAM (1962). Report of a Working Party appointed by the College of General Practitioners. *Brit. med. J.* **1**, 1497.
BIRMINGHAM (1963). Report of a Working Party appointed by the College of General Practitioners. *Brit. med. J.* **2**, 655.
CROMBIE, D. L. Personal communication.
[7] BOMFORD, R. R. (1963). *Proc. R. Soc. Med.* **56**, 316.
ELSOM, K. A. & ELSOM, K. O. (1961). *Arch. environm. Hlth* **3**, 99.
ROBERTS, N. T. (1959). *J. Chron. Dis.* **9**, 95.
[8] BOWLBY, J. (1951). *Maternal Care and Mental Health.* Geneva: WHO.
BOWLBY, J. (1956). *Brit. J. med. Psychol.* **29**. 211.
[9] BOYES, D. A., FIDLER, H. K. & LOCK. D. R. (1962). *Brit. med. J.* **1**, 203.
FIDLER, H. K. & BOYES, D. A. (1959). *Cancer* **12**, 673.
[10] BRESLOW, L. (1959). *Amer. J. publ. Hlth* **49**, 1148.
[11] BRESLOW, L. (1961). *Canad. J. publ. Hlth* **52**, 375.
[12] BRESLOW, L. (1963). *Amer. J. publ. Hlth* **53**, 218.
[13] BROWN, G. W. (1963). *Brit. J. psychiatr. soc. Work* **7**, 5.
BROWN, G. W., MONCK, E. M., CARSTAIRS, G. M. & WING, J. K. (1962). *Brit. J. prev. soc. Med.* **16**, 55.
[14] BULBROOK, R. D. & HAYWOOD. J. L. (1961). *58th Annual Report* of the Imperial Cancer Research Fund. London.
[15] BUTTERFIELD, W. J. H. (1962). *Guy's Hosp. Gaz.* **76**, 470.
BUTTERFIELD. W. J. H. (1962). Personal communication.
[16] CADE, S. (1949). *Brit. J. Radiol.* **22**, 331.
[17] COHEN, A. (1956). *Delinquent Boys.* London.
[18] COLLEGE OF GENERAL PRACTITIONERS (1961). *Brit. med. J.* **2**, 973.
[19] CONN, J. W. & FAJANS, S. S. (1961). *Amer. J. Med.* **31**, 839.
[20] CRAWFORD, M. D. & MORRIS, J. N. (1960). *Brit. med. J.* **2**, 1624.
[21] DAVID, W. D. (1959). *Publ. Hlth Serv. Publ. Wash.* No. **666**.
[22] DAWBER, T. R. (1963). Personal communication.
[23] DAWBER, T. R., KANNEL, W. B., REVOTSKIE, N. & KAGAN, A. (1962). *Proc. R. Soc. Med.* **55**, 265.
DOYLE, J. T., HESLIN, A. S., HILLEBOE. H. E., FORMEL, P. F. & KORNS, R. F. (1957). *Amer. J. publ. Hlth* **47**. Suppl. to No. **4**, p. 25.
[24] DOLL, W. R., JONES, F. A. & PYGOTT, F. (1958). *Lancet* **1**, 657.
[25] DOUGLAS, J. W. B. & BLOMFIELD, J. M. (1958). *Children Under Five.* London.
[26] DUKES, C. E. (1952). *Ann. Eugen.* (Lond.) **17**, 1.
[27] ENGEL, G. (1962). *Psychological Development in Health and Disease.* London.
[28] ENOS. W. F.. HOLMES, R. H. & BEYER, J. (1953). *J. Amer. med. Ass.* **152**, 1090.
[29] FLETCHER. C. M. (1959). *Amer. Rev. resp. Dis.* **80**, 483.
[30] FREMMING, K. H. (1951). *The Expectation of Mental Infirmity in a Sample of the Danish Population.* London: Eugenics Society.
[31] GELFAND, M. (1961). *Medicine in Tropical Africa.* Edinburgh.
[32] GENERAL REGISTER OFFICE (1962). Studies on Medical and Population Subjects. No. 14. *Morbidity Statistics from General Practice.* Vol. 3 (Disease in General Practice). London: HMSO.
[33] GOFMAN. J. W. (1959). *Coronary Heart Disease.* Oxford.
[34] GORDON, J. E. (1958). *Amer. J. med. Sci.* **235**, 337.
[35] GRUENBERG, E. M. (1961). In *Comparative Epidemiology of the Mental Disorders.* Ed. Hoch. P. M. & Zubin, J. New York.
GRUENBERG. E. M. (1963) In press.
[36] HALL. R.. OWEN. S G. & SMART. G. A. (1960). *Lancet* **2**, 187.
[37] HAMES, C. G. & GREENBERG, B. G. (1961). *Amer. J. publ. Hlth* **51**, 374.
[38] HARRIS. H. (1959) *Human Biochemical Genetics.* Cambridge.
[39] DE HAAS, J. H. (1940). *J. Malaya Br. Brit. med. Ass.* **4**. 40.
DE HAAS, J. H. (1954). *Acta paediat.* **43**, Suppl. 100, 374.

[40] HEADY, J. A., MORRIS, J. N., KAGAN, A. & RAFFLE, P. A. B. (1961) *Brit. J. prev. soc. Med.* **15,** 143.

[41] MINISTRY OF HEALTH. *Report 1959,* Part II. London: HMSO.
MINISTRY OF HEALTH. *Report 1961,* Part II. London: HMSO.

[42] HEASMAN, M. A. (1961). Mass Miniature Radiography. *Stud. med. Popul Subj.* No. 17. London: HMSO.
POSNER, E. *et al.* (1963). *Brit. med. J.* **2,** 1157.

[43] HIGGINS, I. T. T. (1959). *Brit. med. J.* **1,** 325.

[44] IMMUNOLOGICAL AND HAEMATOLOGICAL SURVEYS (1959). *Wld Hlth Org techn. Rep. Ser.* **181.**

[45] JONES, F. AVERY (1953). *Lancet* **2,** 556.

[46] KAGAN, A., MILLS, G. L. & PATTISON, D. C. In preparation.

[47] KASS, E. H. (1962). *Ann. intern. Med.* **56,** 46.

[48] KELLGREN, J. H. (1955). *Brit. med. J.* **2,** 1616.

[49] KELLGREN, J. H. & BALL, J. (1959). *Brit. med. J.* **1,** 523.

[50] KELLGREN, J. H. & LAWRENCE, J. S. (1956). *Ann. rheum. Dis.* **15,** 1.
KELLGREN, J. H., LAWRENCE, J. S. & AITKEN-SWAN, J. (1953). *Ann rheum. Dis.* **12,** 5.

[51] KESSEL, W. I. N. (1960). *Brit. J. prev. soc. Med.* **14,** 16.

[52] KILPATRICK, G. S. (1961). *Brit. med. J.* **2,** 1736.

[53] KRAPF, E. E. (1961). In *Teaching of Psychiatry and Mental Health* Public Health Paper No. 9. Geneva: WHO.

[54] LAST, J. M. (1963). *Lancet* **2,** 28.

[55] LAWRENCE, J. S. (1955). *Brit. J. industr. Med.* **12,** 249.

[56] LAWRENCE, J. S. & BALL, J. (1958). *Ann. rheum. Dis.* **17,** 160.
LAWRENCE, J. S. & BALL, J. (1961). *Ann. rheum. Dis.* **20,** 11.

[57] LAWRENCE, J. S., LAINE, V. A. I. & DE GRAFF, R. (1961). *Proc. R. Soc Med.* **54,** 454.

[58] LEAVELL, H. R. & CLARK, E. G. (1958). *Preventive Medicine.* New York

[59] LEYDHECKER, W. (1959). *Docum. ophthal.* **13,** 357.

[60] LOGAN, R. F. L. (1963). *Proc. R. Soc. Med.* **56,** 309.
LOGAN, R. F. L. (1963). Working paper, *European Conference on Morbidity Statistics.* Geneva: WHO.

[61] LOGAN, W. P. D. & CUSHION, A. A. (1958). *Morbidity Statistics from General Practice.* London: HMSO.

[62] MAINLAND, D. (1953). *Amer. Heart J.* **45,** 644.

[63] MAINLAND, D. (1955). *Ann. N.Y. Acad. Sci.* **63,** 474.

[64] McALPINE, S. G., DOUGLAS, A. S. & ROBB, R. A. (1957). *Brit. med. J.* **2,** 483.

[65] *Medical Research.* A Mid-century Survey (1955). London.

[66] MIALL, W. E. (1961). Epidemiology of essential hypertension. In *Pro ceedings of Symposium on Pathogenesis of Essential Hypertension* Prague.

[67] MIALL, W. E. & OLDHAM, P. (1958). *Clin. Sci.* **17,** 409.

[68] MILLAR, M. (1963). *Models and Methods in Psychiatric Research.* Edin burgh.
MILLAR, M. (1963). Personal communication.

[69] MORRIS, J. N. (1941). *Lancet* **1,** 51.

[70] MORRIS, J. N. (1951). *Lancet* **1,** 1, 69.

[71] MORRIS, J. N. (1960). *Mod. Conc. cardiovasc. Dis.* **29,** 625.
MORRIS, J. N. (1961). *Mod. Conc. cardiovasc. Dis.* **30,** 633.

[72] MORRIS, J. N. (1963). *Publ. Hlth Lond.* **77,** 237.

[73] MORRIS, J. N. & CRAWFORD, M. D. (1958). *Brit. med. J.* **2,** 1485.

[74] MORRIS, J. N., HEADY, J. A. & BARLEY, R. G. (1952). *Brit. med. J.* **1,** 503

[75] MORRIS, J. N., HEADY, J. A. & BARLEY, R. G. (1957). *Brit. Heart J* **19,** 227.

[76] MURRAY, R. (1958). In *Cancer,* vol. 3, p. 334. Ed. Raven, R. W. London

[77] OLIVER, M. F. (1961). *Lancet* **2,** 499.
OLIVER, M. F. (1962). *Lancet* **1,** 653.

[78] PERERA, G. A. (1955). *J. Chron. Dis.* **1**, 33.
PERERA, G. A. (1960). *Report of Conference on Arterial Hypertension.* New York: American Heart Association.
[79] PICKERING, G. W. (1955). *High Blood Pressure.* London.
[80] *Proceedings of the Conference on the Preventive Aspects of Chronic Diseases* (1951). Chicago, Ill.
ROSEN, G. (1963). Personal communication.
[81] RUMBALL, A. & ACHESON, E. D. (1963). *Brit. med. J.* **1**, 423.
[82] SCHILLING, R. S. F. (1963). *J. R. Soc. Arts* **111.** In press.
SCHILLING, R. S. F. (1963). Personal communication.
[83] SLATER, E. (1953). *Spec. Rep. Ser. med. Res. Coun., London.* No. **278.**
[84] SOCIAL MEDICINE RESEARCH UNIT AND COLLABORATORS. Work in progress.
[85] STENGEL, E. (1960). *J. ment. Sci.* **106,** 1388.
STENGEL, E. (1963). *Lancet* **1,** 233.
[86] STENGEL, E. (1963). *New Society* **2,** 7.
[86a] REGISTRAR GENERAL. *Statistical Review for 1961, Part III, Commentary,* p. 240.
[87] STROMBERG, V. (1962). *Acta ophthal. Suppl.* 69.
[88] STRONG, J. P., WAINWRIGHT, J. & McGILL, H. C., JR. (1959). *Circulation* **20,** 1118.
[89] THOMAS, C. B., *et al. Collected Papers. The Precursors of Essential Hypertension and Coronary Artery Disease.* Vol. I, 1948-1959. Baltimore.
[90] THORNER, R. M. & REMEIN, Q. R. (1961). *Principles and Procedures in the Valuation of Screening for Disease. Publ. Hlth Monogr.* **67.** Washington, D.C.
[91] TOKUHATA, G. K. (1963). *Publ. Hlth Rep. Wash.* **78,** 121.
[92] TRUSSEL, R. E. & ELINSON, J. (1959). *Chronic Illness in a Rural Area.* Cambridge, Mass.
[93] WALKER, J. B. & KERRIDGE, D. (1961). *Diabetes in an English Community.* Leicester.
[94] WILLIAMS, R. J. & SIEGEL, F. L. (1961). *Amer. J. Med.* **31,** 325.
[95] WILSON, C. (1962). In *Renal Disease.* Ed. Black, D. A. K. Oxford.
[96] WILSON, J. M. G. (1961). *Mon. Bull. Min. Hlth Lab. Serv.* **20,** 2, 214.
WILSON, J. M. G. (1963). *Mon. Bull. Min. Hlth Lab. Serv.* **22,** 16.
[97] WILSON, J. M. G. (1963). *Lancet* **2,** 51.
WILSON, J. M. G. Personal communications.
[98] WING, J. K. (1963). *Publ. Hlth Lond.* **77,** 204.
WING, J. K. (1963). Personal communication.

CHAPTER VI

[1] BAIRD, D. (1957). *Brit. med. J.* **1,** 1061. (1958). *Ibid.* **1,** 1477.
[2] BARTON, R. (1961). *Institutional Neurosis.* London.
GOFFMAN, E. (1961). *Asylums.* New York.
Mental Disorders. A Guide to Control Methods. New York: American Public Health Association.
REES, T. P. (1957). *J. ment. Sci.* **103,** 303.
REES, T. P. & GLATT, M. M. (1955). *Practitioner* **175,** 62.
[3] BURGESS, R. C. (1956). *Proc. Nutr. Soc.* **15,** 14.
[4] *Chronic Wld Hlth Org.* (1956). **10,** 20.
[5] CLARKE, C. A. (1962). *Genetics for the Clinician.* Oxford.
[6] COCHRANE, A. L., FLETCHER, C. M., GILSON, J. C. & HUGH-JONES, P. (1951). *Brit. J. industr. Med.* **8,** 53.
[7] COHEN, H. (1943). *Lancet* **1,** 23.
[8] COURT BROWN, W. M. & DOLL, R. (1961). *Brit. med. J.* **1,** 981.
ACHESON, R. M. (1963). *Yale J. Biol. Med.* **36,** 43.

[9] CRAWFORD, T. (1960). In *Pathogenesis and Treatment of Occlusive Arterial Disease.* Ed. McDonald, L. London.

[10] CRAWFORD, T. & LEVENE, C. I. (1952). *J. Path. Bact.* **64**, 523.

CRAWFORD, T. & LEVENE, C. I. (1953). *J. Path. Bact.* **66**, 19.

[11] CURWEN, M. P., KENNAWAY, E. L. & KENNAWAY, N. M. (1954). *Brit. J. Cancer* **8**, 181.

[12] DAVIES, J. N. P. (1960). *Amer. Heart J.* **59**, 600.

[13] DOLL, R., JONES, F. AVERY & BUCKATZSCH, M. M. (1951). *Spec. Rep. Ser. med. Res. Coun., Lond.* No. **276**.

[14] DOLL, R. & BUCH, J. (1950). *Ann. Eugen. Lond.* **15**, 135.

DOLL, R. & KELLOCK, T. D. (1951). *Ann. Eugen. Lond.* **16**, 231.

[15] DUGUID, J. B. (1946). *J. Path. Bact.* **58**, 207.

DUGUID, J. B. (1954). *Lancet* **1**, 891.

DUGUID, J. B. (1949). *Lancet* **2**, 925.

[16] HEADY, J. A. & MORRIS, J. N. (1959). *J. Obstet. Gynaec. Brit. Emp.* **66**, 577.

[17] JENNINGS, D. (1940). *Lancet* **1**, 395, 444.

[18] JONES, F. AVERY (1957). *Brit. med. J.* **1**, 719, 786.

[19] KREYBERG, L. (1955). *Brit. J. Cancer* **9**, 495.

KREYBERG, L. (1962). *Acta path. microbiol. Scand. Suppl.* 157.

[20] KURLAND, L. T. (1957). *Neurology* **7**, 641.

[21] LEE, J. A. H. (1961). *Lancet* **2**, 815.

HARDING, H. E. (1962). *Brit. med. J.* **2**, 1028. (Appendicitis.)

[21a] LEE, J. A. H. (1962). *Brit. med. J.* **1**, 1737.

LEE, J. A. H. (1963). *Brit. med. J.* **2**, 623. (Leukaemia.)

[22] LOGAN, W. P. D. (1950). *Popul. Stud.* **4**, 132.

[23] LOWE, C. R. & McKEOWN, T. (1962). *Lancet* **1**, 1086.

[24] MACMAHON, B. (1962). *Bull. Wld Hlth Org.* **26**, 579.

[25] McCONNEL, R. B. (1961). In *Clinical Aspects of Genetics.* Ed. Jones, F. Avery. London.

[26] MORRIS, J. N. (1951). *Lancet* **1**, 1, 69.

[27] MORRIS, J. N. & CRAWFORD, M. D. (1958). *Brit. med. J.* **2**, 1485.

MORRIS, J. N. & CRAWFORD, M. D. (1961). *Lancet* **1**, 47.

[28] MORRIS, J. N., HEADY, J. A. & BARLEY, R. G. (1952). *Brit. med. J.* **1**, 503.

[29] MORRIS, J. N. & TITMUSS, R. M. (1944). *Lancet* **2**, 841.

[30] MORRISON, S. L. & MORRIS, J. N. (1959). *Lancet* **2**, 864.

MORRISON, S. L. & MORRIS, J. N. (1960). *Lancet* **2**, 829.

[30a] NEEL, J. V. (1962). In *The Use of Vital and Health Statistics for Genetic and Radiation Studies.* Geneva: WHO.

[31] OSTFELD, A. M. & PAUL, O. (1963). *Lancet* **1**, 575.

[32] MIALL, W. E. & OLDHAM, P. D. (1963). *Brit. med. J.* **1**, 75.

[33] PICKERING, G. W. (1959). In *Significant Trends in Medical Research.* Ciba Symposium. Ed. Wolstenholme, G. E. W. & O'Connor, M. London.

[34] PLATT, R. (1963). *Lancet* **1**, 899.

[35] RATHER, L. J. (1959). In *The Historical Development of Physiological Thought.* Ed. Brooks, C. M. & Cranefield, P. F. New York.

[36] REGISTRAR GENERAL, ENGLAND AND WALES (1927). *Dec. Suppt. Part II. Occupational Mortality for 1921.* London: HMSO.

[37] ROBERTS, J. A. FRASER (1952). *Eugen. Rev.* **44**, 71.

ROBERTS, J. A. FRASER (1961). *Brit. med. Bull.* **17**, 241.

ROTH, M. (1963). *Brit. med. J.* **1**, 321.

[38] SHEARN, M. A. (1961). *Lancet* **2**, 1206.

[39] SOCIAL MEDICINE RESEARCH UNIT AND COLLABORATORS. Work in progress.

[40] *Statistical Report on the Health of the Army, 1943-1945* (1948). London: HMSO.

[41] STEWART, A., WEBB, J. & HEWITT, D. (1958). *Brit. med. J.* **1**, 1495.

[42] *Transactions of the 5th Meeting of the International Society of Geographical Pathology* (1955). New York.
[43] WOLF, S. (1961). *Perspect. Biol. Med.* **4**, 288.
[44] WOOLF, B. (1950). Personal communication.

CHAPTER VII

[1] ABEL-SMITH, B. & TITMUSS, R. M. (1956). *The Cost of the National Health Service in England and Wales.* London.
[2] ALLISON, A. C. (1954). *Brit. med. J.* **1**, 290.
ALLISON, A. C. (1956). *Ann. hum. Genet.* **21**, 67.
[3] BERKSON, J. (1962). *Amer. J. publ. Hlth* **52**, 1318.
[4] *Build and Blood Pressure* (1959). Society of Actuaries. Chicago, Ill.
[5] CAUDILL, W. (1958). *Effects of Social and Cultural Systems in Reactions to Stress.* SSRC Pamphlet No. 14. New York.
CAUDILL, W. (1958). *The Psychiatric Hospital as a Small Society.* Cambridge, Mass.
[6] CIBA SYMPOSIUM ON CONGENITAL MALFORMATIONS (1960). Ed. Wolstenholme, G. E. W. & O'Connor, C. M. London.
EBERT, J. D. (1961). *J. chron. Dis.* **13**, 91.
[7] CLARKE, R. D. (1961). *J. Inst. Actu.* **87**, 196.
CLARKE, R. D. (1961). Personal communication.
[8] CLAY, J. (1844). *Report of the Commission for Enquiry into the State of Large Towns and Populous Districts. Appendix,* p. 41. London.
[9] COMFORT, A. (1956). *The Biology of Senescence.* London.
COMFORT, A. (1963). In *Man and his Future.* Ed. Wolstenholme, G. E. W. London.
[10] COWDRY, E. V. (1933). *Arteriosclerosis.* New York.
[11] DALY, C. (1959). *Brit. J. prev. soc. Med.* **13**, 14.
[12] DAVIDSON, S. & PASSMORE, R. (1963). *Human Nutrition and Dietetics.* 2nd ed. Edinburgh.
[13] DOLL, R. & HILL, A. B. (1962). In *Smoking and Health.* Royal College of Physicians. London.
DOLL, R. & HILL, A. B. Personal communications.
[14] DOLL, R. (1963). In *Epidemiology 1962.* Ed. Pemberton, J. London.
[15] DUBLIN, T. D. & BLUMBERG, B. S. (1961). *Publ. Hlth Rep. Wash.* **76**, 499.
DUBLIN, T. D. (1963). Personal communication.
[16] DUBOS, R. J. (1953). *The White Plague.* London.
[17] FARR, W. (1864). *Evidence to Royal Commission on Condition of Mines.* London.
[17a] ROSEN, G. (1943). *History of Miners' Diseases.* New York.
[18] GALDSTON, I. (1949). Ed. *Social Medicine: Its Derivations and Objectives.* Cambridge, Mass.
[19] GAVIN, H. (1848). *Sanitary Ramblings.* London.
[20] GREENWOOD, M. (1935). *Epidemics and Crowd Diseases.* London.
GREENWOOD, M. (1948). *Medical Statistics from Graunt to Farr.* Cambridge.
[21] GRUENBERG, E. In press.
[22] HEADY, J. A., MORRIS, J. N., KAGAN, A. & RAFFLE, P. A. B. (1961). *Brit. J. prev. soc. Med.* **15**, 143.
[23] JONES, H. B. (1960). In *Handbook of Ageing and the Individual.* Ed. Birren, J. E. Chicago, Ill.
[24] KEYS, A. (1963). In *Atherosclerosis and its Origin.* Ed. Sandler, M. & Bourne, G. H. New York. In press.
[24a] KNOX, G. (1963). *Brit. J. prev. soc. Med.* **17**, 121.
KNOX, G. (1964). *Brit. J. prev soc. Med.* In press. (Leukaemia.)
[25] LEW, E. A. (1962). Personal communication.
[26] LEWIS, A. J. (1960). *Amer. J. Psychiat.* **117**, 289.

[27] MAYER, J. (1960). *Amer. J. publ. Hlth* **50**, No. 3, Part 2, 5.
MAYER, J. (1961). *Amer. J. clin. Nutr.* **9**, 530.
[28] McCOLLUM, E. V., ORENT-KEILES, E. & DAY, H. G. (1939). *The Newer Knowledge of Nutrition.* New York.
[29] MEDICAL RESEARCH COUNCIL. *Report for the Year 1959-60*, p. 22. London: HMSO.
[30] MORRIS, J. N. (1949). *Foundation* (S. Africa) **2**, 7.
[31] MORRIS, J. N. (1959). *Arch. intern. Med.* **104**, 903.
[32] MORRIS, J. N. (1961/62). *Yale J. Biol. Med.* **34**, 199.
[33] MORRIS, J. N. (1963). *Proc. R. Soc. B.* In press.
[34] MYRIANTHOPOULOS, N. C. (1959). *Publ. Hlth Rep. Wash.* **74**, 1098.
[35] ØDEGÅRD, Ø. (1946). *J. ment. Sci.* **92**, 35.
ØDEGÅRD, Ø. (1953). *Acta psychiat. scand.* Suppl. **80**.
[36] PENROSE, L. (1963). *Biology of Mental Defect.* London.
[37] RAPOPORT, R. N. (1963). In *The Encyclopaedia of Mental Health.* New York.
[38] REGISTRAR GENERAL, ENGLAND AND WALES. *Area Mortality, 1951.* London: HMSO.
[39] REGISTRAR GENERAL. *Occupational Mortality Supplement, 1949-53.* London: HMSO.
[40] REGISTRAR GENERAL. *Tables, Medical Part I 1961 and corresponding volumes.* London: HMSO.
[41] REGISTRAR GENERAL. *Population Tables.* London: HMSO.
[42] REGISTRAR GENERAL. *Commentary for 1959 and corresponding volumes.* London: HMSO.
[43] ROBERTS, J. A. F. (1961). *Brit. med. Bull.* **17**, 241.
[44] ROSEN, G. (1958). *A History of Public Health.* New York.
[45] SCHILLING, R. S. F. (1963). *Proc. R. Soc. Arts* **111**. In press.
[46] SNOW, J. (1855). *On the Mode of Communication of Cholera.* 2nd ed. Reprinted, 1936, with Appendix of 1856. New York.
[47] SOCIAL MEDICINE RESEARCH UNIT AND COLLABORATORS. Work in progress.
[48] TERRIS, M., OALMANN, M. C. (1960). *J. Amer. med. Ass.* **174**, 1847. (Cancer of cervix.)
UNITED STATES. *Vital Statistics.* Annual Volumes. Department of Health, Education and Welfare, Washington.
[49] VERNON, H. M. (1939). *Health in Relation to Occupation.* London.
[50] WOLF, S. (1960). *Mod. Conc. cardiovasc. Dis.* **29**, 599.
[51] WOLFF, H. G. (1960). In *Stress and Psychiatric Disorder.* Ed. Tanner, J. M. Oxford.
HINKLE, L. E. & WOLFF, H. G. (1957). In *Explorations in Social Psychiatry.* Ed. Leighton, A. H., Clausen, J. A. & Wilson, R. N. New York.
HINKLE, L. E. & WOLFF, H. G. (1957). *Arch. intern. Med.* **99**, 442.
[52] WORLD HEALTH ORGANIZATION (1961). *International Work in Health Statistics.* Ed. Gear, H. S., Biraud, Y. & Swaroop, S. Geneva: WHO.
[53] YERUSHALMY, J. (1963). *Amer. J. publ. Hlth* **53**, 148.

Modern Epidemic

[1] ACHESON, R. M. (1961). *Brit. J. prev. soc. Med.* **15**, 49.
ACHESON, R. M. (1962). *Yale J. Biol. Med.* **35**, 143.
[2] ALEKSANDROW, D. (1962). *Cardiol. prat.* **13**, 96.
[3] ASTRUP, T. (1956). *Lancet* **2**, 565.
GREIG, H. B. W. (1956). *Lancet* **2**, 16.
[4] BRONTE-STEWART, B. & KRUT, L. H. (1962). *J. Atheroscler. Res.* **2**, 317.
[5] BRUNNER, D. & MANELIS, G. (1960). *Lancet* **2**, 1049.
[6] CHAPMAN, J. M., GOERKE, L. S., DIXON, W., LOVELAND, D. B. & PHILLIPS, E. (1957). *Amer. J. publ. Hlth* **47**, Suppl. to No. 4, p. 33.

[7] CORNFIELD, J. (1962). *Fed. Proc.* **21,** No. 4, Part II, 58.
[8] DAWBER, T. R., KANNEL, W. B., REVOTSKIE, N. & KAGAN, A. (1962). *Proc. R. Soc. Med.* **55,** 265; *Fed. Proc.* **21,** No. 4, Part II.
[9] ECKSTEIN, R. W. (1956). *Fed. Proc.* **15,** 54.
[10] EPSTEIN, F. H. (1961). In *Modern Trends in Cardiology.* Ed. Jones, A. Morgan. London.
[11] MCDONALD, G. A. & FULLERTON, H. W. (1958). *Lancet* **2,** 600.
[12] GALDSTON, I. In preparation.
[13] GROEN, J. (1958). *Ned. melk-en Zuiveltisdschr.* **12,** 282.
[14] HEADY, J. A., MORRIS, J. N., KAGAN, A. & RAFFLE, P. A. B. (1961). *Brit. J. prev. soc. Med.* **15,** 143.
[15] KARVONEN, M., ORMA, E., KEYS, A., FIDANZA, F. & BROZEK, J. (1959). *Lancet* **1,** 492.
[16] MANN, G. V. (1957). *Amer. J. Med.* **23,** 463. (Review.)
MANN, G. V., TEEL, K., HAYES, O., MCNALLY, A. & BRUNO, D. (1955). *New Engl. J. Med.* **253,** 349.
[17] MARR, J. W. & BRAMWELL, E. M. Social Medicine Research Unit. In preparation.
[18] MORRIS, J. N. (1951). *Lancet* **1,** 1, 69.
[19] MORRIS, J. N., HEADY, J. A., RAFFLE, P. A. B., ROBERT, C. G. & PARKS, J. W. (1953). *Lancet* **2,** 1053, 1111.
[20] MORRIS, J. N. & CRAWFORD, M. D. (1958). *Brit. med. J.* **2,** 1485.
[21] MORRIS, J. N. (1959). *Arch. intern. Med.* **104,** 903.
MORRIS, J. N. (1959). *Lancet* **1,** 303.
[22] MORRIS, J. N. (1960). *Mod. Conc. cardiovasc. Dis.* **29,** 625.
MORRIS, J. N. (1961). *Mod. Conc. cardiovasc. Dis.* **30,** 633.
MORRIS, J. N. (1961/62). *Yale J. Biol. Med.* **34,** 359.
[23] MOYNAHAN, E. J. (1961). *Lancet* **1,** 673.
MCKUSICK, V. A. & MURPHY, E. A. (1963). In *Genetic Factors in the Etiology of Myocardial Infarction.* Ed. James, T. N. & Keyes, J. W. London.
[24] OLIVER, M. F. (1961). In *Modern Trends in Cardiology.* Ed. Jones, A. Morgan. London.
[25] OLIVER, R. M. (1963). Personal communication.
[26] PILKINGTON, T. R. E. & KOERSELMAN, H. (1961). *Lancet* **1,** 1019.
[27] RAFFLE, P. A. B. Personal communications.
[28] REGISTRAR GENERAL, ENGLAND AND WALES. *Occupational Mortality.* 1949-53. London: HMSO.
[29] SOCIAL MEDICINE RESEARCH UNIT. Work in progress.
GARDNER, M., KAGAN, A. R., MILLS, G. L. & PATTISON, D. C. In preparation.
[30] TEPPERMAN, J. & PEARLMAN, D. (1961). *Circulat. Res.* **9,** 576.
[31] ZUKEL, W. J., LEWIS, R. H., ENTERLINE, P. E., PAINTER, R. C., RALSTON, L. S., FAWCETT, R. M., MEREDITH, A. P. & PETERSON, B. (1959). *Amer. J. publ. Hlth* **49,** 1630.
ZUKEL, W. J., LEWIS, R. H., ENTERLINE, P. E., PAINTER, R. C., RALSTON, L. S., FAWCETT, R. M., MEREDITH, A. P. & PETERSON, B. (1960). *J. Amer. med. Ass.* **172,** 1261.

Exploring Essential Hypertension

[1] BUCHAN, T. W., HENDERSON, W. K., WALKER, D. E., SYMINGTON, J. & MCNEIL, I. H. (1960). *Hlth Bull. Edinb.* **18,** 3.
[2] *Build and Blood Pressure Study* (1959). Society of Actuaries. Chicago, Ill.
[3] DAHL, L. K. & LOVE, R. A. (1957). *J. Amer. med. Ass.* **164,** 397.
[4] DAHL, L. K. (1958). *New Engl. J. Med.* **258,** 1152.
[5] HAMILTON, M., PICKERING, G. W., ROBERTS, J. A. F. & SOWRY, G. S. C. (1954). *Clin. Sci.* **13,** 11.

[6] HAMILTON, M., PICKERING, G. W., ROBERTS, J. A. F. & SOWRY, G. S. C. (1954). *Clin. Sci.* **13**, 273.
[7] HAMR, V. (1956). *Pracovnilékařstvi,* **8**, 126.
[8] KASS, E. H. (1962). *Ann. intern. Med.* **56**, 46.
MIALL, W. E., KASS, E. H., LING, J. & STUART, K. L. (1962). *Brit. med. J.* **2**, 497.
[9] KOTACKA, L. (1960). Personal communication.
[10] LEDINGHAM, J. M. (1963). *Lond. Hosp. Gaz.* **66**, Suppl.
[10a] MOSER, M. (1959). *Amer. J. Cardiol.* **4**, 727.
[11] LOVELL, R. R. H., MADDOCKS, I. & ROGERSON, G. W. (1960). *Australas. Ann. Med.* **9**, 4.
[12] LOWE, C. R. & MCKEOWN, T. (1962). *Lancet* **1**, 1086.
[13] MIALL, W. E. & COCHRANE, A. L. (1961). *Path. Microbiol.* **24**, 690.
MIALL, W. E. & COCHRANE, A. L. (1961). In *Pathogenesis of Essential Hypertension.* Prague.
[14] MIALL, W. E. (1959). *Brit. med. J.* **2**, 1204.
MIALL, W. E. & OLDHAM, P. D. (1963). *Brit. med. J.* **1**, 75.
[15] MORRISON, S. L. & MORRIS, J. N. (1959). *Lancet* **2**, 864.
[16] MORRISON, S. L. & MORRIS, J. N. (1960). *Lancet* **2**, 829.
[17] MYASNIKOW, A. L. (1961). In *Pathogenesis of Essential Hypertension.* Prague.
[18] OSTFELD, A. M. & PAUL, O. (1963). *Lancet* **1**, 575.
[19] PAUL, J. R. (1958). *Clinical Epidemiology.* Chicago, Ill.
[20] PHILLIPS, J. H., JR. & BURCH, G. E. (1959). *Amer. J. med. Sci.* **238**, 97.
MCDONOUGH, J. R., GARRISON, G. E. & HAMES, C. G. In press.
[21] PICKERING, G. W. (1961). In *Pathogenesis of Essential Hypertension.* Prague.
[22] PICKERING, G. W. (1963). In *Epidemiology. Reports on Research and Teaching 1962.* Ed. Pemberton, J. London.
[23] PLATT, R. (1959). *Lancet* **2**, 55.
[24] PLATT, R. (1961). *Ann. intern. Med.* **55**, 1.
[25] SØBYE, P. (1948). *Heredity in Essential Hypertension and Nephrosclerosis.* Copenhagen.
[26] STAMLER, J. (1959). *Heart Disease Control Program.* Chicago.
For later data see: STAMLER, J. (1962). *Amer. J. Cardiol.* **10**, 319.
[27] WILSON, C. (1960). *Lancet* **2**, 1077.
[28] WORLD HEALTH ORGANIZATION (1957). Study Group on Atherosclerosis and Ischaemic Heart Disease. *Tech. Rep. Wld Hlth Org.* No. **117.**
[29] WORLD HEALTH ORGANIZATION (1959). Hypertension and Coronary Heart Disease. *Tech. Rep. Wld Hlth Org.* No. 168.
[30] WORLD HEALTH ORGANIZATION (1962). Arterial Hypertension and Ischaemic Heart Disease. *Tech. Rep. Wld Hlth Org.* No. 231.
[31] WORLD HEALTH ORGANIZATION (1963). *Chron. Wld Hlth Org.* **17**, 97.

ROSE, G. A. & HOLLAND, W. W. (1964). *Lancet* **1.** In press. (Sphygmomanometer for population study.)

Multiple Causes

[1] BURGESS, A. & DEAN, R. F. A. (1962). Ed. *Malnutrition and Food Habits.* London.
[2] CLARK, E. G. (1948). *Amer. J. Med.* **5**, 655.
CLARK, E. G. (1955). *J. chron. Dis.* **2**, 311.
[3] CLARKE, C. A. (1962). *Genetics for the Clinician.* Oxford.
[4] DUBOS, R. J. (1951). *Louis Pasteur,* chap. 9. London.
[5] DUBOS, R. J. (1953). *The White Plague.* London.
[6] FOX, W. (1962). *Lancet* **2**, 413, 473.
[7] GALDSTON, I. (1954). In *Beyond the Germ Theory.* Ed. Galdston, I. New York.

[8] GORDON, J. E. (1958). *Amer. J. med. Sci.* **235**, 337.
GORDON, J. (1958). *N.Y. St. J. Med.* **58**, 1911.
[9] GREENWOOD, M. (1948). *Some British Pioneers of Social Medicine.* London.
[10] VON HALLER, A. (1768). Quoted in HANSON, N. R. (1958). *Patterns of Discovery.* Cambridge. (Freely: In Nature varied phenomena are linked into a network rather than a chain; but man can grasp only a chain of relationship because he cannot describe in words more than one relationship at a time.)
[11] HEADY, J. A. & HEASMAN, M. A. (1959). *Social and Biological Factors in Infant Mortality.* London: HMSO.
[12] HEASMAN, M. A. (1961). *Arch. Dis. Childh.* **36**, 390.
[13] KARK, S. L. & STEUART, G. W. (1963). Eds. *A Practice of Social Medicine.* Edinburgh.
[14] KRUSE, H. D. (1954). In *Beyond the Germ Theory.* New York.
[15] LILIENFELD, A. M. (1957). *Publ. Hlth Rep. Wash.* **72**, 51.
[16] MACMAHON, B., PUGH, T. F. & IPSEN, J. (1960). *Epidemiologic Methods.* London.
[17] MAY, J. M. & JARCHO, I. S. (1961). *The Ecology of Malnutrition in the Far and Near East.* New York.
[18] MORRIS, J. N. & HEADY, J. A. (1955). *Lancet* **1**, 343.
MORRIS, J. N. (1961-2). *Yale J. Biol. Med.* **34**, 199.
[19] PAUL, J. R. (1958). *Clinical Epidemiology.* Chicago, Ill.
[20] PHELPS, H. W. & KOIKE, S. (1962). *Amer. Rev. resp. Dis.* **86**, 55.
[21] POND, D. A. & BIDWELL, B. (1954). *Brit. med. J.* **2**, 1520.
POND, D. A. (1961). *Brit. med. J.* **2**, 1377, 1454.
[22] SENN, M. J. (1957). *Canad. med. Ass. J.* **77**, 647.
[23] WINSLOW, C. E. A. (1944). *The Conquest of Epidemic Disease.* Princeton.

Bronchitis

[1] *American Journal of Public Health* (1963). **53**. Suppl. to No. 3.
[2] DALY, C. (1954). *Brit. med. J.* **2**, 687.
[3] DALY, C. (1959). *Brit. J. prev. soc. Med.* **13**, 14.
[4] DEAN, G. (1959). *Brit. med. J.* **2**, 852.
DEAN, G. (1961). *Brit. med. J.* **2**, 1599.
[5] EASTCOTT, D. F. (1956). *Lancet* **1**, 37.
[6] FAIRBAIRN, A. S. & REID, D. D. (1958). *Brit. J. prev. soc. Med.* **12**, 94.
FAIRBAIRN, A. S., WOOD, C. H. & FLETCHER, C. M. (1959). *Brit. J. prev. soc. Med.* **13**, 175.
[7] FLETCHER, C. M. (1959). *Amer. Rev. resp. Dis.* **80**, 483.
FLETCHER, C. M. Personal communications.
[8] FLETCHER, C. M., ELMES, P. C., FAIRBAIRN, A. S. & WOOD, C. H. (1959). *Brit. med. J.* **2**, 257.
[9] HIGGINS, I. T. T. (1957). *Brit. med. J.* **2**, 1198.
[10] HIGGINS, I. T. T., OLDHAM, P. D., COCHRANE, A. L. & GILSON, J. C. (1956). *Brit. med. J.* **2**, 904.
[11] HIGGINS, I. T. T., COCHRANE, A. L., GILSON, J. C. & WOOD, C. H. (1959). *Brit. J. industr. Med.* **16**, 255.
[12] MINISTRY OF HOUSING AND LOCAL GOVERNMENT (1962). *Smoke Control, England & Wales, 1962-66.* London: HMSO.
[13] LAWTHER, P. J. (1958). *Proc. R. Soc. Med.* **51**, 262.
LAWTHER, P. J. Personal communications.
[14] LAWTHER, P. J., MARTIN, A. E. & WILKINS, E. T. (1962). *Epidemiology of Air Pollution.* Geneva: WHO.
[15] MEADOWS, S. (1961). *Brit. J. prev. soc. Med.* **15**, 171.
[16] MEDICAL RESEARCH COUNCIL (1960). *Brit. med. J.* **2**, 1665.
[17] MORRIS, J. N. & CRAWFORD, M. D. (1958). *Brit. med. J.* **2**, 1485.

[18] OLSEN, H. C. & GILSON, J. C. (1960). *Brit. med. J.* **1,** 450.
[19] OSWALD, N. C. & MEDVEI, V. C. (1955). *Lancet* **2,** 843.
[20] REID, D. D. (1958). *Lancet* **1,** 1237, 1289.
[21] REGISTRAR GENERAL (1958). *Dec. Suppl. Occupn. Mortality.* London: HMSO.
[22] ROYAL COLLEGE OF PHYSICIANS (1962). *Smoking and Health.* London.
[23] SCOTTISH HOME AND HEALTH DEPARTMENT (1963). *Bronchitis.* London: HMSO.
[24] SOCIAL MEDICINE RESEARCH UNIT. Work in progress.
[25] WALLER, R. E. & LAWTHER, P. J. (1957). *Brit. med. J.* **2,** 1475.

Rediscovery of Byssinosis

[1] HILL, A. B. (1927). *Rep. industr. Fatig. Res. Bd. Lond.* No. **48.**
HILL, A. B. (1930). *Rep. industr. Hlth Res. Bd. Lond.* No. **59.**
[2] McKERROW, C. B., ROACH, S. A., GILSON, J. & SCHILLING, R. S. F. (1962). *Brit. J. industr. Med.* **19,** 1.
[3] NICHOLS, P. J. (1962). *Brit. J. industr. Med.* **19,** 33.
[4] ROACH, S. A. & SCHILLING, R. S. F. (1960). *Brit. J. industr. Med.* **17,** 1.
[5] SCHILLING, R. S. F. (1956). *Lancet* **2,** 261. Personal communications.
SCHILLING, R. S. F., LAMMERS, B. & WALFORD, J. (1964). In press.

"Ecology" of Mental Disorders

[1] AINSWORTH, M. D. (1962). In *Deprivation of Maternal Care: a Reassessment of its Effects.* Geneva: WHO.
[2] ASTRUP, C. (1957). *Acta psychiat. scand.* **32,** 399.
[3] AMERICAN PUBLIC HEALTH ASSOCIATION (1962). *Mental Disorders: A Guide to Control Methods.* New York.
[4] BERNSTEIN, B. (1960). *Brit. J. Sociol.* **11,** 271.
BERNSTEIN, B. (1961). *Educ. Res.* **3,** 163.
[5] BOWLBY, J. (1952). *Maternal Care and Mental Health.* Geneva: WHO.
BOWLBY, J., AINSWORTH, M., BOSTON, M. & ROSENBLUTH, D. (1956). *Brit. J. med. Psych.* **29,** 211.
[6] BROOKE, E. M. (1959). *J. ment. Sci.* **105,** 893.
BROOKE, E. M. (1960). *Eugen. Rev.* **51,** 4.
BROOKE, E. M. (1960). *Proc. R. Soc. Med.* **53,** 128.
[7] BROWN, G. W. (1963). *Brit. J. psychiat. soc. Work* **7,** 5.
BROWN, G. W. & WING, J. K. (1961). *J. ment. Sci.* **107,** 847.
BROWN, G. W. & WING, J. K. (1962). *Sociol. Rev. Monog.* No. 5.
See also Chap. VI of this text, reference 2.
[8] KAPLAN, A. (1962). *The New World of Philosophy.* London.
[9] CARSTAIRS, G. M. (1959). In *Medical Surveys and Clinical Trials.* Ed. Witts, L. J. London.
[10] CARSTAIRS, G. M. (1963). *This Island Now.* London.
[11] DURKHEIM, E. (1897). *Suicide.* Ed. Simpson, G. (1951). Glencoe, Ill.
[12] FARIS, R. E. L. & DUNHAM, H. W. (1939). *Mental Disorders in Urban Areas.* Chicago, Ill.
[13] FREUD, S. (1930). *Civilisation and its Discontents.*
[14] GOFFMAN, E. (1961). *Asylums.* New York.
[15] GOLDBERG, E. M. (1958). *Family Influences and Psychosomatic Illness.* London.
GOLDBERG, E. M. (1964). In press.
[16] GOLDBERG, E. M. & MORRISON, S. L. (1963). *Brit. J. Psychiat.* **109,** 785.
[17] GRUENBERG, E. M. (1961). In *Comparative Epidemiology of the Mental Disorders.* Ed. Hoch, P. H. & Zubin, J. New York.

[18] GRUENBERG, E. M. (1957). *Amer. J. publ. Hlth* **47**, 944.
GRUENBERG, E. M. (1959). *J. chron. Dis.* **9**, 187.
GRUENBERG, E. M. Personal communications.
[19] GRUENBERG, E. M. (1957). In *Explorations in Social Psychiatry.* Ed. Leighton, A. H., Clausen, J. A. & Wilson, R. N. New York.
[20] HARE, E. H. (1962). In *Aspects of Psychiatric Research.* Ed. Richter, D., Tanner, J. M., Taylor, S. & Zangwill, O. L. London.
[21] HOLLINGSHEAD, A. B. & REDLICH, F. C. (1958). *Social Class and Mental Illness.* New York.
[22] KRAPF, E. E. (1953). *Proc. R. Soc. Med.* **46**, 957.
[23] LAMBO, T. A. (1956). *Brit. med. J.* **2**, 1388.
LAMBO, T. A. (1960). *Brit. med. J.* **2**, 1696.
[24] LAMBO, T. A. (1962). *J. ment. Sci.* **108**, 256.
[25] LEWIS, A. J. (1953). *Brit. J. Sociol.* **4**, 109.
LEWIS, A. J. (1962). *Yale J. Biol. Med.* **35**, 62.
LEWIS, A. J. (1963). *Research and its Application in Psychiatry.* Glasgow.
[26] LEWIS, A. J. (1960). *Amer. J. Psychiat.* **117**, 289.
[27] LEWIS, H. N. (1954). *Deprived Children.* London.
[28] MacMAHON, B. & SOWA, J. M. (1961). In *Causes of Mental Disorder.* Milbank memorial Fund. New York.
[29] MADGE, J. (1963). *The Origins of Scientific Sociology.* London.
[29a] MERTON, R. K. (1957). *Social Theory and Social Structure.* Glencoe, Ill.
MERTON, R. K. (1961). In *Contemporary Social Problems.* Ed. Merton, R. K. & Nisbet, R. A. New York.
[30] MORRIS, J. N. (1951). *J. R. san. Inst.* **71**, 621.
[31] MORRIS, J. N. (1959). *Lancet* **1**, 303.
[32] MYASNIKOW, A. L. (1962). *Cardiol. prat.* **13**, 72.
MYASNIKOW, A. L. (1962). *New York Times,* Nov. 27.
[33] ØDEGÅRD, Ø. (1952). *Psychiat. Quart.* **26**, 212.
[34] ØDEGÅRD, Ø. (1962). *Proc. R. Soc. Med.* **55**, 831.
[35] PASAMANICK, B. & LILIENFELD, A. M. (1955). *J. Amer. med. Ass.* **159**, 155.
PASAMANICK, B. & LILIENFELD, A. M. (1955). *Neurology (Minneap.)* **5**, 77.
[36] PASAMANICK, B. (1961). *Arch. gen. Psych.* **5**, 151.
[36a] PAUL, B. D. (1955). Ed. *Health, Culture and Community* (e.g. p. 71). New York.
[37] PENROSE, L. S. (1963). *The Biology of Mental Defect.* London.
[38] PHILP, A. F. (1963). *Family Failure.* London.
[39] RAPOPORT, R. N. (1960). *Community as Doctor: New Perspectives on a Therapeutic Community.* London.
RAPOPORT, R. N. (1963). In *The Encyclopaedia of Mental Health.* New York.
[40] REID, D. D. (1960). *Epidemiological Methods in the Study of Mental Disorder.* Geneva: WHO.
[41] RIESMAN, D. (1954). *Individualism Reconsidered.* Glencoe, Ill.
[42] ROBERTS, J. A. F. (1961). *Brit. med. Bull.* **17**, 241.
[43] ROSEN, G. (1959). *Milbank mem. Fd. Quart.* **37**, 5.
[44] ROSENMAN, R. H. & FRIEDMAN, M. (1962). *Cardiol. prat.* **13**, 42.
FRIEDMAN, M. & ROSENMAN, R. H. (1959). *J. Amer. med. Ass.* **169**, 1286.
[45] SAINSBURY, P. (1955). *Suicide in London.* London.
[45a] SHEPERD, M. (1957). *A Study of the Major Psychoses in an English County.* Maudsley Monog. No. 3. London.
SHEPERD, M. (1960). *Int. J. soc. Psychiat.* **5**, 26.
[46] SOCIAL MEDICINE RESEARCH UNIT AND COLLABORATORS. Work in progress.
[47] SUSSER, M. W. (1962). In *Society.* Ed. Welford, A. T., Argyle, M., Glass, D. V. & Morris, J. N. London.
[47a] TANNER, J. M. & INHELDER, B. (1960). Ed. *Discussions on Child Development.* (WHO Study Group.) London.
[48] TIZARD, J. (1964). In press.

[49] WING, J. K. (1962). *Brit. J. soc. clin. Psychol.* **1**, 38.
WING, J. K. & BROWN, G. W. (1961). *J. ment. Sci.* **107**, 847.
[50] WOOTTON, B. (1959). *Social Science and Social Pathology.* London.

Cancer in the Reports of the General Register Office

[1] ARMITAGE, P. & DOLL, R. (1957). *Brit. J. Cancer* **11**, 161.
[2] BULBROOK, R. D. & HAYWOOD, J. L. (1961). *58th Annual Report of the Imperial Cancer Research Fund.* London.
[3] CASE, R. A. M. (1956). *Brit. J. prev. soc. Med.* **10**, 159, 172.
[4] CASE, R. A. M. (1958). *Med. Press* **240**, 640. (Adapted.)
[4a] KERMACK, W. O., McKENDRICK, A. G. & McKINLAY, P. L. (1934). *Lancet* **1**, 698. (Cohort analysis.)
[5] WORLD HEALTH ORGANIZATION (1963). *Chron. Wld Hlth Org.* **17**, 228.
[6] CLEMMESEN, J. (1951). *J. nat. Cancer Inst.* **12**, 1.
[7] GENERAL REGISTER OFFICE. Registrar General's *Tables Part I. Medical.* London: HMSO.
[8] GENERAL REGISTER OFFICE. Registrar General's *Tables Part III. Commentary, 1952; 1961; and corresponding annual volumes.* London: HMSO.
[9] GENERAL REGISTER OFFICE. Registrar General's *Area Mortality 1951.* London: HMSO.
[10] GENERAL REGISTER OFFICE. *Registrar General's Decennial Supplement on Occupational Mortality for 1949-53 and for 1930-32.* London: HMSO.
[11] HEWITT, D. (1956). *Brit. J. prev. soc. Med.* **10**, 45.
[12] LEE, J. A. H. (1962). *Brit. med. J.* **1**, 1737.
[13] LOGAN, W. P. D. (1953). *Lancet* **2**, 1199.
[14] MACMAHON, B. & FEINLEIB, M. (1960). *J. nat. Cancer Inst.* **24**, 733.
[15] SHIMKIN, M. B. (1963). *J. Amer. med. Ass.* **183**, 358.
[16] SOCIAL MEDICINE RESEARCH UNIT AND COLLABORATORS. Work in progress.
[17] STOCKS, P. (1958). In *Cancer*, vol. 3. Ed. Raven, R. W. London.
[18] STOCKS, P. (1957). *35th Annual Report of the British Empire Cancer Campaign.* Suppl. to Part 2.
[19] TERRIS, M. & OALMANN, M. C. (1960). *J. Amer. med. Ass.* **174**, 1847.

HEASMAN, M. A. (1962). *Proc. R. Soc. Med.* **55**, 733. (Accuracy of death certification.)

Geographical Pathology

[1] EL BATAWI, M. A. (1962). *Brit. J. industr. Med.* **19**, 126.
[2] CARSTAIRS, G. M. (1955). In *Health, Culture and Community.* Ed. Paul, B. D. & Miller, W. B. New York.
[3] COHEN, A. M., BAVLY, S. & POZNANSKI, R. (1961). *Lancet* **2**, 1399. (Israel.)
[3a] DISCOMBE, G. Personal communication.
[4] DOLL, R. (1959). Ed. *Methods of Geographical Pathology.* Oxford.
[5] DUNGAL, N. (1961). *Lancet* **2**, 1350.
[6] GEAR, H. S. (1959). *S. Afr. med. J.* **33**, 228.
[7] GORDON, T. (1957). *Publ. Hlth Rep. Wash.* **72**, 543.
GORDON, T. Personal communication.
[8] HELLER, H., SOHAR, E. & PRAS, M. (1961). *Path. Microbiol. (Basel)* **24**, 718.
SOHAR, E., PRAS, M., HELLER, J., GAFNI, J. & HELLER, H. (1960). *Harefuah* **59**, 39.
[8a] HIGGINSON, J. (1963). In *Cancer.* Progress volume 1963. Ed. Raven, R. W. London.

[9] LARSEN, N. P. & BORTZ, W. (1959). *Hawaii med. J.* **19**, 159.
KEYS, A., KIMURA, N., KUSUKAWA, A., BRONTE-STEWART, B., LARSEN, N. P. & KEYS, M. H. (1958). *Ann. intern. Med.* **48**, 83.
[10] KALLNER, G. (1958). *Lancet* **1**, 1155.
[11] KRAMER, M. (1961). *Proceedings of the Third World Congress of Psychiatry. Geriatrics Panel.* In press.
[12] KURLAND, L. T. & MULDER, D. W. (1954). *Neurology (Minneap.)* **4**, 355.
[13] KURLAND, L. T., MULDER, D. W. & WESTLUND, K. B. (1955). *New Engl. J. Med.* **252**, 649, 697.
[14] LEIGHTON, A. H., LAMBO, T. A., HUGHES, C. C., LEIGHTON, D. C., MURPHY, J. M. & MACKLIN, D. B. (1963). *Psychiatric Disorder Among the Yoruba.* New York.
[15] LAPICCIRELLA, V., LAPICCIRELLA, R., ABBONI, F. & LIOTTA, S. (1962). *Bull. Wld Hlth Org.* **27**, 681.
[16] MANN, G. V. Personal communication.
[17] MCKUSICK, V. A. & HARRIS, W. S. (1961). *Bull. Johns Hopk. Hosp.* **109**, 241.
[18] MORRIS, J. N. (1960). *Mod. Conc. cardiovasc. Dis.* **29**, 625.
MORRIS, J. N. (1961). *Mod. Conc. cardiovasc. Dis.* **30**, 633.
[19] MORRISON, S. L. (1964). *Hlth Bull. Edinb.* In press.
[20] *Patterns of Incidence of Certain Diseases Throughout the World* (1959) Opportunities for Research through Epidemiology. (Sixth Report., Washington, D.C.
[21] PEMBERTON, J. & WILLARD, H. (1958). Eds. *Recent Studies in Epidemiology.* Oxford.
[22] PEMBERTON, J. (1962). *Epidemiology. Reports on Research and Teaching.* London.
[23] SEGI, M. (1963). *Trends in Cancer Mortality for Selected Sites in 24 Countries 1950-1959.* Sendai, Japan.
[24] SHAPER, A. G. & JONES, K. W. (1962). *Lancet* **2**, 1305.
[25] SOCIAL MEDICINE RESEARCH UNIT AND COLLABORATORS. Work in progress.
[26] *Status of World Health* (1959). (Third Report) S. Rept. 161, 86th Cong. Washington, D.C.
[27] STRONG, J. P. (1962). *Proc. R. Soc. Med.* **55**, 274.
[28] STRONG, J. P., WAINWRIGHT, J. & MCGILL, H. C. (1959). *Circulation* **20**, 1118.
[29] TOOR, M., KATCHALSKY, A., AGMON, J. & ALLALOUF, D. (1957). *Lancet* **1**, 1270.
[30] WITTKOWER, E. D. & FRIED, J. (1959). In *Culture and Mental Health.* Ed. Opler, M. K. New York.
WITTKOWER, E. D., MURPHY. H. B., FRIED, J. & ELLENBERGER, H. (1960). *Ann. N.Y. Acad. Sci.* **84**. 854.
[31] WORLD HEALTH ORGANIZATION. *Annual Epidemiological and Vital Statistics.* Geneva: WHO.
WORLD HEALTH ORGANIZATION. *Bibliography on the Epidemiology of Cancer, 1946-1960.* Geneva: WHO.
[32] WORLD HEALTH ORGANIZATION (1959). Effect of Radiation on Human Heredity. *Wld Hlth Org. techn. Rep. Ser.* No. **166.**
[33] WORLD HEALTH ORGANIZATION. Kagan, A R. & Fejfar, Z. In progress.
[34] WORLD HEALTH ORGANIZATION (1962). *Second Report on the World Health Situation 1957-1960.* Geneva: WHO.
[35] WYNDER, E. L. (1961). *Lancet* **2**, 1347.

Hypotheses

[1] BERKSON, J. (1955). *Proc. Mayo Clin.* **30**, 319.
[2] BERKSON, J. (1963). *Amer. Statist.* **17**, 15.
[3] BOUISSON, M. (1859). *Montpellier méd.* **2**, 539: **3**, 19.
HAMMOND, E. C. Personal communication.

4 BRESLOW, L., HOAGLIN, L., RASMUSSEN, G. & ABRAMS, H. K. (1954).
  Amer. J. publ. Hlth **44,** 171.
5 BRONTE-STEWART, B. & KRUT, L. H. (1962). *J. Atheroscler. Res.* **2,** 317.
6 CLAUSEN, J. A. & KOHN, M. (1954). *Amer. J. Sociol.* **60,** 140.
7 COCKBURN, W. C. (1957). *Amer. J. publ. Hlth* **47,** 819.
8 CORNFIELD, J. (1951). *J. nat. canc. Inst.* **11,** 1269.
  CORNFIELD, J. (1956). *Proc. 3rd Berkeley Symposium* **4,** 135.
9 CORNFIELD, J. & HAENSZEL, W. (1960). *J. chron. Dis.* **11,** 523.
10 DOLL, R. (1959). In *Medical Surveys and Clinical Trials*. Ed. Witts, L. J.
  London.
11 DOLL, R. & HILL, A. B. (1952). *Brit. med. J.* **2,** 1271.
12 DOLL, R. & HILL, A. B. (1956). *Brit. med. J.* **2,** 1071.
13 DORN, H. F. (1953). *Amer. J. publ. Hlth* **43,** 677.
14 FISHER, R. A. (1959). *Smoking. The Cancer Controversy*. Edinburgh.
15 FLETCHER, C. M. (1964). *Proc. R. Soc. Med.* In press.
  FLETCHER, C. M. Personal communication.
16 GOLDBERGER, J. (1914). *Publ. Hlth Rep.* **29,** 1683.
17 GOLDBERGER. J., WARING, C. H. & TANNER, W. F. (1923). *Publ. Hlth
  Rep. Wash.* **38,** 2361.
  GOLDBERGER, J. & WHEELER, G. A. (1920). *Bull. U.S. hyg. Lab.* No. 120.
  U.S. Public Health Service, Washington, D.C.
18 HAMMOND, E. C. (1955). In *The Biological Effects of Tobacco*. Ed.
  Wynder, E. L. Boston.
  HAMMOND, E. C. & HORN, D. (1958). *J. Amer. med. Ass.* **166,** 1159, 1294.
19 HEADY, J. A., DALY, C. & MORRIS, J. N. (1955). *Lancet* **1,** 395.
20 HILL, A. B. (1953). *New Engl. J. Med.* **248,** 995.
21 HILL, A. B. (1962). *J. Inst. Actu.* **88,** Part II, No. 379, 178.
22 HIMSWORTH, H. (1961). In *Clinical Aspects of Genetics*, p. 129. Ed.
  Jones, F. Avery. London.
23 LAWTHER, P. J. Personal communication.
24 LEVIN, M. L., KRAUS, A. S., GOLDBERG, I. D. & GERHARDT, P. R. (1955).
  Cancer **8,** 932.
25 LEWIN, K. (1951). *Field Theory in Social Science*. New York.
26 LILIENFELD, A. M. (1957). *Publ. Hlth Rep. Wash.* **72,** 51.
  LILIENFELD, A. M. (1959). *J. chron. Dis.* **10,** 41.
27 MARUYAMA, M. (1963). *Amer. Scient.* **51,** 164.
28 MASS CONTROL OF DENTAL CARIES BY FLUORIDATION OF A PUBLIC WATER
  SUPPLY (1959). *Seventh Report on The Brantford Fluoridation Caries
  Study*. Ottawa.
29 MCGONIGLE, G. C. M. & KIRBY, J. (1936). *Poverty and Public Health*.
  London.
  WILBER, D. M., WALKLEY, R. P., PINKERTON, T. C. & TAYBACK, M. (1962).
  The Housing Environment and Family Life. Baltimore, Md.
30 MORRIS, J. N. (1956). *Lancet* **1,** 687.
31 MORRIS, J. N. (1961-2). *Yale J. Biol. Med.* **34,** 359.
32 MORRIS, J. N., CRAWFORD, M. D. & HEADY, J. A. (1961). *Lancet* **1,** 860.
33 MORRIS, J. N., CRAWFORD, M. D. & HEADY, J. A. (1962). *Lancet* **2,** 506.
34 MORRIS, J. N. & HEADY, J. A. (1955). *Lancet* **1,** 343.
35 MORRIS, J. N., MARR, J. W., HEADY, J. A., MILLS, G. L. & PILKINGTON,
  T. R. E. (1963). *Brit. med. J.* **1,** 571.
36 MORRISON, S. L. (1959). *J. ment. Sci.* **105,** 999.
37 PAUL, B. D., GAMSON, W. A. & KEGELES, S. S., Ed. (1961). *J. soc. Iss.*
  17, No. 4.
38 POPPER, K. (1947). *Logic of Scientific Discovery*. London.
39 *The Conduct of the Fluoridation Studies in the United Kingdom and the
  Results Achieved after Five Years* (1962). *Rep. publ. Hlth med. Subj.*
  Lond. No. **105.** London: HMSO.
39aBRANSBY, E. R. & FORREST, J. R. (1958). *Mon. Bull. Minist. Hlth Lab.
  Serv.* **17,** 28.

[40] *Smoking and Health* (1962). Royal College of Physicians. London.
[41] SCOTT, E. (1960). *J. Coll. gen. Practit.* **3**, 80.
[42] SHEPS, M. C. (1958). *New Engl. J. Med.* **259**, 1210.
SHEPS, M. (1959). *Biometrics* **15**, 87.
[43] SOCIAL MEDICINE RESEARCH UNIT AND COLLABORATORS. Work in progress.
[44] STRØM, A. (1954). *The Influence of Wartime on Health Conditions in Norway.* Oslo.
STRØM, A. Personal communication.
[45] TAYLOR, S. & CHAVE, S. P. W. (1964). In press.
[46] TERRIS, M. (1962). *Amer. J. publ. Hlth* **52**, 1371.
[47] WHITE, C. & BAILAR, III, J. C. (1956). *Amer. J. publ. Hlth* **46**, 35.
[48] WILKINS, L. T. (1960). *Delinquent Generations.* London: HMSO.
[49] WOOLF, B. (1947). *Brit. J. soc. Med.* **1**, 73.
WOOLF, B. & WATERHOUSE, J. (1945). *J. Hyg., Camb.* **44**, 67.
[50] YERUSHALMY, J. & HILLEBOE, H. E. (1957). *N.Y. St. J. Med.* **57**, 2343.
[51] YERUSHALMY, J. & PALMER, C. E. (1959). *J. chron. Dis.* **10**, 27.

APPENDIX

[1] ALLISON, A. C. (1954). *Brit. med. J.* **1**, 290.
ALLISON, A. C. (1954). *Trans. R. Soc. trop. Med. Hyg.* **48**, 312.
[2] BAKER, G. (1767). *Essay Concerning the Cause of the Endemial Colic of Devonshire.* London. Reissued 1958.
[3] BENGOA, J. M., JELLIFFE, D. B. & PEREZ, C. (1959). *Amer. J. clin. Nutr.* **7**, 714.
[4] BETTELHEIM, B. (1961). *The Informed Heart.* London.
[5] BRADY, J. V. (1958). *Sci. Amer.* **199**, 95.
[6] BROWNING, E. (1960). In *Modern Trends in Occupational Health.* Ed. Schilling, R. S. F. London.
[7] BURNET, F. M. (1953). *The Natural History of Infectious Disease,* 3rd ed. 1962. London.
BURNET, F. M. (1955). *Viruses and Man,* 2nd ed. London.
[8] BUTTERFIELD, W. J. H. (1961). *Brit. med. J.* **1**, 1705.
[9] CASE, R. A. M., HOSKER, M. E., McDONALD, D. B. & PEARSON, J. T. (1954). *Brit. J. industr. Med.* **11**, 75.
[10] CASE, R. A. M. & PEARSON, J. T. (1954). *Brit. J. industr. Med.* **11**, 213.
[11] CLARKE, C. A. (1962). *Genetics for the Clinician.* Oxford.
[12] CLEMENTS, F. W. (1955). *Med. J. Aust.* **2**, 369.
CLEMENTS, F. W. (1960). *Brit. med. Bull.* **16**, 133.
CLEMENTS, F. W. (1963). Personal communication.
[13] CLEMENTS, F. W. & WISHART, J. W. (1956). *Metabolism* **5**, 623.
[14] COOK, J. W., HIEGER, I., KENNAWAY, E. L. & MAYNEORD, W. V. (1932). *Proc. R. Soc. B.* **111**, 455.
[15] COURT BROWN, W. M. & ABBATT, J. D. (1955). *Lancet* **1**, 1283.
[16] DAWBER, T. R., KANNEL, W. B., REVOTSKIE, N. & KAGAN, A. (1962). *Proc. R. Soc. Med.* **55**, 265.
[17] COURT BROWN, W. M. & DOLL, R. (1957). *Spec. Rep. Ser. med. Res. Coun. Lond.* No. **295**. (Radiation.)
DOLL, R., JONES, F. AVERY & BUKATZSCH, M. M. (1951). *Spec. Rep. Ser. med. Res. Coun. Lond.* No. **276**. (Ulcer.)
[18] DRAPER, G., DUPERTUIS, C. W. & CAUGHEY, J. L. (1944). *Human Constitution in Clinical Medicine.* London.
[19] FORD, E. B. (1961). *Genetics for Medical Students.* London.
[20] GIBSON, H. B., HOWELER, J. F., CLEMENTS, F. W. (1960). *Med. J. Aust.* **1**, 875.
[21] GOLDBERG, E. M. (1958). *Family Influences and Psychomatic Illness.* London.
[22] GRAY, P. G. & CARTWRIGHT, A. (1951). *Lancet* **1**, 1170.

23 GREGG, N. M. (1941-2). *Trans. ophthal. Soc. Aust.* **3**, 35.
24 GROEN, J. In COHEN, E. A. (1953). *Human Behaviour in the Concentration Camp.* New York.
25 HARDY, H. L. & TABERSHAW, I. R. (1946). *J. industr. Hyg.* **28**, 197.
26 *Hazards to Man of Nuclear and Allied Radiations* (1956). First Report to Medical Research Council. (1960.) Second Report to Medical Research Council. London: HMSO.
27 MINISTRY OF HEALTH (1960). *Rubella and other Virus Infections during Pregnancy.* Ed. Manson, M. M., Logan, W. P. D. & Loy, R. M. *Rep. publ. Hlth med. Subj. Lond.* No. **101**. HMSO.
28 HENRY, S. A. (1946). *Cancer of Scrotum in Relation to Occupation.* London.
29 HIMSWORTH, H. P. (1949). *Lancet* **1**, 465.
30 HIMSWORTH, H. P. (1949). *Proc. R. Soc. Med.* **42**, 323.
31 HUEPER, W. C. (1942). *Occupational Tumors and Allied Diseases.* Springfield, Ill.
32 HUNTER, D. (1955). *The Diseases of Occupation.* 3rd ed. 1962. London.
33 INGALLS, T. H. (1952). In *The Biology of Mental Health and Disease.* New York.
34 JACKSON, A. D. M. & FISCH, L. (1958). *Lancet* **2**, 1241.
35 JELLIFFE, D. B. (1963). *Amer. J. publ. Hlth* **53**, 905.
36 KANTER, V. B. (1958). In reference No. 21 above.
KANTER, V. B. & SANDLER, J. (1955). *Brit. J. med. Psychol.* **28**, 157.
37 KATZ, L. H. & STANLER, J. (1953). *Experimental Atherosclerosis.* Springfield, Ill.
38 KENNAWAY, E. L. (1955). *Brit. med. J.* **2**, 749.
39 KEYS, A. (1956). *Mod. Conc. cardiovasc. Dis.* **25**, 317.
40 LAL, R. B. & ROY, S. C. (1937). *Indian J. med. Res.* **25**, 239.
HEILIG, R. (1963). Personal communication.
41 LANCASTER, H. O. (1951). *Brit. med. J.* **2**, 1429.
LANCASTER, H. O. & PICKERING, H. (1952). *N.Z. med. J.* **51**, 184.
42 LEVINE, P. (1943). *J. Hered.* **34**, 71.
43 MACMAHON, B. (1962). *J. nat. Canc. Inst.* **28**, 1173. (Leukaemia.)
43a MANSON-BAHR, P. H. (1941). *Manson's Tropical Diseases,* 15th ed. 1960. London.
44 MARGOLIN, S. G. (1951). *Psychoanal. Quart.* **20**, 349.
45 *Mental Disorders. A Guide to Control Methods* (1962). American Public Health Association. New York. (Adapted.)
46 MIRSKY, I. A. (1958). *Amer. J. digest. Dis.* **3**, 285.
47 MOLLISON, P. L. (1961). *Blood Transfusion in Clinical Medicine,* 3rd ed. Oxford.
48 MORRIS, J. N. (1951). *Lancet* **1**, 1, 69.
49 MORRIS, J. N. & TITMUSS, R. M. (1944). *Lancet* **2**, 841.
50 MOURANT, A. E. (1954). *The Distribution of Human Blood Groups.* Springfield, Ill.
51 NEEL, J. V. (1961). *Proceedings of Conference on Genetic Polymorphism and Geographic Variations in Disease.* New York.
52 OLIVER, M. F. & BOYD, G. S. (1961). *Lancet* **2**, 499.
53 OLIVER, M. F. (1962). *Lancet* **1**, 653. Personal communication.
54 PAULING, L. (1960). In *Disease and the Advancement of Basic Science.* Ed. Beecher, H. K. Cambridge, Mass.
55 PYKE, D. A. (1956). *Lancet* **1**, 818.
56 RACE, R. R. & SANGER, R. (1962). *Blood Groups in Man,* 4th ed. Oxford.
57 REGISTRAR GENERAL. *Annual Tables.* London: HMSO.
STEWART, A., PENNYBACKER, W. & BARBER, R. (1962). *Brit. med. J.* **2**, 882.
58 ROBERTS, J. A. F. (1957). *Brit. J. prev. soc. Med.* **11**, 107.
59 SANGHVI, L. M., MISRA, S. N. & BOSE, T. K. (1960). *Circulation* **21**, 1096.
60 SCRIMSHAW, N. S. (1963). *J. Amer. diet. Ass.* **42**, 203.
61 SCRIMSHAW, N. S. & BÉHAR, M. (1959). *Fed. Proc.* **18**, 82.

[62] SIMON, J. (1890). *English Sanitary Institutions.* London. In col. two.
[63] SOCIAL MEDICINE RESEARCH UNIT AND COLLABORATORS. Work in progress.
[64] STAMLER, J. (1962). In *Med. Wld News,* May 11th.
[65] STAMLER, J., PICK, R., KATZ, L. N., PICK, A., KAPLAN, B. M., BERKSON, D. M. & CENTURY, D. (1962). Personal communication.
[66] STEINKE, J., TAYLOR, K. W. & RENOLD, A. E. (1961). *Lancet* 1, 30.
[67] STEVENSON, A. C. (1956). *Ulster med. J.* 25, 101.
STEVENSON, A. C. & FISHER, O. D. (1956). *Brit. J. prev. soc. Med.* 10, 134.
[68] STRONG, J. P. & McGILL, H. C. (1962). *Amer. J. Path.* 40, 37.
[69] SYMPOSIUM ON BERYLLIUM DISEASE (1959). *Arch. industr. Hlth* 19, 100.
[70] SZNAJDERMAN, M. & OLIVER, M. F. (1963). *Lancet* 1, 962.
[71] TROWELL, H. C., DAVIES, J. N. P. & DEAN, R. F. A. (1954). *Kwashiorkor.* London.
[72] VALLANCE-OWEN, J. & WRIGHT, P. H. (1960). *Physiol. Rev.* 40, 219.
[73] VERNON, H. M. (1939). *Health in Relation to Occupation.* London.
[74] WALKER, W. & MURRAY, S. (1954). *Brit. med. J.* 2, 126.
[75] WILKINS, L. T. Personal communication.
[76] WILLIAMS, C. D. (1933). *Arch. Dis. Childh.* 8, 423.
WILLIAMS, C. D. (1955). *R. Soc. Hlth J.* 75, 768.
[77] WILLS, V. G. & WATERLOW, J. C. (1958). *J. trop. Pediat.* 3, 167.
[78] WELSH, J. D. & WOLF, S. (1960). *Amer. J. Med.* 29, 754.
[79] WINSER, D. M. DE R. & STEWART, D. N. (1942). *Lancet* 1, 259.
[80] WOLF, S. & WOLFF, H. G. (1943). *Human Gastric Function.* New York.
WOLFF, H. G. (1953). *Stress and Disease.* Springfield, Ill.
[81] WOOLLAM, D. H. M. (1962). *Brit. med. J.* 2, 236.

GLOSSARY

DORN, H. F. (1951). *Amer. J. publ. Hlth* 41, 271.
DORN, H. F. (1955). *J. chron. Dis.* 1, 638.
HILL, A. B. (1961). *Principles of Medical Statistics.* London.
KRAMER, M. (1957). *Amer. J. publ. Hlth* 47, 826.
LILIENFELD, A. M. (1960). *J. chron. Dis.* 11, 471.
MORRIS, J. N., HEADY, J. A. & BARLEY, R. G. (1952). *Brit. med. J.* 1, 503.
REID, D. D. (1960). *Epidemiological Methods in the Study of Mental Disorders.* Geneva: WHO.
SOCIAL MEDICINE RESEARCH UNIT AND COLLABORATORS. Work in progress.
SPIEGELMAN, M. (1957). *Amer. J. publ. Hlth* 47, 297.
WORLD HEALTH ORGANIZATION (1959). Sixth Report of Expert Committee on Health Statistics. *Techn. Rep. Wld Hlth Org.* No. 164.
YERUSHALMY, J. Personal communication.

INDEX OF SUBJECTS

A

ABO Blood Groups, 130, 189, 253, 298
Abortion, 40, 125, 289
Accidents, Injuries, 36-7, 102, 218, 225
  Industrial, Occupational, 34, 77, 228-9, 270
  Road-Vehicle, 12, 27, 73, 74, 104, 109, 269
Action Research, *see* Experimental Epidemiology
Activity, Need for Exercise of Functions, and Health (" Deficiency" Diseases), 168, 181, 225, *see* Ischaemic Heart Disease and Physical Activity, Maternal Deprivation, Mental Retardation, Obesity, Social Breakdown Syndrome
Affluent Society, Diseases of Affluence, 12, 27, 60-3, 65, 69, 133, 167-8, 169, 225
Age, Age Groups, Epochs, Life Cycle, Phases of Development, 24, 164
  Antenatal Phase, 171, 195, 223, *see* Congenital Malformation, Perinatal Mortality, Reproduction, Stillbirth
  Infancy, *see* Infant Mortality
  Childhood, **5-8,** 12, 24-5, 64-5, 72, 77, 91, 92, 151, 206, 284, 287, 291, 293
  Adolescence, Young People, **26-9,** 55, 71, 91, 147, 154, 251
  Adult Phase, 34, 69, 74, 104, 107
  Middle Age, **1-3,** 11, 20, 29-30, **35-40,** 107, 109, 111, 207, 225
  Old Age, Old People, 41, 63n., 80, 98, 111, 112, 132, 135, 273, *see* Ageing of the Population
Ageing/Disease, 170
Ageing of the Population, 16, 22-6, 41
Air, Atmospheric, Pollution, 72, 166, 199-200, **204-5,** 259
Alcohol, 41, 166, 225
Anaemia, 118, 251, 253, 300
Association of Diseases, 21-2, 157-8, 169-71, 194-5, 219
Atherosclerosis, 143-6, *see* Coronary

Attack Rate, 114, 303
Automation, Computers, 69, 92, 131, 276
Average, Mean/Distribution, Range, 55-6, 62-3, 79, 197

B

Beryllium Disease, 5, 290
Bladder, Cancer of, 170, 230, 234, 285
Blood Pressure, High Blood Pressure, Essential Hypertension, 39, 132, 143, **152-3,** 177, 178, **182-8,** 193, 212, 246
  Syndromes, 152-3, 187
Breast, Cancer of, 37, 74, 115, 130, 230-45 *pass.*
  Prevention, 235
Bronchitis, Chronic Non-Specific Pulmonary Disease, **199-211;** 34, 36-7, 45, 58, 74, 122
  and Air Pollution, *in* Town and Country, 89, 166, 204-5, 209-11, 259
  and Cigarette Smoking, 202-3, 260
  and Heart Disease, 201, 207, 213
  Natural History, 122, 127, 131-2
  International Comparison, 15, 210, 247
  and Poverty, 58, 59, 64, 206-10
  Prevention, 211
  and Sex, 204, 207
Bronchus, Lung, Cancer of, 2, 74, 104, 105, 106, 107-8, 195, 196, 237, 268, 270-1
  and Age, 230-4
  and Air Pollution, *in* Town and Country, 235-6, 246, 267
  History, 2, 17-18, 30, 153-4, 231-5, 253, 255-7
  Pathogenesis, Precursors, 127, 140, 235
  and Sex, 2, 253
  and Smoking, 126, 127, 155, **232-4,** 254, 261-6, 270
Byssinosis, 15, 43, 125, 166, 191, **211-18**

C

Cancer, Malignant Disease, 27, 37, 105, 115, **229-41,** 243-8 *pass.,* **284-7,** *see* Bladder, etc.

Cancer (*contd.*)
  and Age, 230-4
  Diagnosis, 117, 122, 240, 244-5
  and Fertility, 239
  History, Secular Trends, 233, 235
  International Comparison, 243-7
  Morbidity, Registration, 107, 241
  and Occupation, 196, 284
  Pathogenesis, Mechanisms, Processes, 231, 284
  Precancerous Lesions, Precursors, 126, 127, 138-40
  and Sex, 230-1
  and Social Class, 238
Case-Control, Retrospective Study, 131, 233, 261-6
Case-Fatality, 93-5, 305-6
Causes of Chronic Diseases, The Search for, **Chap. VII;** 66, 140
  Agent (Necessary Cause), 190-1, 214-7
  Causes in Host, Personal Causes (Individual Differences), 191-2
  External-Environmental Causes, 191-3
  General, Non-Specific Causes, 160-8, 171, 272
  Mode of Life, Ways of Living, 160-8 *pass.*, 192
  Multiple Causes, Meanings of, Patterns of, Importance of, 171-4 *pass.*, 188-95, 260, 266-8
  Personal Behaviour and Habits, 192, 196-9
  Predispositions, Operation of Causes in Individual, 129-30
Causes Affecting Course of Chronic Diseases, Disability, 97, 135-6, 211
Cerebrovascular Disease, 29, 39, 115, 143-4, 247
Cervix, Cancer of, 105, 122, 127, 138-40, 170, 238, 239
  Prevention, 138-40
Change
  in Character of Disease, 18-22, 144-5
  Demographic, 22-5, 30-3, 41
  in Disease Patterns, Health Problems, 1-2, **Chap. I,** 65-70 *pass.*, 163, 172-82 *pass.*, 196-9, 211-18, 232-5, 252-3, 290, 293
  in Health Services, 32, 75-6, 98, 100-1, 135-40, 199
  in Social Patterns, Technological, 26-9, **68-74,** 181, 224-6, 257, 260, 284
Cholesterol, Blood Level, 126, 129, 132, 169, 250, 294

Chronic Diseases, The "Chronic Sick", 2-3, 10-12, 63n., 79-80, 97, 127, 130, 133-40, 180, 270-3
Class, *see* Social Class
Clinical Medicine and Epidemiology, 3-4, 5-6, 13, 66-7, Chap. III *pass.*, Chap. V *pass.*, 204, 220, 259, **277-8,** Appendix *pass.*, *see* Clustering of Cases, Group
Clustering of Cases, Microepidemics, 132, 170, 183, 219-20, 292
Coalminers, 6, 43, 57, 59, 155, 214
Cohort Analysis, *see* Prospective Study
Colon, Cancer of, 37, 105, 235
Coloured Immigration, Recent, 68, 227, 246, 251
Communication, 55n., 82-3, 87, 116-7
Community Care, 80, 97-101, 130, 136
Community Diagnosis, Social Diagnosis, **Chap. II;** Chap. I *pass.*, 77, 83, 98, 128, 139, 164-5, 199-211 *pass.*, 218, 223-9, 236-8, 253, 291, 293
Complementarity of Disorders, Alternatives; Equivalence, Substitution, 18-22, 124, 157-8, 169, 194, 268, 295
"Completing the Clinical Picture" (Natural History of Disease), **Chap. V**
  1. In Breadth, 49, 83, 111-8, 150-1, 212-13, 219, 295
  2. In Depth, Subclinical Disease, Iceberg Phenomenon, 118-25, 201, 212-13, 289
  see Precursors of Chronic Diseases, *see* Predispositions, Causes
Congenital Malformation, 16, 103, 170, 195, 208, **288-9**
Coronary Atherosclerosis, 22, 129, 131, 143, **145-7,** 207, 272
  and Occupation, 146
Critical Period, 26-9, 67, 195, 223, 227, 273, 288
Culture, 190, 219, 251

D

Death Certification, **Glossary**
Death Rates, Mortality, **Glossary;** 285, 291, 305
  and Age, 24-9, 163-4, 231-4, 291
  and Sex, 1-3, 25-6, 163-4, 294
  and Social Class, 56-60, 65-8

Dependence, 63, 134-5, *see* Poverty
Depression, 22, 219, 225
Deprivation, Social, 29, 63, 166, 190, 219-24, *see* Activity, Equality, Poverty
Demography, 22-6, 30-3, *see* Reproduction
Diabetes, 15, 16, 86, 116-17, 120-2, 127, 137, 296-7
" Secondary " Prevention, 137
Syndromes, 296
Dietary Surveys, 46-7, 62, 197, 258
Diphtheria, 5, 91
Direct and Indirect Test of Hypothesis, 254-66
Disability / Illness / Disease, 11, 80, Chap. V *pass.*, 135-6, 171, 189
Doctors, Physicians,
Cancer of Bronchus in, 107, 263
Certification by, 10, 13, 34-5
in Industry, 84-6
Ischaemic Heart Disease in, 104, 114, 144
Shortage of, 85-6
Drugs, Antibiotics, etc., 69, 73, 93, 281, *see* Hazards

E

Environmental Hygiene, Sanitation; Pollution, 69, 161, 210, *see* Air Pollution
Epidemics, Modern, 2-3, 12, 16-18, 172-82, 253
Epidemic Outbreaks, 68, 199-200, 225, 227, 252, 288, 293, 295, (20, 257)
Epidemiological Control, 211, 216, 285
Equality and Inequality, 56-64, 160-3
Exercise, Physical Activity, 174-82
Expectation of Life, 25, 162-3
Experiment, Epidemiological, 268-273, 281
Controlled, Planned, " Experimental Epidemiology ":
in Health Services, " Action Research ", 99-101, 155, 301
in Prevention of Disease, 138-140, 155, 169, 268-73
Of Nature, Opportunity, 72, 162, 257, **259-60**, 283

F

Family, 42, 59-64 *pass.*, 69, 78, 97, 101, 132-3, 136, 183, 206, 219-27 *pass.*
Limitation, Planning, 30-3 *pass.*, 60

Family (*contd.*)
Marital Roles, 69, 214, 225
Marital Status, 42, 164, 166, *see* Maternal Deprivation, Reproduction
Frequency of Conditions, Rates, **Glossary;** *see* Community Diagnosis, Incidence, etc.

G

General Practice, 38-40, 48-9, 77-81, 117
Genetics, 152, 170-1, 220, 223, 246-7
Glaucoma, 117, 126, 127
Glover Phenomenon, 92
Goitre, Hypothyroidism, 157, 293
Graunt's Law, 13, 15, 163
Group Observation / Application to Individual, 63n., 68, Chap. IV, 129-30, 135-6, 183, 259, 267
Growing Points
of Epidemiology, 40-3, 44-7, 71-4, 119-23, 125-9, 130-3, 140, 149, 187-8, 276, 281
of Health Services, 33, 97, 135-40, 199

H

Hazards of Health Services, of Therapy, 31, 69, 73, 96, 268, 281, 287
Health, Epidemiology of, 8, 53, 71, 163-8 *pass.*, 198, 226-9, 250-1
Health Services, Working of (Organisation of Medical Care, Operational Research), **Chap. III;** 42-3, 131, 135-6, 211, 301
Application of New Knowledge, 86-7, 135, 199
Changes in, 89, 98, 101
see Community Care
Demand for, 27, 82-9 *pass.*
Experimental Action Research, 99-101, 155, 301
see General Practice
see Hospitals
International Comparison, 96-7, *see* Medical Geography
Methods for Study, 76-7
Needs for, 23, 33, 49, 67, **82-3,** 101, 116-17, 122, 135
Supply of, 7, 28, 31, 61, **84-7,** 101
Utilisation of, 38-40, 55, 60, 78, 80-1, 84, **87-9**
Quality of, 89-96

Historical Study, 1-2, **Chap. I;** 284, 288, 291, 297, 299
High Blood Pressure, Hypertension, *see* Blood Pressure
Hospitals, 37, 39-40, 49, 81, 92-4, 97-101, 111-16, *pass.*, 227; Mental Hospitals, 37, 81, 97-101, 220-2, *see* Social Breakdown Syndrome, Therapeutic Community
Housing, 41, 60, 161, 224
Hypertension, *see* Blood Pressure
Hypotheses, Models
  Causes of Chronic Diseases, 188 195, 251-73
  Control and Prevention of Chronic Diseases, 134
  Identification of Syndromes, 154-5
  Multiple Causes, 191-5, 266-8
  Natural History of Chronic Diseases, 134
  Processes of Coronary Artery Disease, 146
  Rise of Disease, Secular Trends, 12-18
  Society, 54
  Working of Health Services, 82, 89

I

Iceberg Phenomenon, Subclinical Disease, *see* " Completing "
Identification of Syndromes, **Chap. VI;** 290, 291, 296
Improvement of Health, 7, Chap. I, *pass.*
Incidence, **Glossary;** 16, 17, 21, 27, 29, 102, 107, 108, 114, 133, 134, 138, 151, 185, 222, 236, 262, 264, 280, 293
Indicators and Measurements, 44-8, 70-4
Individual Chances and Risks, **Chap. IV;** Glossary: 162, 264, 285, 289, 304
Industrial, Occupational, Disease, Hazards, Health, 84-5, 125, 171, 211-18, *see* Accidents
Industrial Pulmonary Disease, 155, 163, 269, *see* Byssinosis
Industrial Revolution, 161, 169, 225
Infant Mortality, Neonatal Mortality, Postneonatal Mortality, 31, 53-60 *pass.*, 64-75 *pass.*, 156-7, 208, 267, 289, 305
Intelligence about Health. Chap. II, *pass.*, 274

Ischaemic (Coronary) Heart Disease, " Coronary Thrombosis ", 2, 37, 74, 104, 108, 114, 122, 128, 172-82
  and Blood Cholesterol Level, 126, 127, 129, 172, 248
  and Cigarette Smoking, 107, 108, 165, 167, 265
  and Coronary Artery Disease, 128, 131, 172
  and Diet, 248, 252, 257
  Geography, 241-2, 248, 294
  History, Secular Trends, 2, 16-18, 181, 252
  and Hypertension, 127, 172, 193
  Natural History, 111-15, 117, 122, 127, 128-9
  and Obesity, 169, 180
  and Physical Activity, 174-82
  Prevention, 86, 109, 181, 266, 272
  and Psychosocial Strain, 225-6
  and Sex, 2, 294
  Syndromes, 173

J

Juvenile Delinquency, 15, 29, 70, 124, 150-1, 225, 266, 280
Juvenile Rheumatism, Rheumatic Heart Disease, 5-7, 58, 87, 118, 190, 280

K

Kwashiorkor, 32, 190, 291

L

Lead Poisoning, 119, 125, 283
Leukaemia, 15, 147-50, 170, 195
  and Radiation, 259, 286-7
Levels of Study, 45-7, 76, 220, 276
Life Table, 26, 186, **Glossary**
Lungs, *see* Bronchitis, Bronchus
Lymphoma, 141, 248, 281

M

Marriage, 42n.
Maternal Deprivation, 223-4, 227
Medical Geography, Cross-Cultural Study, International Comparison, World Medicine, 250
  " Geographical Pathology ", **241-50;** 64, 69, 105, 147-9 *pass.*, 179, 180, 210, 213, 217, 257, 291, 294
  Health Services, 96-7, 181
  Physiology, 182, 183, 250
  Population, 31-2
  Psychology, Mental Disorders, 224-5, 251

Mental Disorders, Psychoneurosis, Psychosis, 34, 36-7, 83-4, 98-101, 104, 132, **218-29**
Estimation of, 48-50
History of, 14, 18-19
Investigation of, 48-50
see Schizophrenia
Mental Retardation, 84, 171, 223
Methods, Methodology, 42-52, 178, see Case-Control Study, Indicators, etc.
Migration, 242, 259, see North/South, Social Mobility
Mode of Life, Ways of Living, and Health, 52-74, 192
Models, see Hypotheses
Mongolism (Down's Syndrome), 16, 103, 157
Morbidity, 36-46, 201-7 pass., see Cancer, etc.
Mortality, see Death Rates
Motor Vehicles, 69, 174-82 pass., see Accidents

N

Natural History of Chronic Diseases, 133-40
Necropsy Study, 48, 111-12. 175
New Diseases, 5, 12-13, 20, 27, 65-74 pass., 225, 290
Newly Common, 15-18
Newly Recognised, 13, 291, see Lymphoma
Rediscovery of Old, 211-18
Norm: Average/Healthy, 167, 250
North/South Trends, 44, 90, 205
Nystagmus, 5, 191

O

Obesity, 40, 130, 165-9 pass., 180, 268
Observer Variation, 49, 187, 212, 250
Old Age, see Age
Onion Principle, 14, 18, 201
Operational Research, Chap. III; see Health Services
Otitis Media, 91, 301

P

Pathogenesis, Mechanisms, Processes of Disease, see Precursors
Pellagra, 280-1
Peptic Ulcer, Duodenal, Gastric, **19-22**, 89, 104, 126, 130, 142-3, 154, 157-8, 189, **295**

Perinatal Mortality, 53, 56, 60, 67, 75, 156-7, 159, 299, 305
Personal Behaviour, Habits, 192, 196-9
Population Explosion, 30-3
Poverty, 60-4, 206-9, 223-4, see Deprivation, Social Class
Precursors of Chronic Diseases, 125-129, 138-40, 202, 211, 219, 235
Predispositions, see Causes, Group
Prematurity, Low Birth Weight, 53, 265, 289
Prevalence, **Glossary;** 101, 108, 114, 134, 137, 291, 303-4
Prevention of Chronic Diseases, 134-40, 270-3, see Bronchitis, etc.
Primary, 91, 138, 285, Communal, Personal, 197-9
Secondary, 101, 136
Tertiary, 135
Prognosis, 113-15, 117, 306
Prospective, Cohort, Study, 23, 30, 131-2, 183, 231-5
of Aetiology, 261-6
of Natural History, 131-2
and Ageing, 131
Prostate
Benign Enlargement of, 41, 94-5
Cancer of, 105, 230, 235, 258
Protein Malnutrition, 32, 190, 291
Psychosomatics, 10, 19, 21, 49, 158, 168, 186, 192, 295
Pyelonephritis, 15, 182, 190

R

Radiation, Ionising, 72, 158n., 170 286-7
Randomisation, the Magic Word, 259, 264
Rates, see Incidence, Prevalence, etc.
Record Linkage, 131, 222
Birth and Death Certificates, 59, 67, 156, 208
Registers of Disease, 41, 130, 241
Reproducibility, 212
Reproduction, 26-8, 30-3, 53-60 pass., 81, 82, 87, 155-7, 239, 288-9, see Perinatal Mortality, etc.
Rheumatism, Chronic, 13, 35, 126
Rise of Disease, 1-2, 8-18, 27-9, 225, 234, see Bronchus, Ischaemic, New
Rubella, and Congenital Malformation, 288-9

S

Schizophrenia, 27, 43, 89, 124, 126, 219-23, 226
Scrotum, Cancer of, 160, 284
Selection, Bias, in Populations, 43-4, 178
Sex Behaviour, 28, 41, 196
Sex Ratio
 in Disease, Mortality, 1-3, 25, 163, 164, 294, 296-7
 in population, 25-6, 112
Sickle-Cell Trait, 170
" Sick - Absence ", " Sickness - Absence ", " Industrial Absenteeism ", 7-12, 21, 34-5
Smoking, Tobacco, 71, 167, 198-9, *see* Bronchus
Social Breakdown Syndrome, Institional Neurosis, 19, 141, 227
Social Class, 52-64, 221-2, *see* Death Rate
Social Disorganisation, Pathology, 27-9, 63n., 70, 77, 161-2, 218-229 *pass.*, 291
Social Group/Aggregate, 226-9
Social Medicine, Social Causes and Consequences of Health and Disease, Social Services for them, 27, 52-74, 160-71 *pass.*, 181, *see* Bronchitis, etc., Causes; Health, other " Social ", etc.
Social Mobility, 43-4, 59, 90, 131, 210, 213-14, 219-22
Standardised Mortality Ratio, 58, 66
Stillbirth, 155, 156-7, 193-4, 267, 289

Stomach, Cancer of, 30, 37, 58, 105, 235, 236, 238, 240
 see Peptic Ulcer
" Stress ", 70, 168, 192, 218-29 *pass.*, 295
Suicide, 14, 225
Surveys, Methods, 40-52

T

Teeth, Dental Caries, 90
 Fluoridation, 269-71
Therapeutic Community, 227
Tonsils, Adenoids, Tonsillectomy, 88, 92
Town and Country; Urban-Rural Comparison, 88-9, 160, 164-6
Tuberculosis, 58, 191

V

Validity, 45, 212
Venereal Disease, 28, 118, 188
Victorian Thunder, 60, 161-3
Vulnerable Groups, 66-8, 135, 137

W

Water
 Hardness and Cardiovascular Disease, 253, 256, 268
 Pollution and Cholera, 160-2, 259-60,
 see Teeth
Work, *and* Physical Health, 34-8, 167-8, 174-82 *pass.*, 204, 209, *see* Industrial, etc.
 and Mental Health, 10, 227-9

Printed by The Central Press (Aberdeen) Ltd.